CHANGE AND CONTINUITY IN THE 2004 ELECTIONS

Paul R. Abramson
MICHIGAN STATE UNIVERSITY

John H. Aldrich
DUKE UNIVERSITY

David W. Rohde
DUKE UNIVERSITY

CQ PRESS

A Division of Congressional Quarterly Inc.
Washington, D.C.

CQ Press
1255 22nd Street, NW, Suite 400
Washington, DC 20037

Phone: 202-729-1900; toll-free, 1-866-427-7737 (1-866-4CQ-PRESS)

Web: www.cqpress.com

Cover design: Brian Barth

∞ The paper used in this publication exceeds the requirements of the American National Standard for Information Sciences—Permanence of Paper for Printed Library Materials, ANSI Z39.48-1992.

Printed and bound in the United States of America

09 08 07 06 05   1 2 3 4 5

Library of Congress Cataloging-in-Publication Data

Abramson, Paul R.
  Change and continuity in the 2004 elections / Paul R. Abramson, John H. Aldrich, David W. Rohde.
    p. cm.
  Includes bibliographical references and index.
  ISBN 1-933116-69-2 (alk. paper)
    1. Presidents—United States—Election—2004. 2. United States. Congress—Elections, 2004. 3. Elections—United States. 4. United States—Politics and government—2001–   I. Aldrich, John Herbert   II. Rohde, David W.   III. Title.

JK5262004 .A27 2005
324.973'0931—dc22   2005033360

To John H. Kessel

Contents

Tables and Figures

Tables

Figures

About the Authors

Paul R. Abramson is professor of political science at Michigan State University. He is the coauthor of *Value Change in Global Perspective* (1995) and author of *Political Attitudes in America* (1983), *The Political Socialization of Black Americans* (1977), and *Generational Change in American Politics* (1975). With John H. Aldrich and David W. Rohde, he has coauthored twelve additional books on presidential and congressional elections published by CQ Press.

John H. Aldrich is the Pfizer-Pratt University Professor of Political Science at Duke University. He is the author of *Why Parties?* (1995) and *Before the Convention* (1980). He is a past president of both the Southern Political Science Association and the Midwest Political Science Association. In 2001 he was elected a fellow of the American Academy of Arts and Sciences.

David W. Rohde is professor of political science and director of the Political Institutions and Public Choice Program at Duke University. He is the author of *Parties and Leaders in the Postreform House* (1991), coeditor of *Home Style and Washington Work* (1989), and coauthor of *Supreme Court Decision Making* (1976).

The authors, from left to right: David W. Rohde, John H. Aldrich, and Paul R. Abramson

Preface

Many Americans view the 2004 elections as a struggle between two warring cultures, with conservative and religious forces narrowly prevailing over liberal and secular forces. Although there may be some truth to this characterization, we see George W. Bush's reelection as a narrow victory for an incumbent who held slightly favorable evaluations among the electorate and who convinced a majority of voters that he was better able to combat terrorism. Some analysts argue that the election marked the consolidation of Republican dominance in both presidential and congressional elections, but we think that there is still a close balance between the Republican and Democratic Parties. This leaves us with a less dramatic interpretation of the election than some have offered, but we believe that the evidence supports our conclusions.

In this book, we rely upon a wide variety of evidence. We begin our study of the 2004 elections by analyzing the election results, and we follow this pattern in our discussion of both the presidential and the congressional elections. We review George W. Bush's and John F. Kerry's campaign appeals and examine the impact of campaign spending in the congressional elections. Surveys are also crucial to our study. We refer extensively to polls conducted in 2004 by six sources. These include two major national exit polls: a survey of 13,610 voters conducted by Edison Media Research and Mitofsky International for a national consortium, and a survey of 5,154 voters conducted by the *Los Angeles Times*. We use the Current Population Survey of approximately 60,000 respondents conducted by the U.S. Bureau of the Census in our study of turnout, and we report on a General Social Survey poll of 2,814 respondents conducted by the National Opinion Research Center to study party identification. We also use six surveys of between 881 and 1,125 respondents conducted by Knowledge Networks to study the concerns of the electorate. However, the National Election Study survey of 1,212 respondents is the most important survey in our analysis. This survey is part of an ongoing series studying the U.S. electorate conducted by the Survey Research Center and the Center for Political Studies (SRC-CPS) of the University of Michigan and funded by the National Science Foundation. In the course of our book, we use all twenty-eight surveys conducted between 1948 and 2004 that are often referred to as the National Election Studies (NES) surveys.

The NES surveys are disseminated through the Inter-university Consortium for Political and Social Research (ICPSR) and can be used by analysts throughout the world. The data we use were made available in March 2005. Unless otherwise indicated, all the tables and figures in chapters 2, 4 through 8, and 10 are based upon surveys provided by the ICPSR and the NES. The standard disclaimer holds: these organizations are responsible neither for our analyses nor for our interpretation of these data.

We are indebted to many people for helping us with this project. First, we would like to thank our research assistants, Suzanne M. Gold and Greg Robinson at Michigan State University and Jill Rickershauser and Jenn Tanaka at Duke University. Several scholars helped with our analysis of survey data. Tom Smith of the National Opinion Research Center provided us with results from the General Social Surveys, and Peter Feaver and Christopher Gelpi of Duke University and Jason Reifler of Loyola University of Chicago allowed us to present results from Knowledge Networks surveys. Nancy Burns and David Howell of the University of Michigan helped us in analyzing the NES data. Gerald M. Pomper of Rutgers University provided us with additional information about his study of candidate campaign visits. Rhodes Cook, editor of the *Rhodes Cook Letter,* allowed us to use early results from *America Votes 26.*

Several scholars also aided us in our study of turnout. Walter Dean Burnham of the University of Texas at Austin provided us with his estimates of the politically eligible population, and Michael P. McDonald of George Mason University provided us with his estimates of the voting-age population and the voting eligible population. In our estimates of turnout for twenty-five democracies, we were assisted by Abraham Diskin of the Hebrew University of Jerusalem; Robert W. Jackman of the University of California, Davis; Lawrence LeDuc and Renan Levine of the University of Toronto; and Dennis Patterson of Texas Technological University. William J. Crotty of Northeastern University assisted in our discussion of political change in New England, and Bruce Cain and Jack Citrin of the University of California, Berkeley, made suggestions that helped us discuss political change in California. David L. Leal of the University of Texas at Austin provided information about the William C. Velazquez Research Institute exit poll of Hispanic voters. We are also grateful to Dennis Patterson for his comments on our brief discussion of Japanese politics and to Kaare Strøm of the University of California, San Diego, for his comments on our discussion of Swedish politics. In addition we thank Richard Keiser at Carleton College and Laurie Rhodebeck at the University of Louisville for their comments as reviewers. Finally, we thank Janet Abramson for editing the manuscript.

In addition to this assistance, we appreciate support from the Department of Political Science at Michigan State University, the Political Institutions and Public Choice Program at Michigan State University, and the Department of Political Science at Duke University.

Once again we are thankful to the staff at CQ Press. Many thanks to Charisse Kiino for her encouragement, to Nancy Geltman for copyediting the manuscript, to Jennifer Campi for managing the book's production, and to David Arthur for providing us with early reports from *America Votes 26.*

This book continues a series of twelve books that began with a study of the 1980 elections. In many places we refer to our earlier books, all of which were published by CQ Press. A good deal of this material is available online through the CQ Voting and Elections Collection, which can be accessed through many academic and public libraries. This material includes large portions of the revised editions of *Change and Continuity in the 1980 Elections, Change and Continuity in the 1984 Elections, Change and Continuity in the 1988 Elections,* and *Change and Continuity in the 1992 Elections.* In addition, the Voting and Elections Collection includes large portions of *Change and Continuity in the 1996 and 1998 Elections* and *Change and Continuity in the 2000 and 2002 Elections.*

Like our earlier books, this one was a collective enterprise in which we divided the labor. Paul Abramson had primary responsibility for chapters 3, 4, 5, and 11; John Aldrich for chapters 1, 6, 7, and 8; and David Rohde for chapters 2, 9, and 10.

We would appreciate feedback from our readers. Please contact us if you disagree with our interpretations, find factual errors, or want further clarification about our methods or our conclusions.

Paul R. Abramson
Michigan State University
abramson@msu.edu

John H. Aldrich
Duke University
aldrich@duke.edu

David W. Rohde
Duke University
rohde@duke.edu

PART 1

The 2004 Presidential Election

Presidential elections in the United States are ritual reaffirmations of our democratic values, but they are far more than that. The office of the presidency confers great powers on its occupant, and those powers have expanded during most of the twentieth century. Presidential elections at times have played a major role in determining public policy and in some cases have shaped the course of American history.

The 1860 election, which brought Abraham Lincoln and the Republicans to power and ousted a divided Democratic Party, focused on whether slavery should be extended to the western territories. After Lincoln's election, eleven southern states attempted to secede from the Union, the Civil War erupted, and the U.S. government abolished slavery completely. Thus an antislavery plurality (Lincoln received only 40 percent of the popular vote) set in motion a chain of events that freed some four million black Americans.

The 1896 election, in which Republican William McKinley defeated the Democrat and Populist William Jennings Bryan, beat back the challenge of western and agricultural interests to the prevailing financial and industrial power of the East. Although Bryan mounted a strong campaign, winning 47 percent of the popular vote to McKinley's 51 percent, the election set a clear course for a policy of high tariffs and the continuation of the gold standard for American money.

Lyndon B. Johnson's 1964 landslide over Republican Barry M. Goldwater provided the clearest set of policy alternatives of any election in the twentieth century.[1] Goldwater had offered "a choice, not an echo," advocating far more conservative social and economic policies than Johnson. When Johnson received 61 percent of the popular vote to Goldwater's 38 percent, he saw his victory as a mandate for his Great Society programs, the most far-reaching social legislation since World War II. The election also appeared to offer a clear choice between escalating American involvement in Vietnam and restraint. But American involvement in Vietnam expanded after Johnson's election, leading to growing opposition to Johnson within the Democratic Party, and four years later he did not seek reelection.

WHAT DID THE 2004 ELECTION MEAN?

Some scholars have argued that elections have become less important, and there is some truth in their arguments.[2] Still, presidential elections do offer important choices on public policy, and those choices were sharper in 2004 than in most presidential contests. William Crotty argues in *A Defining Moment,* his edited book on the 2004 elections, that although all presidential elections are important, "some . . . are more important in terms of their consequences for the nation than others; so it was to be with the election of 2004." Crotty writes, "Two opposing visions of the United States and its future were presented to the American public; one would prevail and set the country's course domestically and in relation to the international community for years, if not decades and generations, to come. They had little in common."[3] He notes that all of the contributors to his book share "the unifying belief . . . that the 2004 presidential election was extraordinarily important, nothing less than a marking point in American electoral history."[4]

The importance of the 2004 election arises not only from the sharp policy differences between George W. Bush and John F. Kerry that were contested during the campaign but also from the policies that Bush had pursued during his presidency. As Michael Nelson has pointed out, many politicians and pundits counseled Bush to govern in a bipartisan manner. Instead he promoted policies designed to appeal to conservatives, while antagonizing more liberal Americans. Bush, Nelson writes, chose

> to pursue a conservative Republican agenda of dramatically cutting taxes, toughening national educational standards, involving faith-based initiatives in the administration of federal social programs, promoting oil production in the Alaskan wilderness, restricting certain forms of abortion, limiting embryonic stem cell research, banning human cloning, developing a national missile defense system, implementing business-friendly regulatory policies, withdrawing from controversial environmental and military treaties, and, after 9/11, launching a "war on terror" that included invasions of Afghanistan and Iraq.[5]

The election also created sharp choices because Kerry took positions clearly different from Bush's, especially on domestic policy. As Patricia Conley writes, Kerry

> supported abortion rights and federal funding for abortion and abortion counseling; he said that he would appoint only judges who would not overturn *Roe v. Wade.* Kerry opposed the death penalty except for terrorists. . . . Kerry argued for tougher vehicle emissions standards and opposed drilling in the Arctic National Wildlife Refuge. He opposed a constitutional amendment banning gay marriage and argued that individual states should decide. He would let gays serve openly in the military.

Kerry also proposed expanding health insurance to cover children and allowing prescription drugs to be imported from Canada, where they cost less. Conley concludes, "He opposed giving younger workers the choice of placing their Social Security payroll tax in individual retirement accounts and opposed raising the retirement age or reducing payments." [6]

Kerry and Bush also differed on foreign policy, but their differences were smaller. Along with a majority of his fellow Democrats, Kerry had voted to authorize Bush to use force against Iraq. The war against Iraq had been launched mainly because of the threat that Iraq had, or was developing, weapons of mass destruction, but no such weapons were discovered. During the campaign, Kerry tried to make the case that Bush had exercised poor judgment in attacking, but voters were confused by his criticism of Bush, given his own vote to authorize the use of force. Kerry attempted to explain his later vote against additional funding for the war, saying, "I actually did vote for the $87 billion before I voted against it," a statement that may have made sense to experts on Senate procedures, but not to the public. Kerry also criticized Bush's diplomatic efforts, claiming that he would have tried to enlist more international aid to rebuild Iraq. Kerry promised to strengthen American alliances and to make greater use of diplomacy. [7] But he would not withdraw American troops, saying instead that the war, once under way, needed to be brought to a successful conclusion.

American voters clearly saw the 2004 election as important. In 2000, a Pew Center poll reported that only 45 percent of the electorate thought that the election "really mattered"; in 2004, 63 percent thought so. [8] Moreover, the percentage of Americans who voted rose about four percentage points. In this election, Bush won more votes than any other candidate in American history, although we should not forget that Kerry also won more votes than any previous presidential candidate.

Unlike 2000, when George W. Bush won fewer popular votes than Al Gore, Bush won a majority in 2004, the first presidential candidate in twelve years to do so. Moreover, the Republicans gained three seats in the U.S. House of Representatives and, more important, four seats in the Senate, where the election gave the GOP a comfortable, if not filibuster-proof, majority.

Bush saw his victory as a mandate to continue pursuing his policy agenda. In a forty-minute news conference two days after his reelection, Bush declared, "Let me put it to you this way: I earned capital in this campaign, political capital, and I intend to spend it." [9] At a postelection victory rally Bush promised to revamp the tax system, to move toward an "ownership society" in which younger workers could invest part of their Social Security payroll taxes in private accounts, and to facilitate creating health savings accounts. [10]

Social conservatives were hoping for dramatic reforms, including a constitutional amendment banning same-sex marriage and transformation of the U.S. Supreme Court through the appointment of justices who would overturn the decisions that had established abortion rights. [11] After the election, Richard Viguerie, one of the pioneers of conservative direct mail, said, "Now comes the revolution. . . . If you don't implement a conservative agenda now, when do you?" According to James C. Dobson, the founder of Focus on the Family, a Protestant evangelical group, conservatives "now had four years to pass an amendment banning same-sex marriage, to stop abortion and end embryonic stem-cell research, and most of all to remake the Supreme Court." [12]

Eight months after the election, on July 1, 2005, Associate Justice Sandra Day O'Connor, a swing voter on the Court, announced that she planned to retire, giving Bush the opportunity to appoint a replacement who could move the Court in a conservative direction. His July 19 nomination of John G. Roberts Jr., a fifty-year-old judge on the U.S. Court of Appeals for the District of Columbia Circuit, would replace a swing voter with a solid conservative. Bush, according to Adam Nagourney, "moved to plant the conservative imprint on the Supreme Court that has been a central aim of his presidency, but with a member of the Washington legal establishment designed to frustrate any Democratic effort to block Mr. Bush's replacement for Justice Sandra Day O'Connor." [13] Indeed, Roberts drew such widespread support that when Chief Justice William H. Rehnquist died on September 3, Bush nominated Roberts to be chief justice. Roberts was overwhelmingly confirmed three weeks later by a vote of 78 to 22. On October 3, Bush nominated White House counsel Harriet E. Miers, to fill O'Connor's seat. As Miers had never been a judge, Bush argued that her appointment would increase the diversity of the Court. It also meant that she had no track record by which her views could be judged. The early reaction to Miers was lukewarm, especially among conservatives.[14] On October 31, four days after Miers withdrew, Bush nominated 3rd Circuit appeals court judge Samuel A. Alito Jr., who has a solid conservative record.

Does Bush have a mandate to carry out conservative reforms? Obviously it is in the interest of every winning candidate to claim a mandate in order to increase the chances that his or her initiatives will be adopted. It is also clear that mandates are subject to interpretation—whether a mandate exists is not a matter of meeting some clear standard but rather a function of whether the media and other observers say that one exists. To Bush's advantage, the day after the election, a number of media outlets discussed the White House's claim of a Bush mandate, a claim enhanced by the GOP gains in Congress. As we will see in our review of the evidence, however, there is substantial evidence that the 2004 election did not provide a mandate.

Mandate or not, many observers see the 2004 contest as a turning point in American politics. Crotty believes that the contest provided "a defining moment": "The election redistributed political power, restructures the parties' coalitions and, in this case, established the Republican Party as the dominant political force in America." [15] Nelson argues, "By any standard, the elections of 2004 made George W. Bush a majority president in the narrow sense—that is, the head of a united party governing for at least the first two years of his second term. But there is another, more important sense in which Bush can be described as a majority president: he is the leader, and one of the builders, of the nation's new majority party." [16]

James W. Ceaser and Andrew E. Busch take this argument farther: "No one could call the 2004 election a landslide, but the Republicans emerged from the election ascendant as the nation's majority party." [17] They argue that a realignment has occurred in American politics.[18] "A realignment," they write, "can be conceived simply as a major change in the underlying strength of the two parties during a specified period of time. By this definition, a realignment has already taken place in the time period between the 1960s or 1979, when the Democratic Party was in the clear majority, and today, when the Republican Party holds an edge." [19]

In an article published after the election, Fred Barnes points out that Karl Rove, Bush's chief political strategist, stated in 2003 that the question of whether the Republicans would become the majority party would be decided by the 2004 election. Barnes writes, "Even by the cautious reckoning of Rove . . . Republicans now have both an operational majority in Washington (control of the White House, Senate, and House of Representatives) and an ideological majority in the country (51 percent for a center right president). They also control a majority of governorships, a plurality of state legislatures, and a rough plurality in the number of state legislators." According to Barnes, "Rove says that under Bush a 'rolling realignment' favoring the Republicans continues, and he's right. So Republican hegemony in America is now expected to last for years, maybe decades." [20]

Barnes cites Walter Dean Burnham who, he correctly notes, is America's leading theorist about party realignments. Burnham argues that a Republican breakthrough occurred in 1994, when the GOP gained control of the U.S. House of Representatives for the first time in forty years.[21] The Republicans held the House and made gains in both the 2002 and 2004 elections. The 2004 election "consolidates it all," according to Burnham. The 2004 election, Burnham maintains, "may be the most important of my lifetime" (he was born in 1930). Bush's reelection, as well as Republican gains in the House and Senate, was "very, very impressive," and it will be very difficult for the Democrats to overcome "the huge weight of Republican strength." [22]

Arguments that the Republicans have become the majority party are not based only on the 2004 results. As early as 1969, Kevin P. Phillips, in his widely read book *The Emerging Republican Majority,* argued that the Republicans could become the majority party, mainly by winning support in the South.[23] Between 1969 and 1984, the Republicans won three of the four presidential elections, winning by massive landslides in 1972, when Richard M. Nixon overwhelmed George S. McGovern, and in 1984, when Ronald Reagan triumphed over Walter F. Mondale. In 1985 President Reagan himself proclaimed that a Republican realignment was at hand. "The other side would like to believe that our victory last November was due to something other than our philosophy," he asserted. "I just hope that they keep believing that. Realignment is real." [24]

Reagan won 59 percent of the popular vote in November 1984, which certainly gave him reason for exuberance. George H. W. Bush's victory in 1988, with 53 percent of the popular vote, raised the possibility of continued Republican dominance. But in 1992 Bush won only 37 percent of the vote, a twenty-two-point decline from Reagan's high-water mark. Not only was the Republican winning streak broken, but the party had suffered one of the greatest popular vote defeats since the Civil War. And in 1996 Bob Dole won only 41 percent of the popular vote.

Obviously the 1992 and 1996 presidential elections called into question the claims that there had been a pro-Republican realignment. But Bill Clinton won only 43 percent of the popular vote in 1992 and just 49 percent in 1996. Moreover, the divided partisan outcome that left Congress in GOP hands in 1996 suggests that a substantial number of Clinton voters voted for Republican House and Senate candidates. The 2000 election was the third consecutive contest in which the winner failed to gain a majority of the popular vote: although Bush won the presidency in 2000, he won only 47.9 percent of the popular vote, less than Gore's 48.4 percent. Some scholars argued that voters had reservations about both parties. That raised the possibility that past voting patterns were breaking down, a condition that political scientists have called a "dealignment." But as we have seen, after the 2004 election many scholars and pundits were again ready to conclude that a pro-Republican realignment had occurred.

What do the terms *realignment* and *dealignment* mean? Political scientists define *realignment* in different ways, but they are all influenced by V. O. Key Jr., who began by developing a theory of "critical elections" in which "new and durable electoral groupings are formed." [25] Elections such as those of 1860, in which Lincoln's victory brought the Republicans to power; 1896, in which, according to many scholars, McKinley's victory solidified Republican dominance; and 1932, which brought the Democrats under Franklin D. Roosevelt to power, are obvious candidates for such a label.

But later Key argued that partisan changes take place over a series of elections—a pattern he called "secular realignment." During these periods, "shifts in the partisan balance of power" occur.[26] In this view, the realignment that first brought the Republicans to power might have begun in 1856, when the Republicans displaced the Whigs as the major competition to the Democrats, and might have been consolidated by Lincoln's reelection in 1864 and Ulysses S. Grant's election in 1868. The realignment that consolidated Republican dominance in the late nineteenth century may well have begun in 1892, when Democrat Grover Cleveland won the election but the Populist Party, headed by James B. Weaver attracted 8.5 percent of the popular vote, winning four states and electoral votes in two others. In 1896 the Populists supported Bryan and were co-opted by the Democrats, but the electorate shifted to the Republicans. The pro-Republican realignment might have been consolidated by McKinley's win over Bryan in 1900 and by Theodore Roosevelt's victory in 1904.

Though the term *New Deal* was not coined until 1932, the New Deal realignment, forged by Franklin D. Roosevelt during the 1930s, may be seen as beginning in Herbert C. Hoover's 1928 triumph over Alfred E. Smith, the first Roman Catholic to be nominated by the Democratic Party. Although badly defeated, Smith carried two New England states, Massachusetts and Rhode Island, which later became the most Democratic states in the nation.[27] As Key points out, the beginnings of the shift toward the Democratic Party can be seen in Smith's defeat.[28] The New Deal coalition was not created by the 1932 election, but after it, and it was consolidated by Roosevelt's 1936 landslide over Alfred M. Landon and his 1940 defeat of Wendell Willkie.

Although scholars disagree about how long it takes to create a partisan alignment, they all agree that durability is an essential element of realignment. As James L. Sundquist writes, "Those who analyze alignment and realignment are probing beneath the immediate and transitory ups and downs of daily politics and periodic elections to discover fundamental shifts in the structure of the party system." [29] According to Lawrence G. McMichael and Richard J. Trilling, a realignment is "a significant and durable change in the distribution of party support over relevant groups within the electorate." [30]

Not all scholars believe that the concept of realignment is useful. In 1991 Byron E. Shafer edited a volume that contained several chapters questioning its utility.[31] More recently, David R. Mayhew has published a monograph critiquing scholarship on realignment, and his book has received widespread critical acclaim.[32] Mayhew cites fifteen claims made by scholars of realignment and then examines the work of those who have claimed to identify periods when realignments occurred. The periods they identify, he argues, do not fit well with the criteria they have established. Finally, Mayhew disputes the argument that the 1896 election was critical, arguing that from a statistical standpoint there was little distinctive about it.

Although we disagree with many of Mayhew's arguments, this is not the place for an extensive discussion. We would, however, make four basic points: First, although Mayhew has discussed fifteen criteria for identifying realignments, he mentions only two of the five that guide our discussion.[33] Second, although it is scarcely crucial to our discussion, we believe that there is substantial evidence that the 1896 election was critical in establishing Republican dominance.[34] Third, we disagree with the argument that increases in turnout are not related to past realignments. Finally, there has been excellent research that employs the concept of realignment, such as the work of David W. Brady, Peter F. Nardulli, and Gary Miller and Norman Schofield.[35]

In our view, partisan realignments in the United States have had five basic characteristics. First, party realignments have always involved changes in the regional bases of party support. Between 1852 and 1860 the Republicans replaced the Whigs. In all of the elections between 1836 (when the Whigs first opposed Democrat Martin van Buren) and 1852, the Whigs drew at least some of their support from the South. The last Whig candidate to be elected, Zachary Taylor in 1848, won sixty-six of his electoral votes from the fifteen slave states.[36] In his 1860 victory Lincoln did not win a single electoral vote from any of the slave states. As James M. McPherson writes, "Republicans did not even have a ticket in ten southern states, where their speakers would have been greeted with a coat of tar and feathers—or worse—if they dared to appear." [37] But Lincoln won all of the electoral votes in seventeen of the eighteen free states, as well as a majority of the electoral votes in New Jersey. Subsequent realignments have not involved this degree of regional polarization, but they all display regional shifts in party support.

Second, past realignments appear to have involved changes in the social bases of party support. Even during a period when one party is becoming dominant, some social groups may be moving to the losing party. During the 1930s, for example, Roosevelt gained the support of industrial workers, but at the same time he lost support among business owners and professionals.

Third, past realignments have been characterized by the mobilization of new groups into the electorate. Between Calvin Coolidge's Republican landslide in 1924 and Roosevelt's third term victory in 1940, turnout among the voting-age population rose from 44 percent to 59 percent. Although some long-term forces were pushing turnout upward, the sharp increase between 1924 and 1928, and again between 1932 and 1936, resulted at least in part from the mobilization of new groups into the electorate. Ethnic groups that were predominantly Catholic were mobilized to support Smith in 1928, and industrial workers were mobilized to support Roosevelt in 1936.

Fourth, past realignments have occurred when new issues have divided the electorate. The clearest example is the emergence of the Republican Party, which reformulated the controversy over slavery to form a winning coalition. By opposing the extension of slavery into the territories, the Republicans contributed to divisions within the Democratic Party. No issue since slavery has divided America as deeply, and no subsequent realignment has ever brought a new political party to power. But subsequent realignments have always been based on the division of the electorate over issues.

Last, most political scientists argue that partisan realignments occur when voters change not just their voting patterns but the way they think about the political parties. For example, during the Great Depression, in 1932, many voters who thought of themselves as Republicans voted against Hoover. Many of these voters returned to the Republican side in subsequent elections, but others began to think of themselves as Democrats. Likewise, in 1936 some voters who thought of themselves as Democrats may have voted against Roosevelt. Some of these voters returned to the Democratic fold in subsequent elections, but others began to think of themselves as Republicans.

During the three Republican victories of the 1980s, some of these changes occurred. As we will see, there were shifts in the regional bases of party support and in the distribution of party loyalties among the electorate. There were further shifts among some social groups (especially southern whites) away from the Democratic Party, and some political observers argued that the Republicans had established a winning position on issues that brought out votes in presidential elections.

Despite these changes, however, the Republicans never emerged as the majority party among the electorate, although they came close to parity in the mid-

1980s. Moreover, although the Republicans gained control of the U.S. Senate between 1981 and 1987, they never came close to winning control of the House of Representatives. Clearly, if a realignment occurred, it was incomplete, leading some scholars, such as Michael Nelson, to speculate about the possibilities of a "split-level realignment," a pattern in which the Republicans became the dominant party in presidential elections while Democratic dominance of the House remained intact.[38] And Byron E. Shafer argued that a "new electoral order" had been achieved. The 1988 election, he maintained, had institutionalized a new division in American politics, a new system that had begun twenty years earlier with the controversy over the Vietnam War. "What was to emerge instead of realignment," he wrote, "was a different type of political order; one in which there was a new Republican majority to lay claim to the presidency; an old Democratic order to keep the House, and a wavering Democratic majority to strive to hold on to the Senate." [39] But this order was disrupted by Clinton's election in 1992 and ended with the Republican capture of the House in 1994.

Clinton's victories in 1992 and 1996 and the narrowness of Bush's electoral vote majority in 2000 call into question the thesis that there has been a pro-Republican realignment. Despite the proclamations of Republican hegemony that we quoted at the beginning of this introduction, we should remember that Bush defeated Kerry by only 2.4 percent of the popular vote and that the Republican gains in the House resulted solely from a partisan redistricting plan carried out in Texas in 2003. After Bush's 2000 victory, John B. Judis and Ruy Teixeira published a book, *The Emerging Democratic Majority,* expressing a contrarian view that gained a good deal of media attention. Teixeira does not seem discouraged by Bush's 2004 victory, for he still holds to the thesis that the Democrats will become the winning party in the future, a view espoused by *Donkey Rising,* the online newsletter he edits.[40]

Even though the Republicans swept the presidency, the House, and the Senate in 2004, their narrow presidential victory should encourage the Democrats. After all, Bush won only narrowly in 2000 and 2004, but Clinton's 1992 and 1996 victories were resounding. On the other hand, the large vote for H. Ross Perot in 1992 and the sizable vote for Perot and other minor-party candidates in 1996 raise prospects of the breakdown of the traditional party system. Therefore, despite the GOP success in 2004, some might argue that the term *dealignment,* introduced by Ronald Inglehart and Avram Hochstein in 1972, may provide a better description of current political realities than *realignment.*[41]

A dealignment is a condition in which old voting patterns break down without being replaced by newer ones. Most scholars who use this term stress the weakening of party loyalties as a key component. As Russell J. Dalton, Paul Allen Beck, and Scott C. Flanagan point out, dealignment was originally viewed as a stage preliminary to a new partisan alignment. But, they argue, dealignment "may be a regular feature of electoral politics." [42] As Dalton and Martin P. Wattenberg write, "Whereas realignment involves people changing from one party to another, dealignment concerns people gradually moving away from all parties."

The large Perot vote in 1992, they argue, may have come mainly from voters who have few feelings—either positive or negative—toward the political parties. The movement away from the parties worries many political observers. "Many scholars," Dalton and Wattenberg write, "express concern about potential dealignment trends because they fear the loss of the stabilizing, conserving equilibrium that party attachments provide to electoral systems." [43]

The concept of dealignment is not restricted to U.S. politics. Bo Särlvik and Ivor Crewe have characterized the 1970s as "the decade of dealignment" in British politics. [44] And Harold Clarke and his colleagues suggest that Canadian politics may have reached a stage of "permanent dealignment." "A dealigned party system," they write, "is one in which volatility is paramount, where there are frequent changes in electoral outcomes, as well as lots of individual flexibility." [45]

Raising questions about prospects for realignment and dealignment leads to several basic questions that we will ask throughout our book. First, have the Republicans established dominance in presidential elections? After winning three elections in a row during the 1980s, the GOP lost in 1992 and 1996. The Republicans regained the White House in 2000, but with an extremely close and controversial vote count. In 2004 they won a majority of the vote, albeit a very narrow majority. Are the scholars we cite at the start of this chapter correct in their predictions of Republican dominance, bearing in mind that none of those predictions was based upon the evidence provided by the National Election Study surveys?

Second, what are the Democrats' prospects for rebuilding a presidential majority? Were Clinton's victories based on something genuinely new, or did they resemble those of past Democratic winners? Given what was viewed as a healthy economy in fall 2000, why was Gore unable to hold the presidency for the Democrats? And why did Kerry lose in 2004, even though only about one voter in four thought the nation's economy had improved in the previous year and only about two voters in five thought that the war in Iraq had been worth the cost? [46]

Finally, what ended the Democrats' congressional dominance, and are they likely ever to regain it? With the 1992 election, the Democrats had won control of the U.S. House of Representatives in twenty consecutive elections, by far the longest period of dominance in history. [47] The Republicans have now won six consecutive victories from 1994 through 2004. Can the Republicans extend this winning streak and become the dominant party in the House, as the Democrats were for four decades?

SURVEY RESEARCH SAMPLING

Our book relies heavily on surveys of the American electorate. It draws on telephone polls conducted during the election year, two exit polls, and interviews conducted in respondents' homes by the National Opinion Research Center and the U.S. Bureau of the Census. But for the most part we rely on 1,212 in-person interviews conducted in the respondents' homes during the two months before and the two months after the 2004 election.[48] The Survey Research Center (SRC) and Center for Political Studies (CPS) of the University of Michigan conducted that survey. The SRC has conducted surveys using national samples in every presidential election since 1948 and in every midterm election since 1954; these surveys are generally known as the National Election Studies (NES). Since 1952 the NES surveys have measured party identification and feelings of political efficacy. The CPS, founded in 1970, has developed valuable questions for measuring issue preferences. The NES data are the best and most comprehensive source of information about the issue preferences and party loyalties of the American electorate.

Readers may question our reliance on the NES survey of approximately 1,200 adults when there are some 202 million Americans of voting age. Would we obtain similar results if all adults had been surveyed?[49] The NES surveys use a procedure called "multistage probability sampling" to select the particular individuals to be interviewed. The procedure ensures that the final sample is likely to represent the entire population of U.S. citizens of voting age, except for Americans living on military bases, in institutions, or abroad.[50]

Given the probability procedures used to conduct the NES surveys, we are able to estimate the likelihood that the results represent the entire population of non-institutionalized U.S. citizens living in the United States. Even though the 2004 survey sampled only one American in 168,000, its representativeness depends far more on the size of the sample than on the size of the population being studied, provided the sample is drawn properly. With samples of this size, we can be fairly confident (confident to a level of .95) that the results we find will fall within four percentage points of the results we would get if the entire population had been surveyed.[51] For example, when we find that 24 percent of the sample in the 2004 NES survey said that the nation's economy had gotten better in the past year, we can be reasonably confident that between 20 percent (24 – 4) and 28 percent (24 + 4) thought that the nation's economy had improved. The actual result could be less than 20 percent or more than 28 percent. But a confidence level of .95 means that the odds are 19 to 1 that the proportion of the entire electorate falls within this range. The range of confidence becomes somewhat larger when we look at subgroups of the electorate. For example, with subsets of about 500 (and results in the 50 percent range) the confidence error rises to +/– six percentage points. Because the likelihood of error grows as our subsamples become smaller, we often supplement our analysis with reports of other surveys.

Somewhat more complicated procedures are necessary to determine whether the difference between two groups is likely to reflect the relationship that would be found if the entire population were queried. The probability that such differences reflect real differences in the population is largely a function of the size of the groups being compared.[52] Generally speaking, when we compare the results of the 2004 sample with the results of an earlier NES sample, a difference of four percentage points is sufficient to be reasonably confident that the difference is real. For example, back in 1984, when Reagan was reelected by a landslide, 44 percent of the electorate thought the economy had improved; in 2004, when Bush was reelected in a squeaker, only 24 percent thought it had improved. Because this is a difference of twenty percentage points, we can be quite confident that Americans had a more positive view of the economy in 1984 than they did in 2004.

When we compare subgroups of the electorate sampled in 2004 with other subgroups sampled that year (or with subgroups sampled in earlier years), a larger percentage point difference is necessary for us to be reasonably confident that differences do not result from chance. For example, when we compare men with women, a difference of about just over five points is necessary because in most NES surveys there will be about 750 women and 700 men. When we compare whites with blacks, a difference of nine points is necessary because only about 200 blacks are sampled in most NES surveys. For example, in 2004, 30 percent of the men but only 18 percent of the women surveyed thought the nation's economy had improved in the past year, a difference of twelve percentage points. Therefore, we can be confident that women were less likely than men to think the economy had improved. And 27 percent of the whites but only 6 percent of the blacks said the economy had improved, a difference of twenty-one points. Obviously, we can be extremely confident that blacks had a less favorable view of the economy than whites.

This discussion provides only a ballpark guide to judging whether reported results are likely to represent the entire population. Better estimates can be obtained using formulas presented in many statistics textbooks. To make such calculations, or even a rough estimate of the chances of error, the reader must know the size of the groups being compared. For this reason, we always report in our tables and figures either the number of cases on which our percentages are based or the information necessary to approximate the number of cases.[53]

THE 2004 CONTEST

Chapters 1 and 2 follow the chronology of the 2004 campaign itself. We begin in chapter 1 with the struggle for the Democratic Party's presidential nomination. As often happens when an incumbent president is seeking reelection, Bush faced no opposition for his party's nomination. On the Democratic side, there were ten candidates for the nomination, and at least seven had some prospects of success in winning it. After Gore announced on December 15, 2002, that he would not seek the Democratic Party nomination, there was no clear favorite. We begin by examining the decisions of candidates to run for the Democratic nomination. As we will see, most of them held, or had held, high political office. Despite a growing tendency for nonpoliticians to seek the presidency, only two of the candidates seeking the Democratic nomination—Al Sharpton and Wesley K. Clark—had never held political office, and only Clark had a chance of winning.

We then examine the regularities of the "nomination system of 1972," as well as the unique features of the 2004 contest. We study the rules structuring the nomination of candidates, showing that the electorate has a far larger role than it did before the reforms introduced after the 1968 elections. We examine the process by which the Democratic field was winnowed to Kerry and Edwards by early March, with Edwards barely hanging on. By March 3, Edwards had withdrawn from the competition and endorsed Kerry, setting in motion a chain of events that would lead to Kerry's choosing him as his running mate. And although there were many ways in which the contest for the 2004 Democratic nomination was similar to others of the post-1968 era, it had distinctive features. First, there was the unusual candidacy of Howard Dean, the former governor of Vermont, who relied heavily upon the Internet to raise money and mobilize supporters. Second, because a growing number of contests were held early in the delegate selection season, the contest was the most heavily frontloaded in the modern campaign era, and that had a great deal to do with Kerry's success in capturing the nomination.

Having gained their parties' nominations, Bush and Kerry faced the task of winning the 270 electoral votes necessary to win the general election. We discuss the strategic context that confronted them as the general election campaign began, explaining that the Republicans appeared to have an advantage based upon the past pattern of state-by-state results and showing how both campaigns focused on the same set of "battleground" states. We see that in many respects the general election campaign began in early March, shortly after Kerry had effectively secured the Democratic nomination. Polls showed that the election was likely to be close; we explain how each candidate had both advantages and problems. We examine attacks on Kerry's military record in Vietnam by the Swift Boat Veterans for Truth and consider whether his failure to reply immediately to the charges was a tactical error. We analyze the three presidential debates and one vice-presidential debate and look at how the presidential debates, especially the first, helped Kerry pull even with Bush in the polls. We then discuss the candidates' final campaign efforts, differentiating between the "air war"—the campaign on television—and the "ground war" that emphasizes registration and turnout efforts. Both campaigns and their allies made major efforts to turn out their supporters, and we examine the techniques they used. Finally, we turn to the question of whether the campaign mattered.

Chapter 3 presents and interprets the election results. Bush's narrow win marked an improvement over his first election, in which he received fewer popular votes than Gore. All the same, as we will see, the results in 2004 were very similar to those in the 2000 contest. We examine the rules for electing the president, showing that the candidate who wins the plurality of the popular vote is very likely to win the majority of the electoral vote needed to gain a victory. We then look at the pattern of results since World War II, showing that there has been a great deal of volatility, although with an advantage for the Republicans.

We turn next to the state-by-state results, examining the winning candidates' margins of victory over the past seven elections. We discuss partisan change in the post–World War II South and explain how the South was transformed into one of the most Republican regions of the country. We will see that although there have been other regional shifts as well, regional differences are substantially smaller than they were before World War II. Finally, we turn to the electoral vote balance between the Democrats and Republicans. We argue that neither party is in a dominant position and that each has a mixture of problems and opportunities.

Chapter 1

The Nomination Struggle

On March 3, 2004, Sen. John Edwards, N.C., withdrew from competition for the Democratic presidential nomination, effectively ensuring that Sen. John F. Kerry, Mass., would be nominated. This was six days earlier than both of the major-party nomination contests had effectively ended in 2000. Although Rev. Al Sharpton of New York and Rep. Dennis J. Kucinich, Ohio, continued their campaigns, only Edwards had even an outside chance at the nomination. His withdrawal set in motion events that would lead to Kerry's selecting Edwards as his vice-presidential running mate.

Twenty years earlier, the incumbent president, Ronald Reagan, was unopposed for nomination, just as President George W. Bush was in 2004. In 1984 a large field contended on the Democratic side for the nomination to oppose Reagan, just as occurred twenty years later. The eventual Democratic nominee in 1984, former vice president Walter F. Mondale, defeated a surprisingly strong challenge from a little-known senator, Gary Hart, Colo., again paralleling 2004. Mondale, however, did not have his nomination ensured until after the last primaries were completed, in June of that year. Although Hart ran a stronger campaign against Mondale than Edwards and the other Democrats did against Kerry, a major reason that the 2004 campaign was destined to end much sooner than the campaign of twenty years earlier was that the process known as "frontloading" was only beginning in 1984.

"Frontloading" is the term for the selection of delegates by the states to the national nominating conventions earlier and earlier in the year. Although frontloading began in the 1984 campaign, more delegates were still selected at the end of the campaign than at the beginning (five states, including California, held their primaries on June 5 of that year).[1] The effect of frontloading on the campaigns since has consistently been to speed up the choice of nominees, to months before their party's national conventions. As a further result, candidates have had to raise money, attract attention, and win popular support before the first primary (sometimes called the "invisible primary"), shaping and limiting the pool of candidates who can realistically imagine winning nomination. The 2004 contest was the most frontloaded since 1968, when many of the delegates who eventually supported Hubert H. Humphrey had been chosen in 1967.[2]

In many other respects the presidential nomination contests of 2004 looked similar not only to those of 1984, but to all of those that have been fought since 1972. Reforms in the late 1960s and early 1970s had brought about a new form of nomination campaign, one that required public campaigning for resources and votes. The system was sufficiently different from that which preceded it, and sufficiently in place by the 1972 campaign, that we refer to it as the "new nomination system of 1972." It has shaped many aspects of all subsequent contests, and we will examine similarities that have endured over its thirty-two-year existence. Each contest, of course, differs from all others because of the differing electoral contexts (for example, the state of the economy, of war and peace) and different contenders. And in the new nomination system, the rules change to some degree every four years, as well. The changes in rules, and the strategies that candidates adopt in light of those rules, combine with the context and contenders to make each campaign unique.

In 2004, as in 2000, the changes that had the most impact on candidate strategy and the ultimate outcome of the nomination contest were the dates on which each state held its presidential primary or caucuses. Many states, including some of the largest (for example, California and New York), did not start holding their primaries as early as possible until 2000. As we said, frontloading became one of the most important forces shaping the campaigns of 1996, 2000, and 2004. Learning from the experiences of their predecessors, the candidates in 2004 carefully designed their strategies around the frontloaded campaign. This confluence of circumstances accounts for the most striking aspects of the 2004 campaign—its early beginning and remarkably early conclusion. This confluence also helps us understand why Kerry won, rather than Edwards or some other candidate.

In this chapter, we examine some of the regularities of the campaigns since 1972 and see how they helped shape the 2004 nomination contests. Next we turn to the first step of the nomination process, the decisions of politicians to become—or not to become—presidential candidates. Then we will examine some of the rules of the nomination system they face. Finally we consider how the candidates ran and why Kerry succeeded in his quest.

WHO RAN

A first and important regularity of the nomination campaign is that when incumbents seek renomination, only a very few candidates will contest them, and perhaps no one will at all. In 1972, although President Richard M. Nixon did face two potentially credible challengers to his renomination, they were so ineffective that he was essentially uncontested. Gerald R. Ford in 1976, Jimmy Carter in 1980, and George H. W. Bush in 1992 faced one, or at most two, credible challengers. Bush was expected to have little difficulty defeating his challenger, Pat Buchanan, but had some difficulties at first, in part because he had not anticipated any struggle. Still, he defeated Buchanan rather easily.[3] Ford and Carter, however, had great difficulty defeating their opponents, Reagan and Sen. Edward M. "Ted" Kennedy, D-Mass., respectively. Those two campaigns, while demonstrating that incumbents are not assured of victory, nonetheless demonstrate the power of presidential incumbency because both incumbents were victorious despite facing the strongest imaginable challengers and despite being relatively weak incumbents.[4] But Ronald Reagan in 1984, Bill Clinton in 1996, and George W. Bush in 2004 were actually unopposed.

The second major regularity in the nomination system concerns the other set of contests, those in which the party has no incumbent seeking renomination. In such cases a relatively large number of candidates run for the nomination. Ten important Democrats sought their party's 2004 nomination, though only nine were still actively campaigning by January 1, 2004.[5] A nine-candidate field is typical for parties that do not have an incumbent president seeking the nomination. There have been nine such campaigns since 1980, and the number of major candidates that were in the race as the year began varied remarkably little: seven in 1980 (R); eight in 1984 (D); eight (D) and six (R) in 1988; eight in 1992 (D); eight in 1996 (R); and six in 2000 (R). Yet on the Democratic side in 2000, only Vice President Al Gore and former senator Bill Bradley, N.J., sought their party's nomination, even though numerous others seriously considered doing so.[6]

The ten Democrats who ran were retired general Wesley K. Clark; Howard Dean, former governor of Vermont; Edwards; Rep. Richard A. Gephardt, Mo.; Sen. Bob Graham, Fla.; Kerry; Rep. Dennis J. Kucinich; Sen. Joseph I. Lieberman, Conn. (Gore's running mate in 2000); Carol Moseley-Braun, former senator from Illinois; and the Rev. Alfred "Al" Sharpton Jr. Table 1-1 provides some further information about these contenders. This set of candidates illustrates the first two regularities: Few or none challenge incumbents, but many seek the nomination when there is no incumbent running. They also illustrate well several other major regularities.

A third regularity is that of the many who run in nomination contests without incumbents, only a few put their current office at risk to do so. Clark, Dean, Moseley-Braun, and Sharpton did not hold an elective office at the time. Kerry and Lieberman were not up for reelection to the Senate in 2004. Gephardt and Edwards would have been, but both had announced their retirement from office regardless of the outcome of their presidential bid. And although Graham did not announce his decision not to seek reelection to the Senate until December 2003, a month after he withdrew from the presidential race, there were indications as early as April that he might not run for reelection.[7] Thus, only Kucinich faced the unenviable prospect that he might have to choose between his current House seat and continuing a campaign for the presidency. However he had won with 74 percent of the vote in his 2002 election to the House and had no trouble retaining his seat in 2004.

TABLE 1-1   Major Candidates for the Democratic Nomination, 2004

Candidate	State	Year of birth	Year of election to highest office
Current or former U.S. senators			
John Edwards	North Carolina	1953	1998
Bob Graham	Florida	1936	1986
John F. Kerry	Massachusetts	1943	1984
Joseph I. Lieberman	Connecticut	1942	1988
Carol Moseley-Braun	Illinois	1947	1992 (Defeated in 1998)
Former governor			
Howard Dean	Vermont	1948	1992 (Did not run for reelection in 2002)
Current members of the U.S. House			
Richard A. Gephardt	Missouri	1941	1976
Dennis J. Kucinich	Ohio	1946	1996
Other			
Wesley K. Clark (four star general, retired 2000)	Arkansas	1944	None
Rev. Alfred "Al" Sharpton Jr.	New York	1954	None

Sources: CQ's Politics in America: The 107th Congress, ed. Brian Nutting and H. Amy Stern (Washington, D.C.: CQ Press, 2001); *Marquis Who's Who in America, 2005* (Providence, N.J.: Marquis Who's Who, 2004).

A fourth regularity is that of the candidates who were politicians, most held, or had recently held, high political office. This list (counting the nine Democrats who held political posts) included five senators and a governor. This regularity follows from "ambition theory," developed originally by Joseph A. Schlesinger to explain how personal ambition and the pattern and prestige of office will tend to emerge from political offices that provide the strongest electoral bases.[8] This base for the presidential candidates includes the offices of vice president, senator, governor, and of course the presidency itself. Note that Gephardt (who had resigned as minority leader of the House after Democratic losses in the 2002 midterm elections) and Kucinich were the only members of the U.S. House actually to run for the nomination. House members do not have a strong electoral base from which to run for the presidency and ordinarily must forgo a safe House seat to do so. As a result, few run and fewer still are strong contenders.[9]

TABLE 1-2   Current or Most Recent Office Held by Declared Candidates for President, Two Major Parties, 1972–2004

Office held	Percentage of all candidates who held that office	Number 1972–2004	Number 2004
President	7	7	1
Vice president	4	4	0
U.S. senator	38	39	5
U.S. representative	12	12	2
Governor	19	20	1
U.S. cabinet	4	4	0
Other	8	8	1
None	9	9	1
Total	101	103	11

Sources: The list of candidates between 1976 and 1992 is found in *Congressional Quarterly's Guide to U.S. Elections,* 4th ed. (Washington, D.C.: CQ Press, 2001), 562. Those in 1972 may be found in ibid., 522–525. Candidates for 1996 are listed and discussed in Paul R. Abramson, John H. Aldrich, and David W. Rohde, *Change and Continuity in the 1996 and 1998 Elections* (Washington, D.C.: CQ Press, 1999), 13. Year 2000 candidates are discussed in *CQ Weekly,* January 1, 2000, 22. Year 2004 candidates are listed in *Congressional Quarterly Weekly,* Fall 2003 Supplement, vol. 61, no. 48.

Most candidates in 2004, as in all earlier campaigns under the new nominating system, emerged from one of the strong electoral bases. Table 1-2 shows the data for 2004 and for all campaigns from 1972 through 2004 combined. Sixty-eight percent of all candidates emerged from the four offices that provide a strong electoral base, with nearly as large a percentage, 64 percent, in 2004.[10]

These contenders now prepared for the difficult and complicated task of actually conducting their campaigns. How they ran depended on the other candidates and on the rules (both formal and informal) of the nomination campaign. Knowing the list of candidates, we now turn to consider the remarkably complex game of nomination politics that characterizes campaigning in the new nomination system of 1972. As we shall see, frontloading is but one of the many features of this game.

THE RULES OF THE NOMINATION SYSTEM

The method that the two major parties use for nominating presidential candidates is unique and amazingly complicated. To add to the complication, the various formal rules, laws, and procedures for the nomination are changed—sometimes in large ways and invariably in numerous small ways—every four years. Beyond the formal rules lie informal standards and expectations, often set by the news media or the candidates themselves, that help shape each campaign. As variable as the rules are, however, the nomination system of 1972 has one pair of overriding characteristics that define it as a system: Beginning in 1972, for the first time, (1) the major-party presidential nominees have been selected in public and by the public; (2) as a result, all serious candidates have pursued the nomination by seeking the support of the public through the various communication media.

The complexity of the nomination contests is a consequence of four major factors. The first of these, federalism, or the state as the unit of selection for national nominees, began in 1824, the first year state legislatures nominated presidential candidates to challenge the congressional caucus. The second, the rules concerning the selection (and perhaps instruction) of delegates to the convention, and third, the rules concerning financing the campaign, are the (often revised) products of the reform period. The final factor is the way that candidates react to these rules and to their opponents. This last factor is the invariable consequence of keen competition for a highly valued goal.

Federalism or State-Based Delegate Selection

National conventions to select presidential nominees were first held for the 1832 election, and for every nomination from then to today, the votes of delegates attending the conventions have determined the nominees.[11] Delegates have always been allocated at the state level; whatever other particulars may apply, each state selects its parties' delegates through procedures adopted by state party organizations, by state law (which governs primary elections, as well as their dates, rules, and procedures), or both. Votes at the convention are cast by state delegation, and in general the state (including the District of Columbia, various territories, and for the Democrats, even Americans living abroad) is the basic unit of the nomination process. Thus there are at least fifty-one separate delegate selection contests in each party (plus procedures for the remaining units). There is no national primary, nor is there serious contemplation of one.

That there are more than fifty separate contests in each campaign creates numerous layers of complexity, two of which are especially consequential. First, each state is free to choose delegates using any method consistent with the general rules of the national party. Many states choose to select delegates via a primary election, which is a state-run election like any other, except that each primary selects delegates for only one party's convention. (It also is often an election to select the party's nominees for the various other electoral offices.) The Democratic Party requires that its party's primaries be open only to those who register as Democrats.[12] States not holding primaries use a combination of caucuses and conventions. Caucuses are simply local meetings of party members. Those attending the caucuses typically report their preferences for the presidential nomination (and must do so on the Democratic side) and choose delegates from their midst to attend higher-level conventions, perhaps at the county level, then the congressional district and state, and eventually national-level conventions.

In addition to selecting delegates, caucuses and subsequent conventions may endorse platform proposals and conduct other party business.

The second major consequence of federalism is that the states are free (within bounds; see below) to choose when to hold their primaries or caucuses. As a result, they are spread out over time. New Hampshire's has been the first primary in the nation since the state began to hold primaries in 1920, and state law requires that New Hampshire's primary be held before any other state's. A more recent tradition, which began in 1976, is that Iowa holds the first caucuses, in advance of the New Hampshire primary (a "tradition" challenged by other states, which have tried, from time to time, to schedule even earlier caucuses). The primary season in 2004 ended, as usual, in early June. In prior years, the season had ended with something of a flourish because the June primaries included the largest single prize, California. Even when California moved the date of its primary to earlier in the year, delegate selection was still spread over essentially the same time as in earlier years. The result has been a months-long process that features dramatic ebbs and flows of candidates' fortunes, albeit a more truncated one in the last three campaigns than in earlier ones. The lengthy and dynamic nature of this fifty-plus-event season preceded the reforms that created the nomination system of 1972, but those reforms have greatly accentuated the importance of length and have enhanced the dynamism.[13]

Since the 1980 campaign the Democratic Party has required that all its state parties select their delegates within a three-month "window." Designed to reduce the length of the primary campaign, the requirement exempted Iowa and New Hampshire, to respect their "traditions." The Republicans had no such rules until 2000, but many (although not all) states followed the Democratic example. Because primary elections are run by state governments, and to reduce the considerable expense involved, it is usually the case that both party primaries are held at the same time and thus within the confines of the Democratic window. Starting in 2000 and continuing in 2004, both parties have windows. There are differences between the two parties, however.

The Democratic Party window was pushed back to begin on its earliest date ever, February 3, and it ended on June 8. The Republican window in 2004 started at the same time but ended a week later, on June 15. Perhaps more important, the Republicans did not exempt Iowa and New Hampshire. Of course, because the GOP nomination was uncontested, the differences between the two parties were moot. Should such differences persist in 2008, however, when both nominations will be open and presumably strongly contested, difficulties, perhaps especially over the New Hampshire primary, may arise.

The Nomination System of 1972: Delegate Selection

Through 1968, presidential nominations were won by appeals to the party leadership. To be sure, public support and even primary election victories could be important in a candidate's campaign, but their importance would lie in the credibility they would give to the candidacy in the eyes of party leaders. But the 1968 Democratic nomination, as so many other events that year, was especially tumultuous, with the result that the Democratic Party began a series of reforms, initiated by proposals from the McGovern-Fraser Commission, as adopted by the party convention in 1972, that created one of the two major components of the new nomination system, that concerning delegate selection. Although it was much less aggressive in reforming its delegate selection procedures, the Republican Party did so to a certain degree. Moreover, the most consequential results of these reforms for our purposes—the proliferation of presidential primaries and the media's treatment of some (notably the Iowa) caucuses as essentially primary-like—spilled over to the Republican side in full measure.

In 1968 Sens. Eugene J. McCarthy, D-Minn., and Robert F. Kennedy, D-N.Y., ran highly visible, public, primary-oriented campaigns in opposition to the policies of President Lyndon B. Johnson, especially the conduct of the war in Vietnam. Before the second primary, in Wisconsin, Johnson surprisingly announced, "I shall not seek and I will not accept the nomination of my party for another term as your President." [14] Vice President Hubert H. Humphrey took Johnson's place in representing the party establishment and the policies of the Democratic Party. Humphrey, however, waged no public campaign, winning nomination without entering a single primary,[15] and his nomination split an already deeply divided party. Whether Humphrey would have won the nomination had Bobby Kennedy not been assassinated the night he defeated McCarthy in California, effectively eliminating McCarthy as a serious contender, is unknowable. The chaos, and even violence, that accompanied Humphrey's nomination made it clear to Democrats, however, that the nomination process should be opened to more diverse candidacies and that public participation should be more open and more efficacious, perhaps even determinative.

The two most significant consequences of the reforms were the increased decisiveness of the public in each state's delegate selection proceedings (delegates would now be bound to vote for the candidate whom they were chosen to support) and the proliferation of presidential primaries.[16] Caucus-convention procedures were made more timely, better publicized, and in short, more primary-like. Until recently, the media treated Iowa's caucuses as critical events, and the coverage of them was similar to the coverage of primaries—how many "votes" were "cast" for each candidate, for example. At the state level, many party officials concluded that the easiest way to conform to the new Democratic rules in 1972 was to hold a primary election. Thus the number of states (including D.C.) holding Democratic primaries increased from fifteen in 1968, to twenty-one in 1972, to twenty-seven in 1976, with the number of Republican primaries increasing comparably. By 1988 thirty-six states held Republican primaries (thirty-four did on the Democratic side), which selected three of every four delegates to the Republican convention that year. In 2000 forty-three states conducted Republican primaries, and Democratic primaries were held in forty states. In 2004 thirty-five states held a Democratic Party primary. The sixteen caucuses were typically held in small states (and D.C.), with the two largest exceptions being North Carolina and Michigan. Thus it is fair to say that the parties' new nomination systems have come to be based largely on primaries.

The only major exception to this conclusion is that about one in five delegates to the Democratic National Convention is chosen because he or she is an elected officeholder or a Democratic Party official. Supporters of this reform to party rules (first used in 1984) wanted to ensure that the Democratic leadership would have a formal role to play at the conventions of the party. These "superdelegates" may have played a decisive role in the 1984 nomination of Walter F. Mondale. They have not played a pivotal role in subsequent nomination contests, but because they make up nearly 20 percent of the votes, it is always possible that they may be decisive in future contests.

The delegate selection process has, as noted, become considerably more front-loaded, and this has changed nomination politics.[17] The rationale for frontloading is clear enough: California's (actual or near) end-of-season primary was last consequential in the 1964 Republican and the 1972 Democratic nomination contests. Once candidates, the media, and other actors realized, and reacted to, the implications of the reformed nomination system, the action shifted to the earliest events of the season, and nomination contests, especially those involving multiple candidates, were effectively completed well before the end of the primary season. More and more state parties and legislatures realized the advantages of frontloading, bringing more attention from the media, more expenditures of time and money by the candidates, and more influence to their states if they held primaries earlier rather than later.

If the rationale for frontloading was clear by 1996, when it first became controversial, the consequences were not. Some argued that long-shot candidates could be propelled to the front of the pack by gathering momentum in Iowa and New Hampshire and, before the well-known candidates could react, lock up the nomination early. The alternative argument was that increasing frontloading helps those who begin the campaign with the advantages associated with being a front-runner, such as name recognition, support from state and local party or related organizations, and most of all, money.

Indeed, as the primary season has become more frontloaded, the well-known, well-established, and well-financed candidates have increasingly come to dominate the primaries. Sen. George S. McGovern, S.D., and Jimmy Carter won the Democratic nominations in 1972 and 1976, even though they began as little-known and ill-financed contenders. George H. W. Bush, successful in the 1980 Iowa Republican caucuses, climbed from being, in his words, "an asterisk in the polls" (where the asterisk is commonly used to indicate less than 1 percent support) to become Reagan's major challenger and eventual vice-presidential choice. And Gary Hart nearly defeated former vice president Mondale in 1984. In 1988 the two strongest candidates at the start of the Republican race, George H. W. Bush and Bob Dole, contested vigorously, with Bush winning, while Gov. Michael S. Dukakis, Mass., was the best-financed and best-organized Democrat and won nomination surprisingly easily. Clinton's victory in 1992, then, appeared to be the culmination of the trend toward insuperable advantage for the strongest and best-financed candidates. Clinton was able to withstand scandal and defeat in the early going and eventually cruise to victory.

The 1992 campaign of former senator Paul Tsongas, D-Mass., illustrates one important reason for Clinton's victory. Tsongas defeated the field in New Hampshire, and as usual, the victory and its consequent media attention opened doors to fund-raising possibilities unavailable to him even days earlier. Yet Tsongas faced the dilemma that taking the time to raise the funds and use them to increase the chances of winning votes would allow too many primaries to pass without his competing. Conversely, if he campaigned in those primaries, he would not have the opportunity to raise and direct the funds he needed to be an effective competitor. Frontloading had, simply, squeezed too much into too short a post–New Hampshire time frame for a candidate to be able to capitalize on early victories as, say, Carter had done in winning nomination and election in 1976. The events of 1996 supported the alternative argument—that increased frontloading benefits the front-runner—also, even though it took nearly all of Dole's resources to effect his early victory.

This lesson was not lost on the candidates for 2000. George W. Bush, especially, was able to learn from Dole's experience and act on the lesson. In particular, he began his quest in 1999 (or earlier!) as a reasonably well regarded governor but one not particularly well known to the public outside of Texas (although, of course, sharing his father's name made him instantly recognizable). He was, at that point, only one of several plausible contenders. Bush, however, worked hard to receive early endorsements from party leaders and raised considerable sums of money well in advance of his competition. When others sought to match his early successes in this "invisible primary," they found that he had sewn up a great deal of support. Many, in fact, withdrew before the first vote was cast, suddenly realizing just how Bush's actions had lengthened the odds against them. Bush therefore was able to win nomination at the very opening of the primary season. Incumbent vice president Al Gore, on the other side, benefited from the same dynamics of the invisible primary, although in the more classical role of one who started the nomination season as the odds-on favorite and therefore the one most able to shut the door on his opposition well before most voters cast their ballots.[18]

The Nomination System of 1972: Campaign Finance

The second aspect of the reform of the presidential nomination process began with the Federal Election Campaign Act of 1971, but it was the amendments to the act of 1974 and 1976 that dramatically altered the nature of campaign financing. The Watergate scandal included revelations of substantial abuse in raising and spending money in the 1972 presidential election (facts discovered in part because of the implementation of the 1971 act). The resulting regulations limited contributions by individuals and groups, virtually ending the power of individual "fat cats" and requiring presidential candidates to raise money in a broad-based campaign. Small donations for the nomination could be matched by the federal government, and candidates who accepted matching funds would be bound by limits on what they could spend (a provision that effectively limited Dole's campaign efforts in spring 1996, after he had won the primaries but before the nominating conventions).

These provisions, created by the Federal Election Commission to monitor campaign financing and regulate campaign practices, altered the way nomination campaigns were funded. Still, just as candidates learned over time how to contest most effectively in the new delegate selection process, so too did they learn how to campaign in light of the financial regulations. Perhaps most important, presidential candidates learned—though it is not as true for them as for congressional candidates—that "early money is like yeast, because it helps the dough rise." [19] They believed in both 1996 and 2000 that a great deal of early money was necessary to compete effectively.[20]

The costs of running presidential nomination campaigns have escalated dramatically since 1972. The spike is not, of course, unique to the new presidential nomination system. The costs of campaigning for all major offices have escalated dramatically. But a special chain of strategic reactions has spurred the cost of campaigning for the presidential nomination.

The McGovern-Fraser Commission reforms did not specify that delegates should be chosen via primary elections. Indeed, they indicated a preference for the use of (more open and accessible) caucuses and conventions instead of primaries. The commission, however, sought to achieve a variety of goals, and state parties and legislatures found that compliance with the full set of reform recommendations made the caucus-convention method complicated, whereas compliance via primary elections would be less cumbersome. Increasing numbers of states therefore chose to comply by using primaries. This led to more media coverage of particular events, to the greater possibility of a campaign's developing momentum, and to enhancement of the value of early victories (and harsher costs of early defeats). As we saw earlier, these reactions, in turn, led states to create the frontloaded season that candidates faced in 2004. All of these factors created not only a demand for more money, but also a demand for that money to be raised early, in advance of the primary season. The result, using 2000 for illustration, was that only by raising large sums of money in 1999 could candidates hope to compete effectively in the eleven coast-to-coast primaries held on March 7, 2000.

Bob Dole, in 1996, demonstrated that even the primary victor could not rest on his or her laurels and spend the interim between the primary and general election seasons preparing for the fall. Instead, the victor had to plan on being able to fill that period with expensive, public campaigning. But money that he spent in Republican primary contests could not be replenished with newly raised funds for contesting the unchallenged incumbent on the other side. The reason is that Dole had accepted federal funding and therefore also accepted limits on expenditures. As a result, he was at a comparative disadvantage against an incumbent president who could spend all of his primary season money contesting against Republicans and who also had unparalleled access to the media because of being president. These lessons were not lost on Bush in 2000. He was able to raise huge sums in 1999 and therefore felt free to reject federal funding. Thus he could spend as much money as he could raise during the primary season, especially after he had vanquished his last serious intraparty rival. This lesson was also not lost on Democrats in 2004.

HOW KERRY WON

Although John Kerry had been a national figure since the early 1970s and a senator for twenty years, like most senators he was not a household name. But then, none of the Democratic candidates was. At the very earliest beginnings, he was as close to a front-runner as there was, but certainly not as strong a front-runner as, say, Gore had been in 2000. Perhaps the single biggest surprise of the campaign—and certainly the biggest surprise of the invisible primary season—was the rise to prominence of Howard Dean. Indeed, by the height of the pre-primary season he led in the polls. Of course, that indicated only a small lead over the other candidates. For example, Zogby's poll of September 3–5, 2003 (about the date when pre-nomination campaigns began before the advent of frontloading) had Dean as the first choice of more likely voters in the Democratic primaries than any other candidate. But his figure was 16 percent, compared with Kerry's 13 percent and Lieberman's 12 percent.[21]

Dean was considered a reasonably moderate governor, albeit of Vermont, one of the most liberal states in the country. Dean focused his attention, however, on opposing the Bush administration's foreign policies, especially the war in Iraq. While most prominent Democrats, including Kerry, emphasized their support for the troops, the war on terrorism, and even the war in Iraq (while opposing how the administration was conducting it), Dean took a four-square position against the Iraq war. This not only brought him a lot of media attention in the pre-primary season (very useful for a little-known candidate), but it also made him a favorite of liberal Democrats.

Dean's early campaign introduced one new feature to campaigns—or more accurately, developed a new feature further than anyone had before him. That feature was the use of the Internet, especially for generating resources. Dean and his staff showed how rapidly money could be raised and how volunteers could be motivated through the Web. At some level this further "democratizes" the campaign, by gathering relatively small donations from a very large number of donors who evidently give in the absence of any personal commitment from the candidate. Before the campaign finance reforms, candidates could raise money rapidly if they could convince a few rich fat cats to bankroll them. Later (as we described above), Carter's campaign showed how to use early primary victories to attract subsequent resources from the more general public. But as we also discussed earlier, the cost was time—time spent raising money was time not spent winning voters over to one's side. This time-budget constraint became particularly binding as frontloading increased. But through Internet fund-raising, via secure credit card donations (and Web-based appeals created by staff), individuals could respond to events without the long, begging phone calls to political action committees and the like that so consumed the time and energy of candidates. The success of the Dean endeavor, to the tune of some $50 million by the first primary, led Dean to follow Bush in 2000 (and 2004) in choosing not to accept federal matching funds. Kerry (and Moseley-Braun and Sharpton) also chose to decline.

A typical media cycle is for newly discovered candidates to receive lots of positive attention, followed by a turn to criticism, as the "novelty factor" wears off. Reasonably well-known candidates with substantial track records have public images that are not so much shaped by this "news cycle"; that is to say, unlike what happens with a well-known contender, most people learned about Dean from the news media in 2003 and early 2004. Thus he was perceived to be "the" liberal and antiwar candidate of the campaign, although he described himself as representing "the Democratic wing of the Democratic Party."

While Dean was formulating his campaign strategy, emerging from the pack, and establishing his position on the left, Kerry's campaign seemed at times to be stuck, as his efforts to provide nuanced positions, such as a policy on the war in Iraq (explaining why he voted for the war but against funding it, for instance), did not attract much in the way of positive media attention. As a result, Kerry narrowly trailed Dean in the polls as 2003 closed. And success in the pre- or invisible-primary season is based on such indirect measures as money raised, media attention, and popular poll standings.

Of course, all of these indirect measures are useful if they help the candidate win and help him turn out supporters in the primary or caucus. The "invisible" campaign ends when there are tangible, "visible" results. That first happens in the Iowa caucuses. Although early indications were that Dean would do surprisingly well, Kerry made Iowa—and Dean—a point of heavy focus. A third candidate, Edwards, also had a great deal riding on Iowa. He was little known, inexperienced not just in presidential but in any sort of politics, and as a result lightly regarded. However, Edwards proved to be a very effective campaigner. In addition, while Dean and Kerry were sparring with each other, Edwards provided a stark contrast by his positive campaigning. And Iowa was particularly important to him because the following event, in New Hampshire, was on the home turf of three New Englanders (including Lieberman), leaving Edwards little opportunity for gathering support.

However the dynamics of popular support may actually have gone (especially in a low-turnout caucus), it appeared that Dean lost support, while Kerry and Edwards gained ground. As Table 1-3 shows, Kerry won in Iowa with 37 percent to Edwards's 33 percent, with Dean in third place with 17 percent. New

TABLE 1-3 Democratic Presidential Caucus Results, 2004

State	Date	Total vote	Clark	Dean	Edwards	Kerry	Kucinich	Sharpton	Uncommitted	Other	Winner
Iowa	1/19/2004	124,331	0.1%	17.4%	32.6%	37.1%	1.0%	0.0%	0.2%	11.7%	Kerry
New Mexico	2/3/2004	102,096	20.4%	16.4%	11.2%	42.6%	5.5%	X	0.5%	3.4%	Kerry
North Dakota	2/3/2004	10,558	23.7%	11.7%	9.7%	50.8%	2.9%	0.3%	X	0.9%	Kerry
Michigan	2/7/2004	163,769	6.7%	16.5%	13.4%	51.8%	3.2%	7.0%	0.3%	1.2%	Kerry
Washington	2/7/2004	23,528	3.3%	30.0%	6.7%	48.3%	8.3%	0.1%	3.4%	X	Kerry
Maine	2/8/2004	18,259	3.6%	27.1%	7.0%	47.1%	13.8%	0.1%	1.2%	0.1%	Kerry
District of Columbia	2/14/2004	9,126	1.0%	17.5%	10.2%	46.9%	3.3%	20.0%	0.2%	0.9%	Kerry
Nevada	2/14/2004	3,582	X	16.8%	10.4%	62.9%	6.7%	0.7%	2.5%	X	Kerry
Hawaii	2/24/2004	4,073	0.5%	7.3%	12.5%	47.1%	31.2%	X	1.1%	0.3%	Kerry
Idaho	2/24/2004	4,920	X	11.1%	23.0%	55.4%	3.7%	X	6.9%	X	Kerry
Minnesota	3/2/2004	51,518	0.3%	2.0%	27.0%	50.7%	17.0%	0.6%	2.2%	0.1%	Kerry
Kansas	3/13/2004	2,000	0.7%	6.7%	8.7%	71.9%	10.2%	X	1.7%	X	Kerry
Alaska	3/20/2004	500	X	11.1%	2.6%	47.8%	26.5%	X	12.0%	X	Kerry
Wyoming	3/20/2004	665	X	3.1%	4.2%	77.4%	6.1%	0.8%	8.4%	X	Kerry
Colorado	4/13/2004	12,000	0.3%	2.5%	0.9%	63.7%	13.0%	0.0%	19.6%	X	Kerry
North Carolina	4/17/2004	17,809	X	5.9%	51.6%	27.1%	11.7%	3.2%	0.6%	X	Edwards

Sources: CQ Weekly, July 24, 2004 Supplement, vol. 62, no. 28; The Rhodes Cook Letter, August 2004, 19–20.

Note: All total vote numbers are estimates; X indicates no data or that the candidate was not on the ballot in that state.

Hampshire was thus critical if Dean was to recover at all. But Kerry defeated him 38 percent to 26 percent (see Table 1-4). It was common to attribute Dean's slide in his neighboring state to a speech he gave to Iowa supporters the night of the Iowa caucuses, when it was becoming clear that he had lost. He encouraged his supporters by saying "We will not give up! We will not give up in New Hampshire! We will not give up in South Carolina! We will not give up in Arizona or New Mexico, Oklahoma, North Dakota, Delaware, Pennsylvania, Ohio, Michigan!" He concluded with a long, loud "Yeahhhhh" that was replayed and replayed on news media—and can still be found on Web logs ("blogs") as of this writing.[22] Conversely one might argue, first, that Dean never was able to translate his pre-primary season "lead" into on-the-ground support, and second, that his third-place showing in Iowa was more consequential than his "war cry" in generating his campaign's downward momentum.

Victories in Iowa and New Hampshire pushed Kerry to clear front-runner status. He employed the strategy that has proved successful in the frontloaded era—gain early success and back it with a strong organization and lots of resources to transform early success into rapid victory. To be sure, when the "window" opened on February 3, Kerry did not win all seven events (five primaries and two caucuses) that night. He did, however, win five of them, with Edwards winning the South Carolina primary and Clark the Oklahoma primary (in a near-tie with Edwards). From that point on, however, Kerry won forty of forty-two contests. Edwards and others continued to battle Kerry through "Super Tuesday," the term given to the day on which the most primaries, selecting the most delegates, occur. That was March 2, 2004, with nine primaries and one caucus, including those in such large states as California, New York, and Ohio. Once Kerry won all of those by large-to-massive margins (except for Dean's home state of Vermont, which Dean did win), the race was effectively over. The next day Edwards, the most viable remaining opponent, announced his withdrawal and endorsed Kerry.

Kerry's earlier decision to decline federal funding was to prove critical: He was able to raise about two hundred million dollars from campaign events and advertising between early March and his party's end-of-July convention, with which to contest the general election campaign. Although that campaign would not formally begin until the fall, or at least until after the two national party conventions, in practice the spring and summer were given over not just to preparing for, but also to actually conducting, the general election campaign, if at a slightly more leisurely pace than would be the case in September.

THE CONVENTIONS

While the five months from Kerry's primary victory until his formal nomination were primarily given over to keeping as much public attention as possible focused on his candidacy (that is, to running a general election campaign, attempting to match that of Bush), there were still preparations to make. The

TABLE 1-4 Democratic Presidential Primary Results, 2004

State	Date	Total vote	Clark	Dean	Edwards	Kerry	Kucinich	Sharpton	Uncommitted	Other	Winner
New Hampshire	1/27/2004	219,787	12.4%	26.3%	12.1%	38.4%	1.4%	0.2%	X	9.3%	Kerry
Arizona	2/3/2004	238,942	26.5%	14.0%	6.9%	42.6%	1.6%	0.5%	X	7.8%	Kerry
Delaware	2/3/2004	33,291	9.5%	10.4%	11.0%	50.4%	1.0%	5.7%	X	11.9%	Kerry
Missouri	2/3/2004	418,339	4.4%	8.7%	24.6%	50.6%	1.2%	3.4%	1.0%	6.1%	Kerry
Oklahoma	2/3/2004	302,385	29.9%	4.2%	29.5%	26.8%	0.8%	1.3%	X	7.4%	Clark
South Carolina	2/3/2004	293,843	7.2%	4.8%	45.1%	29.8%	0.5%	9.7%	X	2.9%	Edwards
Tennessee	2/10/2004	369,385	23.1%	4.4%	26.5%	41.0%	X	1.7%	0.7%	2.0%	Kerry
Virginia	2/10/2004	396,181	9.2%	7.0%	26.6%	51.5%	1.3%	3.2%	X	1.1%	Kerry
Wisconsin	2/17/2004	826,250	1.5%	18.2%	34.3%	39.6%	3.3%	1.8%	0.1%	1.1%	Kerry
Utah	2/24/2004	34,854	1.4%	3.8%	29.8%	55.2%	7.4%	X	0.9%	1.5%	Kerry
California	3/2/2004	3,107,629	1.6%	4.2%	19.8%	64.4%	4.7%	1.9%	X	3.4%	Kerry
Connecticut	3/2/2004	130,023	1.2%	4.0%	23.7%	58.3%	3.2%	2.5%	0.8%	6.3%	Kerry
Georgia	3/2/2004	626,738	0.7%	1.8%	41.4%	46.8%	1.2%	6.2%	X	1.9%	Kerry
Maryland	3/2/2004	481,476	0.9%	2.6%	25.5%	59.6%	1.8%	4.5%	1.8%	3.3%	Kerry
Massachusetts	3/2/2004	615,188	0.5%	2.8%	17.6%	71.8%	4.1%	1.0%	0.7%	1.5%	Kerry
New York	3/2/2004	715,633	0.5%	2.9%	20.1%	61.2%	5.1%	8.0%	X	2.2%	Kerry
Ohio	3/2/2004	1,193,339	1.0%	2.5%	34.1%	51.8%	9.0%	X	X	1.5%	Kerry
Rhode Island	3/2/2004	35,759	0.7%	4.0%	18.6%	71.2%	2.9%	X	1.2%	1.5%	Kerry
Vermont	3/2/2004	82,881	3.3%	53.6%	6.2%	31.6%	4.1%	X	X	1.3%	Dean
Florida	3/9/2004	753,762	1.4%	2.8%	10.0%	77.2%	2.3%	2.8%	X	3.6%	Kerry
Louisiana	3/9/2004	161,653	4.4%	4.9%	16.1%	69.7%	1.5%	X	X	3.4%	Kerry
Mississippi	3/9/2004	76,298	2.5%	2.6%	7.3%	78.4%	0.1%	5.2%	1.8%	1.3%	Kerry
Texas	3/9/2004	839,231	2.2%	4.8%	14.3%	67.1%	1.8%	3.7%	X	6.0%	Kerry

State	Date	Votes									Winner
Illinois	3/16/2004	1,217,515	1.6%	3.9%	10.8%	71.7%	2.3%	3.0%	X	6.7%	Kerry
Pennsylvania	4/27/2004	787,304	X	10.1%	9.7%	74.1%	3.8%	X	X	2.2%	Kerry
Indiana	5/4/2004	317,211	5.5%	6.8%	11.2%	72.8%	2.2%	X	X	1.4%	Kerry
Nebraska	5/11/2004	71,572	X	7.5%	14.0%	73.3%	2.1%	1.9%	X	1.1%	Kerry
West Virginia	5/11/2004	246,056	3.6%	4.2%	13.4%	69.2%	2.4%	X	X	7.1%	Kerry
Arkansas	5/18/2004	266,848	X	X	X	66.6%	5.2%	X	23.2%	5.1%	Kerry
Kentucky	5/18/2004	229,805	2.8%	3.6%	14.5%	60.1%	2.0%	2.2%	9.2%	5.6%	Kerry
Oregon	5/18/2004	368,544	X	X	X	78.6%	16.3%	X	X	5.1%	Kerry
Alabama	6/1/2004	217,228	X	X	X	75.0%	4.2%	X	3.3%	X	Kerry
South Dakota	6/1/2004	84,405	X	5.7%	X	82.3%	2.4%	X	6.0%	3.5%	Kerry
Montana	6/8/2004	91,914	4.4%	X	9.1%	68.0%	10.4%	X	X	8.2%	Kerry
New Jersey	6/8/2004	208,176	X	X	X	92.1%	4.4%	X	X	3.5%	Kerry

Sources: CQ Weekly, July 24, 2004 Supplement, vol. 62, no. 28; The Rhodes Cook Letter, August 2004, 19–20.

Note: An X indicates no data or that the candidate was not on the ballot in that state.

most important preparation was to select a running mate—or technically, to decide on a person whom he would "recommend" to the national convention delegates that they nominate for vice president.[23] Edwards had impressed many by a forceful presentation of his vision for America and his consistently positive presentation of reasons to support him, avoiding negative campaigning against opponents. It made him an attractive candidate to many, and after deliberate and lengthy consideration, Kerry chose him. Thus, two of the important decisions that national party conventions reach were already in place, waiting for the delegates to ratify them.

In the nineteenth century and the first half of the twentieth, political decisions were reached at the national conventions themselves (albeit rarely by the delegates; usually by the political bosses who controlled "their" delegations). Presidential nominations are still made on the convention floor, but it is rare in this new nomination system for there to be any doubt when the convention opens about who the nominee will be. Indeed, whereas it used to be the case that presidential nominees spent the night after their formal nomination deciding on their running mate, the early date by which presidential nominees are now known permits them the opportunity to select their running mate carefully, well in advance. Other important actions of the convention are the approval of delegates as having been appropriately chosen, the selection of rules to govern the party for the next four years, and the adoption of the party platform. Any of these could, in principle, become controversial at the convention, but they rarely do. With so many primaries, set by state law, most questions about delegate credentials are resolved well before the convention. Parties appoint committees to develop rules and platforms in advance, typically resolving controversies at that point.

All of these attempts to reduce the possibilities of controversy and conflict are intentional. Conventions today are designed to showcase the party, and especially its nominees, in as positive a light as possible. In that sense, the centerpiece of the convention is no longer the roll call of states as they vote on the presidential nomination or debate over the content of the party platform, but the acceptance speech by the successful nominee. The candidate makes a nationally televised, prime-time speech that helps to define his image and explain what he stands for.

Both candidates benefited from smoothly run conventions in 2004. The Democratic convention was held in Boston from July 26 through 29. Kerry, in an attempt to address a long-running perception of liberal Democrats as weak on defense, opened his speech with a salute and the statement that he was reporting for duty. This and what followed reminded the public that he is a decorated navy hero from his service in Vietnam and were intended to divert attention away from his being a Massachusetts Democrat and toward the events of the day instead, especially the war in Iraq. That war and the wars in Afghanistan and against terrorism constituted one of Kerry's two major themes. The other was the economy.

Ever since 1936 the party of the president has held its convention after the challenging party's. It is unusual, however, for the incumbent party's nominating convention to be held at the end of August, instead of shortly after the out-party's convention (typically held, as in 2004, in late July).[24] The 2004 Republican convention took place in New York City, August 30 through September 2. The move to the end of August–early September meant three things: First, by meeting in Madison Square Garden, only three miles from Ground Zero, the site of the World Trade Center, at the beginning of September, just eight days before the third anniversary of 9/11, Bush could remind voters of his commitment to fighting terrorism. Second, the convention would lead almost immediately into the general election campaign. If, as Bush did (but Kerry did not), the nominee got a boost in the polls from the convention and its media coverage, then it would help launch him at least a little more strongly into the fall campaign. Third, it helped Bush by enabling him to continue to spend nomination season money throughout August.

When they formally receive the nomination, the major-party candidates receive full federal funding, $74.6 million in 2004, and accept limits on spending. A late-August convention meant that Bush could legally continue spending money raised for his nomination, saving the general election funds for later. Even though Bush and Kerry had declined federal funding for the presidential nomination campaign, they both accepted it for the general election. Kerry had to choose between spending as little money as possible in August, and thereby losing momentum generated by the convention, or spending money in August that would reduce the amount he had left for later in the fall. It is possible that the little-to-no "convention bounce" (jump in poll standings) that Kerry experienced after the Democratic convention was due to his choice to try to spend as little as possible in August, a choice that was complicated by attacks on him focused on his Vietnam service. But that was a part of the general election campaign, to which we turn in the next chapter.

Chapter 2

The General Election Campaign

Once they have been nominated, candidates choose their general election campaign strategies based on their perceptions of what the electorate wants, the relative strengths and weaknesses of their opponents and themselves, and their chances of winning. A candidate who is convinced that he has a dependable lead may choose strategies very different from those used by a candidate who believes he is seriously behind. A candidate who believes that an opponent has significant weaknesses is more likely to run an aggressive, attacking campaign than one who does not perceive such weaknesses.

After the 2004 conventions, the race was close. Most observers, and both candidates' organizations, believed that either George W. Bush or John F. Kerry could win (although most also thought that Bush had a real advantage) and that the campaign could really make a difference. Part 2 of this book will consider in detail the impact of particular factors (including both issues and evaluations of Bush's job performance) on the voters' decisions. In this chapter we provide an overview of the campaign—an account of its course and a description of the context within which strategic decisions were made.

THE STRATEGIC CONTEXT AND CANDIDATES' CHOICES

One aspect of the strategic context that candidates must consider is the track record of the parties in recent presidential elections. In presidential races, the past is certainly not entirely prologue, but it is relevant. From this perspective, the picture was slightly more encouraging for the Republicans than for the Democrats. From 1952 through 2000 there had been thirteen presidential elections, and the Republicans had won eight of them. Similarly, the GOP had won three of the five races since 1984, and the two biggest Electoral College victories during that period also belonged to the Republicans.

The nature of the American system for electing presidents requires that we examine the state-by-state pattern of results. U.S. voters do not directly vote for president or vice president. Rather, they vote for a slate of electors pledged to support a presidential and a vice-presidential candidate. Moreover, in every state except Maine and Nebraska, the entire slate of electors that receives the most popular votes is selected. In no state is a majority of the vote required. Since the 1972 election, Maine has used a system in which the winner of a plurality in the whole state wins two electoral votes. In addition, the plurality-vote winner in each of Maine's two House districts receives that district's single electoral vote. Beginning in 1992, Nebraska has allocated its five electoral votes in a similar manner: The statewide plurality-vote winner gains two votes, and the winner of a plurality in each of the state's three congressional districts gains one vote.

If larger states used the district plan employed by Maine and Nebraska, the dynamics of the campaign would be different.[1] For example, candidates might then target specific congressional districts and would probably campaign in all large states, regardless of how well they were doing in the statewide polls. But given the winner-take-all rules employed in forty-eight states and the District of Columbia, candidates cannot safely ignore the pattern of past state results. A state-by-state analysis of the five presidential elections from 1984 through 2000 suggests that the Democrats did not face an easy task in the effort to win the 270 electoral votes required for victory.

As Figure 2-1 reveals, sixteen states voted Republican in all five of these elections. Only one state, Minnesota, and the District of Columbia were equally loyal to the Democrats (see chapter 3 on long-term voting patterns). These perfectly loyal states provided a prospective foundation of 135 electoral votes for the Republicans, to only 13 for the Democrats. Less problematic for the Democratic candidates were the next groups of states: Five states, with a total of 64 electoral votes, had voted Republican in every election but one. Balancing them were eight states, with 86 electoral votes, that had supported the Democrats in four of the five contests.[2] Thus if these states' political leanings were categorized solely on the basis of the last five elections, one might expect that 199 electoral votes were likely to go to the GOP, while only 96 were as likely to go to the Democrats.

If this past pattern had completely controlled the 2004 election, the Democratic ticket would have been at a severe disadvantage. But, of course, things were not that simple, and many factors made Democratic chances considerably better than they had been in the 1980s. Most obviously, the Democrats had *won* two of the three previous elections and had come within an eyelash of winning three straight. Bill Clinton had carried many large states that were not sure things for the GOP, winning comfortable (albeit not overwhelming) majorities in the Electoral College. In particular, the Democrats had pried the largest state, California—which had once leaned Republican—away from the GOP. It now appeared to have a definite Democratic tilt, although it was not a certain victory. That, plus very good prospects in a number of the other big states, formed the basis for a plausible Democratic prospect of victory.

Thus either party could win, and both campaign organizations saw virtually the same states as determining the outcome. These would be the "battleground"

FIGURE 2-1   States That Voted Republican at Least Four out of Five Times, 1984–2000, with Numbers of Electoral Votes

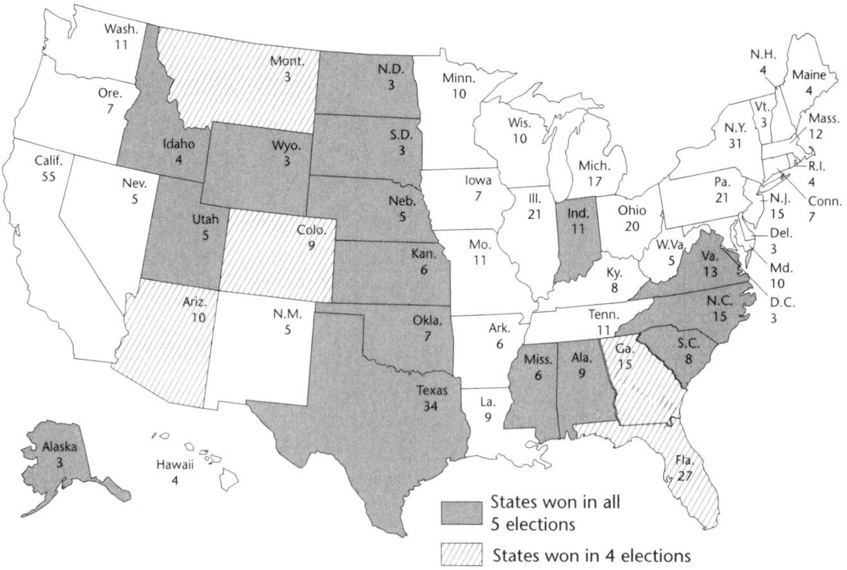

Source: Presidential Elections, 1789–2000 (Washington, D.C.: CQ Press, 2002), 223–227.

states, where both campaign organizations would concentrate the lion's share of their time, money, and effort. Indeed, as early as mid-March the two parties had already focused their attention on a set of eighteen states, and most of the other thirty-two states would be largely ignored until election day.[3] The larger states in this group—particularly Florida, Michigan, Ohio, and Pennsylvania—would be the main focus of their efforts. Many of the remaining states, on the other hand—even large ones such as California, New York, and Texas—would see little evidence that a presidential campaign was in progress. Thus a state perspective, through the lens of the Electoral College, would determine strategy in the 2004 campaign.[4]

FROM THE SPRING TO THE DEBATES

As we saw in chapter 1, Bush's renomination was never in doubt and Kerry had secured his nomination by the first week in March. The day after Kerry's March 2 string of primary victories, Bush made a speech in Los Angeles to kick off his campaign. In it he mentioned Kerry by name for the first time. Thus the general election campaign in effect began at that point, and it would last about eight months. Much of the story we will tell about 2004 will stress similarities to the election of 2000. However, we want to focus first on one of the biggest differences from four years before—the fact of Bush's incumbency.

Ebb and Flow Before the Conventions

Contests with incumbents are different from those without. They tend to unfold in a regular pattern, and the first stage of the pattern centers on the public's attitudes toward the current occupant of the White House. As we will discuss in detail in chapter 7, elections involving incumbents tend to be referendums on presidential performance. During the period 1953–2000, for which we have dependable measurements of the public's evaluation of the presidents' performance, there were nine elections in which an incumbent president could face the electorate. (In three other elections—1960, 1988, and 2000—the incumbent was constitutionally ineligible to run again.) In five of those elections, the president had approval ratings above 50 percent during the spring before the vote—that is, before the general election campaign and even well before the selection of the opposing nominee by his party's convention. In all five instances, the incumbent won comfortably. On the other hand, the incumbent's approval was below 50 percent in four cases. In all of those, he either withdrew from the race or lost.[5]

These data indicate that Bush's approval rating was an important indicator of his prospects for reelection, and in early 2004 the news was decidedly mixed. Between the beginning of March and the end of July (when the Democratic convention was held), Bush's approval rating, measured by the Gallup poll, ranged between 46 percent and 53 percent.[6] Thus the president's standing was right on the historical borderline between victory and defeat, confirming the prospects for a real contest that either major party could win. This moved the race into the second stage of the pattern of incumbent races, in which the public evaluates the opposing candidate and makes a judgment as to whether he is a plausible alternative to the incumbent. In years when approval of the incumbent is quite high (e.g., 1956 or 1964) the electorate doesn't seriously consider the challenger, and the race is in effect over before it begins. Clearly 2004 was not to be one of those years, and Kerry would have the opportunity to make his case for election.

As the campaign began, both candidates had advantages and problems. Even though he had reached a stratospheric 90 percent approval rating in the wake of the 9/11 terrorist attacks, President Bush had again become a polarizing figure, particularly along party lines. In a March *USA Today*/CNN/Gallup poll, Bush's approval rating was 91 percent among Republicans, but only 17 percent among Democrats. This 74-point gap was 18 points greater than the interparty difference in approval of Bill Clinton eight years earlier.[7] The public perceived that the country had economic problems, with the saliency of that issue increasing relative to concerns about terrorism, and support for the war in Iraq was dwindling. As a result of these developments, Kerry took a 52 percent to 44 percent lead over the president in early March.[8] The Bush campaign immediately went on the attack, running ads claiming that Kerry would boost taxes by $900 billion and weaken the Patriot Act (passed after 9/11 to fight terrorists).[9] One of the ads generated particular controversy because it showed scenes from the aftermath of the 2001 attacks. Some critics contended that the Bush campaign was exploiting the tragedy, but the president's campaign staff was elated because the criticism drew attention away from weak economic numbers.[10]

Problems in the Kerry campaign aided the Bush campaign's efforts. In the middle of March, Kerry was scheduled to appear in West Virginia (which has a high proportion of veterans) to talk about national defense. The president's campaign staff prepared an ad that attacked the Democratic candidate for voting against funds for the Iraq war and aired it in West Virginia. At an appearance before a veterans group, a heckler demanded that Kerry explain why he had opposed more funding for the troops. Kerry tried to explain that he cast his vote that way because he had tried, but failed, to include in the package a reduction in Bush's tax cut for the rich. Then, pressed further and losing patience, he uttered a sentence that would haunt him throughout the remainder of the campaign: "I actually did vote for the $87 billion before I voted against it." [11]

Bush's team recognized immediately that their opponent had given them a great gift. It played directly into their efforts to portray Kerry as an indecisive "flip-flopper." They simply added a clip of the Democrat's statement to the ad they were already running. Moreover, the attention that it generated caused the media to run the ad frequently, free of charge. By the end of March, Kerry's lead had been erased, and Bush had moved ahead by four points. Even worse for Kerry, Bush had a six-point lead in seventeen battleground states where the Democrat had had a large lead only six weeks earlier.[12] Then the president's situation was reinforced at the beginning of April, when the Bureau of Labor Statistics reported that 308,000 new jobs had been created in March, the best monthly gain in four years.[13]

Despite the gains for Bush, not all developments were bad for Kerry. One problem that many expected, a significant financial disadvantage, had not materialized. Between the time he secured the nomination in March and the middle of June, Kerry raised over $100 million, more than a million dollars a day.[14] His financial position was reinforced by the spending of independent groups (called "527s" after the section of the tax code that governed their operation). They had spent more than $52 million by the middle of April and continued to raise and spend all the way to the election.[15] Moreover, events continued to cause trouble for Bush. In early May, photographs of the mistreatment of Iraqi prisoners at Abu Ghraib prison appeared in news outlets around the world. Then the commission Bush had appointed to review the events leading up to the 9/11 attacks issued its final report, concluding that there was no evidence of collaboration between Iraq and al Qaeda.[16] By late June, Bush had lost his principal advantage with the voters: respondents to a poll were evenly divided about who would do the best job of handling the U.S. campaign against terrorism.[17] Yet evidence of improvement in the economic situation counteracted the negative foreign news, and Bush maintained a slight lead.[18] The situation did not change during the doldrums of July, as the Democrats prepared to hold their convention in Boston.

The Swift Boat Veterans Attack

As we noted in the previous chapter, the Democrats benefited from a smoothly run convention. Party activists and campaign workers were delighted. Kerry had been presented to the nation as a war hero and experienced senator prepared to lead the country in time of war. Polls immediately after the convention revealed that Kerry's ratings had received a small bounce by historical standards, but he now had a small lead over the incumbent.[19] The candidate and his running mate, Sen. John Edwards of North Carolina, set off on a cross-country campaign swing designed to showcase the ticket and the party's unity. Then the roof fell in.

The most visible of the problems to beset the Democrats was the attack on Kerry by a 527 group called the Swift Boat Veterans for Truth. They contended that Kerry had lied about the events in Vietnam for which he was awarded medals. Initially the veterans group only aired the ads briefly in three states, and that alone would have had little effect. But the ads received intense coverage by the cable news programs and then by the more mainstream media. Most analyses of the charges eventually concluded that they were not supported by the facts,[20] but the damage was done. Beyond just the coverage of the charges, the Democrats were damaged by the campaign's lack of an adequate response to them, and that was partly due to the money dilemma we described in the previous chapter: Because Kerry was officially the Democratic nominee (whereas Bush did not have the same status for the GOP), Kerry could no longer spend funds he had raised privately. If his campaign operation used a significant portion of the $75 million that each major party received in public financing, it might be short of funds during the home stretch leading up to election day in November. The problem, however, wasn't just money. The campaign was divided about how, or even whether, to respond. Some of the staff thought that responding would dignify the charges, and most in the campaign didn't recognize the potential for damage.[21]

The consequences of the Swift Boat ads were reinforced by other problems. During the postconvention campaign swing, a reporter asked Kerry to respond to a Bush challenge: "If Kerry had to do it all over again, knowing what he knew now, would he still have voted in support of the Iraq war?"[22] Kerry responded "Yes," and then tried to explain that he would have supported the authorization to use force, without saying that he agreed with the decision to go to war. The public coverage and the Bush campaign attacks, however, just reinforced the image of Kerry as flip-flopper. By the end of August, all of the benefits of the Democratic convention had dissipated. A *Washington Post* poll showed the race a dead tie at 48 percent each. Moreover, likely voters saw Bush as better by eight points on handling Iraq, and better by eighteen points on handling the war on terrorism. Immediately after the Democratic convention the two candidates had been almost even on both issues.[23]

By this time, at least Kerry had begun to find his voice and hit back. He charged that the Swift Boat Veterans were being used as a front for the Bush campaign and that they were lying about his record. He also began to be more direct in his attacks on the Iraq war, calling it (in the refrain he would use until election day) the "wrong war at the wrong time in the wrong place." [24] Then when Vice President Dick Cheney sought to heighten public concerns about Kerry by saying that if he were elected, "the danger is that we'll get hit again" by terrorists,[25] Kerry responded that it "is outrageous and shameful to make the war on terror an instrument of their politics." [26] But while these responses may have been good for Democratic morale, they didn't immediately benefit the candidate's standing with the voters. The GOP had also had a good convention, and Bush received a bigger bounce in the polls. By the end of September, on the eve of the first debate, all of the major polls showed the president with a lead of four to eight points.[27] Many observers thought that if Bush could solidly defeat Kerry in that debate—which would deal with foreign policy and homeland security, presumably the president's strong suit—it could set him up for a landslide victory.

REVERSAL OF FORTUNE: THE DEBATES EVEN THE RACE

The Bush campaign had always been wary of the potential of the debates to undermine their efforts, whereas Kerry's people hoped that they would give their candidate the chance to gain ground. Thus it took quite a while—until September 20—for the two sides to agree on the number and format of the debates. Most of the major features followed the plan proposed by the nonpartisan Commission on Presidential Debates, although there were some revisions.[28] And there were a great many details hammered out—in thirty-two pages of rules.[29] They settled on three presidential debates and one vice-presidential debate, each lasting ninety minutes. All except the second presidential debate were to have questioning by a moderator; the exception would have a town hall format, with questions submitted in writing by "soft supporters" of the candidates. Ralph Nader and other "minor" candidates were to be excluded from all of the events. Bush and Kerry would face each other one on one.

The first debate took place at the University of Miami. These events are so important because they are televised to millions of people, and the reactions of viewers are often different from those of people on the scene. That was decidedly true in this instance. The networks were airing many split-screen shots showing both candidates while one was answering. Viewers could see both the responses and the other candidate's reactions to them, and many viewers responded negatively to Bush's reactions. While Kerry spoke, "Bush scowled, squinted, clenched his jaw and appeared disgusted as he hunched over his lectern." [30] There were, moreover, many viewers to affect. The audience was about 62 million people, approximately 35 percent more than in the first debate in 2000.[31]

Kerry's advisers had sought to find ways to mitigate their candidate's difficulties and help him connect with the audience. At first they tried to offer him humorous lines to use, but that didn't work well in practice sessions. More successful was their effort to reduce Kerry's tendency to ramble on in response to questions. To get him in the habit of keeping his answers under two minutes (the limit agreed for the debates), they brought in an extremely large buzzer and set it off when Kerry exceeded his time.[32]

The staff efforts seemed to have some positive effects; Kerry's performance received generally good reviews from viewers and the press. He argued that although Saddam Hussein was dangerous, the president had chosen the wrong way to disarm him. When the president tried to follow his campaign's strategy of portraying Kerry as a flip-flopper because of his statement about voting for the $87 billion for the Iraq war, the Democrat responded by saying: "I made a mistake in how I talk about the war. But the president made a mistake in invading Iraq. Which is worse?"[33] Kerry also needled Bush by pointing out that the president's father had written about not invading deep into Iraq during the Persian Gulf War in 1991, noting that the elder Bush "said our troops would be occupiers in a bitterly hostile land. That's exactly where we find ourselves today."[34]

The Bush staff was amazed by the reaction to the debates. Media commentators, both conservative and liberal, nearly unanimously saw Kerry as the clear winner. That reaction was mirrored by the public's judgment reflected in surveys. A *Los Angeles Times* poll of debate watchers saw Kerry as the victor over Bush by 54 percent to 15 percent. Yet despite this collective evaluation, neither the vote intentions of respondents nor their approval ratings for Bush shifted from pre-debate responses.[35]

Many observers expected fireworks in the vice-presidential debate between Edwards and Cheney the following week, but the interaction was subdued and most analysts rated it a draw. Three days later, in the presidential town meeting debate, Bush was more relaxed before the event and performed better. Here, too, most observers rated the debate a tie, although respondents in focus groups saw the candidates as giving "stock responses" and seemed disappointed that they had received little new information.[36]

The stage was set for the final debate. In this encounter, Bush shifted strategy a bit. Instead of focusing on Kerry as a flip-flopper, the president sought to portray him as an extreme liberal, saying to him at one point, "Your record is such that Ted Kennedy, your colleague, is the *conservative* senator from Massachusetts."[37] He also claimed that Kerry had no record of leadership in the Senate. The Democrat attacked the president's tax cuts the previous year, saying that the top 1 percent of Americans got $89 billion in cuts. Bush responded that most of the cuts went to the middle class. One consequential set of responses occurred when the moderator asked whether homosexuality was a choice. Bush said that he didn't know but that consenting adults could live the way they wanted. Kerry noted that Vice President Cheney's daughter, "a lesbian," would probably say "she's being who she was born as. I think if you talk to anybody, it's not choice."[38] After the debate both the vice president and his wife criticized Kerry for using their daughter for political purposes. The candidates also answered a question about the role their religious faith played in their lives, to which Bush responded that those with religious faith and those without were both equally American, although his personal faith had a big impact on him.

Overall the debates appear to have had a substantial impact on the race. Before the first event, Kerry was clearly trailing, and perhaps more important, his campaign staff and his supporters in the country were increasingly pessimistic about their candidate's chances. By the end of the debates the electorate's perceptions of the Democratic standard bearer had changed. Viewers were pleasantly surprised by their impression of Kerry from the contests. They may have been surprised partly because of the low expectations established by the Bush campaign's very effective, negative advertising in previous months. In any event, the proportion of survey respondents in *Washington Post* polls who had a favorable view of Kerry increased twelve percentage points between early September and mid-October. Moreover, Kerry's ratings on this score were virtually the same as Bush's.[39]

Although the situation had improved for the Democrats, it was far from completely positive. Many doubts remained about Kerry, and even some potential voters who were skeptical about Bush thought he was a strong leader. Members of a group of uncommitted voters who agreed to watch the last debate with two *Washington Post* reporters saw as the president's core strength the perception, even by those who didn't like him, "that he is a leader who strikes them as decisive and on the level." In contrast to Bush's perceived sincerity, one participant said he would like to vote for Kerry, but "I just don't know, because I still don't know that I can fully trust him." [40] Kerry had enhanced his competitive position, sufficiently improving his image that at least half of the electorate could see him as a potential commander in chief and a substitute for the current occupant of the White House. But a *New York Times* poll showed the race a virtual tie among likely voters—Bush 47 percent, Kerry 46 percent.[41] With two weeks to go, the election was still either side's to win.

FINAL EFFORTS: AIR WAR AND GROUND WAR

The "air war" is the public face of the campaign, led by the candidates themselves—where the candidates travel, to whom they speak, what their "stump speeches" cover, and especially what their televised advertising emphasizes. This is called the "air war" because it is the campaign that most voters see on the television airwaves, and all of it is, or could easily become, a center of national attention. The "ground war" encompasses the efforts that campaign organizations make to register and turn out voters—telephone and mailed advertisements, and specialized campaigns in "narrow-cast" on cable TV and radio and through churches and other organizations. Here messages are often tailored to particular groups and perhaps even individuals. It is called the "ground war" because it is conducted by a large number of volunteers or low-paid professionals who work on the ground, perhaps going door to door. Although there are occasional media reports about the ground war, it is highly unlikely to become the center of national attention. These two are not completely distinct efforts, of course, and they are certainly joined in that they both require money and other resources. However, their messages and target audiences are often distinct.

The Air War

Candidates develop a standard stump speech that has at its core the central message they wish to present to the voters. It can evolve over the course of the campaign, and it is also modified from day to day. It changes to reflect the concerns and interests of the particular audience and also to reflect a changing major theme of the day that the candidate's campaign hopes will be the message that the national news media report. The latter is an attempt to help shape the campaign's agenda. Most scholarship shows that presidential candidates are not very effective in changing people's preferences on policy—they cannot convert liberals into conservatives or vice versa in the course of a campaign. What they can do, however, is shape the agenda.[42] That is, they can affect what policy dimensions people care about, even though they cannot change what people would like the government to do about those concerns.

As we saw above, the air war had been waged since early March (and, in a less-focused way, even before), and it would continue until November 2. It included the Bush-Cheney attacks on Kerry and the Democrats' responses. It also involved the candidates' efforts in the debates. In Table 2-1 we report what issues the candidates focused on in this aspect of the campaign.[43] The candidates' speeches were read and recorded as to what issues, among the list in the table, the candidate made a major component of his speech that day. These were then averaged over all the candidates' speeches from March through the Democratic convention in July, and then again over the September-through-November general election campaign.

As Table 2-1 indicates, the economy was a dominant concern of Bush and Kerry in both the preconvention and the postconvention periods; it was the major theme in about one-third of the speeches by both of them. Terrorism was a more important subject for Bush than for Kerry in both periods, and it became an even more frequent reference for the president after the conventions. Indeed, in the fall period the combination of terrorism and Iraq accounted for almost half of the issues the president raised. It is appropriate to link these subjects because Bush wanted Iraq to be seen as a part of the war on terrorism, whereas Kerry wanted the two to be seen as distinct and the Iraq war to be seen as harmful to successfully combating terrorism. Kerry also talked slightly less about terrorism and more about Iraq as the campaign neared its end.

Note also that Kerry spoke even more about the economy in the fall than he had in the earlier period. After the election some observers criticized the Democratic candidate for not sufficiently emphasizing the economy. The media may

TABLE 2-1   Issues Raised in Presidential Candidates' Campaign Speeches, March–November 2004

| | Major Issues in Speeches by George W. Bush | | | | | |
| | Through July | | Sept. 1–Nov. 1 | | Total | |
Issue	N	%	N	%	N	%
Economy	47	31.1	64	28.2	111	29.4
Terrorism	31	20.5	82	36.1	113	29.9
Iraq	14	9.3	25	11.0	39	10.3
Other foreign policy or military	7	4.6	5	2.2	12	3.2
Health care	6	4.0	16	7.0	22	5.8
Social Security and Medicare	3	2.0	2	0.9	5	1.3
Education	9	6.0	5	2.2	14	3.7
Taxes	4	2.6	16	7.0	20	5.3
Values	15	9.9	7	3.1	22	5.8
Environment	2	1.3	0	0.0	2	0.5
Other	10	6.6	5	2.2	15	4.0
Civil rights	3	2.0	0	0.0	3	0.8
Total	151	99.9	227	99.9	378	100.0

| | Major Issues in Speeches by John Kerry | | | | | |
| | Through July | | Sept. 1–Nov. 1 | | Total | |
Issue	N	%	N	%	N	%
Economy	40	33.6	43	39.4	83	36.4
Terrorism	13	10.9	9	8.3	22	9.6
Iraq	5	4.2	15	13.8	20	8.8
Other foreign policy or military	10	8.4	4	3.7	14	6.1
Health care	8	6.7	5	4.6	13	5.7
Social Security and Medicare	1	0.8	7	6.4	8	3.5
Education	7	5.9	1	0.9	8	3.5
Taxes	5	4.2	6	5.5	11	4.8
Values	15	12.6	9	8.3	24	10.5
Environment	2	1.7	0	0.0	2	0.9
Other	7	5.9	6	5.5	13	5.7
Civil rights	3	2.5	1	0.9	4	1.8
Energy	3	2.5	3	2.8	6	2.6
Total	119	99.9	109	100.1	228	99.9

Source: Data collected by John H. Aldrich, John Griffin, Jill Rickershauser, and the students in Duke's political science course POL 101AS.

not have accurately conveyed Kerry's emphasis, but it is clear that the subject dominated his speeches. Domestic issues besides the economy were broadly scattered among a wide range of concerns. We do not have measures of what the "narrow-cast" campaign appeals dealt with, but it is at least possible that several of these domestic issues were pursued in that part of the ground war instead of, or in addition to, their discussion in the air war. Neither candidate made values a central theme in his speeches.

Part of the strategy of this generally visible face of the campaigns involved not only what the candidates were to say, but also where they were to go. This was another manifestation of the calculation of which states were the battlegrounds that could decide the winner and which were probably committed to a candidate already. Gerald M. Pomper counted the daily campaign trips of the presidential and vice-presidential candidates between Labor Day and the end of the campaign, and their choices of where to campaign demonstrate the narrow geographic focus of the strategists.[44] Pomper's data show that the top five states (Florida, Iowa, Ohio, Pennsylvania, and Wisconsin) accounted for 57.4 percent of the total of 338 trips by the four candidates. Ohio was number one, with 53 visits (15.7 percent of the total). By contrast, California—the largest state, with 55 electoral votes, 20 percent of the number needed to win—got only a single visit (from John Edwards).

The air war hit a fever pitch in the last week of the campaign. Combined spending on advertising in that week was $60 million, about one-fourth of the total for the election.[45] Reflecting the contrasts in messages discussed above, Bush emphasized the terrorism issue and his personal determination in the face of it. In Miami, two days before the voting, he said, "If you believe America should fight the war on terrorism with all her might and lead with unwavering confidence, . . . I ask you, come stand with me." Kerry, on the other hand, continued to focus primarily on economic matters. Campaigning in New Hampshire, he said: "I pledge to you that I will be a president who fights as hard for your jobs as I do for my own." [46]

The Ground War and the Turnout Efforts

A central focus of the ground war was the effort by both candidates' organizations and their allies to maximize turnout among supporters. Given the closeness of the 2000 outcome in Florida, and the small number of undecided voters in 2004, the campaigns believed that every vote could be crucial, and their efforts were unprecedented. They allocated far more money to turnout efforts than in the past. For example, the Bush side budgeted $125 million for voter mobilization, about three times the amount in 2000. The Democrats allocated around $60 million, more than twice the 2000 level.[47] Moreover, both parties' efforts, especially the Democrats', were supplemented by the activities of allied groups such as America Coming Together (ACT). Labor unions also supplemented Democratic Party efforts; the AFL-CIO alone planned to spend $45 million in sixteen battleground states.[48]

ACT claimed to have raised about $125 million, and it employed up to 2,500 workers to register new voters and stay in contact with them throughout the campaign. The group said it made 16 million phone calls in just the last three weeks leading up to election day, sent 23 million pieces of mail, and delivered 11 million fliers.[49] Other allied independent groups reinforced this pro-Democratic effort, and there were additional groups supporting the GOP, as well. The Progress for America Voter Fund and its parent organization raised over $50 million and spent nearly $19 million to run commercials in eleven states and on national cable channels. They also sent millions of pieces of mail and thousands of e-mails to influence potential voters.[50]

The Bush campaign made a particular effort to encourage participation by conservative Christian voters. Karl Rove, the president's chief political strategist, believed that Bush lost the 2000 popular vote because millions of evangelical Christians failed to go to the polls.[51] He was determined that 2004 would not repeat this pattern, and from 2001 on, he sought to build bridges to the Christian right. Incumbent presidents have the advantage that they can build political support not just with words but with actions, and Bush took many actions designed to please the Christian right and to be visible to them, without making those actions a major part of the more public appeals of the air war. They included the ban on "partial-birth" abortions, limits on embryonic stem cell research, opposition to Oregon's "right to die" law, and especially support for a constitutional amendment banning same-sex marriage. These efforts touched a responsive chord. Tom Minnery, of Focus on the Family, called Bush "the most openly Christian president we have had in our lifetimes."[52] The strategy was reinforced by the independent efforts of Christian right groups participating in referendum campaigns in the eleven states that had bans on gay marriage on their ballots.

DID THE CAMPAIGN MATTER?

It is appropriate to ask whether the general election campaign made any difference, and the answer depends on the yardstick one uses to measure the campaign's effects. Did the campaign determine the winner? Did it affect the choices of a substantial number of voters? Did it put issues and candidates' positions clearly before the voters? Would a better campaign by one of the candidates have yielded a different result? Did the campaign produce events that will have a lasting impact on American politics? We cannot provide firm answers to all of these questions, but we can shed light on some of them.

Regarding the outcome and voters' decisions, it seems quite clear that the campaign did indeed have an effect.[53] As recounted above, the relative standings of the candidates ebbed and flowed from March to November, and the changes seemed to be linked in part to events in the campaign. In particular, Bush had a solid lead before the presidential debates and lost it by the conclusion of the third. While we may not be certain of the import of various events during the eight months after Kerry secured the Democratic nomination, or the magnitude of their impact, we can conclude that either of the major candidates could have won if the voting had taken place at a different date during the period.

Another perspective on these questions is offered by data from the 2004 National Election Study (NES) survey. Table 2-2 shows the percentage of major-

TABLE 2-2   Percentage of Major-Party Voters Who Voted for Bush, by Time of Vote Decision and Party Identification, 2004

Party identification	Knew all along %	(N)	Through conventions %	(N)	After conventions; before last debate %	(N)	After last debate %	(N)
Strong Democrat	2	(54)	2	(53)	[0]	[7]	9	(23)
Weak Democrat	7	(27)	14	(42)	7	(14)	24	(29)
Independent, leans Democratic	3	(31)	12	(48)	0	(10)	26	(31)
Independent, no partisan leanings	[2]	[9]	[4]	[8]	[2]	[7]	52	(21)
Independent, leans Republican	90	(20)	88	(34)	[8]	[8]	70	(20)
Weak Republican	97	(31)	96	(46)	[7]	[8]	74	(31)
Strong Republican	100	(92)	96	(54)	[3]	[3]	84	(19)
Total	55	(264)	50	(285)	37	(57)	47	(174)

Note: The numbers are weighted. The numbers in brackets are the number of cases where there are fewer than ten total cases.

party voters who voted for Bush, controlling for their party identification and when they claimed to have made their vote choice.[54] Overall, about one-third of the sample (264 out of 780 voters) indicated that they knew all along how they were going to vote. This was nearly three times the proportion (12 percent) that said the same after 2000 when no incumbent was running, but was close to the 29 percent who gave that response in 1996 when Clinton was running as the incumbent. That is the subset within which Bush received the highest percentage. Indeed it is the only one that the president carried. The next group—people who said they decided through the time of the conventions—split evenly. Kerry won the last two groups, albeit the last one (voters who decided after the debates) only narrowly. Overall, the close competition of the race is reflected throughout the campaign.

Finally there is the question of whether a better campaign by a candidate, specifically by Kerry, would likely have led to a different result. Many observers (mostly Democrats) believe that the electorate was dissatisfied with Bush because of the economy and the war and that different strategies or a different Democratic candidate could have brought victory. In our view the answer is not clear one way or the other. Both the electoral context and campaign strategy had an impact on the outcome. The most important thing to note about context is that Bush was president in time of war and that all four wartime presidents who ran for office were reelected.[55] Voters are risk-averse, and "switching horses" in war is risky. The major national exit poll for 2004 showed that voters believed things were not going well in Iraq, but by 51 percent to 45 percent they still thought that going to war was the right thing to do.[56]

Another aspect of security that was important to the campaign was perceptions about the war on terror. We have seen that this was the issue that Bush emphasized most, and it was here that Kerry had his greatest disadvantage. When exit pollers asked whether Iraq was part of the war on terror, respondents said yes by 55 percent to 42 percent. And in response to questions about whether they trusted the two candidates to handle terrorism, regarding Bush they said yes by 58 percent to 40 percent, and regarding Kerry they said no by the same margin. In contrast, on handling the economy, supposedly the Democrats' best issue, voters indicated that they didn't trust either candidate to do the job, but they exhibited slightly more confidence in Bush (49 percent yes, versus 51 percent no) than in Kerry (45 percent to 53 percent).

Kerry was in a difficult strategic situation in the wake of 9/11, and any other Democrat would have faced similar difficulties. In addition, there were real divisions within the Democratic Party over whether the war in Iraq was justified and over what course the United States should follow given that the country was committed. Moreover, as we saw above, contrary to what some critics argued after the fact, Kerry made the economy the central issue in his public appeals.

Kerry had significant weaknesses, which the GOP campaign exploited. The failure to quickly and effectively counter the Swift Boat Veterans' ads clearly hurt, although given the money situation, spending a lot on ads in August might have produced an even worse situation in October. Still worse for the Democrats was that Kerry had a substantial record in Congress within which the Republicans could find votes and positions that permitted them to portray him as vacillating and two-faced, whether the labels were justified or not. Rove called the Kerry decisions first to support the $87 billion in Iraq funding and then to vote against it "the gift that kept on giving." [57] In the context of national concerns about contesting the war on terror, the flip-flopper image hurt. It is not clear, however, that alternative candidates such as Edwards or Dean would not have been similarly vulnerable, or even more so, to effective GOP attacks.

Finally, it is worth noting that the Democratic mobilization efforts were very effective. Unfortunately for the Democrats, the GOP effort was even more effective. In Ohio, the pivotal state, ACT and the Democratic organization exceeded their expectations. For example, in Cuyahoga County (Cleveland), where ACT had set a target of about 350,000 votes, Kerry actually received over 433,000.[58] Indeed, Kerry received more votes in Ohio than any Democratic presidential candidate in history. This successful effort was, however, overwhelmed by the Republican campaign that turned out more GOP voters than ever before and produced the narrow victory for the president in that essential state. So despite Kerry's significant problems, it is not clear that different choices by his campaign, or another standard-bearer for the Democrats, could have changed the outcome.

Chapter 3

The Election Results

As the general election campaign ended, it was clear that the election was likely to be close. The average (mean) results of nineteen national polls conducted during the week before the election showed George W. Bush winning 51.2 percent of the major-party vote. But seven of those polls showed Bush with 50 percent of the major-party vote, and one showed John F. Kerry with a one point lead over Bush.[1] According to the average results of seventeen political experts polled over the course of the campaign, Bush would receive 50.5 percent of the major-party vote.[2] Bush fared a bit better in various academic models. For example, in October 2004 James E. Campbell presented the results of forecasts for the presidential election from seven models; he reported that the median prediction was for Bush to receive 53.8 percent of the major-party vote.[3] Likewise, the mean results of ten academic models also showed Bush winning 53.8 percent of the major-party vote.[4]

These academic models rely partly on public opinion data, since they include measures of presidential approval, but they also employ economic indicators. On the other hand, voting projections based on recent polls are more current. Regardless of how one predicted the results, it seemed clear that either Bush or Kerry could win and that the result might depend upon which campaign was better able to get its supporters to the polls.

Exit poll results prematurely leaked on election day (November 2) suggested that Kerry would win. But after the polls closed it became apparent that the contest would be very close, hinging largely on the results in Pennsylvania, Florida, and Ohio. After the networks projected Kerry the winner in Pennsylvania and Bush the victor in Florida, Ohio's 20 electoral votes became crucial. The television networks remembered their two early and withdrawn projections of the Florida contest in 2000, in which the networks first "called" Florida for Al Gore, withdrew that call, next called Florida for Bush, and then withdrew their second call. In 2004, the networks were determined to be more cautious. "It seemed like a three-way game of chicken," according to George Stephanopoulos, a 1992 campaign adviser for Bill Clinton and an analyst for ABC News. "Kerry didn't want to concede. Bush didn't want to claim victory until Kerry conceded, and he didn't want to claim victory until the networks gave it to him." [5] At 12:41 a.m. EST on Wednesday, November 3, the Fox News Channel projected Bush the winner in Ohio, and NBC made the same projection at 1 a.m. According to their counts, Bush had 269 electoral votes. According to Tom Brokaw of NBC News, the race was "all but over." [6] On the other hand, although ABC, CBS, and CNN declared that Bush had won Nevada, both NBC and Fox kept Nevada in their "undecided" columns, and they had Bush stuck at 269 votes, one shy of victory, for nearly four hours.

In the final tally, Bush won thirty-one states, and Kerry won nineteen states and the District of Columbia. Bush was the first presidential winner since George H. W. Bush in 1988 to win a majority of the popular vote, but his 2.4 percent margin of victory was the narrowest popular-vote win for an incumbent in American history.[7] Even so, nine of the twenty-six incumbents who ran for reelection were defeated, and so being reelected is a significant achievement.

While clearly besting his minority-vote victory in 2000, Bush's 2.4 percent margin was substantially smaller than that of any other Republican winner since 1980. Reagan won by 9.7 points over Jimmy Carter in 1980; in 1984 he defeated Walter F. Mondale by 18.2 points; and in 1988 George H. W. Bush defeated Michael S. Dukakis by 7.7 points. Although Bill Clinton failed to win a majority of the popular vote in either election, he defeated Bush by 5.6 points in 1992 and Bob Dole by 8.5 points in 1996. Table 3-1 presents the official 2004 election results by state.[8] Compared with 2000, Bush gained 2.8 percent of the total vote. The gain resulted, in part, from the reduced share of the vote that went to third-party and independent candidates. With 99.0 percent of the votes going to the major-party candidates, compared with 96.2 percent in 2000, Bush was able to score gains in forty-eight of the fifty states, as well as the District of Columbia, while Kerry's share of the total vote was greater than Gore's had been in twenty-six states, as well as D.C.

As Figure 3-1 shows, Bush won 286 electoral votes to Kerry's 251. His electoral vote margin was the fourth closest in the forty-five elections since 1828, the first election in which a vast majority of states chose their presidential electors by popular vote.[9]

The most striking feature of the 2004 result is its similarity to that of 2000. Only three of the fifty states switched sides. Iowa and New Mexico narrowly voted Democratic in 2000, but they narrowly voted Republican in 2004. New Hampshire narrowly voted Republican in 2000 but narrowly voted Democratic four years later. Bush gained fifteen electoral votes between 2000 and 2004, and eight of the fifteen came from the switches among these three states. The remaining seven-vote gain resulted from a net increase in House seats among the twenty-nine states he won in both 2000 and 2004, which was part of the reapportionment of House seats following the 2000 Census.

TABLE 3-1 Presidential Election Results, by State, 2004

State	Total vote	George W. Bush Republican	John F. Kerry Democrat	Other	Rep. or Dem. Plurality	Percentage Rep.	Percentage Dem.
Alabama	1,883,449	1,176,394	693,933	13,122	482,461 R	62.5	36.8
Alaska	312,598	190,889	111,025	10,684	79,864 R	61.1	35.5
Arizona	2,012,585	1,104,294	893,524	14,767	210,770 R	54.9	44.4
Arkansas	1,054,945	572,898	469,953	12,094	102,945 R	54.3	44.5
California	12,421,852	5,509,826	6,745,485	166,541	1,235,659 D	44.4	54.3
Colorado	2,130,330	1,101,255	1,001,732	27,343	99,523 R	51.7	47.0
Connecticut	1,578,769	693,826	857,488	27,455	163,662 D	43.9	54.3
Delaware	375,190	171,660	200,152	3,378	28,492 D	45.8	53.3
Florida	7,609,810	3,964,522	3,583,544	61,744	380,978 R	52.1	47.1
Georgia	3,301,875	1,914,254	1,366,149	21,472	548,105 R	58.0	41.4
Hawaii	429,013	194,191	231,708	3,114	37,517 D	45.3	54.0
Idaho	598,447	409,235	181,098	8,114	228,137 R	68.4	30.3
Illinois	5,274,322	2,345,946	2,891,550	36,826	545,604 D	44.5	54.8
Indiana	2,468,002	1,479,438	969,011	19,553	510,427 R	59.9	39.3
Iowa	1,506,908	751,957	741,898	13,053	10,059 R	49.9	49.2
Kansas	1,187,756	736,456	434,993	16,307	301,463 R	62.0	36.6
Kentucky	1,795,882	1,069,439	712,733	13,710	356,706 R	59.5	39.7
Louisiana	1,943,106	1,102,169	820,299	20,638	281,870 R	56.7	42.2
Maine	740,752	330,201	396,842	13,709	66,641 D	44.6	53.6
Maryland	2,386,678	1,024,703	1,334,493	27,482	309,790 D	42.9	55.9
Massachusetts	2,912,388	1,071,109	1,803,800	37,479	732,691 D	36.8	61.9
Michigan	4,839,252	2,313,746	2,479,183	46,323	165,437 D	47.8	51.2
Minnesota	2,828,387	1,346,695	1,445,014	36,678	98,319 D	47.6	51.1
Mississippi	1,152,145	684,981	458,094	9,070	226,887 R	59.5	39.8
Missouri	2,731,364	1,455,713	1,259,171	16,480	196,542 R	53.3	46.1
Montana	450,445	266,063	173,710	10,672	92,353 R	59.1	38.6
Nebraska	778,186	512,814	254,328	11,044	258,486 R	65.9	32.7
Nevada	829,587	418,690	397,190	13,707	21,500 R	50.5	47.9

(Table continues on next page)

TABLE 3-1 (continued)

State	Total vote	George W. Bush Republican	John F. Kerry Democrat	Other	Rep. or Dem. Plurality	Percentage Rep.	Percentage Dem.
New Hampshire	677,738	331,237	340,511	5,990	9,274 D	48.9	50.2
New Jersey	3,611,691	1,670,003	1,911,430	30,258	241,427 D	46.2	52.9
New Mexico	756,304	376,930	370,942	8,432	5,988 R	49.8	49.0
New York	7,391,036	2,962,567	4,314,280	114,189	1,351,713 D	40.1	58.4
North Carolina	3,501,007	1,961,166	1,525,849	13,992	435,317 R	56.0	43.6
North Dakota	312,833	196,651	111,052	5,130	85,599 R	62.9	35.5
Ohio	5,627,908	2,859,768	2,741,167	26,973	118,601 R	50.8	48.7
Oklahoma	1,463,758	959,792	503,966		455,826 R	65.6	34.4
Oregon	1,836,782	866,831	943,163	26,788	76,332 D	47.2	51.3
Pennsylvania	5,769,590	2,793,847	2,938,095	37,648	144,248 D	48.4	50.9
Rhode Island	437,134	169,046	259,760	8,328	90,714 D	38.7	59.4
South Carolina	1,617,730	937,974	661,699	18,057	276,275 R	58.0	40.9
South Dakota	388,215	232,584	149,244	6,387	83,340 R	59.9	38.4
Tennessee	2,437,319	1,384,375	1,036,477	16,467	347,898 R	56.8	42.5
Texas	7,410,765	4,526,917	2,832,704	51,144	1,694,213 R	61.1	38.2
Utah	927,844	663,742	241,199	22,903	422,543 R	71.5	26.0
Vermont	312,309	121,180	184,067	7,062	62,887 D	38.8	58.9
Virginia	3,198,367	1,716,959	1,454,742	26,666	262,217 R	53.7	45.5
Washington	2,859,084	1,304,894	1,510,201	43,989	205,307 D	45.6	52.8
West Virginia	755,887	423,778	326,541	5,568	97,237 R	56.1	43.2
Wisconsin	2,997,007	1,478,120	1,489,504	29,383	11,384 D	49.3	49.7
Wyoming	243,428	167,629	70,776	5,023	96,853 R	68.9	29.1
District of Columbia	227,586	21,256	202,970	3,360	181,714 D	9.3	89.2
United States	122,295,345	62,040,610	59,028,439	1,226,296	3,012,171 R	50.7	48.3

Source: Richard M. Scammon, Alice V. McGillivray, and Rhodes Cook, *America Votes 26, 2003–2004: Election Returns by State* (Washington, D.C.: CQ Press, 2006), 9. Based on reports of the secretaries of state of the 50 states and the District of Columbia.

FIGURE 3-1   Electoral Votes by State, 2004

States carried by Bush   States carried by Kerry

Source: Richard M. Scammon, Alice V. McGillivray, and Rhodes Cook, *America Votes 26, 2003–2004: Election Returns by State* (Washington, D.C.: CQ Press, 2006), 9.

Note: Bush won 286 electoral votes; Kerry won 251 electoral votes. One elector from Minnesota voted for Edwards.

THE ELECTION RULES

In 2004 Bush won a majority of both the popular and electoral vote, and one might conclude that he would have won under most election rules. But we would argue that the crucial, steady reduction in the independent and third-party vote between 1992 and 2004 is in large part a result of the U.S. election rules. In 1992, H. Ross Perot won 18.9 percent of the popular vote; in 1996 his support dropped to 8.4 percent. In 2000, Ralph Nader won only 2.7 percent of the vote, and other minor-party candidates and independents won .6 percent. In 2004, minor-party candidates (including Nader) were reduced to a bare 1.0 percent of the vote. Partly because of these independent and third-party candidates, Clinton was able to win with only 43.0 percent of the popular vote, and he was still short of a majority when he was reelected in 1996 with 49.2 percent. In 2000 Bush won with only 47.9 percent of the popular vote, even though Gore had won 48.4 percent.

As we saw in chapter 2, voters do not vote directly for president. Rather, they vote for a slate of electors pledged to support certain presidential and vice-presidential candidates. Moreover, in every state except Maine and Nebraska, the slate that receives the most popular votes is elected. In no state is a majority required to win. In 2004 Bush did win a majority of the popular vote in twenty-nine states, and he would have won 274 electoral votes if a majority-vote victory had been required. In 2000 he won a majority in only twenty-six states and would have won only 217 electoral votes, of the required 270, if states had a majority-vote requirement.

The plurality-vote, winner-take-all system usually transforms a plurality of the popular vote into a majority of the electoral vote. And it takes a majority of the electoral vote to produce a winner. If there is no majority winner, the House of Representatives, voting by state delegation, chooses among the three candidates with the largest numbers of electoral votes. But the House has not chosen a winner since 1825, mainly because the plurality-vote system is very likely to produce a winner in the Electoral College as well as a two-party system. In forty-two of the forty-five elections from 1828 through 2004, the candidate with the most popular votes has won a majority of the electoral vote. The three other elections, 1876, 1888, and 2000, were all very close.[10] During this period there have been fourteen elections in which a candidate won a plurality of the vote, but not a majority, and won a majority of the electoral vote.[11]

The system places a heavy burden on third-party or independent candidates. A successful third-party candidate usually receives a far smaller share of the electoral vote than of the popular vote.[12] We can see this by reviewing the fates of the four most successful third-party or independent candidacies (in popular-vote terms) since World War II: those of George C. Wallace (who won 13.5 percent of the popular vote in 1968), John B. Anderson (who won 6.6 percent in 1980), and H. Ross Perot (who won 18.9 percent in 1992 and 8.4 percent in 1996). In 1980 and 1992 Anderson and Perot, respectively, had some modest regional support. Both fared better in New England than elsewhere, and both fared worst in the South.[13] Perot also did well in the mountain states.[14] He even came in second in two states: Maine, where he came in ahead of Bush, and Utah, where he came in ahead of Clinton.[15] In 1996 Perot fared somewhat better in New England, but regional differences were small. None of these candidates, however, won any electoral votes. Wallace, in contrast, had a regional base of support in the South. Even though he won a smaller share of the popular vote than Perot in 1992, Wallace came in first in five states (winning a majority in Alabama and Mississippi) and gained forty-six electoral votes (including one faithless elector from North Carolina). But even Wallace won only 8.5 percent of the electoral vote, less than his popular-vote share.[16]

The U.S. plurality-vote system can be seen as a confirmation of Duverger's law, a proposition advanced by Maurice Duverger in the 1950s. According to Duverger, "the simple-majority single-ballot system favours the two-party system."[17] In other words, a plurality-vote system with no runoffs tends to favor the dominance of two political parties.[18] Indeed, Duverger argued that "the American procedure corresponds to the usual machinery of the simple-majority single-ballot system. The absence of a second ballot and of further polls, particularly in the presidential elections, constitutes in fact one of the historical reasons for the emergence and the maintenance of the two-party system."[19]

According to Duverger, this principle applies for two reasons. First, the plurality-vote system has a "mechanical" effect: Third parties may earn a large number of votes nationally but fail to gain a plurality of the vote in many electoral units. Second, some voters who prefer a candidate or party they think cannot win will cast their vote for their first choice between the major-party candidates. This behavior is called "sophisticated" or "strategic" voting. William H. Riker defines strategic voting as "voting contrary to one's immediate tastes in order to obtain an advantage in the long run." [20] As we have demonstrated, a substantial number of voters who most preferred a third-party or independent candidate in the 1968, 1980, 1992, 1996, and 2000 elections wound up voting for one of the major-party candidates.[21] There were probably a small number of strategic voters in 2004 as well. Using the "feeling thermometers" in the 2004 National Election Survey, we found that 5 percent of the electorate preferred Nader to both Bush and Kerry. But among the thirty-two voters who preferred Nader to both major-party candidates, only one voted for him; 58 percent voted for Kerry, 19 percent for Bush, and 19 percent for other candidates.

Of course, we do not know what the results would have been if the rules had been different. Although Bush won more popular votes than Kerry, we cannot know what the results would have been if the system provided that the president must be elected by a majority of the popular vote. For example, Kerry devoted almost no effort in the nation's second-largest state, Texas, since he had no chance of winning its 34 electoral votes. On the other hand, Bush spent little effort in the nation's largest and third-largest states, California and New York, since he had very little chance of winning their 55 and 31 electoral votes. We should be even more cautious in concluding that the 2000 election results were illegitimate because Gore won more popular votes than Bush: Both candidates campaigned to win a majority of the electoral votes, not a majority of the popular votes.

A strong case can be made for eliminating the Electoral College.[22] But change through a constitutional amendment is unlikely, since gaining the approval of three-fourths of the states would be difficult, especially given that the system overrepresents the smaller states. Maine and Nebraska both have district systems for choosing their electors, and other states could choose that system through legislation. But most states do not want to diminish their potential influence by making it likely that their electoral vote will be split. For example, in 2004 a ballot proposal in Colorado would have divided the state's electoral vote according to proportional representation. Its opponents argued that a proportional representation system would diminish Colorado's importance in selecting the president. Rather than making it highly likely that the plurality-vote winner in Colorado would receive all nine of the state's electoral votes, it seemed likely that if the amendment passed (and survived court challenges) five of its votes would go to the winner and four to the loser. The proposal failed by a margin of 65 percent to 35 percent. The main problem with the present, winner-take-all system is that it focuses the vast majority of the campaigning on a small number of states, but despite this disadvantage it seems unlikely that the system will be changed.

THE PATTERN OF RESULTS

Two fundamental facts emerge from the 2004 presidential election results. First, consistent with the election results themselves, the postwar pattern reveals a close balance between the two parties, but with an edge for the Republicans. The Republicans have won nine of the fifteen elections held since World War II, and the Democrats have won six. In addition, the Republicans have won a majority of the vote seven times since the war ended (1952, 1956, 1972, 1980, 1984, 1988, and 2004), whereas the Democrats have won a popular-vote majority only twice (1964 and 1976). Finally, the average (mean) level of Republican presidential support has been 49.1 percent, whereas the average level of Democratic support has been 46.2 percent.

The Republican advantage goes along with a considerable pattern of volatility since World War II. Table 3-2 shows the presidential election results since 1832, the first election in which parties used national nominating conventions to select their candidates. From 1832 through 1948 we find four periods in which the same party won three or more elections in a row. The Republicans won six elections in a row from 1860 through 1880, although Rutherford B. Hayes beat Samuel J. Tilden by a single electoral vote, and Tilden won a majority of the popular vote. The Republicans also won four elections from 1896 through 1908, as well as three from 1920 through 1928. And the Democrats won five straight elections from 1932 through 1948.

After 1948 a period of volatility began. From 1952 through 1984 neither party was able to win more than two elections in a row. The Republicans won in 1952 and 1956, the Democrats in 1960 and 1964, and the Republicans in 1968 and 1972. In all three cases the second win was by a bigger margin than the first (substantially bigger in 1964 and 1972). Volatility increased in 1980, when the Democrats, who won the White House in 1976, failed to hold it. The 1980 and 1984 elections reverted to the pattern of a win followed by a bigger win, and Reagan's second win was by a substantially bigger margin than his first. Then in 1988 George H. W. Bush's election gave the Republicans three elections in a row, breaking the pattern of postwar volatility. With Clinton's victory in 1992 volatility returned, and as with previous postwar elections, Clinton won in 1996 by a larger—though only slightly so—margin. George W. Bush's defeat of Al Gore in 2000 continued the postwar pattern of volatility, and Bush, who trailed his opponent in 2000, slightly improved his popular-vote share in 2004.

The 1976 and 1980 elections are the only successive elections in the twentieth century in which incumbent presidents lost.[23] But two periods in the nineteenth century were actually more volatile than postwar America. The incumbent party lost four elections from 1840 through 1852, a period of alternation between the Democrats and the Whigs, and again between 1884 and 1896, a period of alternation between the Republicans and the Democrats. Both these periods were followed by party realignments. Although many Whigs, including Abraham Lincoln himself, became Republicans, the Republican Party was not just the Whig Party

TABLE 3-2   Presidental Election Results, 1832–2004

Election	Winning candidate	Party of winning candidate	Success of incumbent political party
1832	Andrew Jackson	Democrat	Won
1836	Martin Van Buren	Democrat	Won
1840	William H. Harrison	Whig	Lost
1844	James K. Polk	Democrat	Lost[a]
1848	Zachary Taylor	Whig	Lost
1852	Franklin Pierce	Democrat	Lost
1856	James Buchanan	Democrat	Won
1860	Abraham Lincoln	Republican	Lost
1864	Abraham Lincoln	Republican	Won
1868	Ulysses S. Grant	Republican	Won[b]
1872	Ulysses S. Grant	Republican	Won
1876	Rutherford B. Hayes	Republican	Won
1880	James A. Garfield	Republican	Won
1884	Grover Cleveland	Democrat	Lost
1888	Benjamin Harrison	Republican	Lost
1892	Grover Cleveland	Democrat	Lost
1896	William McKinley	Republican	Lost
1900	William McKinley	Republican	Won
1904	Theodore Roosevelt	Republican	Won
1908	William H. Taft	Republican	Won
1912	Woodrow Wilson	Democrat	Lost
1916	Woodrow Wilson	Democrat	Won
1920	Warren G. Harding	Republican	Lost
1924	Calvin Coolidge	Republican	Won
1928	Herbert C. Hoover	Republican	Won
1932	Franklin D. Roosevelt	Democrat	Lost
1936	Franklin D. Roosevelt	Democrat	Won
1940	Franklin D. Roosevelt	Democrat	Won
1944	Franklin D. Roosevelt	Democrat	Won
1948	Harry S. Truman	Democrat	Won
1952	Dwight D. Eisenhower	Republican	Lost
1956	Dwight D. Eisenhower	Republican	Won
1960	John F. Kennedy	Democrat	Lost
1964	Lyndon B. Johnson	Democrat	Won
1968	Richard M. Nixon	Republican	Lost
1972	Richard M. Nixon	Republican	Won
1976	Jimmy Carter	Democrat	Lost
1980	Ronald Reagan	Republican	Lost

(Table continues on next page)

TABLE 3-2   (continued)

Election	Winning candidate	Party of winning candidate	Success of incumbent political party
1984	Ronald Reagan	Republican	Won
1988	George H. W. Bush	Republican	Won
1992	Bill Clinton	Democrat	Lost
1996	Bill Clinton	Democrat	Won
2000	George W. Bush	Republican	Lost
2004	George W. Bush	Republican	Won

Sources: Presidential Elections: 1789–2000 (Washington, D.C.: CQ Press, 2002); Richard M. Scammon, Alice V. McGillivray, and Rhodes Cook, *America Votes 26, 2003–2004: Election Returns by State* (Washington, D.C.: CQ Press, 2006).

[a] The Whigs are classified as the incumbent party in 1844 based on their having won the 1840 election. In fact, their presidential candidate, William Henry Harrison, had died a month after taking office and his vice president, John Tyler, was officially expelled from the Whig Party in 1841.

[b] The Republicans are classified as the incumbent party in 1868 based on their having won the 1864 election. (Technically, Lincoln had been elected on a Union Ticket.) In fact, after Lincoln's assassination in 1865, Andrew Johnson, a War Democrat, became president.

renamed. The Republicans had transformed the political agenda by capitalizing on opposition to slavery in the territories.[24]

The 1896 contest, the last of four incumbent losses, is usually considered a critical election because it solidified Republican dominance.[25] Although the Republicans had won all but two elections since the Civil War, many of their victories were by narrow margins. In 1896 the Republicans emerged as the clearly dominant party, gaining a solid hold in Connecticut, Indiana, New York, and New Jersey, states that they had frequently lost between 1876 and 1892. After William McKinley's defeat of William Jennings Bryan in 1896, the Republicans established a firmer base in the Midwest, New England, and Mid-Atlantic states. They lost the presidency only in 1912, when the GOP was split, and in 1916, when Woodrow Wilson ran for reelection.

The Great Depression ended Republican dominance. The emergence of the Democrats as the majority party was not preceded by a series of incumbent losses. The Democratic coalition, forged in the 1930s, relied heavily on the emerging working class and the mobilization of new groups into the electorate.

As the emergence of the New Deal coalition demonstrates, a period of electoral volatility is not a necessary condition for a partisan realignment. Nor, perhaps, is it a sufficient condition. In 1985 Reagan himself proclaimed that a realignment had occurred. Political scientists were skeptical about that claim, mainly because the Democrats continued to dominate the U.S. House of Representatives. With George H. W. Bush's victory in 1988, however, some agreed that a "split-level" realignment had occurred.[26]

Although Bush's election suggested that Republican dominance might have arrived, Clinton's 1992 victory called that thesis into question, and his 1996 victory cast further doubt on the idea that a realignment had occurred. On the other hand, the Republicans' capture of the House and Senate in 1994, and their ability to hold both chambers in the next five elections, countered any claim that Democratic dominance had been established. After the 2000 elections the Republicans held control of the House, the Senate, and the presidency for the first time since 1953, although they temporarily lost control of the Senate between June 1991 and January 1993.[27] The closeness of the 2000 election calls into question any claim of Republican dominance. The 2004 election was likewise extremely close, although the Republicans can be encouraged by their gains in the Senate. Even so, the narrowness of Bush's win over Kerry weakens any claim that the Republicans have emerged as a majority party.

STATE-BY-STATE RESULTS

Because states deliver the electoral votes needed to win the presidency, the presidential election can be viewed as fifty-one separate contests, one for each state and one for the District of Columbia. As we saw in chapter 2, the candidate with the most votes wins all of a state's electoral votes. Regardless of how a state decides to allocate its electors, the number of electors is the sum of its senators (two) plus its number of representatives in the House.[28] There are 538 electors, and a majority is required to be elected by the Electoral College. In 2004, the number of electors ranged from a low of 3 in Alaska, Delaware, Montana, North Dakota, South Dakota, Vermont, Wyoming, and the District of Columbia, to a high of 55 in California.

Because each state, regardless of population, has two electoral votes for its senators, the larger states are underrepresented in the Electoral College and the smaller states are overrepresented. In 2004 the nine largest states, which had 52 percent of the population in the 2000 Census, had only 45 percent of the electoral votes. The twenty smallest states and the District of Columbia contained 10 percent of the population and had 16 percent of the electoral votes. Some have argued that the overrepresentation of the smaller states gives the Republicans an advantage. In both of the last elections, Bush tended to do better in smaller states. In 2000, the thirty states that Bush carried yielded an average of 9.0 electoral votes, while the twenty states (plus D.C.) that Gore carried yielded an average of 12.7 votes. In 2004, the thirty-one states that Bush carried yielded an average of 9.2 electoral votes, and the nineteen states (plus D.C.) that Kerry carried yielded an average of 12.6. But even in 2000, the tendency of the Republicans to win smaller states played a negligible role in Bush's minority victory.[29]

Even though small states are overrepresented in the Electoral College, presidential candidates tend to focus on the larger states unless polls indicate that they are unwinnable. Despite being underrepresented in the Electoral College, California provides one-fifth of the votes necessary to win the presidency. Even so, in 1992 George H. W. Bush quit campaigning in California in early September because the polls showed that Bill Clinton had a commanding lead. In contrast, in 1996 Bob Dole campaigned in California during the final weeks of the campaign, although the strategy may have been aimed at helping the Republicans retain control of the U.S. House of Representatives. In 2000 George Bush spent some last-minute resources in California, but in 2004 he spent few resources in that state, even though John Kerry's lead, according to the polls, though comfortable, was not large. As we saw in chapter 2, during the last weeks of the 2004 campaign both candidacies focused heavily on three large states—Florida, with 27 electoral votes, Pennsylvania with 21, and Ohio with 20.

States are the building blocks of winning presidential coalitions, but state-by-state results can be overemphasized and may sometimes be misleading. First, as we saw, in forty-two of the forty-five elections between 1828 and 2004, the candidate with the largest number of popular votes has also won a majority of the electoral vote. Thus, candidates can win by creating a broad-based coalition throughout the nation, although they must also consider whether they are likely to win specific states. Moreover, given the nature of national television coverage, candidates must run national campaigns. They can make appeals targeted to specific states and regions, but the national media broadcast the appeals. And presidential debates, which have been held in every election since 1976, also reach a nationwide audience.

Second, state-by-state results can be misleading, and the comparisons may even conceal change. To illustrate this point we can compare the results of two close Democratic victories—John F. Kennedy's defeat of Richard M. Nixon in 1960 and Jimmy Carter's defeat of Gerald R. Ford in 1976. There are many parallels between these two Democratic victories. In both 1960 and 1976 the Republicans did very well in the West, and both Kennedy and Carter needed southern support to win. Kennedy carried six of the eleven states of the old Confederacy (Arkansas, Georgia, Louisiana, North Carolina, South Carolina, and Texas) and gained five of Alabama's 11 electoral votes for a total of 81 electoral votes.[30] Carter carried ten of these states (all but Virginia) for a total of 118 electoral votes.

The demographic basis of Carter's support was quite different from Kennedy's, however. In 1960, only 29 percent of African Americans in the South were registered to vote, compared with 61 percent of whites. According to our analysis of the National Election Studies (NES), only about one in fifteen of the Kennedy voters in the South was black. In 1976, 63 percent of African Americans in the South were registered to vote, compared with 68 percent of whites.[31] We estimate that about one out of three southerners who voted for Carter was black. A simple state-by-state comparison would conceal this massive change in the social composition of the Democratic presidential coalition.

Third, state-by-state comparisons do not tell us why a presidential candidate received support. Of course, such comparisons can lead to interesting speculation, especially when dominant issues are related to regional differences. They

FIGURE 3-2   Bush's Margin of Victory over Kerry, 2004

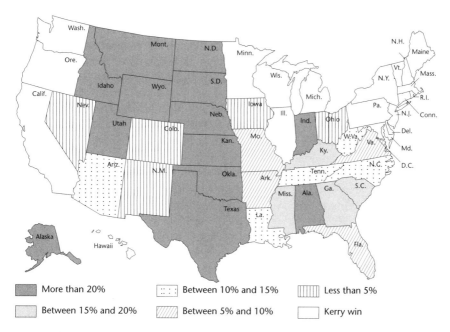

■	More than 20%	▨	Between 10% and 15%	▥	Less than 5%
■	Between 15% and 20%	▨	Between 5% and 10%	□	Kerry win

Source: Richard M. Scammon, Alice V. McGillivray, and Rhodes Cook, *America Votes 26, 2003–2004: Election Returns by State* (Washington, D.C.: CQ Press, 2006), 9.

can even lead to hyperbolic comparisons of "red" states versus "blue" states.[32] But it is also necessary to turn to surveys, as we do in part 2, to understand the dynamics of electoral change.

With these qualifications in mind we can turn to the state-by-state results. In our earlier books we have presented maps displaying Reagan's margin of victory over Carter in 1980, Reagan's margin of victory over Mondale in 1984, George H. W. Bush's margin over Dukakis in 1988, Clinton's margin over Bush in 1992, Clinton's margin over Dole in 1996, and George W. Bush's margin over Al Gore in 2000.[33] In Figure 3-2 we show Bush's margin over Kerry in 2004. These maps clearly reveal differences among the five Republican victories and also show continuities in Clinton's victories.

In 1980 Reagan did far better in the West than in other regions. We consider eighteen states to be western from the standpoint of presidential elections (see note 30), and Reagan won all of them except Hawaii. He carried thirteen of them by twenty percentage points or more. Outside the West, Reagan carried only a single state (New Hampshire) by a twenty-point margin. Although he carried ten southern states (all except Carter's home state of Georgia), he carried many of them by narrow margins.

In 1984 Reagan won by a far larger margin than in 1980, carrying every state except Minnesota. Although he still had a massive margin of victory in the West, Reagan now had a massive margin in many more states, and he carried seventeen states outside the West by at least twenty points. He made his biggest gains in the South. In 1980 he carried none of the southern states by a twenty-point margin. In 1984 he carried ten of them by twenty points or more and Tennessee by sixteen. Although southern blacks voted overwhelmingly for Mondale, his losses in the South were massive. Whereas in 1980 Carter had won more than one-third of the southern white vote, only about one white southerner in four voted for Mondale.

The 1988 results show a clear improvement for the Democrats. Dukakis won two New England states (including his home state of Massachusetts), gaining nearly half the vote in this region. He carried three midwestern states (Iowa, Minnesota, and Wisconsin). Dukakis fared somewhat worse than Carter in the border states, where he won only West Virginia. Like Mondale, Dukakis lost all eleven southern states.

George H. W. Bush's overall margin of victory over Dukakis was much smaller than Reagan's margin over Mondale in 1984, and it was somewhat smaller than Reagan's margin over Carter. Bush's best region was the South, and he was far less dominant in the West than Reagan. Bush won five southern states with a margin of twenty points and three others by fifteen to twenty points. He won the three remaining states by a margin of ten to fifteen points. Bush won every southern state by more than his national margin (7.7 points) and carried the South as a whole by 17.5 points.

Of the eighteen western states, Bush actually lost three, and he won by less than ten percentage points in five others, including California, which he carried by only 3.5 points. If we restrict our attention to the eight mountain states, we find that Bush carried five by a margin greater than twenty points, but he carried the remaining three by less than ten points. The combined results for these states show Bush with a 16.8 point margin over Dukakis, slightly smaller than his margin in the South. Bush's margin in all eighteen western states was only 7.5 points, slightly less than his national average.

In 1992, as in 1988, the South was the best region for the Republicans. Clinton lost seven of the eleven southern states, and he carried three others by less than five points, winning by a wider margin only in his native Arkansas. For all eleven states, Bush won 42.6 percent of the popular vote, compared with 41.2 percent for Clinton, and the South was the only region where Bush won a majority of the electoral vote, gaining 108 of the South's 147 electors. Among the eighteen western states, Bush and Clinton each won nine. Clinton even won four of the eight mountain states, although three of his victories were by less than five percentage points. But the mountain states were Perot's best region, and he won 25.2 percent of the vote there. Bush won 38.1 percent of the vote in those states; Clinton 36.3 percent. Because he won by nearly 1.5 million votes over Bush in California, Clinton fared better in the eighteen western states than Bush. He carried 41.2 percent of the vote in all the western states, compared with 36.2 percent for Bush. Clinton's margin there was the same as his national average. Perot also did well in New England, carrying 23.3 percent of the vote. But Clinton won all six New England states, the first time a Democrat had carried all of them since Johnson's 1964 landslide. Clinton won 44.4 percent of the total vote, while Bush won only 31.7 percent.

In 1996 Dole's share of the major-party vote slipped slightly in the South, compared with Bush's, but he still won seven states, carrying 96 of the region's 147 electoral votes. Bill Clinton actually won slightly more of the popular vote in these states than Dole, carrying 46.2 percent to Dole's 46.1 percent. Dole did better than Clinton in the mountain states. Although Perot won 12 percent of the vote or more in Idaho, Montana, and Wyoming, his overall share of the vote in the mountain states fell to 8.7 percent, and Dole appears to have been the beneficiary. Dole carried five of these eight states, winning 23 of their 40 electoral votes. He also won a plurality of their popular vote, winning 46.4 percent to Clinton's 42.6 percent. But Clinton won California by 1.3 million votes. In the eighteen western states, Clinton received 46.7 of the popular vote, Dole 42.1 percent.

Clinton's greatest margin of victory was in New England and the Mid-Atlantic states. He carried every midwestern state except Indiana, winning Illinois and Minnesota by fifteen percentage points. He won California and Washington by more than ten percentage points, and he carried traditionally Democratic Hawaii by more than twenty points. Clinton won by a narrow margin in Arizona, but that ended an eleven-election winning streak for the Republicans. Arizona had been the only state to have voted the same way in every presidential election since Dwight D. Eisenhower's victory in 1952.

In 2000 there were once again clear regional differences, with Democratic strength concentrated in the Northeast, the Midwest, and the Pacific Coast states. But George W. Bush also had regional areas of strength. First of all, he carried every southern state, although he won only his home state of Texas by more than twenty percentage points. His victory in Florida, by a margin of 537 votes out of nearly six million cast, was contested for thirty-six days before Gore was forced to concede. Overall, Bush won 54.4 percent of the vote in the South, while Gore won only 43.4 percent. Bush's largest margins of victory occurred in the prairie and mountain states. He won four of the eight mountain states by twenty points or more, although he narrowly lost New Mexico. In these eight states, Bush won 54.8 percent to Gore's 39.7 percent, a larger margin than in the South. But Gore won five of the eighteen states that we classify as western, defeating Bush in California by 1.3 million votes. As a result, for all eighteen western states Bush held only a small margin of victory, capturing 48.2 percent of the vote to 46.7 percent for Gore. Gore's best region was New England, where he carried two states by over twenty percentage points and won 56.1 percent of the vote to Bush's 37.0 percent.

In 2004 Bush again won all eleven southern states, although he carried only two of them by twenty percentage points or more. He won 56.8 percent of the vote in the South, compared with 42.5 percent for Kerry. As in 2000, he won four of the mountain states by a margin of twenty points, but this time he narrowly carried New Mexico. For the mountain states as a whole, Bush won 56.7 percent of the vote and Kerry won 42.0 percent, so that Bush's margin in the mountain West was only slightly larger than his margin in the South. But Kerry won California by 1.2 million votes. As a result, Bush's overall total in the western states was only 50.8 percent, compared with 47.9 percent for Kerry. As in 2000, the best region for the Democrats was New England, where they carried all six states, winning three of them by margins of twenty points or more. Overall, Kerry won 57.7 percent of the vote in New England, compared with only 40.8 percent for Bush.

As we will see, state-by-state variation in 2004 was about the same as it was in 2000. The South is now a Republican region, but the Republicans do not dominate that region. In both 1992 and 1996 the Republicans lost four southern states (Arkansas, Georgia, Louisiana, and Tennessee in 1992, and Arkansas, Florida, Louisiana, and Tennessee in 1996).

However, the Democrats would still have won in both 1992 and 1996 had they not carried a single southern state. Lyndon B. Johnson in 1964 was the only other Democratic winner since World War II who would have won without southern electoral votes. But Johnson won a popular and electoral vote landslide over Barry M. Goldwater.

It is instructive to compare Clinton's victories in 1992 and 1996 with Jimmy Carter's victory. Although Carter won many southern states by narrow margins, his electoral vote victory depended heavily on southern electoral votes. Of the 297 votes he won, 118 came from southern states. Of the 370 electoral votes that Clinton won in 1992, only 39 came from the South; of the 379 votes he won in 1996, only 51 did.

Likewise it is instructive to compare George W. Bush's wins in 2000 and 2004 with Richard Nixon's 1968 victory. Nixon won five southern states, losing five to Wallace and one to Hubert H. Humphrey. All the same, 57 of Nixon's 301 electoral votes came from the South, and without southern support he would not have won an electoral vote majority. In 2000, Bush won 147 of his 271 electoral votes from the South; in 2004, 153 of his 286 votes were from that region.

Clearly, the South has been transformed from the most Democratic region of the country to one of the most Republican. But perhaps the most striking feature of postwar presidential elections has been the decline of regional differences, which can be demonstrated by statistical analysis. Joseph A. Schlesinger has analyzed state-by-state variation in presidential elections from 1832 through 1988, and we have updated his analyses through 2004. Schlesinger's measure is the standard deviation among the states in the percentage voting Democratic. State-by-state variation in 2004 was 8.39, slightly lower than the 8.51 variation recorded in 2000. Although 2000 and 2004 elections reveal the highest level of variation since 1968 (9.50), they are well below the 11.96 level recorded in the 1964 contest between Johnson and Goldwater. But Schlesinger's analysis also clearly reveals the relatively low level of state-by-state variation in all fifteen postwar elections. According to his analysis (as updated), all fifteen of the presidential elections from 1888 through 1944 displayed more state-by-state variation than any of the fifteen postwar elections. To a large extent, the decline in state-by-state variation has been a result of the transformation of the South.[34]

ELECTORAL CHANGE IN THE POSTWAR SOUTH

The South is a growing political region that has undergone dramatic political change. Even though five of the eleven southern states have lost congressional representation since the end of World War II, Florida and Texas have both made spectacular gains. In the 1944 and 1948 elections, Florida had only 8 electoral votes, but by the 2004 election it had 27. In 1944 and 1948, Texas had 23 votes, but in 2004 it had 34. Since World War II ended the South's electoral vote total has grown from 127 to 153.

The political transformation of the South was a complex process, but the major reason for the change was simple. As V. O. Key Jr. brilliantly demonstrated in *Southern Politics in State and Nation* (1949), the major factor in southern politics is race. "In its grand outlines the politics of the South revolves around the position of the Negro. . . . Whatever phase of the southern political process one seeks to understand, sooner or later the trail of inquiry leads to the Negro." [35] And it is the changed position of the Democratic Party toward African Americans that has smashed Democratic dominance in the South.[36]

Between the end of Reconstruction (1877) and the end of World War II (1945) the South was a Democratic stronghold. In fifteen of the seventeen elections from 1880 through 1944, all eleven southern states voted Democratic. In his 1920 victory over James M. Cox, the Republican Warren G. Harding narrowly carried Tennessee, but the ten remaining southern states voted Democratic. The only major southern defections came in 1928, when the Democrats ran Alfred E. Smith, a Roman Catholic, and the Republican candidate, Herbert C. Hoover, won five southern states. Even then, six of the most solid southern states—Alabama, Arkansas, Georgia, Louisiana, Mississippi, and South Carolina—voted for Smith, even though all but Louisiana were overwhelmingly Protestant.[37]

After Reconstruction ended in 1877, many southern blacks were prevented from voting, and in the late nineteenth and early twentieth centuries several southern states changed their voting laws to further disfranchise blacks. The Republicans ceded those states to the Democrats. Although the Republicans had black support in the North, they did not attempt to enforce the Fifteenth Amendment, which bans restrictions on voting on the basis of "race, color, or previous condition of servitude."

In 1932 a majority of African Americans in the North remained loyal to the Republicans, although by 1936 Franklin D. Roosevelt had won the support of northern Democrats. But Roosevelt made no effort to win the support of southern blacks, most of whom remained disfranchised. Even as late as 1940 about 70 percent of the nation's blacks lived in the states of the old Confederacy. Roosevelt carried all eleven of those states in each of his four victories. His 1944 victory, however, was the last contest in which the Democrats carried all eleven southern states.

World War II led to a massive migration of African Americans from the South, and by 1948 Truman, through his support for the Fair Employment Practices Commission, made explicit appeals to blacks. In July 1948 he issued an executive order ending segregation in the armed services.[38] These policies led to defections by the "Dixiecrats" and cost Truman four southern states (Alabama, Louisiana, Mississippi, and South Carolina). But he still won all seven of the remaining southern states. In 1952 and 1956 Democratic candidate Adlai E. Stevenson de-emphasized appeals to blacks, although Eisenhower made inroads in the South. In 1960 Kennedy played down appeals to African Americans and, as noted above, southern support was crucial in his win over Nixon.[39] Kennedy may also have strengthened his campaign by choosing a Texan, Lyndon B. Johnson, as his running mate. Clearly, Johnson helped Kennedy win Texas, which he carried by only two percentage points.

But if Johnson as running mate aided the Democrats in the South, Johnson as president played a different role. His explicit appeals to African Americans helped end Democratic dominance in the South. Barry M. Goldwater, the Republican candidate, had voted against the Civil Rights Act in 1964, creating a sharp difference between the two presidential candidates. In 1968, Hubert H. Humphrey, who had been a champion of black demands throughout his political career, carried only one southern state, Texas, which he won with only 41 percent of the vote. He was probably aided by George Wallace's candidacy, since Wallace carried 19 percent of the Texas vote. Wallace's third-party candidacy carried Alabama, Arkansas, Georgia, Louisiana, and Mississippi, while Nixon carried the remaining five southern states. Nixon carried every southern state in 1972, and his margin of victory was greater in the South than outside it. Although Carter won ten of the eleven southern states (all but Virginia) he carried a minority of the vote among white southerners.

In 1980, as noted earlier, Reagan carried every southern state except Georgia, Carter's home state. In his 1984 reelection Reagan carried all the southern states, and his margin of victory in the South was greater than his margin outside it. In 1988 George H. W. Bush carried all eleven southern states, and the South was his strongest region. As we saw, Clinton made some inroads in the South in 1992 and somewhat greater inroads in 1996. All the same, the South was the only predominantly Republican region in 1992, and in 1996 Dole won a majority of the electoral vote only in the South and mountain states. In 2000 the South was the only region where George W. Bush carried every state, and over half of his electoral votes came from that region. In 2004 Bush carried every southern state, along with all of the states of the mountain West. Once again, more than half of his electoral votes came from the states of the old Confederacy. As we noted above, the Democrats have not won all eleven southern states since the end of World

War II. The Republicans have carried all these states in five postwar elections (1972, 1984, 1988, 2000, and 2004). The transformation of the South is clearly the most dramatic change in postwar American politics.

OTHER REGIONAL CHANGES

There have been other regional changes, although none is as dramatic or important as the change in the South. First, there has been a shift toward the Republicans in the mountain West. But this change has been little studied, partly because those states are sparsely populated and yield few electoral votes. Since World War II, Arizona, Colorado, Nevada, New Mexico, and Utah have all gained at least one electoral vote, and only Montana has lost an electoral vote. After the war, these states contributed 32 electoral votes, but even with postwar growth they still contribute only 44. And the shift in these states has not been as dramatic because they never had a long history of voting Democratic. Granted, even as far back as 1892 three of the then-five mountain states voted for James B. Weaver, the Populist candidate, and all six of the mountain states supported the Democratic and Populist candidacy of William Jennings Bryan in 1896. In 1916, all eight mountain states voted to reelect Woodrow Wilson, perhaps because he seemed more opposed to American entry into the war in Europe than his Republican opponent, Charles Evans Hughes. Although all the western states voted Republican in 1920, 1924, and 1928, like most states, they voted for FDR in 1932 and 1936, and only Colorado voted Republican in 1940. In 1944, six of the eight mountain states voted to reelect Roosevelt, and only Colorado and Wyoming voted for Thomas E. Dewey. In 1948, Harry S. Truman carried all eight mountain states, the last time the Democrats swept the region.

In fact, writing in 1987, Eric R. A. N. Smith and Peverill Squire observed that since 1952 the Democratic candidates had only won twice—in 1960, when Kennedy won Nevada and New Mexico, and 1964, when Johnson won every mountain state except Arizona. They concluded, "The Mountain states have been a solid part of the Republican presidential coalition since 1952." [40] And the Republicans swept the mountain West in 1988. But as we saw, their hold weakened in 1992 and 1996. Even in 2000, Gore won New Mexico, although his 366-vote margin was the smallest of any state. In 2004 Bush carried New Mexico by less than one percentage point, and the Republicans once again swept the region.

The reasons for the Republican edge in the mountain West have been far less studied than change in the South,[41] but Arthur H. Miller concludes that "the realignment which has been occurring in the Mountain West reflects a combination of shifting social demographics, political attitudes and partisan evaluations." [42] Even though Goldwater carried only a single mountain state in 1964, his candidacy may have led voters to identify the Democratic Party with unpopular welfare policies, and McGovern's candidacy in 1972 may have increased negative views of the Democrats. "In short," Miller writes, "the growth in negative evaluations of Democratic party performance, a dramatic shift toward conservative social welfare policy preferences, and a professionalization of the population of this region . . . provide a description of the major forces that produced the Mountain realignment in voting behavior and party identification." [43]

Although the South and mountain West have moved to the Republicans since World War II, the six New England states (see note 13) have moved to the Democrats. These states have been losing representation since 1960. Maine lost one electoral vote after 1960; between 1960 and 1992 Massachusetts lost four; and Connecticut lost one vote after the 2000 Census. The remaining three states had the same number of votes in 2004 as they had in 1960. Even after the 1950 Census, these states still had a total of forty electoral votes; by the 2004 election they had only thirty-four.

From the first time the Republicans contested the presidency, in 1856, through Taft's election in 1908, all six New England states voted Republican in all fourteen elections. Five of them voted for Woodrow Wilson in 1912, when the GOP was split. But five of the states voted Republican in 1916, and all voted Republican in the GOP landslides of 1920 and 1924. As we noted earlier in our book (introduction to part 1), in 1928 Massachusetts and Rhode Island both voted for Al Smith, the first Catholic to head a major-party ticket. But in 1932, in the first of FDR's four wins, New England was the most Republican region. Hoover carried only five states, and four of them were in New England. In 1936 Alfred E. Landon carried only two states, Maine and Vermont, and the Republican candidate carried them, along with some midwestern and prairie states, in both 1940 and 1944. In 1948 Truman carried Massachusetts and Rhode Island, but Dewey won the four remaining New England states. In his two electoral vote landslides Eisenhower swept New England, but even Kennedy carried only three of the New England states, Connecticut, Rhode Island, and his native Massachusetts. In his 1964 landslide Johnson swept New England, and in his 1968 loss Humphrey carried four of the six New England states. In 1972, George S. McGovern lost forty-nine states, but his one win came in Massachusetts. And in his narrow win in 1976, Carter carried Maine and Rhode Island, with Ford winning the remaining New England states.

In 1988, Dukakis, the incumbent Democratic governor of Massachusetts, carried Rhode Island and his home state. But ever since 1992, the Democrats have been extremely successful in New England, carrying all six states in 1992, 1996, and 2004, and winning every state except New Hampshire in 2000.

The changes in New England may have been facilitated by the decline of the liberal wing of the Republican Party. As Nichol C. Rae writes, "While liberal Republicanism was disintegrating as a national political force, its position in several state parties was also weakened by the effects of realignment-dealignment and the transformation of the party system. This was even true in former liberal Republican strongholds such as in lower New England." [44] Rae compares the failure of liberal Republicans in Massachusetts to deal with changing national forces with the relative success of liberal Republicans in Connecticut. But at the presidential level Massachusetts has voted consistently Democratic in the last five elections, and Connecticut has voted Democratic in the past four.

Finally, we can turn to California. Granted, it is a single state, not a "region," but with 55 electoral votes it provides more electoral votes than either the mountain West or New England. Although its relative growth is slowing, California's electoral vote total more than doubled from 25 after the 1940 Census to 55 after the 2000 Census.

Between 1856 and 1928 California seldom voted Democratic, but it was not consistently Republican either. It voted Democratic in 1856, 1892, and 1916, when its 13 electoral votes were enough to swing the election to Wilson. And it voted for FDR in all four of his victories and gave Truman a very narrow margin over Dewey in 1948. But then it began voting Republican, supporting the GOP presidential candidate in nine of the ten elections between 1952 and 1988. In seven of those elections the Republican ticket included a resident of California.[45] But in those elections California did not vote very differently from the nation as a whole: its average level of Republican support was 51.6 percent, only a tenth of a percentage point more Republican than the nation as a whole. In 1968 California voted four points more Republican than the nation as a whole, but in four elections—1956, 1972, 1984, and 1988—it voted less Republican.[46]

But California shifted toward the Democratic Party between 1988 and 1992, and by early September 1992 George H. W. Bush quit campaigning in California. Even with Perot winning 21 percent of the vote, Clinton defeated Bush by thirteen percentage points. He defeated Dole by the same margin in 1996. Although Gore defeated George W. Bush by a half a percentage point in the nation as a whole, he won by 12 percent in California. And while Bush defeated Kerry by 2.4 percent of the national vote, Kerry won by just under a ten-point margin in California.

One of the reasons for this change is the state's growing Hispanic population, which increased from 19 percent in 1980 to 33 percent in 2005.[47] Granted, Latinos are much less likely to be citizens than non-Latinos, and even those who are citizens are less likely to register and to vote. According to estimates by Mark Baldassare, based on exit polls, in 1990 only 4 percent of California voters were Latinos; by 2000, 14 percent were. In 1990, 82 percent of all voters were white non-Latinos; by 2000 the figure fell to 71 percent.[48] According to the Edison Media Research/Mitofsky International exit poll conducted in 2004, 21 percent of California voters were Hispanic, and only 65 percent were non-Hispanic whites. The poll showed that 66 percent of Hispanics voted for Kerry, and only 32 percent for Bush.[49]

Baldassare argues that "observers . . . speculate that California has become so predictably Democratic and liberal in voting that it has become an irrelevant player in national politics." But, he writes, "We find the current, popular view that California has become a one-party state off base. In reality, the more significant political trend is the growth and flourishing of the un-party state, which is a result of the public's distrust in its political and governance system." [50] He argues that the Democrats have not made major gains in party registration and that many Californians are fiscal conservatives who distrust big government. On the other hand, Baldassare points out, the Republicans' emphasis on social issues, especially their views on restricting abortion, run counter to the views of many independents who do not want the government to interfere in the private lives of individuals.

THE ELECTORAL VOTE BALANCE

The Republicans dominated presidential elections from 1972 through 1988. After his relatively narrow win over Humphrey in 1968, Nixon swept forty-nine states in his victory over McGovern four years later. Carter won a narrow victory in 1976, but the Republicans swept most states in the Reagan and Bush elections, winning forty-nine states in Reagan's triumph over Mondale.

As a result of these victories, in which the Republicans carried many states over the course of the five elections,[51] some scholars argued that the Republicans had an electoral vote "lock." According to Marjorie Randon Hershey, the Republicans had won so many states during this period that they had a "clear and continuing advantage in recent presidential elections."[52] That advantage, Hershey argued, came mainly from Republican strength in many small states, which are overrepresented in the Electoral College. But Michael Nelson argued that the Republicans did not have an electoral vote advantage, and James C. Garand and T. Wayne Parent argued that the Electoral College was biased toward the Democrats.[53] I. M. Destler concludes that if there is any Electoral College bias, it is very small. His advice is, "Target specific states if you like, but above all win 51% of the popular vote. An electoral college victory is very, very likely."[54] Using substantially different procedures, Andrew Gelman, Jonathan N. Katz, and Gary King also concluded that since the 1950s, partisan biases created by the Electoral College have been negligible.[55]

We tested for the possibility of a pro-Republican bias in the Electoral College in 1992 and 1996 by assuming that Clinton and George H. W. Bush won the same percentage of the popular vote in 1992, and that Clinton and Dole won the same percentage of the popular vote in 1996. We found a slight pro-Republican bias in 1992, but no pro-Republican bias in 1996.[56] The 2000 result clearly demonstrates a pro-Republican bias, since George W. Bush won even while trailing Al Gore by .45 points, just under half a percentage point. To assume that Bush and Gore each received the same percentage of the popular vote, we added .225 percentage points to Bush's total in each state and subtracted .225 percentage points from Gore's. This would have led to Bush's winning Florida by a safer margin, although he would have won by less than half a percentage point. But this slight shift would have moved Iowa, New Mexico, Oregon, and Wisconsin from Gore's column to Bush's, adding thirty electoral votes to Bush's total.

FIGURE 3-3   Results of the 1988, 1992, 1996, 2000, and 2004 Elections

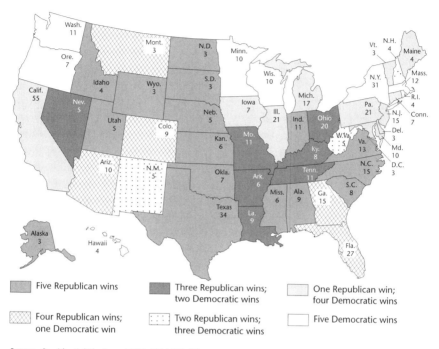

	Five Republican wins		Three Republican wins; two Democratic wins		One Republican win; four Democratic wins
	Four Republican wins; one Democratic win		Two Republican wins; three Democratic wins		Five Democratic wins

Source: Presidential Elections, 1789–2000 (Washington, D.C.: CQ Press, 2002); Richard M. Scammon, Alice V. McGillivray, and Rhodes Cook, *America Votes 26, 2003–2004: Election Returns by State* (Washington, D.C.: CQ Press, 2006).

In 2004, Bush won by a 2.4 percentage point margin over Kerry. We therefore subtracted 1.2 percentage points from Bush's percentage in each state and added 1.2 percentage points to Kerry's. This hypothetical exercise switched three states, Iowa, New Mexico, and Ohio. Subtracting 32 electoral votes from Bush's electoral vote total and adding them to Kerry's would have made Kerry the winner. This exercise suggests that in 2004 the Electoral College may have had a slightly pro-Democratic bias, because if the popular vote had been tied, the Democrats would have won.

But if there are partisan biases, they do not appear to be systematically in favor of either party, and they are small. Even small biases, however, can lead to a "wrong winner," as they appear to have done in 1876, 1888, and 2000.[57] Despite the election of a "wrong winner" in 2000, the likelihood of such a winner is smaller than it was before World War II, when the Democrats often won southern states by large popular-vote majorities.

Today's presidential elections are national in scope, and the Electoral College provides no significant barrier to either political party. Figure 3-3 illustrates the results of the last five elections, showing the electoral votes for each state in 2004 and 2008. It also shows the number of times each state has voted Republican or Democratic in these elections.

First, there are sixteen states, which yield 135 electoral votes, that the Republicans have won in all five elections. Six of them are in the South, and they include all four prairie states, three of the eight mountain states, and Alaska, Indiana, and Oklahoma. There are five additional states that the Republicans have won in four of these five contests, and they are worth 64 electoral votes. Two of these states are in the South and three are mountain states. On the Democratic side, there are eight states, as well as the District of Columbia, that the party has won in all five elections, yielding 92 electoral votes. They include two New England states, New York, two midwestern states, and the two northwestern states, as well as Hawaii. And there are eleven states, yielding 163 electoral votes, that the Democrats have won in four of the five contests. Most important, several large states are in this group, including California, Illinois, Michigan, New Jersey, and Pennsylvania. Of the remaining states, seven voted Republican in three of these contests, yielding 70 votes. Finally, there are three small states, yielding 14 votes, that voted Democratic in three of these elections.

On balance, there are twenty-eight states, yielding 269 electoral votes, that have voted Republican more often than they have voted Democratic. There are twenty-two states, plus the District of Columbia, that have voted Democratic more often than they have voted Republican, and they also have 269 electoral votes.

This mixture shows problems and opportunities for both parties. The Republicans have strong prospects in the South, but they may have overinvested in that region. For example, the conservative appeals that helped George H. W. Bush and George W. Bush in the South may have cost them votes in California. The Democrats have demonstrated that they can win without the South, but many of Clinton's victories in the Midwest were in states that he won by relatively narrow margins. The potential for the Republicans to gain a lock on the presidency has disappeared, but the Democrats have no hold on the presidency either.

To assess the future prospects of the major parties we must go beyond analyzing official election statistics. We must attempt to understand the reasons why, at least until 2004, electoral politics was being fought among a shrinking percentage of the electorate, and we must determine why some Americans are likely to vote, whereas others are not. To determine how social coalitions have changed over time, as well as the issue preferences of the electorate, we must turn to surveys. We also need surveys to assess the extent to which Bush's reelection resulted from narrowly positive evaluations of his performance as president, and the extent to which it resulted from voters' approving his policies. And we must study surveys to examine the way partisan loyalties have changed during the postwar years. Part 2 of our study uses survey data to examine the prospects for change and continuity in American electoral politics.

Voting Behavior in the 2004 Presidential Election

The collective decision reached on November 2, 2004, was the product of 202 million individual decisions.[1] Two questions faced American citizens eighteen years old and older: whether to vote and, if they did, how to cast their ballots. How voters make up their minds is one of the most thoroughly studied subjects in political science—and one of the most controversial.[2]

Voting decisions can be studied from at least three theoretical perspectives.[3] First, voters may be viewed primarily as members of social groups. Voters belong to primary groups of family members and peers; secondary groups such as private clubs, trade unions, and voluntary associations; and broader reference groups such as social classes and ethnic groups. Understanding the political behavior of these groups is the key to understanding voters, according to the pioneers of this approach, Paul F. Lazarsfeld, Bernard R. Berelson, and their colleagues. Using a simple "index of political predisposition," they classified voters according to religion (Catholic or Protestant), socioeconomic level, and residence (rural or urban) to predict how they would vote in the 1940 presidential election. Lazarsfeld and his colleagues maintained that "a person thinks, politically, as he is, socially. Social characteristics determine political preference." [4] This perspective is still popular, although more so among sociologists than political scientists.[5]

A second approach analyzes psychological variables. To explain voting behavior in the 1952 and 1956 presidential elections, Angus Campbell, Philip E. Converse, Warren E. Miller, and Donald E. Stokes, scholars at the University of Michigan Survey Research Center developed a model of political behavior based on psychological variables, which was presented in their classic book *The American Voter.*[6] They focused on attitudes most likely to have the greatest effect on the vote just before the moment of decision, particularly attitudes toward the candidates, the parties, and the issues. Party identification emerged as the most important social-psychological variable that influences voting decisions. The Michigan approach is the most prevalent among political scientists, although many de-emphasize its psychological underpinnings. The work of Philip E. Converse provides an outstanding example of this tradition.[7] Warren E. Miller and J. Merrill Shanks's *The New American Voter* provides an excellent example of this approach and is especially valuable for understanding the long-term forces that have transformed the American electorate.[8]

A third approach draws heavily upon the work of economists. According to this perspective, citizens weigh the costs of voting against the expected benefits when deciding whether or not to go to the polls. And when deciding for whom to vote, they calculate which candidate favors policies closest to their policy preferences. Citizens are thus viewed as rational actors who attempt to maximize their expected utility. Anthony Downs and William H. Riker helped to found the rational choice approach.[9] The writings of Riker, Peter C. Ordeshook, John A. Ferejohn, and Morris P. Fiorina provide excellent examples of this point of view.[10]

In our view, however, none of these perspectives provides a complete answer to questions of how voters decide whether to vote and for whom. Although individuals belong to groups, they are not always influenced by their group memberships. Moreover, classifying voters by groups does not explain why they are influenced by social factors. Placing too much emphasis on social-psychological factors can lead us away from studying the political forces that shape political behavior. And while the assumptions of economic rationality may lead to clearly testable propositions, the data used to test them are often weak, and the propositions that can be tested are often of limited importance.[11]

Therefore, we have chosen an eclectic approach that draws on insights from each viewpoint. Where appropriate, we employ sociological variables, but we also use social-psychological variables, such as party identification and feelings of political efficacy. The rational choice approach guides our study of the way issues influence voting behavior.

Part 2 begins with an examination of the most important decision of all: whether to vote. One of the most profound changes in postwar American politics has been the decline of electoral participation. Although turnout among the voting-age population grew fairly consistently between 1920 and 1960, it fell in 1964 and in each of the next four elections. Turnout rose slightly in 1984, but it dropped to a postwar low in 1988, and even though it rose in the three-way Bush-Clinton-Perot contest of 1992, it fell to its lowest postwar level in 1996. Despite extensive mobilization efforts in 2000, turnout rose only two points compared with 1996. In 2004, with even greater mobilization efforts, turnout among the voting-age population rose four points. By comparing turnout among the voting-age population and the U.S. population eligible to vote, we will shed light on some of the reasons that turnout declined between 1960 and 2004.

Although turnout is low in the United States compared with other advanced democracies, it is not equally low among all social groups, and we examine group differences in detail, using both the 2004 National Election Study (NES) data and the 2004 Current Population Survey conducted by the U.S. Bureau of the Census. Drawing mainly on a social-psychological perspective, we will use the NES surveys to study changes in attitudes that have contributed to the decline of electoral participation. And we will examine the reasons that turnout rose in 2004. Finally, we will examine whether low levels of turnout, as well as the increase in turnout in 2004, have implications for a partisan realignment.

In chapter 5 we examine how social forces influence the vote. We rely mainly on the NES survey of 800 voters, but we also employ an exit poll of 13,660 voters conducted for a consortium of television networks and newspapers by Edison Media Research/Mitofsky International (EMR/MI) and a national exit poll of 5,154 voters conducted by the *Los Angeles Times.* Using these polls we were able to analyze the impacts of race, gender, marital status, region, urbanicity, age, occupation, social class, education, income, union membership, religion, and religious commitment. We examine Hispanic support for the parties, noting that there is considerable controversy about the extent to which George W. Bush made gains among Hispanics. By using both exit polls we were able to examine the relationship between sexual preferences and the vote.

We then used NES surveys to analyze changing social patterns during the postwar years, at times using a survey of the U.S. civilian population conducted by the National Opinion Research Center in 1944. The impact of those social forces has changed considerably during the postwar years. Support for the Democratic coalition among white southerners has eroded dramatically, and support has also dropped among working-class whites. Although support among white union members has remained relatively high, the proportion of voters living in households with a union member has declined markedly since World War II. Jews remain strongly Democratic, although even here there has been some slippage. Blacks, on the other hand, have remained solidly Democratic and became even more Democratic as a result of the 1964 contest between Democrat Lyndon B. Johnson and Republican Barry M. Goldwater. We argue that the failure of a Catholic candidate to win the votes of a majority of white Catholics was a major obstacle that Kerry could not overcome, especially when compared with John F. Kennedy's success in winning four out of five Catholic voters in 1960. Finally, although some remnants of the New Deal coalition remain, we discuss the reasons the New Deal coalition has broken down since the early and mid-1960s.

Chapter 6 examines attitudes toward the candidates and the issues. Because this was so clearly an election dominated by the two major-party candidates, we do not provide an extensive discussion of voter attitudes toward the most visible independent candidate, Ralph Nader. We do discuss the major concerns of the electorate in 2004, using the NES surveys to compare them with the concerns of the electorate in all previous elections between 1972 and 2000. As might be expected, the major change in 2004 was the concern over terrorism, Islamic extremists, and homeland security, which was the major concern of two-fifths of the electorate.

We then discuss the electorate's issue preferences, partly to determine whether voters met the criteria for having voted on the basis of the issues. We employed seven, seven-point issue scales used in 2004, in which respondents were asked to place themselves, Bush, and Kerry. Most voters could place themselves on the scales, but fewer could place both candidates; an even smaller share saw a difference between them; and on average only about half saw that Kerry was more "liberal" than Bush. Still, what we found compares favorably with most of the previous eight elections. Unlike 2000, when the electorate was on balance closer to George W. Bush than to Al Gore on these seven-point scales, in 2004 the electorate was closer to Kerry than to Bush. In determining whether Americans voted according to their issue preferences we examined all voters who had a position on an issue and then divided them into two categories: The first category comprised those who placed both candidates on the scales, saw a difference between them, and recognized that Kerry was more "liberal" than Bush. Those who did not meet all three of these conditions we placed in the second category. We found that among voters who met all three of our criteria for issue voting, a substantial majority voted for the candidate whom they had placed closest to their position; among those who did not meet the three conditions, voting according to issue preferences was essentially random. We next built a "balance of issues" measure based on the summary scores of respondents on all seven issues. We found that the electorate as a whole was tilted in a noticeably Republican direction, even though Kerry was, on average, closer to the typical respondent.

We spend some timing discussing the abortion issue, not only because it is divisive but because the NES survey asked voters both to choose their own policy preference and to say where Bush and Kerry stood on this issue. The vast majority of respondents chose one of the four policy preferences offered, and their preferences were clearly related to their vote. But we further examined those voters who placed both Bush and Kerry, saw a difference between them, and saw that Kerry was more "pro-choice" than Bush. Among these voters there was a very strong relationship between opinions about abortion and the way they voted; among those who did not meet the three conditions, there was no relationship between preferences about abortion and their vote. We end this chapter by examining the importance of social and moral issues in 2004, questioning the EMR/MI exit poll results concerning "moral values." We turn instead to national polls conducted over the course of the election year, which strongly suggest that voters were concerned mainly with the economy and to a lesser degree with the war in Iraq and the war against terrorism.[12]

We then turn to how presidential performance influences voting decisions. Recent research suggests that many voters decide to vote on the basis of "retrospective evaluations" of the incumbents. In other words, what candidates have done in office—not what candidates promise to do if elected—affects how voters decide. In chapter 7 we examine the role of retrospective evaluations in the past nine presidential elections. Voters' negative evaluations of Gerald R. Ford's performance in 1976 played a major role in the election of Jimmy Carter, just as negative evaluations of Carter played a major role in electing Ronald Reagan. To a very large extent George H. W. Bush's defeat in 1992 resulted from negative evaluations of his performance as president. And positive evaluations of Clinton's presidency played a major role in his reelection in 1996. The 2000 contest appears to be an exception, since positive evaluations of Clinton and the Democratic Party were nearly as high as they were four years earlier, but the Democratic share of the major-party vote fell from 54.7 percent to 50.3 percent. Perhaps because he did not emphasize the accomplishments of the Clinton administration, Gore was unable to capitalize on the good economic conditions in fall 2000.

To the extent that we can make comparisons with earlier elections, we found that, as in previous elections, few voters thought the government was doing a good job solving what they considered the most important issue. The division between those who thought it was doing a good job, and those who thought it was doing a bad or a very bad job was relatively close. That result is similar to the one in 2000 and not too dissimilar to the views of the electorate in 1976, 1984, and 1996. Although the 2004 NES study did not ask which party would do a better job handling the most important problem, it did ask which party would better handle the nation's economy, the war on terrorism, and keeping us out of war. The Republicans did best on the question of handling terrorism. We examine the relationship between economic evaluations and the vote, and because foreign policy and the fight against terrorism were so important to voters in 2004 we added a discussion of the relationship between foreign policy evaluations and the vote.

We examined presidential approval using the nine NES presidential election year surveys between 1972 and 2004. Only two presidents had lower levels of approval than George W. Bush did in the fall of the election year (Carter in 1980 and the senior Bush in 1992), and both were defeated. In 2004 Bush was at a tipping point, with 51 percent approving of the job he was doing as president and 49 percent disapproving, and that contributed to the very close outcome. We build a summary measure of retrospective evaluations, but without a question asking which party would do a better job solving the problem the voter thought was the most important, we cannot directly compare the results with the previous seven elections (1976 through 2000) for which this measure can be constructed. Even so, our substitute measure is very strongly related to the vote. Moreover, when we compare the impacts of issues and retrospective evaluations, we find that both factors are important, although retrospective evaluations are more strongly related to voters' choices than their issue preferences.

As we note in chapter 7, we cannot fully understand the voting decision unless we examine the factors that shape issue preferences and influence retrospective evaluations. Of all these factors, the single most important is party identification, which for most voters provides a powerful means to reach preliminary judgments. How closely do voters identify with a political party? And how does this identification shape issue preferences and evaluations of the incumbent and the incumbent party? Chapter 8 explores the impact of party loyalties on voting choices during the postwar era, using the NES surveys to examine change between 1952 and 2004; we also briefly use the General Social Surveys (GSS) conducted by the National Opinion Research Center to study change between 1972 and 2004.[13] We found that there has been a modest shift toward the Republicans since Reagan was first elected in 1980, although the Democrats still hold an edge. We used the NES surveys to discuss party identification separately among the white and black electorates, since the patterns of postwar change among these groups differed dramatically.

We will examine the role of party loyalties in shaping issue preferences, retrospective evaluations, and voting preferences. As we will see, the relationship between party identification and retrospective evaluations was very strong in 2004, although we need to be cautious in making comparisons with earlier years. The relationship between party identification and the vote was also very strong in 2004. Moreover, the percentage of strong partisans increased, with both the NES and GSS showing the highest percentage of strong Republicans since each of these surveys began measuring party identification.

Chapter 4

Who Voted?

Before discovering how people voted in the 2004 presidential election, we must answer a more basic question. Who voted? Turnout is lower in the United States than in any other industrialized democracy, with the possible exception of Switzerland. In Table 4-1 we present estimates of postwar turnout in twenty-five democracies, including the United States. The United States clearly ranks last, if legislative elections are examined, but U.S. congressional elections, especially midterm elections, are not comparable to legislative elections in most parliamentary systems.[1] However turnout in U.S. presidential elections is also clearly lower than turnout in parliamentary elections in every other democracy except Switzerland. It is also clearly lower than turnout in presidential elections in five of the six other democracies that hold presidential elections, and Ireland, the only democracy with comparable turnout, chooses a president who is largely a figurehead.[2]

In 2004 George W. Bush won 62 million votes, while John F. Kerry won 59 million, so the approximately 80 million Americans who did *not* vote could easily have elected any presidential candidate.[3] Both parties did a good job of turning out their supporters, although there is some evidence that the Republicans did a better job. With the outcome so close, it seems possible that increased turnout could have changed it. Before turning to the 2004 presidential election, however, we must place the study of turnout in a broader historical context.[4]

TURNOUT FROM 1828 THROUGH 1920

Historical records can be used to determine how many people voted in presidential elections, and we can derive meaningful estimates of turnout as early as 1828, the first election in which the vast majority of states chose their presidential electors by popular vote. Turnout is calculated by dividing the total number of votes cast for president by the voting-age population.[5] But should the turnout denominator be all people who are old enough to vote? Or should it include only people

TABLE 4-1   Turnout in National Elections, 1945–2003 (in percentages)

Country	National Parliamentary	Presidential
Australia (24)	94.5	
Belgium (18)	92.5	
Austria (18)	90.9	(10) 90.9
Italy (15)	89.8	
Luxembourg (12)	89.7	
Iceland (17)	89.5	(5) 84.7
Malta (14)	88.2	
New Zealand (20)	87.5	
Netherlands (18)	86.6	
Denmark (23)	86.0	
Sweden (18)	85.7	
Germany (15)	85.0	
Norway (15)	80.4	
Greece (16)	79.9	
Israel (16)	77.8	
Spain (8)	75.7	
Finland (17)	76.5	(9) 74.0
United Kingdom (16)	75.2	
France (16)	74.8	(7) 81.8
Portugal (11)	73.6	(6) 69.3
Ireland (16)	72.6	(6) 57.6
Japan (22)	70.7	
Canada (18)	70.0	
Switzerland (14)	56.6	
United States (29)	44.6	(14) 55.6

Sources: For all the countries except Australia, Canada, Japan, Israel, New Zealand, and the United States, the results are from International Institute for Democracy and Electoral Assistance, *Voter Turnout in Western Europe* (Stockholm, Sweden: Publications Office International IDEA, 2004), 90. For Australia, the results are from the International Institute for Democracy and Democratic Assistance, accessed at www.idea.int/vt/country_view.cfm.CountryCode=AU (accessed May 23, 2005). The results for Canada are from Elections Canada, *Voter Turnout at Federal Elections and Referendums, 1867–2000,* accessed at www.elections.ca/ (accessed April 26, 2005); the results for Israel are from The State of Israel, *The Knesset: The Israeli Parliament, 2005,* accessed at www.Knesset.gov.il/index.html (accessed April 22, 2005). The New Zealand results are from "New Zealand Elections," accessed at www.absoluteastromoy.com/encyclopedia/N/Ne?_New_Zealand_elctions.htm (accessed May 23, 2005). The results from Japan are from the Association for Promoting Fair Elections (Tokyo, 2004). For the United States, turnout is based upon the U.S. Census Bureau, *Statistical Abstract of the United States, 2004–2005,* 124th ed. (Washington, D.C.: U. S. Government Printing Office, 2004), Table 409, 257, also available online at www.census.gov.statab/www/.

Note: Numbers in parentheses are the number of parliamentary or presidential elections. For all countries with bicameral legislatures, we report turnout for the lower house. For all countries except the United States, we calculate turnout based on voter registration lists. For the United States turnout is based upon the voting-age population.

who are eligible to vote? The answer to this question will greatly affect our estimates of turnout in all presidential elections through 1916 because few women were eligible to vote before 1920.

Although women gained the right to vote in the Wyoming territory as early as 1869, even by 1916 only eleven of the forty-eight states had fully enfranchised women, and they were mainly western states with relatively small populations.[6] Because women were already voting in some states, it is difficult to estimate turnout before 1920. Clearly women should be included in the turnout denominator in the states where they had the right to vote. Including them in the states where they could not vote leads to very low estimates of turnout.

In Table 4-2 we present two sets of turnout estimates. The first column, which presents results compiled by Charles E. Johnson Jr., calculates turnout by dividing the number of votes cast for president by the voting-age population. The second, based on Walter Dean Burnham's calculations, measures turnout by dividing the total presidential vote by the total number of Americans eligible to vote. Burnham excludes blacks before the Civil War, and from 1870 on he excludes aliens where they were not able to vote. But the main difference between Burnham's estimates and Johnson's is that Burnham excludes women from the turnout denominator in those states where they could not vote.

Most political scientists would consider Burnham's calculations more meaningful than Johnson's. For example, most political scientists argue that turnout was higher in the nineteenth century than it is today. But whichever set of estimates one employs, the pattern of change is the same. There was a large jump in turnout after 1836, when both the Democrats and the Whigs began to employ popular appeals to mobilize the electorate. Turnout jumped markedly in 1840, the "Log Cabin and Hard Cider" campaign, in which William Henry Harrison, the hero of the Battle of Tippecanoe (1811), defeated the incumbent Democrat, Martin van Buren. Turnout waxed and waned after 1840, but it rose substantially after the Republican Party, founded in 1854, polarized the nation by taking a clear stand against extending slavery into the territories. In Abraham Lincoln's election in 1860, four out of five white men went to the polls.

Turnout rose and fell after the Civil War, peaking in the 1876 contest between Rutherford B. Hayes, the Republican winner, and Samuel J. Tilden, the Democratic candidate. As the price of Hayes's contested victory, the Republicans agreed to end Reconstruction. Once they lost the protection of federal troops, many African Americans were prevented from voting. Although some southern blacks could still vote in 1880, overall turnout among them dropped sharply, which in turn reduced southern turnout. Turnout began to fall nationally by 1892 but rose in the 1896 contest between William Jennings Bryan (Democrat and Populist) and William McKinley, the Republican winner. It dropped again in the 1900 rematch between the two men.

By the late nineteenth century, African Americans were denied the franchise throughout the South, and poor whites often found it difficult to vote as well.[7] Throughout the country, registration requirements, which were in part designed

TABLE 4-2   Turnout in Presidential Elections, 1828–1916

Election year	Winning candidate	Party of winning candidate	Percentage of voting-age population who voted (Johnson)	Percentage eligible to vote who voted (Burnham)
1828	Andrew Jackson	Democrat	22.2	57.3
1832	Andrew Jackson	Democrat	20.6	56.7
1836	Martin Van Buren	Democrat	22.4	56.5
1840	William H. Harrison	Whig	31.9	80.3
1844	James K. Polk	Democrat	30.6	79.0
1848	Zachary Taylor	Whig	28.6	72.8
1852	Franklin Pierce	Democrat	27.3	69.5
1856	James Buchanan	Democrat	30.6	79.4
1860	Abraham Lincoln	Republican	31.5	81.8
1864[a]	Abraham Lincoln	Republican	24.4	76.3
1868	Ulysses S. Grant	Republican	31.7	80.9
1872	Ulysses S. Grant	Republican	32.0	72.1
1876	Rutherford B. Hayes	Republican	37.1	82.6
1880	James A. Garfield	Republican	36.2	80.6
1884	Grover Cleveland	Democrat	35.6	78.3
1888	Benjamin Harrison	Republican	36.3	80.5
1892	Grover Cleveland	Democrat	34.9	78.3
1896	William McKinley	Republican	36.8	79.7
1900	William McKinley	Republican	34.0	73.7
1904	Theodore Roosevelt	Republican	29.7	65.5
1908	William H. Taft	Republican	29.8	65.7
1912	Woodrow Wilson	Democrat	27.9	59.0
1916	Woodrow Wilson	Democrat	32.1	61.8

Sources: The estimates of turnout among the voting-age population are based on Charles E. Johnson Jr., *Nonvoting Americans,* ser. P-23, no. 102 (U.S. Department of Commerce, Bureau of the Census, Washington, D.C.: U.S. Government Printing Office, 1980), 2. The estimates of turnout among the population eligible to vote are based on calculations by Walter Dean Burnham. Burnham's earlier estimates were published in U.S. Department of Commerce, Bureau of the Census, *Historical Statistics of the United States: Colonial Times to 1970,* ser. Y-27-28 (Washington, D.C.: U.S. Government Printing Office, 1975), 1071–1072. The results in the table, however, are based on Burnham's "The Turnout Problem," in *Elections American Style,* ed. A. James Reichley (Washington, D.C.: Brookings Institution Press, 1987), 113–114.

[a] The estimate for the voting-age population is based on the entire U.S. adult population. The estimate for the eligible population excludes the eleven Confederate states that did not take part in the election.

to reduce fraud, were introduced. Because individuals were responsible for getting their names on the registration rolls before the election, the procedure created an obstacle that reduced electoral participation.[8]

Introducing the secret ballot also reduced turnout. Before this innovation, most voting in U.S. elections was public. The parties printed their own ballots, which differed from each other in size and color; hence any observer could see how each person voted. In 1856 Australia adopted a law calling for a secret ballot to be printed and administered by the government. The "Australian ballot" was first used statewide in Massachusetts in 1888. By the 1896 election, nine out of ten states had followed Massachusetts's lead.[9] Although the secret ballot was introduced to reduce fraud, it also reduced turnout. When voting was public, men could sell their votes, but candidates were less willing to pay for a vote if they could not see it delivered. Ballot stuffing was also more difficult when the state printed and distributed the ballots.

As Table 4-2 shows, turnout trailed off rapidly in the early twentieth century. By the time of the three-way contest between Woodrow Wilson (Democrat), William Howard Taft (Republican), and Theodore Roosevelt (Progressive) only three out of five politically eligible Americans went to the polls (column 2). In 1916, turnout rose slightly, but just over three-fifths of eligible Americans voted (column 2), and only one-third of the total adult population went to the polls (column 1).

TURNOUT FROM 1920 THROUGH 2004

It is easier to calculate turnout after 1920, and we have provided estimates based on U.S. Bureau of the Census Statistics, as well as turnout among the politically eligible population. These two methods of estimating turnout lead to relatively similar estimates, although differences have increased since 1972. We prefer focusing on turnout based on the voting-age population for three basic reasons: First, it is difficult to estimate the size of the eligible population, even though excellent attempts have been made by Walter Dean Burnham and by Michael P. McDonald and Samuel L. Popkin.[10] But their estimates differ, with McDonald and Popkin reporting higher levels of turnout than Burnham in all five elections between 1984 and 2000. Second, even though only citizens can vote in present U.S. elections, citizenship is not a constitutional requirement of voting. National legislation determines how long it takes to become a citizen, and state laws impose citizenship as a condition of voting. Lastly, the incarceration rate has grown markedly during the past three decades, and all but two states disfranchise prisoners. Only Maine and Vermont allow prisoners to vote, and fourteen states disfranchise some or all ex-felons. In his 2004 estimates, McDonald excludes a total of four and a half million prisoners, persons on probation, and parolees from his turnout denominator.

To exclude noneligible adults from the turnout denominator leads to misleading comparisons, especially when U.S. turnout is compared with turnout levels in other democracies. Approximately one out of ten voting-age Americans cannot vote, whereas in the United Kingdom only about one in fifty is disfranchised. About one in seven black males is disfranchised because of a felony conviction. As Thomas E. Patterson writes in a critique of McDonald and Popkin, "To ignore such differences, some analysts say, is to ignore official efforts to control the size and composition of the electorate." [11]

In Table 4-3 we show the percentage of the voting-age population that voted for the Democratic, Republican, and minor-party and independent ("Other") candidates between 1920 and 2004. The table also shows the percentage that did not vote, as well as the overall size of the voting-age population. In Figure 4-1 we show the percentage of the voting-age population that voted in each of these twenty-two elections, as well as the politically eligible population between 1920 and 1944 and the voting-eligible population between 1948 and 2004 (see note 10).

In 2004, George W. Bush received more votes than any presidential candidate in American history, and John F. Kerry received the second largest number. But these numbers are less impressive once one considers that the voting-age population was 221 million and that only 55.3 percent of the voting-age population voted. According to our calculations, only 28.0 percent of the voting-age population voted for Bush. In eleven of these elections, the winning candidate received a higher percentage. In 1960, the highest-turnout election during these years, Richard M. Nixon, the losing candidate, received a larger share of the vote.[12]

As Figure 4-1 reveals, turnout among the voting-age population increased in seven of the ten election intervals between 1920 and 1960. Two of the exceptions—1944 and 1948—resulted from the dislocations during and after World War II. Specific political conditions account for increases in turnout in certain elections. The jump in turnout between 1924 and 1928 resulted from the candidacy of Alfred E. Smith, the first Catholic candidate to receive a major-party nomination, and the increase between 1932 and 1936 resulted from Franklin D. Roosevelt's efforts to mobilize the lower social classes, especially the industrial working class. The extremely close contest between Nixon and the second Catholic candidate, John F. Kennedy, partly accounts for the high turnout in 1960, when turnout rose to 62.8 percent of the voting-age population and was slightly higher among the politically eligible population and the voting eligible population.[13] This was far below the percentage of eligible Americans that voted between 1840 and 1900, although it was the highest level of the voting-age population that had ever voted in a presidential election. Nonetheless, U.S. turnout in 1960 was still well below the average turnout attained in most advanced democracies (see Table 4-1).

As short-term forces drove turnout upward in specific elections, so long-term changes were driving turnout upward from 1920 through 1960. For example, women who came of age before the Nineteenth Amendment often failed to exercise their right to vote, but women who came of age after 1920 had higher levels of turnout and gradually replaced older women in the electorate.[14] Because all states restricted voting to citizens, immigrants enlarged the voting-age population but could not increase the number of voters until they became citizens. But after 1921, as a result of restrictive immigration laws, the percentage of the population that was foreign born declined. Moreover, levels of education rose throughout the twentieth century, a change that boosted turnout. Americans

TABLE 4-3   Percentage of Adults Who Voted for Each Major Presidential Candidate, 1920–2004

Election year	Democratic candidate		Republican candidate		Other candidates	Did not vote	Total	Voting-age population
1920	14.8	James M. Cox	*Warren G. Harding*	26.2	2.4	56.6	100	61,639,000
1924	12.7	John W. Davis	*Calvin Coolidge*	23.7	7.5	56.1	100	66,229,000
1928	21.1	Alfred E. Smith	*Herbert C. Hoover*	30.1	.6	48.2	100	71,100,000
1932	30.1	*Franklin D. Roosevelt*	Herbert C. Hoover	20.8	1.5	47.5	100	75,768,000
1936	34.6	*Franklin D. Roosevelt*	Alfred M. Landon	20.8	1.5	43.1	100	80,174,000
1940	32.2	*Franklin D. Roosevelt*	Wendell Willkie	26.4	.3	41.1	100	84,728,000
1944	29.9	*Franklin D. Roosevelt*	Thomas E. Dewey	25.7	.4	44.0	100	85,654,000
1948	25.3	*Harry S. Truman*	Thomas E. Dewey	23.0	2.7	48.9	100	95,573,000
1952	27.3	Adlai E. Stevenson	*Dwight D. Eisenhower*	34.0	.3	38.4	100	99,929,000
1956	24.9	Adlai E. Stevenson	*Dwight D. Eisenhower*	34.1	.4	40.7	100	104,515,000
1960	31.2	*John F. Kennedy*	Richard M. Nixon	31.1	.5	37.2	100	109,672,000
1964	37.8	*Lyndon B. Johnson*	Barry M. Goldwater	23.8	.3	38.1	100	114,090,000
1968	26.0	Hubert H. Humphrey	*Richard M. Nixon*	26.4	8.4	39.1	100	120,285,000
1972	20.7	George S. McGovern	*Richard M. Nixon*	33.5	1.0	44.8	100	140,777,000
1976	26.8	*Jimmy Carter*	Gerald R. Ford	25.7	1.0	46.5	100	152,308,000
1980	21.6	*Jimmy Carter*	Ronald Reagan	26.8	4.3	47.2	100	163,945,000
1984	21.6	Walter F. Mondale	*Ronald Reagan*	31.3	.4	46.7	100	173,995,000
1988	23.0	Michael S. Dukakis	*George H. W. Bush*	26.9	.5	49.7	100	181,956,000
1992	23.7	*Bill Clinton*	George H. W. Bush	20.6	10.8	44.9	100	189,493,000
1996	24.1	*Bill Clinton*	Bob Dole	19.9	4.9	51.1	100	196,789,000
2000	24.8	Al Gore	*George W. Bush*	24.5	1.9	48.8	100	205,813,000
2004	26.7	John F. Kerry	*George W. Bush*	28.0	.6	44.7	100	221,257,000

Sources: For the voting-age population between 1920 and 1928, see U.S. Bureau of the Census, *Statistical Abstract of the United States, 1972,* 92nd ed. (Washington, D.C.: U.S. Government Printing Office, 1972), Table 597, 373; for the voting-age population between 1932 and 2000, see U.S. Bureau of the Census, *Statistical Abstract of the United States, 2004–2005,* 124th ed. (Washington, D.C.: U.S. Government Printing Office, 2004), Table 409, 257. Also available online at www.census.gov/statab/www/. For the voting-age population in 2004, see Michael P. McDonald, "2004 Voting-Age and Voting-Eligible Population Estimates and Voter Turnout," http://elections.gmu.edu/Voter_Turnout_2004.htm (accessed July 25, 2005). For the number of votes cast for presidential candidates, as well as the total vote cast for all elections between 1920 and 2000, we employed *Presidential Elections: 1789–2000* (Washington, D.C.: CQ Press, 2002), 136–200. For the number of votes cast for each presidential candidate in 2004, as well as the total number of votes, we employed Richard M. Scammon, Alice V. McGillivray, and Rhodes Cook, *America Votes 26, 2003–2004: Election Returns by State* (Washington, D.C.: CQ Press, 2006), 9.

Note: The names of the winning candidates are italicized.

FIGURE 4-1   Percentages of the Voting-Age Population and of the Politically Eligible and Voting-Eligible Population That Voted for President, 1920–2004

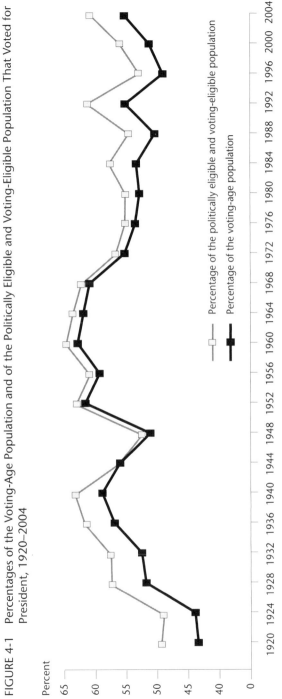

Percent

Percentage of the politically eligible and voting-eligible population

Percentage of the voting-age population

1920 1924 1928 1932 1936 1940 1944 1948 1952 1956 1960 1964 1968 1972 1976 1980 1984 1988 1992 1996 2000 2004

Sources: For the voting-age population, see Table 4-3. For the politically eligible population between 1920 and 1944, see Walter Dean Burnham, "The Turnout Problem," in *Elections American Style*, ed. A. James Reichley (Washington, D.C.: Brookings Institution Press, 1987), 113–114. For the voting-eligible population between 1944 and 2000, see Michael P. McDonald and Samuel L. Popkin, "The Myth of the Vanishing Voter," *American Political Science Review* 95 (December 2001) : 966. For 2004, see Michael P. McDonald, "2004 Voting-Age and Voting-Eligible Population Estimates and Voter Turnout," accessed at http://elections.gmu.edu/Voter_Turnout_2004.htm, July 25, 2005.

who have attained higher levels of education are much more likely to vote than those with lower education levels.

Between 1960 and the century's end, changes that tended to increase turnout occurred. After the passage of the Voting Rights Act of 1965, turnout rose dramatically among African Americans in the South, and their return to the voting booth spurred voting among southern whites. Less-restrictive registration laws introduced during the past three decades have made it easier to vote. The National Voter Registration Act, better known as the "motor-voter" law, which went into effect in January 1995, may have added nine million additional registrants to the rolls.[15]

Despite these changes, turnout declined after 1960, as can be seen in Figure 4-1. By 1960 generational replacement among the female electorate had largely run its course. In the 1960s and 1970s, immigration laws were reformed, again increasing the noncitizen population. Of course, levels of education continued to increase, a change that should have pushed turnout upward.

Except for a small increase in turnout in 1984, however, turnout among the voting-age population continuously declined from 1960 through 1988.[16] Turnout rose almost five percentage points in 1992, perhaps partly as a result of H. Ross Perot's candidacy.[17] But in 1996 turnout fell some six percentage points, reaching only 48.9 percent. In 2000 the expectation that the election would be close led both candidates and their supporters to make major efforts to mobilize supporters, but turnout rose only 2.3 percentage points. As we saw in chapter 2, the 2004 election was also expected to be close, and there were unprecedented efforts to increase turnout. Turnout did increase by 4.1 percentage points, but it was still 7.5 percentage points lower than turnout among the voting-age population in the Kennedy-Nixon contest.

TURNOUT AMONG SOCIAL GROUPS

Although turnout was relatively low in 2004, especially when compared with other advanced democracies, it was not equally low among all social groups. To compare turnout among social groups, we rely on the National Election Study (NES) survey conducted by the Survey Research Center and the Center for Political Studies of the University of Michigan.[18] The NES survey is based exclusively on whether or not respondents said that they voted.[19] In 2004, actual votes counted showed a turnout among the politically eligible population of about 60 percent, whereas in the 2004 NES, 76 percent said that they had voted.

There are three basic reasons that the NES surveys overestimate turnout: First, even though they are asked a question that provides reasons for not voting, some nonvoters falsely claim to have voted.[20] Validation efforts, in which the NES checked voting and registration records, suggest that about 15 percent of the respondents who say that they voted have not done so, whereas only a handful of actual voters say that they did not vote.[21] Second, the NES surveys do not perfectly represent the voting-age population. Lower socioeconomic groups, which have very low turnout, are underrepresented. Third, during presidential years the same respondents are interviewed before and after the election. Being interviewed before an election provides a stimulus to vote and thus increases turnout among the NES sample.[22]

Race, Gender, and Age

Table 4-4 compares reported turnout among social groups, using the NES survey. Our analysis begins by comparing African Americans with whites.[23] As the table shows, whites were nine percentage points more likely to report voting than blacks. As we pointed out in note 21, all eight vote validation studies showed that blacks were more likely to overreport voting than whites, so it seems likely that these differences are greater than the NES surveys suggest.[24] Of course, racial differences in turnout are far smaller than they were before the Voting Rights Act of 1965. The first Current Population Survey of U.S. turnout, conducted in 1964, found that whites were 12.5 percentage points more likely to vote than non-whites.[25] Racial differences in turnout may have been smallest in 1984, when Jesse Jackson's first presidential candidacy mobilized African Americans to vote.[26]

But racial differences were relatively small in 2004. According to the Current Population Survey, 67.2 percent of white non-Hispanic citizens and 60.0 percent of black citizens reported voting.[27] Given the relatively small number of black respondents in the NES survey, we cannot make many comparisons among blacks. Southern blacks were less likely to vote than blacks outside the South.[28] African Americans who had not graduated from high school had lower turnout than those who had graduated. Finally, as in most surveys, black women were more likely to report voting than black men. All of these differences were found in the Current Population Survey.

The NES studies include only citizens. As our table shows, Hispanic citizens were less likely to vote than non-Hispanic citizens.[29] The Current Population Surveys include noncitizens, but their recent publications allow analysts to calculate turnout for both the voting-age population and the voting-age-citizen population. In 2004, according to the Current Population Survey, only 28.0 percent of voting-age Hispanics voted; among voting-age Hispanic citizens, however, 47.2 percent said that they voted. Even this latter figure, however, is far below the percentages of non-Hispanic white citizens and of black citizens who reported voting.[30]

Table 4-4 shows that white women were somewhat more likely to vote than white men. In all presidential elections through 1976, surveys consistently showed men more likely to vote than women. The 1980 presidential election seems to mark a historical turning point at which the participation advantage of men was eliminated. In recent Current Population Surveys, women have been slightly more likely to vote than men. In 2004, for example, among voting-age citizens, women were 3.3 percentage points more likely to vote than men; among non-Hispanic white citizens, women were 2.5 percentage points more likely to

TABLE 4-4 Percentage of the Electorate Who Reported Voting for President, by Social Group, 2004

Social group	Voted	Did not vote	Total	(N)[a]
Total electorate	76	24	100	(1,066)
Electorate, by race				
African American	70	30	100	(169)
White	79	21	100	(769)
Hispanic (of any race)	63	37	100	(76)
Whites, by gender				
Female	81	19	100	(397)
Male	77	23	100	(371)
Whites, by region				
New England and				
Mid-Atlantic	78	22	100	(153)
North Central	80	20	100	(233)
South	76	24	100	(181)
Border	79	21	100	(42)
Mountain and Pacific	82	18	100	(161)
Whites, by urbanicity				
Inner city or large city	76	24	100	(156)
Suburb	80	20	100	(227)
Small town	83	17	100	(189)
Rural area	79	21	100	(146)
Whites, by birth cohort				
Before 1939	82	18	100	(147)
1940–1954	86	14	100	(203)
1955–1962	86	14	100	(129)
1963–1970	77	23	100	(98)
1971–1978	76	24	100	(95)
1979–1986	57	43	100	(94)
Whites, by social class				
Working class	66	34	100	(230)
Middle class	85	15	100	(456)
Whites, by occupation				
Unskilled manual	61	39	100	(87)
Skilled manual	69	31	100	(142)
Clerical, sales, other				
white collar	82	18	100	(193)
Managerial	85	15	100	(93)
Professional and				
semi-professional	89	11	100	(170)

(Table continues on next page)

TABLE 4-4 (continued)

Social group	Voted	Did not vote	Total	(N)[a]
Whites, by level of education				
Not high school graduate	58	42	100	(90)
High school graduate	74	26	100	(248)
Some college	80	20	100	(215)
College graduate	93	7	100	(131)
Advanced degree	94	6	100	(86)
Whites, by annual family income				
Less than $15,000	62	38	100	(72)
$15,000–$24,999	74	26	100	(77)
$25,000–$34,999	70	30	100	(81)
$35,000–$49,999	84	16	100	(111)
$50,000–$69,999	80	20	100	(123)
$70,000–$89,999	91	9	100	(102)
$90,000–$119,999	88	12	100	(83)
$120,000 and over	88	12	100	(81)
Whites, by union membership[b]				
Member	85	15	100	(158)
Nonmember	78	22	100	(609)
Whites, by religion				
Jewish	95	5	100	(22)
Catholic	81	19	100	(208)
Protestant	79	21	100	(399)
No preference	76	24	100	(124)
White Protestants, by religious commitment				
Medium to low	81	19	100	(123)
High	77	23	100	(127)
Very high	90	10	100	(61)
White Protestants, by religious tradition				
Mainline	79	21	100	(134)
Evangelical	79	21	100	(170)
Whites, by social class and religion				
Working-class Catholics	68	32	100	(60)
Middle-class Catholics	85	15	100	(131)
Working-class Protestants	67	33	100	(119)
Middle-class Protestants	83	17	100	(229)

[a] Numbers are weighted.
[b] Respondent or a family member in a union.

vote; and among black citizens, women were 7.5 percentage points more likely to vote.[31]

Of course, we do not need surveys to study turnout among the various regions of the country. Because the Census Bureau estimates the voting-age population of each state, we can measure turnout by dividing the total number of votes cast for president in each state by its voting-age population. In 2004, turnout varied a great deal, from a low of 44.3 percent in Hawaii to a high of 73.0 percent in Minnesota.[32] Historically, the South has had low turnout, but differences between the South and other regions have been diminishing. According to our estimates, 52.2 percent of the voting-age population in the South voted; outside the South, 56.6 percent did.[33]

Official election statistics do not present results according to race, and so we need surveys to compare turnout among blacks and whites in each region. As we have already noted, southern blacks were less likely to vote than blacks elsewhere. As Table 4-4 shows, white turnout, too, was lower in the South. Seventy-six percent of southern whites reported voting; among whites elsewhere, 81 percent did. The relatively low level of turnout in the South results partly from the lower level of education in that region.[34] Though regional turnout differences still exist, they have declined dramatically during the past three decades. According to the 1964 Current Population Survey, southern whites were fifteen percentage points less likely to vote than whites outside the South, and nonwhite southerners were twenty-eight percentage points less likely to vote than nonwhites outside the South. But regional differences were small in 2004. White non-Hispanic citizens living in the South were as likely to report voting as whites outside the South, and southern black citizens were only 2.5 percentage points less likely to say that they voted than blacks outside the South.

As with regional differences, we do not need surveys to determine relative levels of turnout in urban, suburban, and rural areas, but voting records do not provide information by race. Table 4-4 presents the percentages who said that they voted according to urbanicity.[35] There is relatively little difference, although whites who lived in small towns were the most likely to say that they voted.

As in previous surveys, the 2004 NES survey found that turnout was very low among the young. Among the cohort born after 1978 (aged 18 to 26), fewer than three out of five claimed to have voted, and even the cohorts born between 1963 and 1970 and between 1971 and 1978 had relatively low levels of turnout. In the 2004 Current Population Survey, reported turnout among the entire citizen population was 63.8 percent; among citizens between the ages of 18 and 24, only 46.7 percent said that they voted. Older Americans do not disengage from politics as once was thought. Even in surveys that find older Americans less likely to vote, the lower turnout results from their lower levels of formal education.[36]

Young Americans are more likely to have higher levels of formal education than their elders, and one might therefore expect them to have higher levels of turnout. As we saw, they do not. As they age, young Americans tend to participate more, although the reasons why their participation increases are not well understood.[37]

Social Class, Income, and Union Membership

As Table 4-4 shows, there were clear differences between the working class (manually employed workers) and the middle class (nonmanually employed workers). Middle-class whites were nineteen percentage points more likely to report voting than working-class whites.[38] Although this distinction between the working class and the middle class is crude, it appears to capture a politically meaningful division because when we further divide respondents according to occupation, we find that clerical, sales, and other white-collar workers (the lowest level of the middle class) are more likely to vote than skilled manual workers.

Family income is also related to electoral participation, with reported voting very low among whites with annual family incomes of less than $15,000.[39] Reported turnout was very high among whites with annual family incomes of $70,000 and above. Americans with higher levels of income are more likely to have higher levels of education, and both income and education contribute to voting. The 2004 Current Population Survey also revealed a strong relationship between income and reported turnout. However, education has a greater effect on turnout than income does.[40]

Surveys over the years have found a weak and inconsistent relationship between union membership and turnout. Being in a household with a union member may create organizational ties that encourage voting, and in 2004 union leaders made a concerted effort to mobilize their members to support Democratic candidates. As Table 4-4 reveals, in 2004 whites in union households were more likely to report voting than whites in households with no union members.

Religion

In the postwar years Catholics have been more likely to vote than Protestants, although the difference has declined. As Table 4-4 reveals, in 2004 white Catholics had only marginally higher levels of reported turnout than white Protestants. Jews have a higher level of education than gentiles, and postwar surveys show they have higher levels of turnout. The 2004 NES survey shows Jews to have the highest level of turnout among the three basic religious groups, although the number of Jews sampled is too small to reach reliable conclusions. Whites with no religious preference are somewhat less likely to vote than any of the basic religious groups.

In recent elections, fundamentalist Protestants have launched get-out-the-vote efforts to mobilize their supporters, and we examined turnout among white Protestants in some detail.[41] David C. Leege and Lyman A. Kellstedt, for example, argue that religious commitment is an important factor in voting behavior.[42] We classified white Protestants according to their level of commitment. To receive a score of "very high" on this measure respondents had to report praying several

times a day and attending church at least once a week, to say that religion provided "a great deal" of guidance in their lives, and to believe that the Bible is literally true or the "word of God." [43] White Protestants with "very high" levels of
religious commitment were very likely to report voting.

Beginning in 1990 the NES has asked detailed questions that allow us to distinguish among Protestant denominations and thus to conduct analyses of religious differences that could not be conducted earlier. We can now divide Protestants into four groups: evangelical, mainline, ambiguous affiliation, and
nontraditional. Most white Protestants can be classified into the first two categories which, according to Kenneth D. Wald, make up over two-fifths of the total
U.S. adult population.[44] According to R. Stephen Warner, "The root of the [main-
line] liberal position is the interpretation of Christ as a moral teacher who told
his disciples that they could best honor him by helping those in need." In contrast, Warner writes, "the evangelical position sees Jesus (as they prefer to call
him) as one who offers salvation to anyone who confesses in his name." Liberal,
or mainline, Protestants stress the importance of sharing their abundance with
the needy, whereas evangelicals see the Bible as a source of revelation about Jesus,
"treasure it and credit even its implausible stories. Liberals argue that these stories are timebound, and they seek the deeper truths that are obscured by myths
and use the Bible as a source of wisdom." [45]

In classifying Protestants as mainline or evangelical, we rely on their denomination. For example, Anglicans, Congregationalists, and most Methodists and
Presbyterians are classified as mainline, whereas Baptists, Pentecostals, and many
small denominations are classified as evangelicals.[46] In 1992, 1996, and 2000
white mainline Protestants were more likely to report voting than evangelicals. As
we saw in chapter 2, in 2004 fundamentalist churches launched a massive get-
out-the-vote effort, and in 2004 white evangelicals were as likely to report voting
as white mainline Protestants. Given the relatively low levels of education among
evangelicals, turning out at the same rate as mainline Protestants is an impressive
achievement.

In Table 4-4 we can note the differences between white Protestants and white
Catholics by looking at the combined effect of class and religion. The table reveals
no differences between working-class Catholics and working-class Protestants
or between middle-class Catholics and middle-class Protestants. But among
both Catholics and Protestants, middle-class whites are more likely to vote than
working-class whites.

Education

We found a strong relationship between education and reported electoral participation. Reported participation is very high among whites who have graduated
from college, and low among whites who have not graduated from high school.
Strong differences were also discovered by the 2004 Current Population Survey.
Among white non-Hispanic citizens who have graduated from college, 82.7 per-

cent voted; of those who had not graduated from high school, only 40.3 percent did. As Raymond E. Wolfinger and Steven J. Rosenstone demonstrate, formal education is the most important variable in explaining turnout in the United States.[47] Better-educated Americans have skills that reduce the information costs of voting and can acquire information about how to vote more easily than less-educated Americans; the better-educated are also more likely to develop attitudes that contribute to political participation, especially the view that citizens have a duty to vote and that they can influence the political process.

As Table 4-4 shows, among whites who did not graduate from high school,[48] fewer than three out of five claimed to have voted, whereas among college graduates (including those with advanced degrees) over nine out of ten said that they voted. Even though surveys may somewhat exaggerate the relationship between formal education and electoral participation, the tendency of better-educated Americans to be more likely to vote is one of the most extensively documented relationships in voting research.[49]

WHY HAS TURNOUT DECLINED?

Despite the four-point increase in turnout between 2000 and 2004, turnout is still substantially below its high in the Kennedy-Nixon contest of 1960. Among the voting-age population, turnout was 7.5 points lower in 2004, and among the voting-eligible population it was 3.5 points lower.

The research of McDonald and Popkin provides important clues about why turnout among the voting-age population has declined. According to their estimates, in 1960 noncitizens made up only about 2 percent of the adult population, but by 2004 they made up 8 percent.[50] Moreover, in 1960 fewer than half a million people were ineligible to vote because they were incarcerated or convicted felons; in 2004, about four and a half million were disfranchised for these reasons,[51] another factor that would tend to reduce turnout among the voting-age population.

Still, given that education is strongly related to voting, and given that education levels have risen continuously during the past four decades, it is difficult to explain the decline of turnout. In 1960, 43 percent of whites aged twenty-five and older, and only 20 percent of blacks of that age, had graduated from high school. By 2003, 86 percent of whites were high school graduates, and 80 percent of blacks were. In 1960, 8 percent of whites were college graduates and only 3 percent of blacks were; by 2003 those percentages had grown to 27 percent among whites and 17 percent among blacks.[52] Clearly, turnout within educational groups must have been declining so fast that the effect of rising education levels was canceled out. This suggests that the decline of turnout since 1960 resulted from the offsetting of some forces that stimulated turnout by others that depressed it.

Analysts have studied the decline of turnout extensively. Some have focused on social factors, such as the changing levels of education among the electorate, while others have studied political attitudes, such as changes in partisan loyalties, as a major source of turnout decline. Some scholars have examined institutional changes, such as the easing of registration requirements. Others have pointed to the behavior of political leaders, arguing that they are making less effort to mobilize the electorate. Certain changes, such as the rise in education levels and the easing of registration requirements should have increased turnout in national elections. Because turnout declined in spite of those forces, Richard A. Brody views the decline of turnout as a major puzzle for students of political participation.[53]

We begin to explore this puzzle by examining the relationship between education and turnout among whites in all presidential elections from 1960 through 2004. (African Americans have substantially lower levels of formal education than whites, and southern blacks have only been enfranchised since 1965. Therefore, including blacks in our analysis would obscure the relationships we are studying.) We divided whites into four educational levels: college graduates, some college, high school graduates, and those who had not graduated from high school.

The NES surveys show no decline in turnout among college graduates, but they do show declines in all the remaining four categories, with the greatest decline in the two lowest education categories. Several studies of earlier Census Bureau surveys also suggest that turnout declined most among Americans who are relatively disadvantaged.[54]

Ruy A. Teixeira's analysis of Census surveys shows a ten-point drop in turnout among college graduates from 1964 to 1988, although the decline was greater among those who had not graduated from college.[55] And Jan E. Leighley and Jonathan Nagler show that turnout declines were greater among manually employed workers. Leighley and Nagler argue that studies of turnout should focus on income, since government policies affect Americans differentially according to their income levels; their analyses suggest that the decline of turnout was consistent across all income groups.[56]

It is the rise in education levels that creates the greatest problem in accounting for the decline of turnout. Although the increase in education did not prevent turnout from declining, it did play a role in slowing the decline. As we saw, between 1960 and 2003 there was a remarkable increase in education levels among the white electorate. According to the NES surveys, the percentage of whites who had not graduated from high school fell from 47 percent in 1960 to 12 percent in 2004. During this period the percentage who had graduated from college rose from 11 percent to 28 percent. Among whites who could be classified by education, reported turnout fell 2.5 percentage points between 1960 and 2004. An estimate based on an algebraic standardization procedure suggests that if education levels had not increased, turnout would have declined 22 percentage points.[57] Although this procedure provides only a preliminary estimate of their impact, it suggests that the decline of turnout would have been much greater if education levels had not increased.

Other social factors also tended to slow the rate of decline. In a comprehensive attempt to explain the decline of turnout between 1960 and 1988, Teixeira studied changes in turnout using the NES surveys. He found that increases in income and the growth of white-collar employment tended to retard the decline of turnout. But the rise in education levels, according to Teixeira's estimates, was far more important than those two changes, its influence being three times as great as the impact of occupational and income levels combined.[58]

Steven J. Rosenstone and John Mark Hansen, too, have used NES surveys to develop a comprehensive explanation for the decline of turnout during these years. Their analyses also demonstrate that the increase in formal education was the most important factor preventing an even greater decline in voter participation. They also examined the effects of easing registration requirements. They found that reported turnout declined eleven percentage points from the 1960s through the 1980s, but that turnout would have declined sixteen points if it had not been for the combined effects of rising education levels and liberalized election laws.[59]

Although some forces slowed the decline of electoral participation, other forces contributed to it. After 1960 the electorate became younger, as the baby boom generation (generally defined as Americans born between 1946 and 1964) came of age. As we have seen, young Americans have lower levels of turnout, although as baby boomers have aged (by 2004 they were between the ages of forty and fifty-eight) one might have expected turnout to rise. The proportion of Americans who were married declined, and because married people are more likely to vote than the unmarried, this change reduced turnout. Church attendance declined, reducing the ties of Americans to their communities. Teixeira identifies these three changes as major shifts that contributed to the decline of turnout and argues that the decline of church attendance was the most important of them.[60] Rosenstone and Hansen also examined changes that tended to reduce turnout, and their analysis suggests that a younger electorate was the most important factor reducing electoral participation.[61]

Warren E. Miller argues that the decline of turnout resulted mainly from the entry of a post–New Deal generation into the electorate.[62] That change, Miller argues, resulted not only from the youth of these Americans but also from generational differences that contributed to lower levels of electoral participation. During the late 1960s and early 1970s a series of events—the Vietnam War, Watergate, and the failed presidencies of Gerald R. Ford and Jimmy Carter— created a generation that withdrew from political activity. Robert D. Putnam also argues that civic disengagement was largely a result of the baby boom generation and that generational succession reduced other forms of civic activity as well. Putnam writes, "The declines in church attendance, voting, political interest, campaign activities, associational membership, and social trust are attributable almost entirely to generational succession." [63]

Most analysts agree that attitudinal change has contributed to the decline of electoral participation. Our own analysis has focused on the effect of attitudinal change, and we have examined the erosion of party loyalties and what George I. Balch and others have called "feelings of external political efficacy," that is, the belief that political authorities will respond to attempts to influence them.[64] These are the same two fundamental attitudes that Teixeira studied in his first major analysis of the decline of turnout, and they are among the attitudes studied by Rosenstone and Hansen.[65] We found these attitudinal changes to be important in explaining the decline of turnout, as Teixeira did.[66] We have estimated the impact of changes in party identification and feelings of external political efficacy in all the presidential elections between 1980 and 2000.[67] Although the effects of the decline in party loyalties and the erosion of political efficacy have varied from election to election, these variables have always played a major role in accounting for the decline of electoral participation. And they also strongly affected the decline of turnout between 1960 and 2004.

The measure of party identification that we use is based on a series of questions designed to measure attachment to a partisan reference group.[68] In chapter 8 we discuss how party identification contributes to the way people vote. But party loyalties also contribute to *whether* people vote. Strong party loyalties contribute to psychological involvement in politics, as Angus Campbell and his colleagues argue.[69] Party loyalties also reduce the time and effort needed to decide how to vote and thus reduce the cost of voting.[70]

Between 1952 and 1964, the percentage of whites who were strong party identifiers never fell below 35 percent. The percentage of white strong party identifiers fell to 27 percent in 1966, and continued to fall through 1978, when only 21 percent identified strongly with either party. Since then party identification has rebounded, and the greatest increase was between 2002 and 2004, mainly because of a four-point increase in the percentage of strong Republicans. Partisan strength appeared to have reached 1952-to-1964 levels. But there was one major change. In the 1952–1964 period the percentage of independents who leaned toward a party was about 15 percent; in 2004, it was 29 percent. As we will see, in 2004 independents with no party leanings were less likely to vote than weak partisans, and so the growth of the former group tended to reduce overall levels of turnout. For a detailed discussion of party identification from 1952 through 2004, along with tables showing the distribution of party identification among whites and blacks during those years, see chapter 8.

Feelings of political effectiveness also contribute to electoral participation. Citizens may expect to gain benefits if they believe that the government is responsive to their demands. Conversely, those who believe that political leaders will not or cannot respond to their demands may see little reason for voting. In twelve of the thirteen elections between 1952 and 2000, Americans with high feelings of political efficacy were the most likely to vote, and in all thirteen, those with low feelings of political efficacy were the least likely to vote.

From 1960 to 1980 scores on feelings of political efficacy declined markedly. Scores on our measure are based on responses to the following two statements: "Public officials don't care much what people like me think," and "People like me

TABLE 4-5   Percentage of Whites Who Reported Voting for President, by Strength of Party Identification and Sense of External Political Efficacy, 2004

Scores on external political efficacy index	Strength of Party Identification							
	Strong partisan		Weak partisan		Independent who leans toward a party		Independent with no partisan leaning	
	%	(N)	%	(N)	%	(N)	%	(N)
High	96	(113)	83	(82)	84	(64)	64	(17)
Medium	94	(53)	81	(47)	71	(73)	45	(11)
Low	90	(97)	81	(80)	61	(87)	35	(34)

Note: Numbers in parentheses are the totals on which the percentages are based. Numbers are weighted.

don't have any say about what the government does." [71] In 1956 and 1960, 64 percent of whites were classified as feeling highly efficacious and only 15 percent scored low. After 1960, the percentage began to fall, reaching an all-time low in 1996, when only 35 percent of whites scored high and 46 percent scored low. Overall levels of efficacy were somewhat higher in 2000 and 2004. In 2004, 36 percent scored high on feelings of political efficacy, and the percentage scoring low fell to 39 percent.

Although strength of partisan loyalties and feelings of political effectiveness are both related to political participation, they are usually weakly related to each other. In 2004, strong and weak partisans did have somewhat higher feelings of political effectiveness than independent leaners and independents with no partisan leanings. Table 4-5 shows the combined impact of these attitudes on reported electoral participation among whites in 2004.

Reading down each column we see that among independents who lean toward a party and independents with no party leanings, whites with high levels of political efficacy were more likely to report voting than those with medium levels, and those with medium levels were more likely to vote than those with low feelings of political efficacy. Among strong partisans, whites with high and medium levels of efficacy were somewhat more likely to vote than those with low levels. Reading across each row, we see that at all three efficacy levels, strong partisans were more likely to vote than any other group; at all three levels, turnout was lowest among independents with no partisan leanings. Although our past research has found no consistent difference in turnout between weak partisans and independents who leaned toward a party,[72] in 2004 weak partisans were more likely to vote than independents with no party leanings among whites with both medium and low levels on the political efficacy measure. These attitudes have a strong cumulative effect. Among whites with strong party loyalties and high feelings of political effectiveness, nineteen out of twenty said that they voted; among independents with no partisan loyalties and low feelings of political effectiveness, only one in three claimed to have voted.

The declines in party loyalties and feelings of political efficacy clearly contributed to the decline of turnout. Among whites who could be classified on both of these measures in 1960 and 2004, turnout fell 4.0 percentage points. A preliminary assessment of the effects of these factors can be derived through an algebraic standardization procedure.[73] Our analyses suggest that the combined impact of this attitudinal change accounts for 80 percent of the decline in turnout, with the decline in feelings of political efficacy being about three times as important as the decline of party identification.

Our estimates demonstrate that these attitudinal changes are important, but they are not final estimates of their impact. We do not claim to have solved the puzzle of declining political participation. Comprehensive analyses, such as those conducted by Teixeira and by Rosenstone and Hansen, are needed to study the 1992, 1996, 2000, and 2004 NES results. As Teixeira demonstrates, a comprehensive estimate of the impact of attitudinal change must calculate the contribution that attitudinal change would have made to the decline of turnout had there been no social forces retarding the decline. In Teixeira's analysis, for example, the decline in party loyalties and the erosion of feelings of political efficacy contributed 62 percent of the decline in turnout between 1960 and 1980. But these attitudinal changes contributed only 38 percent of the decline that would have occurred if changes in education levels, income, and occupational patterns had not slowed it.

We analyzed the combined effects of rising education levels, the erosion of feelings of political efficacy, and the decline of party identification between 1960 and 2004. Our estimates show that attitude change would have accounted for just under 60 percent of the decline that would have occurred if rising education levels had not slowed the decline.[74]

A comprehensive analysis of the impact of attitudinal factors would take into account other factors that might have eroded turnout. As has been well documented, there has been a substantial decline of trust during the past four decades,[75] a decline that may be occurring in a large number of democracies.[76] In 1964, when political trust among whites was highest, 77 percent of whites said the government in Washington could be trusted to do what is right just about always or most of the time, and 74 percent of blacks endorsed that view.[77] Political trust reached a very low level in 1980, when only 25 percent of whites and 26 percent of blacks trusted the government. Trust rebounded during the Reagan years, but it fell after that, and by 1992 trust was almost as low as it had been in 1980. Trust rose in 1996 and again in 2000. It rose again in 2004, when 50 percent of whites and 34 percent of blacks trusted the government.

Back in 1964, 63 percent of whites and 69 percent of blacks said the government was run for the benefit of all.[78] By 1980, only 20 percent of whites and 19 percent of blacks trusted the government on this question. Once again, trust rose during the Reagan years, but it fell after that, and by 1992 trust had fallen back to the 1980 level among whites, and blacks were less trusting than they were twelve years earlier. But trust rose in 1996 and again in 2000. In 2004, however, trust rose among whites while falling somewhat among blacks: 44 percent of whites, but only 27 percent of blacks, said the government was run for the benefit of all.

Although many scholars have studied the decline of trust, this decline has had little impact on the decline of turnout. In most years, including 2004, Americans who distrust the government are as likely to vote as those who are politically trusting. With both of these questions, whites who were politically trusting were only about three or four percentage points more likely to report voting than whites who were politically distrustful.

WHY TURNOUT ROSE IN 2004

Although turnout was low in 2004, there was a substantial increase over 2000. As we saw, turnout among the voting-age population rose by 4.1 percentage points. According to McDonald's estimates turnout rose 4.7 percent among the voting-eligible population, while Burnham maintains that it rose 6.4 percent among politically eligible Americans.[79] Burnham points out that there were twenty-one pairs of elections between 1920 and 2004 and that the increase in turnout between 2000 and 2004 was the third-largest "surge" since 1920.[80]

Scholars will also need to examine short-term forces that may have contributed to the increase in turnout between 2000 and 2004. We have already examined some possibilities elsewhere. It has been argued that the Republicans were especially successful in turning out their supporters. That may be true, but there was no relationship between Bush's gains at a state-by-state level and state-by-state increases in turnout. Likewise, eleven states held referendums to ban marriages between same-sex partners, but it does not appear that the presence of such a proposal on the ballot did much to affect turnout.[81] As we saw in chapter 2, 2004 saw unprecedented get-out-the-vote efforts, especially in the battleground states.

Research by Rosenstone and Hansen points to the importance of political parties in mobilizing voters, and it may shed light on the increase in turnout. These researchers present a fascinating analysis that focuses on the effect of political parties on the participation of the electorate. But there are problems with their interpretation. The percentage of Americans who said they had been contacted by a political party actually increased after the 1960 election. In 1960, 22 percent of the electorate said they had been contacted by a political party; in 1980, 32 percent said they had been contacted.[82] In 1992, only 20 percent said they had been contacted by a political party, but turnout was higher in 1992 than in 1980. The percentage saying they had been contacted by a party grew in 1996 and in 2000, and it increased slightly between 2000 and 2004. In 2004, 38 percent of the electorate said they had been contacted, with whites being twice as likely (51 percent) to be contacted as blacks (27 percent). As in previous elections, Americans who were contacted by a party were more likely to report voting than those who were not. Among whites who were contacted by a political party ($N = 391$), 90 percent said that they voted; among those who said they were not contacted ($N = 374$), only 68 percent did. But even though there was a strong relationship between being contacted and voting, and even though the percentage contacted by a party was higher in 2004 than in 1960, turnout declined over the course of these decades.[83]

In most elections, Americans who think the election will be close are more likely to vote than those who think the winner will win by quite a bit.[84] Although the differences are usually not large, the percentage who think the election will be close varies greatly from election to election. Orley Ashenfelter and Stanley Kelley Jr. report that the single most important factor accounting for the decline of turnout between 1960 and 1972 was "the dramatic shift in voter expectations about the closeness of the race in these two elections." [85] These percentages do vary dramatically, but in some elections the relationship between perceptions of closeness and voting is very weak. In 1996, only 52 percent of whites thought the contest between Bill Clinton and Bob Dole would be close, but in 2000, 88 percent thought that the contest between Al Gore and George W. Bush would be. And in 2000, whites who thought the election would be close were twenty-four percentage points more likely to report voting than those who thought the winner would win by "quite a bit." In 2004, 82 percent of whites and 78 percent of blacks thought the Bush-Kerry contest would be close. But there was no difference in voting between whites who thought the election would be close and those who thought it would not be.

DOES LOW TURNOUT MATTER?

For the past two decades, Democratic leaders have debated the importance of increasing turnout. Some argue that low turnout was a major reason for Democratic presidential losses. The Democrats could win, they argued, if they could mobilize disadvantaged Americans. In 1984 the Democrats made major get-out-the-vote efforts, but turnout increased less than one percentage point, and in 1988 turnout among the voting-age population reached a postwar low. Other Democrats argued that the main problem the party faced was defections by its traditional supporters. Of course, increasing turnout and attempting to win back defectors are not mutually exclusive strategies, but they can lead to contradictory tactics. For example, mobilizing African Americans may not be cost free if doing so leads to defections among white Democrats.

As James DeNardo has pointed out, from 1932 through 1976 there was only a weak relationship between turnout and the percentage of the vote won by Democratic presidential candidates.[86] In our analyses of the 1980, 1984, and 1988 presidential elections, we argued that under most reasonable scenarios increased turnout would not have led to Democratic victories.[87] In 1992 increased turnout went along with a Democratic victory, although not an increased share in the

Democratic vote. Our analyses suggest that Clinton benefited from increased turnout but that he gained more by converting voters who had supported George H. W. Bush four years earlier.[88] Despite a six-point decline in turnout between 1992 and 1996, Clinton was easily reelected. Even so, there is some evidence that the decline of turnout cost Clinton votes.[89]

Given the closeness of the 2000 contest, it seems more plausible that a more successful get-out-the-vote effort by the Democrats might have swung the election to Gore. Pointing to CBS polls conducted both before and after the election, Gerald M. Pomper argues, "If every citizen had actually voted, both the popular and the electoral votes would have led to an overwhelming Gore victory." [90] A CBS poll issued on November 5, two days before the election, showed that Americans who expected not to vote favored Gore by a 42 percent to 28 percent margin over Bush. A CBS poll released on November 13 showed that Americans who regretted not voting favored Gore by a 53 percent to 33 percent margin over Bush. This latter evidence is questionable, however, for although the electoral vote outcome was not definitive, Gore was trailing Bush in the Florida popular vote.

We begin our discussion by examining turnout among party identifiers. In 1980, 1984, and 1988, strong Republicans were more likely to vote than strong Democrats.[91] In 1992 differences were small because turnout increased more among Democrats than among Republicans. But in 1996 and 2000 we once again found that strong Republicans were more likely to vote than strong Democrats. The Republican turnout advantage varies from year to year, among other partisanship categories. In 2000 weak Republicans were no more likely to vote than weak Democrats, although independents who leaned Republican were more likely to vote than independents who leaned Democratic.

In Table 4-6 we present the percentage of the electorate who reported voting according to party identification, issue preferences, and retrospective evaluations of Bush and the Republican Party's performance. Turning first to party identification, we find a clear Republican advantage. Strong Republicans were more likely to vote than strong Democrats, and weak Republicans were more likely to vote than weak Democrats. There was turnout parity only among independents who felt closer to one of the major parties. This turnout advantage for the Republicans could result from the greater success that the Republican leaders and their allies had in mobilizing their supporters, although the NES survey shows that Republicans were only slightly more likely to be contacted by a political party than Democrats were.[92]

How would Kerry have fared if the GOP had not enjoyed this turnout advantage? If strong Democrats had been as likely to vote as strong Republicans, and if weak Democrats had been as likely to vote as weak Republicans, and if the Democrats in these two groups had been as likely to vote for Kerry as strong and weak Democrats who did vote, Kerry would have gained 3.4 percent of the vote. Depending on the states in which these increased votes were cast, Kerry would have won the election. Of course, it would be unwarranted to reach any firm con-

TABLE 4-6   Percentage of the Electorate Who Reported Voting for President, by Party Identification, Issue Preferences, and Retrospective Evaluations

Attitude	Voted	Did not vote	Total	(N)[a]
Electorate, by party identification				
Strong Democrat	84	16	100	(168)
Weak Democrat	72	28	100	(156)
Independent, leans Democratic	70	30	100	(180)
Independent, no partisan leanings	50	50	100	(101)
Independent, leans Republican	71	29	100	(125)
Weak Republican	83	17	100	(139)
Strong Republican	94	6	100	(180)
Electorate, by scores on the balance of issues measure[b]				
Strongly Democratic	90	10	100	(79)
Moderately Democratic	74	26	100	(146)
Slightly Democratic	71	29	100	(197)
Neutral	58	42	100	(92)
Slightly Republican	76	24	100	(217)
Moderately Republican	82	18	100	(190)
Strongly Republican	84	16	100	(141)
Electorate, by scores on the summary measure of retrospective evaluations toward the incumbent party[c]				
Strongly opposed	90	10	100	(162)
Moderately opposed	72	28	100	(157)
Slightly opposed	73	27	100	(114)
Neutral	65	35	100	(103)
Slightly supportive	55	45	100	(65)
Moderately supportive	77	23	100	(305)
Strongly supportive	89	11	100	(127)

[a] Numbers are weighted.
[b] Chapter 6 describes how the "balance of issues" measure was constructed.
[c] Chapter 7 describes how the "summary measure of retrospective evaluations" was created.

clusion about the consequences of increased turnout based on reported turnout among relatively small samples of partisan groups.

In chapter 6 we will examine the issue preferences of the electorate. Our measure is based on respondents' position on seven issues: (1) reducing or increasing government services; (2) decreasing or increasing defense spending, (3) government job guarantees, (4) government aid for blacks, (5) protecting the environment, (6) the role of diplomacy versus military force, and (7) the role of women in society. In 1980 there was no systematic relationship between policy preferences and turnout, but in 1984, 1988, 1992, and 1996 respondents with pro-Republican views were more likely to vote than those with pro-Democratic views. Obviously, that tendency of respondents with pro-Republican views could not have affected the outcome in the two elections the Democrats won, and in 1984 Ronald Reagan won by such a massive margin that it is difficult to imagine that this relationship of policy preferences to turnout cost Walter F. Mondale the election. Although we estimate that the turnout advantage of Americans with pro-Republican views cost Michael S. Dukakis two percentage points, turnout gains would be unlikely to have overcome George H. W. Bush's 7.7 percentage point margin. In 2000 the only Republican turnout advantage was that respondents who were slightly Republican were more likely to vote than those who were slightly Democratic. But this difference is unlikely to have affected the outcome, since more than three out of five members of both groups voted for Gore.[93]

As Table 4-6 shows, in 2004 there was no systematic relationship between issue preferences and reported turnout. In fact, respondents who were strongly Democratic were more likely to vote than those who were strongly Republican. On the other hand, respondents who were moderately Republican were more likely to vote than those who were moderately Democratic, and respondents who were slightly Republican were more likely to vote than those who were slightly Democratic. But all of these differences were small (ranging from five to eight points). Given these weak and inconsistent relationships, it is apparent that differential turnout among respondents with different issue preferences was unlikely to have affected the outcome. But we should not discount the possibility that there might have been differential turnout on some issues that could have contributed to Bush's reelection. For example, Bush won nine of the eleven states where a proposal to ban same-sex marriages was on the ballot, but of those nine states Ohio was the only one where the outcome was expected to be close. Turnout increased nine percentage points in Ohio, which, as we saw in chapter 2, was the most heavily contested state. We do not know the extent to which the presence of this ballot proposition contributed to increased turnout or whether the voters brought to the polls by this proposal were crucial for Bush's 2.1 percentage point margin over Kerry.

In chapter 7 we will discuss the retrospective evaluations of the electorate. Voters, some argue, make their decisions based not just on their evaluations of policy promises, but on their evaluation of how well the party in power has been performing. For 2004 our measure of retrospective evaluations has three components: (1) an evaluation of Bush's performance as president; (2) an assessment of how good a job the government is doing in solving the most important problem facing the country; and (3) the respondent's assessment as to which party would do a better job of dealing with the economy, terrorism, and keeping the United States out of war. As we point out in chapter 7, the summary measure of retrospective evaluations that we employed in elections between 1980 and 2000 cannot be reproduced with the 2004 NES survey, and therefore one must be cautious in comparing the results in Table 4-6 with similar tables for earlier elections.[94]

In 1980 respondents who expressed negative views toward Carter and the Democrats were more likely to vote than those with positive views; but these biases cannot account for Reagan's 9.7 percentage point margin over Carter. In 1984 and 1988 respondents with positive views of the Republicans were more likely to vote than those with negative views, although in 1992, these biases were eliminated. In 1996 respondents with pro-Republican views were more likely to vote, and the bias probably cost Clinton about one percentage point. But in 2000 there were no consistent biases between retrospective evaluations and political participation.

In 2004, as in 2000, there was no consistent relationship between retrospective evaluations and reported participation. Respondents who were strongly Democratic and strongly Republican were equally likely to vote, although respondents who were moderately Republican were five points more likely to vote than those who were moderately Democratic. On the other hand, respondents who leaned Democratic were eighteen points more likely to vote than those who leaned Republican. Correcting for differential turnout according to scores on our measure of retrospective evaluations has virtually no effect on turnout.

Of these three variables, only turnout differences among party identifiers could have cost Kerry the election. Because strong Republicans are always likely to vote, the biggest increase in turnout was found among weak Republicans, who registered a ten-point increase between 2000 and 2004.

Clearly, in most elections increased turnout is unlikely to affect the outcome, unless one makes unrealistic assumptions about increased participation. Of course, there can be conditions under which turnout does increase dramatically, but it is hard to imagine ones under which turnout would surge among Democrats without also rising among Republicans. The 1928 contest provides an excellent example. In 1924, only 12.7 percent of the voting-age population voted for John W. Davis, the Democratic candidate, but in 1928, 21.1 percent voted for Al Smith. Unfortunately for the Democrats, turnout surged for the Republican candidates as well. In 1924, 23.7 percent of the voting-age population voted for Calvin Coolidge; in 1928, 30.1 percent voted for Herbert Hoover (Table 4-3).

It seems unlikely that increased turnout would have altered the outcome of most presidential elections, although given the remarkably close results in 2000 and 2004, these contests may be exceptions. Given that in most contests increased turnout would not have affected the outcome, some analysts might argue that low turnout does not matter. Moreover, a number of scholars have argued that in many elections the policy preferences of Americans who do not vote have been similar to those who do go to the polls. That is to say, turnout has been low in postwar elections, but in most of them the voters have reflected the sentiments of the electorate as a whole.[95]

Despite this evidence, we cannot accept the conclusion that low turnout is unimportant. We are especially concerned that turnout is low among the disadvantaged. Some observers believe this is so because political leaders structure policy alternatives in a way that provides disadvantaged Americans with relatively little choice. Frances Fox Piven and Richard A. Cloward, for example, acknowledge that the policy preferences of voters and nonvoters are similar, but they argue that this similarity exists because of the way that elites have structured policy choices. "Political attitudes would inevitably change over time," they argue, "if the allegiance of voters from the bottom became the object of partisan competition, for then politicians would be prodded to identify and articulate the grievances and aspirations of the lower-income voters in order to win their support, thus helping them to give form and voice to a distinctive political class." [96]

We cannot accept this argument either, mainly because it is highly speculative and there is little evidence to support it. The difficulty in supporting this view may partly result from the nature of survey research because questions about public policy are usually framed along the lines of controversy as defined by mainstream political leaders. Occasionally, however, surveys pose radical policy alternatives, and they often ask open-ended questions that allow respondents to state their policy preferences. We find no concrete evidence that low turnout leads American political leaders to ignore the policy preferences of the electorate.

Nevertheless, low turnout can scarcely be helpful for a democracy. Even if low turnout seldom affects electoral outcomes, it may undermine the legitimacy of elected political leaders. The existence of a large bloc of nonparticipants in the electorate may be potentially dangerous because it means that many Americans have weak ties to the established parties and leaders. The prospects for electoral instability, and perhaps political instability, thus increase. [97]

Does the low turnout in American elections provide clues about the prospects for a partisan realignment? Low turnout in 1980 led scholars to question whether Reagan's victory presaged a pro-Republican realignment. As Pomper pointed out at the time, "Elections that involve upheavals in party coalitions have certain hallmarks, such as popular enthusiasm." [98] In 2004 turnout increased, but it was still well below the level attained in other advanced industrialized democracies.

Past realignments have been characterized by increases in turnout. As Table 4-2 shows, turnout rose markedly between 1852 and 1860, a period when the Republican Party formed, replaced the Whigs, and gained the presidency. Turnout rose in the Bryan-McKinley contest of 1896, generally considered a realigning election (see Table 4-2). And turnout rose markedly after 1924, increasing in 1928 and again in 1936, a period when the Democrats emerged as the majority party (see Table 4-3 and Figure 4-1).

The increase in turnout in 2004 gave Republicans hope that the election was the beginning of GOP dominance. As Rhodes Cook writes, "Obviously it is much too soon to say whether the election of 2004 will be remembered as a watershed event, one that seals Republican dominance for a generation. But with its sky high turnout, it already suggests a different legacy. By galvanizing voters as no election in decades, it just might launch a whole new era of voter engagement in the electoral process. If that happens, the election of 2004 would qualify for 'greatness' not in partisan terms, but in civic terms. And for the health of the nation's democratic processes, that would be all to the good." [99]

Chapter 5

Social Forces and the Vote

More than 122 million Americans voted for president in 2004. Although voting is an individual act, group memberships influence voting choices because individuals with similar social characteristics may share political interests. Group similarities in voting behavior may also reflect past political conditions. The partisan loyalties of African Americans, for example, were shaped by the Civil War; black loyalties to the Republicans, the party of Lincoln, lasted through the 1932 presidential election. The steady Democratic voting of southern whites, the product of those same historical conditions, lasted even longer, perhaps through 1960.

It is easy to see why group-based loyalties persist over time. Studies of pre-adult political learning suggest that partisan loyalties are often transmitted from generation to generation. And because religion, ethnicity, and to a lesser extent social class are often transmitted from generation to generation, social divisions have considerable staying power. Moreover, the interaction of social group members with each other may reinforce similarities in political attitudes and behaviors.

Politicians often think in group terms. They recognize that to win they need to mobilize the social groups that have supported them in the past and that it may be helpful to cut into their opponent's social bases of support. The Democrats think in group terms more than the Republicans do because since the 1930s the Democrats have been a coalition of minorities. To win, the Democrats need a high level of support from the social groups that have traditionally supported their broad-based coalition.

The 1992 election was unique, however. Bill Clinton earned high levels of support from only two of the groups composing the coalition forged by Franklin D. Roosevelt in the 1930s—African Americans and Jews. Most of the other New Deal coalition groups gave less than half of their votes to Clinton. Fortunately for him, in a three-way contest it took only 43 percent of the vote to win. Despite a second candidacy by H. Ross Perot, the 1996 election was much more of a two-candidate fight, and Clinton won 49 percent of the popular vote. Clinton gained ground among the vast majority of the groups that we will analyze below, making especially large gains among union members (a traditional component of the New Deal coalition) and Hispanics. In many respects, Democratic presidential losses during the past three decades can be attributed to the party's failure to hold the loyalties of the New Deal coalition groups. In winning in 1992 and 1996, Clinton only partly revitalized that coalition.

In 2000 Al Gore won only one percentage point less of the popular vote than Clinton had won in 1996, while George W. Bush won seven points more than Bob Dole had won. Among most groups, Gore won about the same share of the vote as Clinton but Bush won a larger share than Dole. As a result, group differences were smaller than in previous elections.

This chapter analyzes the voting patterns of groups in the 2004 presidential election. To put the 2004 election in perspective, we will examine the voting behavior of groups during the entire postwar period. By studying the social bases of party support since 1944, we will discover the long-term trends that have weakened the New Deal coalition and thus will be better able to understand the distinctive character of Bush's victory.

HOW SOCIAL GROUPS VOTED IN 2004

Our basic results on how social groups voted in the 2004 election are presented in Table 5-1.[1] Among the 800 respondents in the 2004 National Election Study (NES) survey who said they voted for president, 49.4 percent said they voted for George W. Bush, 49.0 percent for John F. Kerry, .2 percent for Ralph Nader, and 1.3 percent for other candidates, very close to the actual result. The NES survey is the best source of data for analyzing change over time, but the total number of reported voters was smaller than in any previous election we have studied because the size of the sample itself was smaller.[2] Because the number is so small we will frequently supplement these analyses by referring to the exit poll of 13,610 voters conducted by Edison Media Research/Mitofsky International (EMR/MI),[3] and we also rely upon a national poll of 5,154 voters conducted by the *Los Angeles Times*.[4] Exit polls clearly have some major advantages, but they also have limitations that make them less useful to political scientists than the NES surveys.[5]

Race, Gender, and Region

Political differences between African Americans and whites are far sharper than any other social cleavage.[6] According to the NES survey, 88 percent of blacks supported Kerry; among whites, only 41 percent did. The EMR/MI poll reported virtually identical results—although in the exit poll blacks make up a somewhat smaller percentage of the voters—and the *Los Angeles Times* poll reported very similar results. According to the NES survey, a fourth of Kerry's total vote came from black voters; according to the exit polls, about one out of five did. Even if we use the lower percentage, black voters cast 12 million of the 59 million votes

TABLE 5-1 How Social Groups Voted for President, 2004 (in percentages)

Social group	Bush	Kerry	Other	Total	$(N)^a$
Total electorate	49	49	2	100	(800)
Electorate, by race					
African American	10	88	3	101	(114)
White	58	41	1	100	(604)
Hispanic (of any race)	31	67	2	100	(49)
Whites, by gender					
Female	55	44	1	100	(321)
Male	60	37	2	99	(283)
Whites, by region					
New England and Mid-Atlantic	52	45	3	100	(118)
North Central	58	42	1	101	(185)
South	66	34	0	100	(137)
Border	56	44	0	100	(34)
Mountain and Pacific	54	43	3	100	(131)
Whites, by urbanicity					
Inner city or large city	45	51	3	99	(119)
Suburb	60	40	1	101	(181)
Small town	53	46	1	100	(156)
Rural areas	69	29	3	101	(115)
Whites, by birth cohort					
Before 1939	53	47	0	100	(119)
1940–1954	63	37	0	100	(171)
1955–1962	56	42	2	100	(110)
1963–1970	72	27	1	100	(74)
1971–1978	51	46	3	100	(72)
1979–1986	42	51	7	100	(55)
Whites, by social class					
Working class	55	44	1	100	(151)
Middle class	57	41	2	100	(385)
Whites, by occupation					
Unskilled manual	60	40	0	100	(53)
Skilled manual	52	46	2	100	(98)
Clerical, sales, other white collar	66	32	2	100	(157)
Managerial	65	33	3	101	(79)
Professional and semi-professional	44	54	1	99	(149)

(Table continues on next page)

TABLE 5-1   (continued)

Social group	Bush	Kerry	Other	Total	$(N)^a$
Whites, by level of education					
Not high school graduate	48	52	0	100	(52)
High school graduate	59	39	2	100	(180)
Some college	63	35	2	100	(171)
College graduate	61	38	2	101	(122)
Advanced degree	44	56	0	100	(80)
Whites, by annual family income					
Less than $15,000	50	46	5	101	(44)
$15,000–$24,999	37	58	4	99	(57)
$25,000–$34,999	55	45	0	100	(56)
$35,000–$49,999	47	53	0	100	(89)
$50,000–$69,999	67	30	3	100	(99)
$70,000–$89,999	66	34	0	100	(93)
$90,000–$119,999	57	43	0	100	(74)
$120,000 and over	65	31	4	100	(71)
Whites, by union membership[b]					
Member	42	57	1	100	(134)
Nonmember	62	36	2	100	(469)
Whites, by religion					
Jewish	19	81	0	100	(21)
Catholic	50	49	1	100	(166)
Protestant	69	30	1	100	(311)
No preference	43	53	4	100	(93)
White Protestants, by religious commitment					
Medium to low	57	40	3	100	(100)
High	74	26	0	100	(98)
Very high	89	11	0	100	(55)
White Protestants, by religious tradition					
Mainline	61	39	0	100	(104)
Evangelical	77	22	1	100	(134)
Whites, by social class and religion					
Working-class Catholics	32	68	0	100	(41)
Middle-class Catholics	56	42	2	100	(110)
Working-class Protestants	73	27	0	100	(79)
Middle-class Protestants	66	32	2	100	(188)

[a] Numbers are weighted.
[b] Respondent or a family member in a union.

that Kerry received. Neither the NES survey nor the EMR/MI poll showed any meaningful slippage in black support for the Democratic presidential candidate.

Because race is such a profound social division, we examine whites and blacks separately.[7] We turned to exit polls to examine differences among blacks but were stymied because the published reports based upon these polls presented only one comparison among blacks. The EMR/MI poll sampled about 1,500 black voters, and the *LA Times* poll sampled approximately 500, so they both potentially provide data for analyzing differences among blacks. The EMR/MI poll shows that 75 percent of nonwhite females voted for Kerry; among nonwhite males, 67 percent did.

As Table 5-1 shows, among respondents (of any race) who identified themselves as Hispanic, 67 percent voted for Kerry, a larger percentage than voted for Gore in the 2000 NES survey. The EMR/MI poll tells a different story, however. It shows Kerry winning 65 percent of the Hispanic vote, but comparisons with 2000 show substantial Republican gains. According to CNN, Latino support for Bush increased by nine points between 2000 and 2004; according to the *New York Times*, his support among Hispanics increased twelve points. It seems quite likely that these polls tell a more accurate story, although there is debate about the magnitude of Bush's gain.[8] The *LA Times* poll shows Bush doing substantially better among Latinos, for Kerry won only 54 percent of their vote while Bush won 45 percent, although that poll provided no comparisons with earlier elections. Both of these polls show substantially different results than a national poll conducted by the Willie C. Velazquez Research Institute, which found that only 31 percent of Hispanics voted for Bush.[9] After a careful review of the evidence from pre-election polls, as well as Latino voting in Texas, David L. Leal and his colleagues concluded that both the EMR/MI and *Los Angeles Times* polls exaggerated the level of Hispanic support for Bush.[10] Of course, Hispanics are not a homogeneous group. Cubans in South Florida usually vote Republican, for example.[11] Moreover, both exit polls demonstrate that Hispanics make up a small share of the electorate. In the EMR/MI poll, only 3 percent of the voters were Latinos, and in the *Los Angeles Times* poll only 5 percent were.

Gender differences in voting behavior have been pronounced in some European societies, but historically they have been weak in the United States.[12] Gender differences emerged in 1980, however, and they grew through 2000. For example, according to the exit polls, in 1976 Jimmy Carter gained 50 percent of the female vote and 50 percent of the male vote, while Gerald R. Ford won 48 percent of the female vote and 48 percent of the male vote. But in every subsequent presidential election, women have been more likely to vote Democratic than men. According to exit polls, the "gender gap" was 8 points in 1980, 6 points in 1984, 4 points in 1992, 11 points in 1996, and 12 points in 2000.

According to the EMR/MI poll in 2004, 51 percent of women voted for Kerry, and 44 percent of men did, a gap of seven points. Among white women, 44 percent voted for Kerry, while among white men, 37 percent did, once again revealing a seven-point difference. The *LA Times* poll found an even smaller gender gap: It showed 50 percent of the women voting for Kerry and 46 percent of the men. But no comparison was presented of white women and white men. It is noteworthy that in both exit polls just about half of all women voted for Kerry, while among all males Bush had a clear majority.

As the gender gap began to emerge, some feminists hoped that women would play a major role in defeating the Republicans. But as we pointed out over two decades ago, a gender gap does not necessarily help the Democrats.[13] For example, in the 1988 election George H. W. Bush and Michael S. Dukakis each won half the female vote, but Bush won a clear majority of the male vote. Bush benefited from the gender gap in the 1988 election.

Bill Clinton clearly benefited from the gender gap in both 1992 and 1996. In 2000, however, George W. Bush was the beneficiary. According to our analyses of the 2000 NES survey, the votes of white women were equally divided between Bush and Gore, with 48 percent for Gore and 50 percent for Bush. Among white men, only 39 percent voted for Gore, while 57 percent voted for Bush. The Voter News Service (VNS) exit poll showed a similar result.[14] Among white women, 48 percent voted for Gore, while 49 percent voted for Bush; among white men, only 36 percent voted for Gore, and 60 percent voted for Bush.

As Table 5-1 reveals, the 2004 NES revealed relatively modest gender differences, with white women only seven points more likely to vote for Kerry than white men were. Among all women, the NES survey shows that 53 percent voted for Kerry, while 46 percent of the men did. According to the exit poll, 51 percent of all women voted for Kerry, while 44 percent of the men did, once again revealing a seven-point gap. The NES survey leads to the same conclusion as the exit polls: while Kerry may have won a slight majority of the female vote, Bush clearly won a majority of the male vote.

In studying previous elections, we found that the gender gap was greatest among women with higher socioeconomic status, but that was not true in 2004. On the other hand, as with our analyses of NES presidential election surveys between 1984 and 2000, we found clear differences between women who were married and those who were single.[15] Among all women who had never been married ($N = 68$), 68 percent voted for Kerry; among all women who were married ($N = 238$), 45 percent did, a twenty-three-point gap. As in most earlier years, however, this gap is partly attributable to the very large number of black women who had never married. Among white women who had never been married ($N = 36$), 50 percent voted for Kerry; among white women who were married, 40 percent did, a gap of only ten points.

Both exit polls also showed Bush doing well among married women. According to the EMR/MI poll, married women, who made up 31 percent of the total population, voted 55 percent for Bush and only 44 percent for Kerry. Among married women with children (28 percent of the total population) 59 percent voted for Bush and only 40 percent for Kerry. According to the *LA Times* poll, 67 percent of married women voted for Bush, while only 35 percent of single women did. Perhaps single women objected to Republican social policies, but they may well have been outvoted by so-called security moms, who believed that Bush would better protect the nation's domestic tranquility.

The exit polls also reveal a very large gap according to sexual orientation. According to the EMR/MI poll, 77 percent of the voters who said they were gay, lesbian, or bisexual voted for Kerry and only 23 percent voted for Bush.[16] According to the *Los Angeles Times* poll, 81 percent of gay, lesbian, and bisexual voters supported Kerry and only 17 percent voted for Bush. But in both of these surveys, only 4 percent of the voters acknowledged being homosexual or bisexual.

Our analysis in chapter 3 shows that overall regional differences were relatively small. There were clear regional differences among whites, however. As Table 5-1 shows, according to the 2004 NES survey Bush won two-thirds of the southern white vote. Unlike 2000, when Bush won a majority of the white vote only in the South and border states, the 2004 NES shows him winning at least a small majority in all five regions. Unfortunately, published exit poll results do not show regional differences controlling by race.

In principle, one can calculate the percentage of voters supporting each candidate, controlling for whether voters live in an urban area, by using official election statistics. That would be a time-consuming exercise and still would not enable us to easily examine differences according to race. It has been well established that Republicans have been doing better in suburban and rural areas, and this pattern is demonstrated in Table 5-1. Kerry did best in inner cities and large cities, although even in these urban areas he won only about half the white vote. He did worst in rural areas, where Bush won nearly seven out of ten votes. The EMR/MI poll shows that Kerry won 54 percent of the vote in cities of over 50,000, 46 percent in the suburbs, but only 25 percent in small cities and rural areas. The *LA Times* poll used four categories. It found that Kerry won 56 percent of the vote in the cities, 47 percent in the suburbs, 41 percent in small towns, and 37 percent in rural areas. In neither poll, however, were the results presented with controls for race.

In recent years, young Americans have been more likely to vote Republican than their elders, and in the 1980, 1984, 1988, 1992, and 1996 elections the Democrats did better among whites who had reached voting age before World War II (born before 1924). That was not the case in 2000, however. In the 2004 NES there were only thirty whites born before 1924, precluding any analysis among this subgroup. Bush did best among voters born between 1963 and 1970, the same group that he scored best with in 2000 (see Table 5-1). These were voters who entered the electorate during the 1980s, and who may have been influenced by the pro-Republican tide during the Reagan years. The one hopeful sign for the Democrats is that they did best among the young, although even among young whites they gained just over half of the vote.

Both exit polls show that Bush did best among voters sixty-five years old and older, although in the *Los Angeles Times* polls these differences were small. Both polls showed that voters aged eighteen to twenty-nine were the most supportive of Kerry: In the EMR/MI poll, 54 percent of them voted for Kerry, and in the *LA*

Times poll 55 percent did. But Democratic hopes of winning by mobilizing young voters were dashed for two reasons: First, even among the young, Kerry held only a small edge over Bush. Second, according to the EMR/MI poll, young voters made up only 17 percent of the electorate, the same share as in 2000.[17]

Social Class, Education, Income, and Union Membership

Traditionally the Democratic Party has done well among the relatively disadvantaged. It has done better among the working class, voters with lower levels of formal education, and the poor. Moreover, since the 1930s most union leaders have supported the Democratic Party, and union members have been a mainstay of the Democratic presidential coalition. In 2004 there were clear differences between union members and nonmembers, and all three polls that we examine show a tendency for voters with higher incomes to vote more Republican than those with lower incomes. But differences between the better educated and the less well educated were weak and inconsistent, and since World War II social class differences in voting behavior have been declining. In 2000 the tendency of the working class to vote more Democratic than the middle class disappeared, at least among the white electorate, and the relationship was very weak in 2004.

In both 1992 and 1996, Clinton won a plurality of the vote among working-class whites, and in 1996 he won a majority of the votes among whites who were unskilled manual workers. But in 2000 Bush won a majority among working-class whites and did best among whites who were unskilled manual workers. Bush also won a majority among working-class whites in 2004, although he did best among clerical, sales, and other white-collar workers and among managerial workers (see Table 5-1). On balance there were very small differences between the working class and the middle class.

In both of his victories Clinton clearly fared better among the poor than among the more affluent. The relationship between income and voting preferences was weak and inconsistent in 2000. In the 2004 NES survey, the relationship between family income and the vote was once again relatively weak, although whites with annual family incomes of $50,000 and above were more likely to vote for Bush. The EMR/MI poll found a consistent tendency for the more affluent to vote Republican. Although reported income categories in the exit polls are not comparable across time, 2004 appears to show a higher level of income-based polarization than any previous presidential election (1992, 1996, and 2000) for which relatively comparable family income data are available. The *LA Times* poll, however, reveals a very weak relationship between voter income and voting preferences. Among voters with incomes below $20,000, 46 percent voted for Bush; among those with incomes of $75,000 or more, 54 percent did.

In 1992 and 1996, Clinton fared best among whites who had not graduated from high school, whereas George H. W. Bush and Bob Dole both fared best among whites who were college graduates (but without advanced degrees). In 1992, Clinton won over half the major-party vote among whites with advanced degrees, and in 1996 he won almost half the major-party vote. In 2000 there was a weaker relationship between education and voting preferences. Gore did best among whites who had not graduated from high school, while Bush did best among whites with some college education. In 2004, we find that Kerry did best among whites in the highest and lowest education categories. The EMR/MI poll reveals the same pattern among the total electorate, with Kerry winning half the vote among those who were not high school graduates and 55 percent among those with some postgraduate education. And the *LA Times* poll shows that among whites with a college education or more, 50 percent voted for Kerry, while among those without a college degree 45 percent did.

Some scholars of American politics, such as Walter Dean Burnham and Everett Carll Ladd Jr., argue that the Democrats now tend to fare better among the upper and lower socioeconomic groups.[18] The pattern for education seems to support that thesis. The Democrats may be appealing to disadvantaged Americans because of their party's economic policies and to better-educated Americans— especially better-educated women—who may reject the interpretation of traditional values that the Republicans have emphasized in recent elections.

According to the NES surveys, Clinton made major gains among white union households in 1992 and 1996. But the 2000 NES survey shows that Gore slipped twelve percentage points from Clinton's 1996 total, while George W. Bush gained sixteen points over Dole's. In 2004, the NES survey shows, Bush made no gains among union households but gained six points among nonunion households. The two exit polls show substantially different results. According to the EMR/MI poll, among voters who were in union households, 59 percent voted for Kerry, while among those who were not, only 44 percent did, results that are very close to those of the 2000 VNS survey. According to the *LA Times* poll, among members of union households, 56 percent voted for Kerry, while among voters in nonunion households, 45 percent did, although no comparisons with earlier surveys were available.[19]

Comparing the EMR/MI results with previous exit polls that show voting among union families, we calculate that their 2004 results are comparable to differences found between union and nonunion households in elections between 1984 and 2000.

Religion

Religious differences, partly reflecting ethnic differences between Protestants and Catholics, have also played a major role in American politics.[20] Catholics have tended to support the Democrats, and white Protestants, especially outside the South, have tended to favor the Republicans. Throughout the postwar years Jews have consistently voted more Democratic than any other major religious group. In 2004, according to the NES survey, four out of five Jews voted for Kerry, but the number of Jews sampled is too small for this result to be meaningful. The EMR/MI poll sampled about 400 Jews, and 74 percent voted for Kerry, down slightly from 2000. The *Los Angeles Times* sampled about 200 Jewish voters, among whom 74 percent voted for Kerry.

In 2004, the NES survey shows a small slippage in Bush's support among white Catholics but shows him gaining ten points among white Protestants. The poll shows him winning half the vote among white Catholics and over two-thirds among white Protestants. (Among the entire electorate, Bush won just under half the total Catholic vote and just over half the Protestant vote.) But the EMR/MI survey shows Bush making gains among both Catholics and white Protestants, winning 52 percent of the vote of Catholics and 67 percent among white Protestants. The *LA Times* poll shows Bush winning 55 percent of the Catholic vote, and 61 percent of the vote among *all* Protestants. The relatively small difference between Catholics and Protestants revealed in the exit polls is remarkable, especially when one considers that the Democrats were fielding a Catholic presidential candidate for only the third time.[21] The NES data showed that in 1960 John F. Kennedy won 80 percent of the Catholic vote when he ran against Richard M. Nixon (see Figure 5-5).[22] In that year, the Roman Catholic hierarchy attempted to distance itself from the election. In 2004, however, some bishops warned their parishioners not to vote for candidates who supported abortion rights, and some proclaimed that Catholic politicians with unacceptable views should not receive communion in their dioceses. For a Catholic to fail to win majority support among Catholics was a major obstacle that Kerry could not overcome.

Although Bush won a clear majority of white Protestant votes, he was more successful among some than among others. The Republican emphasis on traditional values may have had special appeal to some Protestants with traditional religious values. Bush's policies, such as limiting federal funding for embryonic stem cell research, calling for an amendment to the U.S. Constitution to ban same-sex marriage, and appointing conservatives to federal courts, may have appealed to Christian conservatives. Kerry tried to show that he, too, was committed to religious values, stressing the importance of his membership in the Catholic Church and emphasizing that his religious beliefs included a commitment to good works.

We focus here on differences among white Protestants.[23] For example, in the EMR/MI survey, respondents were asked, "Would you describe yourself as a born-again or evangelical Christian?" Among white Protestants who answered yes, 78 percent voted for Bush; according to our calculations, among white Protestants who answered no, 54 percent did.

As we noted in chapter 4, David C. Leege and Lyman A. Kellstedt argue that religious commitment has an important effect on voting behavior.[24] Table 5-1 reveals that white Protestants with very high levels of religious commitment were much more likely to vote for Bush than those with lower levels of commitment. The variation in the percentage of white Protestants voting for Bush is impressive when one considers that we are looking at a subset of the electorate that is already predisposed to vote Republican, since it is both white and Protestant. As Table 5-1 reveals, 69 percent of all white Protestants voted for Bush, yet there is still a twenty-two-point difference between white Protestants with very high or high levels of religious commitment and those with medium or low levels.

According to Stanley B. Greenberg, "[A]t the center of the Republican world are the white Evangelicals whose faith gives meaning to the modern Republican Party and whose moral system defines what has become known as 'red America.' " [25] Table 5-1 also shows that Bush did better among white evangelicals than among white mainline Protestants. This is also reflected in the EMR/MI result reported above that combines the responses on being "born again" with those on being evangelical.

Both exit polls also show that church attendance was strongly related to the vote. According to the EMR/MI poll, just over one-third of the voters who never go to church voted for Bush, whereas among those who go to church more than once a week, nearly two out of three did. The *LA Times* poll shows that 65 percent of the voters who attended church once a week voted for Bush, but of those who attended less often than that, only 42 percent did. [26] As Morris P. Fiorina and his colleagues have pointed out, the NES surveys suggest that the relationship between church attendance and the tendency to vote Republican grew between 1960 and 1976. [27] However, comparing the EMR/MI results for 2004 with the VNS results for 2000 we found that the relationship between church attendance and the tendency to vote for Bush was the same in both elections.

In most surveys, we can gain additional understanding by combining social class and religion. In the survey that the National Opinion Research Center (NORC) conducted in 1944, and in all the NES surveys conducted between 1948 and 1996, we found that working-class Catholics were always more likely to vote Democratic than any other group and middle-class Protestants were always the most likely to vote Republican. In 2000, however, there was very little difference between these groups. In 2004 we found that working-class Catholics were more likely to vote Democratic than any other group, but working-class Protestants were the least likely to vote Democratic.

HOW SOCIAL GROUPS VOTED DURING THE POSTWAR YEARS

How does the 2004 election compare with other presidential elections? Do the relationships in 2004 result from long-term trends that have changed the importance of social factors? To answer these questions we will examine the voting behavior of social groups that have been an important part of the Democratic presidential coalition during the postwar years. Our analysis begins with the 1944 election between Roosevelt and Thomas E. Dewey and uses a simple measure to assess the effect of social forces.

In his lucid discussion of the logic of party coalitions, Robert Axelrod analyzed six basic groups that make up the Democratic presidential coalition: the poor; southerners; blacks (and other nonwhites); union members (and members of their families); Catholics and other non-Protestants, such as Jews; and residents of the twelve largest metropolitan areas.[28] John R. Petrocik's more comprehensive study identified fifteen coalition groups and classified seven of them as predominantly Democratic: blacks, lower-status native southerners, middle- and upper-status southerners, Jews, Polish and Irish Catholics, union members, and lower-status border state whites.[29] A more recent analysis by Harold W. Stanley, William T. Bianco, and Richard G. Niemi analyzes seven pro-Democratic groups: blacks, Catholics, Jews, women, native white southerners, members of union households, and the working class.[30] Our own analysis focuses on race, region, union membership, social class, and religion.[31]

The contribution that a social group can make to a party's coalition depends upon three factors: the relative size of the group in the total electorate, its level of turnout compared with that of the total electorate, and its relative loyalty to the political party.[32] The larger a social group, the greater its contribution can be. African Americans make up 12 percent of the electorate; the white working class makes up about 30 percent. Thus the potential contribution of blacks is smaller than that of the white working class. The electoral power of blacks is further diminished by their relatively low turnout. However, because blacks vote overwhelmingly Democratic, their contribution to the Democratic Party can be greater than their group size would indicate. And the relative size of their contribution grows as whites desert the Democratic Party.

Race

Let us begin by examining racial differences, which we can trace back to 1944 by using the 1944 NORC study for that year.[33] Figure 5-1 shows the percentages of white and black major-party voters who voted Democratic for president from 1944 through 2004. (All six figures in this chapter are based on major-party voters.) Although most African Americans voted Democratic from 1944 through 1960, a substantial minority voted Republican. The political mobilization of blacks spurred by the civil rights movement and the Republican candidacy of Barry M. Goldwater in 1964 ended that Republican voting, and the residual Republican loyalties of older blacks were discarded between 1962 and 1964.[34]

While the Democrats made substantial gains among blacks, they lost ground among whites. From 1944 through 1964, the Democrats gained a majority of the white vote in three of six elections. Since then, they have never won a majority of the white vote. However, in a two-candidate contest, a Democrat can win with just under half of the white vote, as the 1960 and 1976 elections demonstrate. In the three-way contests of 1992 and 1996, Clinton was able to win with only about two-fifths of the white vote.[35] Even in the two-candidate contests of 2000 and 2004, Gore and Kerry came very close to winning with only about two-fifths of the white vote.

The gap between the two trend lines in Figure 5-1 illustrates the overall difference in the Democratic vote between whites and blacks. Table 5-2 shows the over-

FIGURE 5-1   Major-Party Voters Who Voted Democratic for President, by Race,
1944–2004 (in percentages)

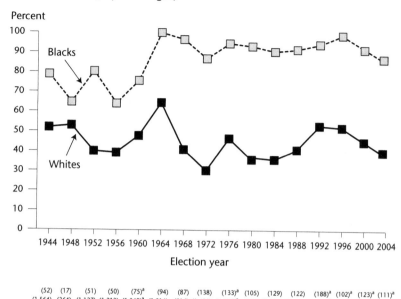

Number of:

Blacks	(52)	(17)	(51)	(50)	(75)[a]	(94)	(87)	(138)	(133)[a]	(105)	(129)	(122)	(188)[a]	(102)[a]	(123)[a]	(111)[a]
Whites	(1,564)	(364)	(1,127)	(1,213)	(1,340)[a]	(1,014)	(816)	(1,430)	(1,459)[a]	(765)	(1,220)	(1,041)	(1,134)[a]	(900)[a]	(851)[a]	(595)[a]

[a]These numbers are weighted.

all level of "racial voting" in all sixteen elections, as well as four other measures of social cleavage.

From 1944 through 1964, racial voting ranged from a low of 12 percent to a high of 40 percent. Racial voting then rose to 56 percent in 1968 (61 percent if Wallace voters are included with Nixon voters) and did not fall to the 40-point level until 1992.[36] But racial voting was high in the last three elections.

Not only did African American loyalty to the Democratic Party increase sharply after 1960, but black turnout rose markedly from 1960 to 1968 because southern blacks (about half the black population during this period) were re-enfranchised. And while black turnout rose, turnout among whites declined. Between 1960, when overall turnout was at its highest, and 1996, when turnout among the voting-age population reached its postwar low, turnout among the white voting-age population dropped by about fifteen percentage points. Even though black turnout fell in 1996, it was still well above its levels before the Voting Rights Act of 1965.

From 1948 through 1960, African Americans never accounted for more than one Democratic vote out of twelve. In 1964, however, Johnson received about one out of seven of his total votes from blacks, and blacks contributed a fifth of the Democratic totals in both 1968 and 1972. In the 1976 election, which saw

TABLE 5-2   Relationship of Social Characteristics to Presidential Voting, 1944–2004

	Election Year															
	1944	1948	1952	1956	1960	1964	1968	1972	1976	1980	1984	1988	1992	1996	2000	2004
Racial voting[a]	27	12	40	25	23	36	56	57	48	56	54	51	41	47	47	49
Regional voting[b]																
Among whites	—	—	12	17	6	−11	−4	−13	1	1	−9	−5	−10	−8	−20	−10
Among entire electorate (NES surveys)	—	—	9	15	4	−5	6	−3	7	3	3	2	0	0	−10	1
Among entire electorate (official election results)	23	14	8	8	3	−13	−3	−11	5	2	−5	−7	−6	−7	−8	−8
Union voting[c]																
Among whites	20	37	18	15	21	23	13	11	18	15	20	16	12	23	12	21
Among entire electorate	20	37	20	17	19	22	13	10	17	16	19	15	11	23	11	18
Class voting[d]																
Among whites	19	44	20	8	12	19	10	2	17	9	8	5	4	6	−6	3
Among entire electorate	20	44	22	11	13	20	15	4	21	15	12	8	8	9	2	4
Religious voting[e]																
Among whites	25	21	18	10	48	21	30	13	15	10	16	18	20	14	8	19
Among entire electorate	24	19	15	10	46	16	21	8	11	3	9	11	10	7	2	5

Note: All calculations are based on major-party voters.

[a] Percentage of blacks who voted Democratic minus percentage of whites who voted Democratic.
[b] Percentage of southerners who voted Democratic minus percentage of voters outside the South who voted Democratic.
[c] Percentage of members of union households who voted Democratic minus percentage of members of households with no union members who voted Democratic.
[d] Percentage of working class that voted Democratic minus percentage of middle class that voted Democratic.
[e] Percentage of Catholics who voted Democratic minus percentage of Protestants who voted Democratic.

FIGURE 5-2   White Major-Party Voters Who Voted Democratic for President, by
Region, 1952–2004 (in percentages)

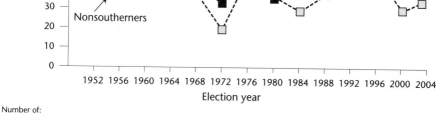

Number of:														
Southerners	(152)	(211)	(279)[a]	(163)	(124)	(267)	(266)[a]	(203)	(221)	(198)	(238)[a]	(231)[a]	(202)[a]	(137)[a]
Nonsoutherners	(975)	(1,002)	(1,061)[a]	(851)	(692)	(1,163)	(1,193)[a]	(562)	(999)	(843)	(897)[a]	(669)[a]	(649)[a]	(458)[a]

[a]These numbers are weighted.

Democratic gains among whites, black voters' portion of the total fell back to one in seven. In 1980 Jimmy Carter received about one in four of his votes from blacks, and in the next three elections about one in five Democratic votes came from blacks. In 1996, about one in six of Clinton's votes came from black voters, and in 2000 about one in five of Gore's votes did. In 2004, as we saw, between a fifth and a fourth of Kerry's total vote came from black voters.

Region

The desertion of the Democratic Party by white southerners is the most dramatic change of postwar American politics. As we saw in chapter 3, regional differences can be analyzed using official election statistics. But official statistics are of limited use in examining race-related differences in regional voting because election results are not tabulated by race. Survey data allow us to document the dramatic shift in voting behavior among white southerners.

As the data in Figure 5-2 reveal, white southerners were somewhat more Democratic than whites outside the South in the 1952 and 1956 contests between Dwight D. Eisenhower and Adlai E. Stevenson and in the 1960 contest between John F. Kennedy and Richard M. Nixon.[37] But in the next three elections, regional differences were reversed, with white southerners voting more Republican than whites outside the South. In 1976 and 1980, when the Democrats fielded Jimmy Carter of Georgia as their standard-bearer, white southerners and whites outside the South voted very much alike. In 1984 and 1988 white southerners were less likely to vote Democratic than whites from any other region. In 1992 Bill Clinton and his running mate, Al Gore, were both from the South. Even so, both George H. W. Bush in 1992 and Bob Dole in 1996 did better among white southerners than among whites in any other region. In 2000 the Democrats ran Al Gore, a southern presidential candidate, but with Joseph A. Lieberman of Connecticut as his running mate. As our figure reveals, George W. Bush did much better than the Democratic team among southern whites. The NES data suggest that regional differences among whites were smaller in 2004 than in 2000, although they clearly show the Republicans doing better among southern whites than among whites outside the South.

Regional differences among whites from 1952 through 2004 are presented in Table 5-2. The negative signs for 1964, 1968, 1972, and 1984 through 2004 reveal that the Democratic candidate fared better among white major-party voters outside the South than he did in the South. As we saw in chapter 3, Wallace had a strong regional base in the South. If we include Wallace voters with Nixon voters, regional differences in 1968 increase markedly, moving from –4 to –12.

Table 5-2 also presents regional voting for the entire electorate. Here, however, we present two sets of estimates: (1) NES results from 1952 through 2004; and (2) results based upon official election statistics (for which we also include measures for 1944 and 1948). Both sets of statistics show that regional differences have been reversed, but their results are often different and in many cases would lead to substantially different conclusions. The 2004 election provides a clear example. The 2004 NES survey shows that voters in the South were as likely to vote Democratic as voters outside the South. But we know that this result is wrong. In fact, the official election statistics show that southern voters were eight percentage points more likely to vote Republican than voters outside the South. The NES results are based on a sample of 800 voters, whereas the official election results comprise the actual results among 122 million voters. It is obvious that the latter are correct. This should remind us of a basic caution in studying elections: Always study the actual election results before turning to survey data.

Surveys are useful in demonstrating the way in which the mobilization of southern blacks and the defection of southern whites from the Democratic Party dramatically transformed the Democratic coalition in the South.[38] According to our analyses of the NES surveys, between 1952 and 1960 Democratic presidential candidates never received more than one out of fifteen of their votes from the South. In 1964 three out of ten of Johnson's southern votes came from black voters, and in 1968 Hubert H. Humphrey received as many votes from southern blacks as from southern whites. In 1972, according to these data, George S. McGovern received more votes from southern blacks than from southern whites.

African Americans were crucial to Carter's success in the South in 1976; Carter received about a third of his southern support from African Americans. Even

FIGURE 5-3   White Major-Party Voters Who Voted Democratic for President, by Union Membership, 1944–2004 (in percentages)

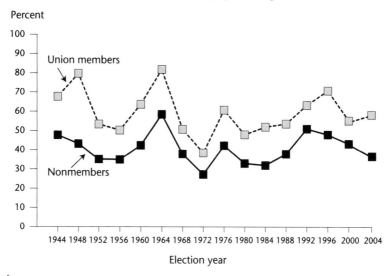

Number of:
Union members[a]   (332) (94) (305) (334) (342)[c] (259) (197) (366) (347)[c] (193) (278) (209) (207)[c] (175)[c] (141)[c] (133)[c]
Nonmembers[b]   (1,215) (266) (815) (877) (979)[c] (755) (617) (1,049) (1,099)[c] (569) (941) (828) (925)[c] (723)[c] (706)[c] (461)[c]

[a]Union member or in a household with a union member.
[b]Not a union member and not in a household with a union member.
[c]These numbers are weighted.

though he won ten of the eleven southern states, he won a majority of the white vote only in his home state of Georgia, and possibly in Arkansas. In 1980 Carter once again won about a third of his southern support from blacks. In 1984 Mondale received about four in ten of his southern votes from blacks, and in 1988 about one in three of the votes Michael S. Dukakis received came from black voters. About a third of Clinton's southern support in 1992 came from black voters, and in 1996 about three in ten of his votes in the South came from African Americans. In 2000 about four in ten of the southern votes Gore received came from black voters. Having a southern running mate appears to have helped Kerry very little among white southerners. According to the NES survey about half the votes he received in the South were cast by blacks.

Union Membership

Figure 5-3 shows the percentages of white union members and nonmembers who voted Democratic for president from 1944 through 2004. In all six elections from 1944 through 1964, a majority of white union members (and members of their households) voted Democratic. For 1968, our figure shows Humphrey receiving a slight majority of the white union vote, although his total would be cut to 43 percent if Wallace voters were included. The Democrats won about three-fifths of the union vote in 1976, when Carter defeated Ford. In 1988 Dukakis appears to have won a slight majority of the white union vote, although he fell well short of Carter's 1976 tally. In 1992 Clinton won three-fifths of the major-party union vote and won nearly half of the total union vote. In 1996 the NES data show him making major gains and winning 70 percent of the major-party vote among white union members. Gore won a majority of the union vote, but he was well below Clinton's 1996 tally. In 2004 Kerry did slightly better than Gore among white union voters, but Bush did somewhat better among non-members. As there are more nonmembers than members, this shift worked to Bush's advantage.

Differences between union members and nonmembers are presented in Table 5-2. Because Wallace did better among union members than nonmembers, including Wallace voters with Nixon voters reduces union voting from thirteen points to ten points. Union voting was highest in 1948, a year when Harry S. Truman's opposition to the Taft-Hartley Act gained him strong union support.[39] Union voting was low in 1992 and 2000, when white union members were only slightly more likely to vote Democratic than nonmembers. Because Bush did better among nonmembers in 2004, the difference between members and non-members rose to twenty-one points. We have also included the results for the entire electorate, but because blacks are about as likely to live in union households as whites are, including blacks has little effect on the results.

The percentage of the total electorate composed of white union members and their families declined during the postwar years. Members of white union households made up 25 percent of the electorate in 1952; by 2004, they made up only 15 percent. Turnout among white union members has declined at about the same rate as turnout among nonunion whites. In addition, in many elections since 1964 the Democratic share of the union vote has been relatively low. All of these factors, as well as increased turnout by blacks, have reduced the total contribution of white union members to the Democratic coalition. Through 1960 a third of the total Democratic vote came from white union members and their families. Between 1964 and 1984 only about one Democratic vote in four came from white union members. In 1988, 1992, and 1996 only about one Democratic vote in five came from white union members, and in 2000 only about one Gore vote in six came from this group. In 2004, with a drop in Democratic support among whites who did not live in union households, the share of Kerry's vote coming from white union members and their families rose back to one vote in five.[40]

Social Class

The broad cleavage in political behavior between manually employed workers (and their dependents) and non–manually employed workers (and their dependents) is especially valuable for studying comparative voting behavior.[41] In all

FIGURE 5-4 White Major-Party Voters Who Voted Democratic for President, by Social Class, 1944–2004 (in percentages)

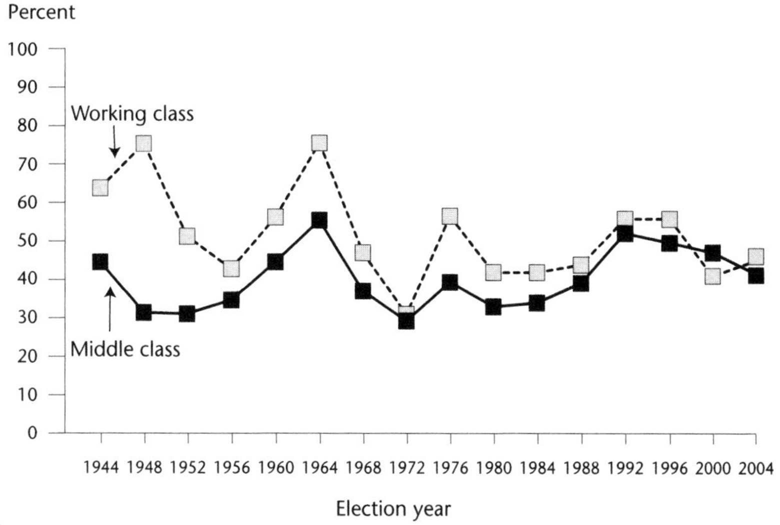

Number of:	1944	1948	1952	1956	1960	1964	1968	1972	1976	1980	1984	1988	1992	1996	2000	2004
Working class	(597)	(134)	(462)	(531)	(579)[a]	(425)	(295)	(587)	(560)[a]	(301)	(473)	(350)	(393)[a]	(279)[a]	(224)[a]	(149)[a]
Middle class	(677)	(137)	(437)	(475)	(561)[a]	(454)	(385)	(675)	(716)[a]	(376)	(634)	(589)	(569)[a]	(507)[a]	(540)[a]	(379)[a]

[a]These numbers are weighted.

fourteen presidential elections between 1944 and 1996, the white working class voted more Democratic than the white middle class. But as Figure 5-4 shows, the percentage of working-class whites who voted Democratic has varied considerably from election to election. It reached its lowest level in 1972, during the Nixon-McGovern contest. Carter regained a majority of the white working-class vote in 1976, but he lost it four years later. Clinton won only about two-fifths of the white working-class vote in 1992, although he did win a clear majority of the major-party vote. In 1996, he won half this vote, and a clear majority of the major-party vote. In 2000 Gore won only two-fifths of the vote among working-class whites, and 2000 is the only election during these years in which the Democratic presidential candidate did better among middle-class whites than among working-class whites. According to the NES data, Kerry did somewhat better in 2004, and Bush did somewhat worse. Even so, the data suggest that Kerry fell short of a majority.

Although levels of class voting have varied over the past six decades, they have clearly followed a downward trend, as Table 5-2 reveals.[42] Class voting was even lower in 1968 if Wallace voters are included with Nixon voters, because 15 percent of the white working class supported Wallace, while only 10 percent of white middle-class voters did. Class voting was very low in 1972, mainly because many working-class whites deserted McGovern. Only in 2000 do we find class voting to be negative.[43] In 2004 the white working class was once again more likely to vote Democratic than the white middle class, but class voting was negligible.

Class voting trends are affected substantially if African Americans are included in the analysis. Blacks are disproportionately working class, and they vote overwhelmingly Democratic. In all the elections between 1976 and 1996, class voting is somewhat higher when blacks (and other nonwhites) are included in our estimates. In 2000 class voting is positive (although very low) when blacks are included in our calculations. In 2004, however, class voting is only one point higher. The overall trend toward declining class voting is dampened somewhat when blacks are included. However, black workers voted Democratic because they were black, not because they were working class. In 2004 middle-class blacks were more likely to vote for Kerry than working-class blacks. Among black middle-class voters ($N = 57$), 89 percent voted for Kerry; among black working-class voters ($N = 41$), 80 percent did. It seems reasonable, therefore, to focus on the decline of class voting among the white electorate.

During the postwar years the proportion of the electorate made up of working-class whites has remained relatively constant, while that of middle-class whites has grown.[44] The percentage of whites in the agricultural sector has declined dramatically. Turnout fell among both the middle and working classes after 1960, but it fell more among the working class. As we saw in chapter 4, only 66 percent of working-class whites claimed to have voted in 2004, while 85 percent of middle-class whites did. Declining turnout and defections from the Democratic Party by working-class whites, along with increased turnout by blacks, have reduced the total white working-class contribution to the Democratic presidential coalition.

In 1948 and 1952 about half the Democratic vote came from working-class whites, and from 1956 through 1964 more than four out of ten Democratic votes came from this social group. Their contribution fell to just over a third in 1968, and then to under a third in 1972. In 1976, with the rise in class voting, the white working class provided nearly two-fifths of Carter's total support, but it provided just over a third in 1980. In 1984 over a third of Mondale's support came from working-class whites, and in 1988 Dukakis gained just over two out of five of his votes from this group. In both 1992 and 1996 three out of ten of Clinton's votes came from working-class whites, but in 2000 only about a fifth of Gore's total vote came from this group. In 2004, with a drop in middle-class support for the Democratic candidate, Kerry received just under a fourth of his vote from working-class whites.

The middle-class contribution to the Democratic presidential coalition amounted to fewer than three votes out of ten in 1948 and 1952, and just under one-third in 1956, stabilizing at just over one-third in the next five elections. In 1980 a third of Carter's support came from middle-class whites. In 1984 Mondale received just under two out of five of his votes from middle-class whites, and in 1988 Dukakis received more than two out of five. In 1992 more than two out of five of Clinton's total vote came from this group, and in 1996 he received nearly half of his vote from this group. In 2000 Gore received two-fifths of his vote from middle-class whites, and in 2004 Kerry received just over two-fifths. In each of the past six presidential elections, the Democrats have received a larger share of their vote from middle-class whites than from working-class whites. The increasing middle-class contribution is due to two factors: first, the middle class is growing; and second, class differences are eroding. The decline of class differences in voting behavior may be part of a phenomenon that is widespread in advanced industrial societies.[45]

Of course, our argument that class-based voting is declining depends on the way we have defined social class. Different definitions may yield different results. For example, in a major study using a far more complex definition that divides the electorate into seven social class categories, Jeff Manza and Clem Brooks, using NES data from 1952 through 1996, conclude that class differences are still important.[46] But their findings actually support our conclusion that the New Deal coalition has eroded. They found, for example, that professionals were the most Republican class in the 1950s, but that by the 1996 election they had become the most Democratic.

Religion

Voting differences among major religious groups have also declined during the postwar years. Even so, as Figure 5-5 reveals, in every presidential election since 1944, Jews have been more likely to vote Democratic than Catholics, and Catholics have been more likely to vote Democratic than Protestants.

A large majority of Jews voted Democratic in every election from 1944 through 1968, and although the percentage declined during Nixon's 1972 landslide, even McGovern won a majority of the Jewish vote. In 1980 many Jews (like many gentiles) were dissatisfied with Carter's performance as president, and some resented the pressure he had exerted on Israel to accept the Camp David peace accord, which returned the Sinai Peninsula—captured by Israel in 1967—to Egypt. A substantial minority of Jews voted for John B. Anderson that year, but Carter still outpolled Ronald Reagan among Jewish voters. Both Mondale in 1984 and Dukakis (whose wife, Kitty, is Jewish) in 1988 won a clear majority of the Jewish vote. The Jewish vote for Clinton surged in 1992, with Clinton winning nine out of ten of the major-party votes, and Clinton won overwhelming support in his 1996 reelection. With Lieberman, an observant Jew, as his running mate, Gore, too, won overwhelming Jewish support in 2000. Even though Bush was strongly pro-Israel in his foreign policy, Kerry won solid support among Jewish voters, although there may have been small Republican gains.

A majority of white Catholics voted Democratic in six of the seven elections from 1944 through 1968. The percentage of Catholics voting Democratic surged in 1960, when the Democrats fielded a Catholic candidate, but it was still very high in Johnson's landslide four years later. Since then, Democratic voting among Catholics has declined precipitously. In 1968 a majority of white Catholics voted

FIGURE 5-5   White Major-Party Voters Who Voted Democratic for President,
by Religion, 1944–2004 (in percentages)

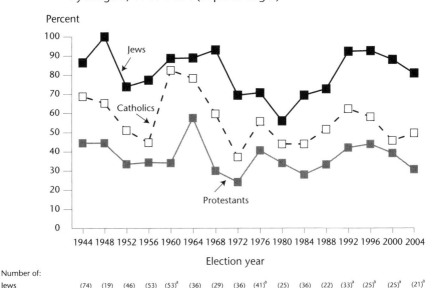

Number of:

Jews	(74)	(19)	(46)	(53)	(53)ᵃ	(36)	(29)	(36)	(41)ᵃ	(25)	(36)	(22)	(33)ᵃ	(25)ᵃ	(25)ᵃ	(21)ᵃ
Catholics	(311)	(101)	(284)	(288)	(309)ᵃ	(267)	(206)	(384)	(378)ᵃ	(188)	(360)	(287)	(301)ᵃ	(279)ᵃ	(269)ᵃ	(164)ᵃ
Protestants	(1,183)	(222)	(770)	(841)	(957)ᵃ	(674)	(533)	(938)	(959)ᵃ	(490)	(709)	(641)	(642)ᵃ	(490)ᵃ	(454)ᵃ	(308)ᵃ

ᵃThese numbers are weighted.

Democratic, although Humphrey's total would be reduced from 60 percent to 55 percent if Wallace voters were included. In 1976, Carter won a majority among white Catholics, but the Democrats did not win a clear majority of the major-party vote among white Catholics again until Clinton's victory in 1992. In his 1996 reelection, Clinton again won over half the major-party vote among white Catholics. In 2000 George W. Bush outpolled Al Gore among white Catholic voters. And, as we noted above, in 2004, even when the Democrats ran a Catholic presidential candidate, Bush outscored Kerry among white Catholic voters.

Our simple measure of religious voting shows considerable change from election to election, although there has clearly been a downward trend since 1968 (see Table 5-2). Even though white Protestants were more likely to vote for Wallace in 1968 than white Catholics were, including Wallace in our totals has little effect on religious voting (it falls from thirty points to twenty-nine points). Religious differences were small in the 1980 Reagan-Carter contest, but since then they have varied. The lowest level of religious voting during this entire period was in 2000. But with the uptick in Catholic support for Kerry and the fall in Protestant voting, religious voting rose in 2004.

Including African Americans in our calculations substantially reduces religious voting. Blacks are much more likely to be Protestant than Catholic, and including blacks adds a substantial number of Protestant Democrats. In 2004 religious voting is reduced from nineteen points to five points when blacks (and other nonwhites) are included.

The Jewish contribution to the Democratic Party has declined, partly because Jews did not vote overwhelmingly Democratic in 1972, 1980, 1984, 1988, and 2004, and partly because the percentage of Jews in the electorate has declined. From 1972 through 1988 Jews made up only about a twentieth of the total Democratic presidential coalition. Despite the upsurge in Democratic voting in 1992, the NES survey shows that Clinton received only 4 percent of his total vote from Jews, and it shows him receiving a similar share in 1996. In 2000 the NES survey shows that Gore received 4 percent of his vote from Jewish voters. However, in all three of these elections, exit polls showed the Democratic presidential candidates receiving a somewhat larger share of their vote from Jewish voters. In 2004, the NES polls showed that Kerry received 4 percent of his vote from Jews. According to our estimates based upon the EMR/MI poll, 5 percent of Kerry's votes came from Jewish voters, and according to the *LA Times* poll, 6 percent did.

Although Jews make up only 2.2 percent of the population, three-fourths of the nation's Jews live in seven large states (New York, California, Florida, New Jersey, Pennsylvania, Massachusetts, and Illinois), which have 182 electoral votes.[47] More important, two of these states are battleground states: Florida, where Jews make up 3.9 percent of the population, and Pennsylvania, where their share is the same as the national average. Jewish electoral influence may be weakened because one-fourth live in New York, where they make up 8.7 percent of the state's population. Although Jews could influence New York's 31 electoral votes, a Democratic candidate who does not win by a comfortable margin in New York is very likely to lose the election.[48]

According to our estimates, based on NES surveys, Truman received about a third of his total vote from white Catholics. Stevenson won three-tenths of his vote from white Catholics in 1952 but only one-fourth in 1956. In 1960, Kennedy received 37 percent of his votes from white Catholics, but the Catholic contribution fell to just below three out of ten votes when Johnson defeated Goldwater in 1964. In 1968, three-tenths of Humphrey's total vote came from white Catholics, but only a fourth of McGovern's vote in 1972 came from this group. Just over a fourth of Carter's vote came from white Catholics in his 1976 victory, but in his 1980 loss to Reagan just over a fifth of his vote came from this source. Mondale received just fewer than three out of ten of his votes from white Catholics, and Dukakis received just over a fifth of his total support from this group. According to our analysis, based on NES surveys, just under a fourth of Clinton's votes in 1992 came from white Catholics, and just over a fourth of his vote in 1996 did. The NES surveys suggest that just over one-fifth of Gore's total vote came from white Catholics.

In 2004, according to the NES surveys, 21 percent of Kerry's support came from white Catholics. The EMR/MI poll reveals similar results, suggesting that 18 percent of Kerry's vote came from white Catholics.[49] These results contrast markedly with NES results for 1960, when Kennedy received nearly twice as large

FIGURE 5-6   White Major-Party Voters Who Voted Democratic for President, by Social Class and Religion, 1944–2004 (in percentages)

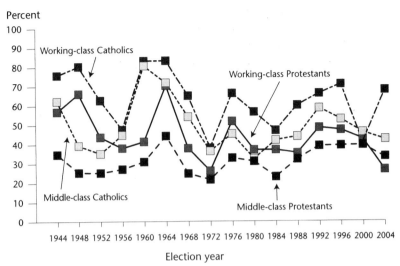

Number of:																
Catholics																
Working class	(152)	(61)	(158)	(168)	(179)[a]	(126)	(83)	(176)	(163)[a]	(76)	(156)	(100)	(100)[a]	(86)[a]	(79)[a]	(41)[a]
Middle class	(130)	(28)	(94)	(96)	(109)[a]	(121)	(96)	(176)	(179)[a]	(96)	(177)	(164)	(166)[a]	(167)[a]	(161)[a]	(108)[a]
Protestants																
Working class	(405)	(59)	(279)	(329)	(374)[a]	(280)	(198)	(383)	(367)[a]	(197)	(286)	(218)	(234)[a]	(159)[a]	(115)[a]	(79)[a]
Middle class	(479)	(91)	(302)	(336)	(405)[a]	(287)	(254)	(430)	(457)[a]	(226)	(359)	(349)	(303)[a]	(256)[a]	(292)[a]	(185)[a]

[a]These numbers are weighted.

a share of his total vote from white Catholics as Kerry did. Of course, the social characteristics of the Catholic community have changed over the span of forty-four years. And there were social issues that may have led Catholics to vote Republican in 2004 that were simply not on the political agenda four decades earlier.

Wilson Carey McWilliams argues that Catholics' deserting the Democratic Party was a crucial factor in the election. "Evangelical voters were so prominent among Bush's supporters," he writes, "that they caught most of the media attention. Catholics, however, played a more pivotal role in the election. A vital element of the New Deal coalition, most Catholic voters are now torn between their church's position on issues such as abortion and homosexuality and its egalitarian teachings on economic and social justice." [50]

As the data reveal, in all of the elections between 1944 and 1996 the effects of class and religion have been cumulative (Figure 5-6). In every one of these fourteen elections, working-class Catholics were more likely to vote Democratic than any other group. In all these elections middle-class Protestants were the most likely to vote Republican. In 2000, middle-class Catholics were the most likely to vote Democratic, but as in past elections, middle-class Protestants were the most likely to vote Republican. In 2004, as in the vast majority of past elections, working-class Catholics were the most Democratic group. Middle-class Protestants were somewhat more likely to vote Republican than middle-class Catholics. All the same, middle-class Protestants are the most consistent group, with a majority supporting the Republicans in all sixteen elections.

The relative importance of social class and religion can be assessed by comparing the voting behavior of middle-class Catholics. Religion was more important than social class in predicting voting choices in 1944, 1956, 1960 (by a considerable margin), 1968, 1972, 1984, 1988, 1992, 1996, 2000, and 2004. Social class was more important than religion in 1948 (by a considerable margin), 1952, 1976, and 1980. And class and religion were equally important in 1964. However, all of these trend lines have been converging, suggesting that traditional sources of cleavage are declining in importance.

WHY THE NEW DEAL COALITION BROKE DOWN

The importance of race increased substantially after 1960, but except for union membership, the other factors we have examined have declined in importance. The effect of region on voting behavior has been reversed, with the Republicans now enjoying an advantage in the South, especially when we compare southern whites with whites outside the South. As the national Democratic Party strengthened its appeals to African Americans during the 1960s, party leaders endorsed policies that southern whites opposed, and many of them deserted the Democratic Party. The migration of northern whites to the South may also have reduced regional differences.

The Democratic Party's appeals to blacks may have also weakened its hold on other white groups that traditionally supported it. Robert Huckfeldt and Carol Weitzel Kohfeld clearly demonstrate that Democratic appeals to blacks weakened the party's support among working-class whites.[51] But the erosion of Democratic support among union members that we find in many elections, as well as eroding support among working-class whites and among Catholics, results from other factors also. During the postwar years, these groups have changed. Although union members do not hold high-paying professional and managerial jobs, they have gained substantial economic advantages. Differences in income between the working class and the middle class have diminished. And Catholics, who often come from more recent immigrant groups than Protestants, have become increasingly middle class, as the proportion of second- and third-generation immigrants has become larger, a trend only partially offset by the growing number of Catholic Hispanics. During the 1950s and 1960s white Catholics were more likely to be working class than white Protestants. In 1976, 1980, and 1984 they were equally likely to be middle class, and in the past five elections they were somewhat more likely to be middle class than white Protestants were.

Not only have these issues changed economically and socially, but the historical conditions that led union members, the working class, and Catholics to become Democrats have receded further into the past. Although the transmission of party loyalties from generation to generation gives historically based coalitions some staying power, the ability of the family to transmit party loyalties has decreased as the strength of party identification weakened.[52] Moreover, with the passage of time, the proportion of the electorate that directly experienced the Roosevelt years has progressively declined. By 2004 only one voter in twenty had entered the electorate before or during World War II. New policy issues, often unrelated to the traditional political conflicts of the New Deal era, have tended to erode party loyalties among traditionally Democratic groups. Edward G. Carmines and James A. Stimson provide strong evidence that race-related issues have been crucial in weakening the New Deal coalition.[53] And more recently, conflicts over social issues such as abortion may have weakened support for the Democratic Party among Catholic voters.[54]

Despite the weakening of the New Deal coalition, the Democrats managed to win the presidency in 1992 and 1996, came very close to holding it in 2000, and came close to regaining it in 2004. In his 1992 victory Clinton boosted his share of the major-party vote among union members, the working class, and even white southerners. Clinton focused his appeals to middle America, and in both 1992 and 1996 he paid as low a price as possible to gain the black vote. Clinton's win in 1992 was the first Democratic win in which blacks made up more than 15 percent of the Democratic vote. In 1996, Clinton once again won with over 15 percent of his vote coming from blacks. But the 1992 election and, to a lesser extent, the one in 1996 were contests in which the white vote was split among three candidates. Our calculations suggest that it would be difficult for the Democrats to win a two-candidate contest in which blacks made up a fifth or more of their total coalition.

Clinton's victory in 1992 seemed to provide an opportunity to forge a new Democratic coalition, perhaps based on some of the components of the old New Deal coalition. But after the Democrats lost both the House and Senate in the 1994 midterm elections, Clinton developed a more reactive strategy that focused on moving to the political center. In some respects, he partly revitalized the New Deal coalition, primarily because of the effort of union leaders to end Republican control of Congress. But in 2000, despite populist appeals by Gore, union voting and religious voting were low, and the white middle class actually voted more Democratic than the white working class. Polarization based on union membership increased in 2004, but given that there are more nonmembers than members, this worked against Kerry, and religious voting increased mainly because of a shift of white Protestants to Bush.

On balance, Kerry won overwhelming support among blacks, solid support among Jews, and a clear majority among union households. However, he failed to gain a majority of the vote among white Catholics, and according to the EMR/MI and *Los Angeles Times* exit polls, he did not win a majority of the vote among the entire Catholic population. For a Catholic presidential candidate to fail to win majority support among Catholics was an obstacle Kerry was unable to overcome.

Perhaps, as James W. Ceaser and Andrew E. Busch argued after the 1992 election, new coalitions will be formed based on common issue positions rather than on the demographic groups that both politicians and political scientists now employ.[55] Turning to the issue preferences of the electorate provides an opportunity to see how a Democratic coalition can be formed and may also suggest strategies that the Republicans can follow to hold the presidency.

Chapter 6

Candidates, Issues, and the Vote

In chapter 5 we discussed the relationship between various social forces and the vote. The impact of such forces is indirect. Even though the New Deal coalition was constructed from members of different groups, people who were members of those groups did not vote Democratic simply because they were African Americans, white southerners, union members, Catholics, or Jews. Rather, they usually voted Democratic because that party offered symbolic and substantive policies and candidates that appealed to their concerns and because the party's platforms and candidates were consistent, encouraging many voters to develop long-term partisan loyalties. The long-term decline in class voting, for example, is evidence of the decreasing importance that members of the working and middle classes assign to the differences between the parties on concerns that divide blue collar and white-collar workers. That race is the sharpest division in American politics today does not mean that blacks vote Democratic simply because they are black; as Supreme Court justice Clarence Thomas and former ambassador Alan Keyes demonstrate, African Americans may also be conservative ideologically and may identify with, and vote for, Republicans.

In this and the following two chapters, we examine some of the concerns that underlie voters' choices for president. Even though scholars and politicians disagree about what factors voters employ, and how they employ them, there is general consensus on several points. First, voters' attitudes or preferences determine their choices. There may be disagreement over exactly which attitudes shape behavior, but most scholars agree that voters deliberately choose to support the candidate they believe will make the best president. There is also general agreement that attitudes toward the candidates, the issues, and the parties are the most important attitudes in shaping the vote.[1] In these three chapters, we start with the considerations that immediately precede voters' casting their ballots and then turn to considerations that occur earlier, ending with the most important long-term attitudinal force shaping the vote, party identification.

In this chapter we look first at the relationship between one measure of candidate evaluation and the vote, the "feeling thermometers" that the National Election Studies (NES) use to measure affect toward the candidates. In this brief analysis we ignore two of the major components underlying these evaluations: voters' perceptions of the candidates' personal qualities and voters' perceptions of the candidates' professional qualifications and competence to serve as president.[2] As we will see, there is a very powerful relationship between thermometer evaluations of candidates and the vote. It might seem obvious that voters support the candidate they like best, but as in 1968, 1980, 1992, 1996, and 2000, the presence of a significant third candidate complicates decision making for many voters.[3]

We see the simple measure of attitudes toward the candidates as the most direct influence on the vote itself; attitudes toward the issues and the parties help to shape attitudes toward the candidates and thus the vote. In that light, we then turn to the first part of our investigation of the role of issues. After analyzing what problems most concerned the voters in 2004, we discuss the two basic forms of issue voting, which are referred to as voting based on "prospective" and "retrospective" issues. In this chapter we investigate the impact of prospective issues. We consider one of the controversies about issue voting: how much information the public has about issues and candidates' positions on them. Our analyses provide an indication of the significance of prospective issues in 2004 and compare their impact with what is shown in earlier election surveys. Chapter 7 examines retrospective issues and the vote, and chapter 8 examines partisan identification and assesses the significance of parties and issues, together, on voting in 2004 and in earlier elections.

ATTITUDES TOWARD THE CANDIDATES

Although the United States has a two-party system, there are still ways that other candidates can appear on the ballot, or they can run a write-in candidacy. The 2004 presidential election was a two-person race for all intents and purposes, but there were actually many other candidates running. The most noteworthy was Ralph Nader, who also ran in 2000 and drew much media attention but a small popular vote (2.7 percent). Nader ran again in 2004, appearing on thirty-five state ballots, plus D.C.'s, and receiving 0.4 percent of the popular vote. The Libertarian Party candidate, Michael Badnarik, was on all but two state ballots, coming in fourth with 0.3 percent of the vote. And there were even more candidates—but it was nonetheless effectively a two-person contest. Since 1980, only the 1984 and 1988 contests were as completely dominated by the two major-party candidates.

Limiting our attention to incumbent president George W. Bush and his Democratic challenger, Sen. John F. Kerry, we want to know why people preferred one candidate to the other and how they therefore voted and, as a further result, why

Bush won reelection. The obvious starting point in two-person races is to imagine that people voted for the candidate they preferred. This may sound truly obvious, but in races with three or more candidates—such as most recent contests—people do not necessarily vote for the candidate they most prefer.[4]

Because there were only two presidential candidates receiving significant numbers of votes in 2004, we can consider it a strictly two-person race in which people all but invariably voted for the candidate they preferred. This close relationship can be demonstrated by analyzing the "feeling thermometer," which we have presented in several earlier books.[5] That measure produces a scale that runs from 0 through 100 degrees, with 0 indicating "very cold" or negative feelings, 50 indicating neutral feelings, and 100 indicating a "very warm" or positive evaluation. Respondents who rank a major-party candidate highest on the feeling thermometer among three candidates vote overwhelmingly for that major-party candidate. On the other hand, respondents who rank a third-party or independent candidate highest often desert that candidate to vote for one of the major-party candidates; we believe this may result from voters' applying strategic considerations to avoid "wasting" their vote on a candidate who has little chance of winning.[6]

In the postelection wave of the NES survey, 98.6 percent of the 296 voters who rated Kerry higher than Bush or Nader voted for Kerry. Three-hundred fifty-two voters rated Bush highest, and 97.7 percent of them reported that they voted for him. Twenty-two tied Bush and Kerry, and their vote was ten for Bush, twelve for Kerry, almost precisely what we would expect, on average, if the voters really were indifferent between them. This finding is commonplace; so it is worth noting that much smaller majorities of the voters preferring them reported voting for third candidates, such as Nader. Nader was an extreme case in 2000, as he received the votes of only three in ten of those who ranked him first on the postelection feeling thermometer. However, no third candidate in this era has held anything like the 95-plus percent of their support that major-party nominees invariably do.[7] In 2004 Nader fared even worse than he did in 2000. In 2000, 10 percent of voters ranked Nader first; in 2004, only 4 percent did. Moreover, as we saw in chapter 3, Nader did very poorly even among those who did rank him first, winning only a single vote among the thirty-one voters who ranked him higher than both Kerry and Bush.

The feeling thermometers are also useful in answering another question: Was Bush the Condorcet winner? Most social choice theorists would agree with the Marquis de Condorcet that if a candidate would defeat all of his or her opponents in head-to-head contests, that candidate should be elected.[8] We term this the "Condorcet criterion." A candidate who meets this criterion and wins the election is a Condorcet winner.

In most U.S. presidential elections, the actual winner was probably the Condorcet winner as well. This may not have been true of all elections, however. William H. Riker argues that Woodrow Wilson, the Democratic standard-bearer in 1912, was probably not the Condorcet winner. A majority may have preferred William Howard Taft, the Republican incumbent, to Wilson, and a majority may have preferred Theodore Roosevelt, a former Republican president running under the Progressive or "Bull Moose" party label, to Wilson. But with the Republican Party split, Wilson won with only 42 percent of the vote.[9] But we have no evidence to test Riker's speculation. In most elections for which we do have evidence on voters' preferences, the actual winner was the Condorcet winner as well.[10]

Using evidence from the 2000 NES feeling thermometers, as well as exit polls, we argued that Bush was probably not the Condorcet winner in 2000.[11] In 2004 Bush received a majority of the popular vote, but this fact does not prove that he was the Condorcet winner, although in the absence of an attractive third-party or independent candidate, it seems likely that he was. We used the feeling thermometer scales to conduct a series of mock elections between Bush and Kerry, Bush and Nader, and Kerry and Nader. In both the preelection and postelection surveys, Bush and Kerry soundly defeat Nader. Among the 1,042 respondents who ranked both Bush and Kerry in the preelection survey, Bush had only a slight edge, 45.9 percent to 44.4 percent, with 7.4 percent rating them the same. In the postelection survey Bush has a slightly larger lead, 48.3 percent to 45.0 percent, with 6.7 percent rating them the same. If one bears in mind that the NES survey itself slightly underestimated Bush's share of the vote (see chapter 5), it seems likely that these thermometer scores may slightly underestimate Bush's strength as well. If so, the evidence that Bush was the Condorcet winner in 2004 is even stronger than these comparisons suggest.

PROSPECTIVE EVALUATIONS

Underlying these evaluations of the candidates are the public's attitudes toward the issues and toward the parties, as well as more specific evaluations of the candidates. We begin by considering the role of issues in elections. Public policy concerns enter into the voting decision in two very different ways. In an election in which an incumbent is running, two questions become important: How has the incumbent president done on policy? And how likely is it that his opponent (or opponents) would do any better? Voting based on this form of policy appraisal is called "retrospective voting"; it will be analyzed in chapter 7.

The second form of policy-based voting involves examining the candidates' policy platforms and assessing which candidate's policy promises conform to what the voter believes the government should be doing. Policy voting, therefore, involves comparing sets of promises and voting for the set that is most like the voter's own preferences. Voting based on these kinds of decisions may be referred to as "prospective voting," for it involves examining the promises of the candidates about future actions. In this chapter we examine prospective evaluations of the two major-party candidates and how these evaluations relate to voter choice.

The past nine elections show some remarkable similarities with respect to prospective evaluations and the vote. Perhaps the most important similarity is in perceptions of where the Democratic and Republican candidates stood on issues. In these elections, the public saw clear differences between the major-party nominees. In all cases, the public saw the Republican candidates as conservative on most issues, and most citizens scored the GOP candidates as more conservative than the voters themselves. And in all nine elections the public saw the Democratic candidates as being liberal on most issues, and most citizens viewed the Democratic candidates as more liberal than the voters themselves. As a result, many voters perceived a clear choice based on their understanding of the candidates' policy positions. The candidates presented—in the 1964 campaign slogan of Republican nominee Barry M. Goldwater—"a choice, not an echo." The *average* citizen faced a difficult choice, however. Many considered the Democratic nominees to be as far to the left as the Republicans were to the right. On balance, the net effect of prospective issues was to give neither party a clear advantage.

One of the most important differences among these elections was in the issues that concerned the public. Each election presented its own mixture of policy concerns. Moreover, the general strategies of the candidates on issues differed in each election.[12] In 1980 Jimmy Carter's incumbency was marked by a general perception that he was unable to solve pressing problems. Ronald Reagan attacked that weakness both directly (for example, by the question he posed to the public during his debate with Carter, "Are you better off today than you were four years ago?") and indirectly. The indirect attack was more future oriented. Reagan set forth a clear set of proposals designed to convince the public that he would be more likely to solve the nation's problems because he had his own policy proposals to end soaring inflation, strengthen the country militarily, and regain respect and influence for the United States abroad.

In 1984 the public perceived Reagan as a far more successful president than Carter had been. He chose to run a campaign focused primarily on the theme of how much better things were by 1984 (as illustrated by his advertising slogan, "It's morning in America"). Walter F. Mondale attacked that claim by arguing that Reagan's policies were unfair and by pointing to the rapidly growing budget deficit. Reagan's reply to Mondale's pledge to increase taxes to reduce the deficit was that he, Reagan, would not raise taxes and that Mondale would do so only to spend them on increased government programs (or, in his words, Mondale was another "tax and spend, tax and spend" Democrat).

The 1988 campaign was more similar to the 1984 than to the 1980 campaign. George H. W. Bush continued to run on the successes of the Reagan-Bush administration and promised no new taxes ("Read my lips," he said. "No new taxes!"). Michael S. Dukakis initially attempted to portray the election as one about "competence" rather than "ideology," arguing that he had demonstrated his competence as governor of Massachusetts. By competent management he would be able to solve the budget and trade deficit problems, for example. Bush, by implication, was less competent. Bush countered that it really was an election about ideology and that Dukakis was just another liberal Democrat from Massachusetts.

The 1992 election presented yet another type of campaign. Bush initially hoped to be able to run as the president who presided over the "new world order," the post-Soviet world, and he used the success of the 1991 Persian Gulf War to augment his claim that he was a successful world leader. Bill Clinton attacked the Bush administration on domestic issues, however, barely discussing foreign affairs at all. He sought to keep the electorate focused on current economic woes, seeking to get the nation moving again. He argued for substantial reforms of the health care system and raised a number of other issues that he expected to appeal to Democrats and to serve as the basis for action, should he become the first Democrat in the White House in twelve years. At the same time, he sought to portray himself not as another "tax and spend," liberal Democrat, but as a moderate "New Democrat."

In 1996 Clinton ran a campaign typical of a popular incumbent, focusing on what led people to approve of his handling of the presidency, and avoided mentioning many specific new programs. While he had a catchy slogan (handed to him by Dole), "Building a bridge to the twenty-first century," his policy proposals were a lengthy series of relatively inexpensive, limited programs. Dole, having difficulties deciding whether to emphasize Clinton's personal failings in the first term or to call for different programs for the future, decided to put a significant tax cut proposal at the center of his candidacy within both of those campaign strategies.

In 2000 the candidates debated a broad array of domestic issues—education, health care, Social Security, and taxes the most prominent among them—often couched in terms of a newfound "problem"—federal government budget surpluses. Typically these issues (except for taxes) have favored Democratic contenders, and Republicans often avoided detailed discussions of all except taxes, on the grounds that to do otherwise would make the issues more salient to voters and highlight Democratic advantages. George W. Bush, however, spoke out on education and other domestic issues, believing he could undercut the traditional Democratic advantage. For his part, Al Gore was advantaged by the belief (backed by public opinion polls) that the public was less interested in tax cuts than usual and more in favor of allocating budget surpluses to buttress popular domestic programs.

In 2004 in contrast, Bush and Kerry had less choice about what issues to consider. With wars in Iraq, in Afghanistan, and against terrorism, neither candidate could avoid foreign policy considerations. Bush, of course, emphasized the successes of his foreign efforts. Kerry did not contest the choice of entering the conflicts, but he did challenge the wisdom of the way in which Bush and his administration justified launching the war in Iraq, as well as the way the conflict was fought. Bush preferred to emphasize that Iraq was a part of the war on terrorism, while Kerry argued that it is was not, and indeed that it was a costly distraction from it. Similarly, 2004 opened with the economy slumping. Democrats, including Kerry, were attacking Bush administration policies, while Bush was countering by saying that the economy was actually improving, in large part because of the success of his policies. As the year wore on, the economy did in fact improve, although not so sharply as to remove all criticism. The cost of the wars, the decline in the economy, and the tax cuts enacted by the Bush administration and the Republican majorities in Congress eliminated the budget surplus that had shaped the 2000 campaign. As a result, and combined with the necessary focus on war and the economy, there was less time for consideration of domestic concerns such as education, health care, tax cuts (in this case, extensions of the recent ones), and Social Security reforms, compared to the 2000 race, although these subjects were not totally ignored. The closeness of the outcome indicates, broadly speaking, that both candidates had strong arguments and nearly equally effective appeals. Note also that such issues as the handling of the war in Iraq and of the economy have both retrospective aspects (how did Bush handle these challenges) and prospective ones (which candidate offers policies on Iraq and the economy that the voter most agrees with). That is, these central issues could be fodder for either approach to thinking about policy-related voting. Furthermore, while there was less room than in 2000 for the candidates to focus on "new" issues that would almost necessarily be exclusively prospective, the media liked to portray the politicians and the public as polarized into "red" and "blue" states (that is, states that are Republican and conservative, or Democratic and liberal, respectively). And Bush did discuss such issues as abortion and gay marriage in "playing toward his base" (that is, in developing enthusiasm among conservative activists and voters), while Kerry, for his part, also played to his base. We will see shortly that there is a good bit of evidence that both kinds of policy-related voting were unusually pronounced in 2004.

THE CONCERNS OF THE ELECTORATE

The first question to ask about prospective voting is, What kinds of concerns moved the public? In 2004 the NES survey asked respondents, "What do you think has been the most important issue facing the United States over the last four years?" A similar question was asked in previous election years.[13] In Table 6-1 we have listed the percentages of responses to the "most important problem" question, in broad categories of concerns over the nine most recent elections.

In the four elections preceding 2004, the public was far more concerned about domestic issues than about foreign or defense policies. This lack of concern about foreign policy might have been due to the end of the cold war, but foreign policy also rated low in 1976, during the cold war.

The great majority of responses concerned domestic issues, and in the eight elections prior to 2004, two categories of domestic issues dominated: From 1976 through 1992, in good times and bad, by far the more commonly cited issue was the economy. In 1972, 1996, and 2000, the most frequently cited problems were in the social issues category, and an absolute majority cited some social welfare problem (such as welfare reform, the environment, or health care) or problem in

TABLE 6-1 Most Important Problem as Seen by the Electorate, 1972–2004 (in percentages)

Problem	1972	1976	1980	1984	1988	1992	1996	2000	2004[a]
Economics	*27*	*76*	*56*	*49*	*45*	*64*	*29*	*19*	*19*
Unemployment/recession	9	33	10	16	5	23	7	5	4
Inflation/prices	14	27	33	5	2	—[b]	—[b]	1	—[b]
Deficit/government spending	1	9	3	19	32	16	13	4	2
Social issues	*34*	*14*	*7*	*13*	*38*	*28*	*56*	*67*	*49*
Social welfare	7	4	3	9	11	17	33	45	4
Public order	20	8	1	4	19	10	23	21	45
Foreign and defense	*31*	*4*	*32*	*34*	*10*	*3*	*5*	*10*	*29*
Foreign	4	3	9	17	6	2	3	6	27
Defense	1	1	8	17	3	1	2	4	3
Functioning of government (competence, corruption, trust, power, etc.)	4	4	2	2	1	2	5	5	3
All others	*4*	*3*	*3*	*3*	*6*	*2*	*4*	*0*	*0*
Total	100	101	100	101	100	100	100	101	100
(N)	(842)	(2,337)	(1,352)	(1,780)	(1,657)	(2,003)	(794)	(907)	(1,033)
"Missing"	(63)	(203)	(56)	(163)	(118)	(54)	(27)	(31)	(32)
Percentage missing	7	7	4	7	7	2	4	3	3

Note: The main categories are in italics. Empty cells = less than 1 percent of responses. "Foreign" in 1972 includes 25 percent who cited Vietnam. "Foreign" in 1980 includes 15 percent who cited Iran. Questions asked of randomly selected half sample in 1972, 1996, and 2000. All of the subcategories are not included. The total percentages for the subcategories, therefore, will not equal the percentages for the main categories. In 1984 total *N* is 1,943 because 46 respondents were not asked this question, being given a shortened questionnaire. In 1992 the total *N* is 2,057, because 431 respondents either had no postelection interview or were given a shortened form via telephone.

[a] For 2004, "foreign" includes the war in Iraq (18 percent), and "public order" includes terrorism, Islamic extremists, and homeland security (42 percent).
[b] Less than 1 percent of responses.

the realm of public order (such as crime, terrorism, or drugs). In 1992 and 1996 nine out of ten respondents named either an economic or a social problem, and in 2000, 86 percent did. From 1972 through 2000 very few cited problems in the "functioning of government" category, such as "gridlock," term limits, other reforms, or government corruption. Finally, in these elections very few—only 3 percent in 2000, for example—cited no problem at all.

In 2004 social issues were once again the largest category of responses; they were selected by nearly half the respondents. Unlike all other elections since 1972, however, social welfare concerns (the largest specific category of concern in 2000) were virtually absent, declining from 45 percent to merely 4 percent of respondents. The various considerations under the rubric "public order" had taken social welfare's place, with public order concerns being selected by 44 percent. Virtually all of these responses (42 percent) were recorded in the category "terrorism, Islamic extremists, homeland security." In second place was foreign policy, selected by slightly more than one in four (primarily Iraq, selected by 18 percent) as their most important concern. In this respect, "9/11 changed everything" by generating new concerns that were salient through the 2004 election. Note, for example, that a higher percentage chose Iraq than chose any international conflict or foreign "hot spot" (the previous high being the 15 percent that chose the ongoing Iranian hostage crisis in 1980) in any election since 1972, when 25 percent said the Vietnam War was their most important concern. And that two in five chose the "terrorism" set of responses was a dramatic difference from any other election. Finally, the general category of economics was the last of the "big three" concerns, being selected by 18 percent of the electorate, its lowest level in the last nine election years, although essentially the same as in 2000.[14] No other category of response was at all common; the "functioning of government" category appeared most frequently, but only 3 percent selected it, and only 3 percent selected no problem at all.

Although the economy and social issues have dominated the concerns of the public over the past three decades, the particular concerns within these broad categories have varied from election to election. With respect to the economy, for example, inflation was a common concern throughout the 1970s, but by 1984 it all but dropped from sight, becoming a literal "asterisk in the polls" by 1992, as it was in 2004. Unemployment has varied as a concern, roughly in tandem with the actual level of unemployment in the nation. Not surprisingly, concern over the federal budget deficit has also tracked closely the rate of growth (or, in 2000, decline) in the actual deficit. Note, however, that the current growth in the deficit has yet to register in the public consciousness, or perhaps it was overwhelmed by war, terrorism, and economic decline and recovery. Similarly, in the social issues category particular concerns have varied from year to year, corresponding to the headlines in the news media and the issues the candidates emphasized in the campaigns. Thus in 1992, not only was H. Ross Perot's (and Clinton's) focus on the deficit reflected in the public, but so too was Clinton's emphasis on the "health care crisis." By 1996 those concerns had waned somewhat, replaced by crime, education, and welfare policy, and education, health care, and the environment loomed large in 2000. By 2004 the ability of the government to address the domestic consequences of terrorism was salient, among other considerations.[15]

The concerns of the electorate are the backdrop of the campaign. In 2004 the relatively low level of concern about the economy was good news for the incumbent. In 1992 the senior Bush had just led the successful removal of Iraqi forces from Kuwait and had presided during an economic downturn and the beginning of a recovery. The public, however, saw the first Gulf War as a matter already in the past and did not believe that the economy had yet recovered significantly. His son had the good fortune to face an electorate that largely believed the economy had recovered, or was well on its way to doing so, and in his case, of course, the second Gulf War was far from over. Still, that he or she is concerned about a problem does not directly indicate which candidate the voter intends to back. A vote, after all, is a choice among alternatives. To investigate the questions of choice we must look at the voters' issue preferences and their perceptions of where candidates stood on the issues.

ISSUE POSITIONS AND PERCEPTIONS

Since 1972 the NES surveys have included a number of issue scales designed to measure the preferences of the electorate and voters' perceptions of the positions the candidates took on the issues.[16] These questions are therefore especially appropriate for examining prospective issue evaluations. We hasten to add, however, that voters' perceptions of where the incumbent party's nominee stands may well be based in part on what the president has done in office, as well as on the campaign promises he makes as the party's nominee. The policy promises of the opposition party candidate may also be judged partly by what his party did when it last held the White House. Nevertheless, the issue scales generally focus on prospective evaluations and are very different from those used to make the retrospective judgments examined in chapter 7.

We use the issue scales to examine several questions: What alternatives did the voters believe the candidates were offering? To what extent did the voters have issue preferences of their own and relatively clear perceptions of the candidates' positions? Finally, how strongly were voters' preferences and perceptions related to their choice of candidates?

Figure 6-1 presents the text of one of the seven-point issue scale questions, along with an example of an illustration presented to respondents as they considered their responses. Figure 6-2 shows the responses to the seven-point issue scales used in the 2004 NES survey. The figure presents the average (median) position of the respondents (labeled *s,* for "self") and their average (median) perception of the positions of Kerry and Bush.[17] Issues asked about in 2004 probed the respondents' own preferences and their perceptions of the major-party nominees' positions on whether government spending should be reduced or increased

FIGURE 6-1   Example of a Seven-Point Issue Scale: Jobs and Standard of Living
Guarantees

Questions the interviewers asked:

Please look at page 9 of the [respondent] booklet

Some people feel the government in Washington should see to it that every person has
a job and a good standard of living. Suppose these people are at one end of a scale,
at point 1. Others think the government should just let each person get ahead on their
own. Suppose these people are at the other end, at point 7. And, of course, some other
people have opinions somewhere in between at points 2, 3, 4, 5, or 6.

Where would you place YOURSELF on this scale, or haven't you thought much about this?

Where would you place GEORGE W. BUSH on this issue?

Where would you place JOHN KERRY (on the issue)?

Source: 2004 National Election Studies, Pre-Election Interview Schedule and Respondent Booklet.

to provide greater social services; whether defense spending should be increased
or decreased; the jobs scale as shown in Figure 6-1; whether the government
should provide aid to blacks or whether they should get ahead on their own;
whether women should play a role equal with men in society or whether they
should stay at home ("a woman's place is in the home"); the tradeoff between jobs
and the environment; and whether the government should intervene militarily or
by diplomacy.[18]

These issues were selected because they were controversial and generally measured long-standing partisan divisions. The average citizen comes out looking
reasonably moderate on these issues—in five out of seven cases the respondents'
own preferences were between the average placements of the two candidates (see
Figure 6-2). On many issues in 2004, the typical citizen was very near the center
of the scale, especially on defense spending, jobs and standard of living, and aid
to blacks. These average citizen stances are quite similar from one election to the
next. There are some changes of course. For example, self-placement on the jobs
scale was rather more conservative in Reagan's initial victory in 1980 than earlier,
and more conservative again in George W. Bush's victory in 2000 than in other
preceding elections, but it moved in a more liberal direction again in 2004. In
another example, on the government spending and services scale the average citizen has typically been just to the left of the middle but scored a bit more liberal
in 2004. In those surveys in which the same women's rights scale as in 2004 was
used (all but 1984), most citizens favored an "equal role" for women, and in both
2000 and 2004 a majority chose the most liberal point possible on this scale.[19]

FIGURE 6-2 Median Self-Placement of the Electorate and the Electorate's Placement of Candidates on Issue Scales, 2004

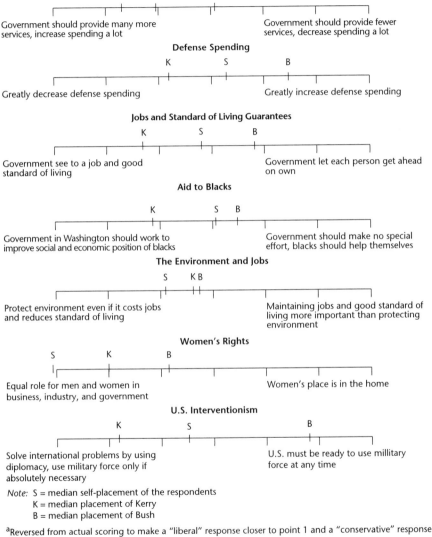

Note: S = median self-placement of the respondents
K = median placement of Kerry
B = median placement of Bush

[a]Reversed from actual scoring to make a "liberal" response closer to point 1 and a "conservative" response closer to point 7.

The average citizen has been about one point to the pro-environment side of the midpoint of that scale since it was introduced for the 1996 election survey. The military-versus-diplomacy scale is new to 2004, and here the average respondent is one-half point on the diplomacy side from the midpoint.

The public has seen the Democratic candidate as more liberal, and the Republican candidate as more conservative, than the average person on every issue scale used between 1980 and 2004, although (perhaps reflecting the low level of campaign attention to this issue) the public as a whole saw Bush and Kerry as taking essentially the same position on the environment. In that case the two are effectively indistinguishable, on average. With that single exception, however, over the entire set of issue scales since 1972, the results show that the typical citizen has seen the candidates as taking very different positions. In 2004 the candidates were placed about 1.8 units apart, 30 percent of the maximum difference possible. And if we exclude the tiny differences seen on the environmental scale, the average over the other six issues is a difference of 2.1, over one-third of the maximum possible. On the diplomacy-versus-military scale, the difference was 3.4 units, and it was nearly two and a half points on defense spending and the jobs and standard of living guarantees scales. These are quite large differences, among the largest we have observed over the past nine election surveys. No matter how polarized the public may have been in 2004, they saw the two candidates as very polarized on most issues.[20]

Voters saw clear differences between the candidates, but the average voter faced a difficult choice. Kerry was seen as to the left of the average respondent, and Bush was seen as to the right. On average, Kerry was 0.5 units to the left and Bush 1.3 units to the right of the average citizen. Kerry thus held an advantage, and he was in an especially favorable position on the diplomacy/military scale (and the women's rights scale). Except for the aid to blacks scale, Bush had a less-clear advantage on any issue. However, as we will see in the next chapter, Bush received positive marks for his handling of the wars in which the United States was engaged, so the theoretical advantage was muted by performance advantages for Bush. Of course, we cannot at this point go much farther on these overall figures. The choice is not made by the average voter, choosing based on what the respondents as a whole thought the candidates offered, but it is made by individual voters, considering what they think about the issues. To consider a voter's choices, we must look beyond the averages.

ISSUE VOTING CRITERIA

The Problem

Because voting is an individual action, we must look at the preferences of individuals to see whether prospective issues influenced their votes. In fact, the question of prospective voting is controversial. Angus Campbell and the other authors of the classic study of the American electorate, *The American Voter,* point out that the public is often ill-informed about public policy and may not be able to vote on the basis of issues.[21] They asked what information voters would need before an issue could influence the decision of how to vote, and they answered by posing three conditions: First, the voters must hold an opinion on the issue; second, they must see what the government is doing on the issue; and third, they must see a difference between the policies of the two major parties. According to those authors' analysis, only about one-quarter to one-third of the electorate in 1956 could meet the three conditions.

Although it is impossible to replicate the analysis in *The American Voter,* we can adapt its authors' procedures to the 2004 electorate. In some ways, recent NES data focus more directly on the actual choice citizens must make—a choice among the candidates. The first criterion is whether respondents claim to have an opinion on an issue.[22] It is measured by whether they placed themselves on the issue scale. Second, the respondents should have some perception of the positions taken by the candidates on the issue. This was measured by whether they could place both major-party candidates on that issue.[23] Although some voters might perceive the position of one candidate and vote on that basis, prospective voting involves a comparison between or among alternatives, so the expressed ability to perceive the stands of the contenders seems a minimal requirement of prospective issue voting. Third, the voter must see a difference between the positions of the candidates. Failing to see a difference means that the voter perceived no choice on the issue. The reason might be that the candidates failed to address the issue in the campaign, as might have been true about the environment issue in 2004. It may also be that the candidates in fact took very similar positions on the issue, and respondents were thus, on average, responding to that similarity. We believe that was more true of the candidates in 1976 than in other recent campaigns.

A voter might be able to satisfy these criteria but misperceive the offerings of the candidates. This leads to a fourth condition, which we are able to measure more systematically than was possible in 1956: Do the respondents accurately perceive the relative positions of the two major-party candidates—that is, do they see Bush as more "conservative" than Kerry? This criterion does not demand that the voter have an accurate perception of what the candidate proposes, but it does expect the voter to see that Kerry, for instance, favored more spending on social services than Bush did.

The Data

In Table 6-2 we report the percentages of the sample that met the four criteria on the seven issue scales used in 2004.[24] We also show the average proportion that met the criteria for all scales and compare those averages to comparable averages for all issue scales used in the eight preceding elections.[25] As can be seen in column I of Table 6-2, most people felt capable of placing themselves on the issue scales, and that capability was common to all election years.[26]

For all seven issues, fewer people could place both the candidates and themselves on an issue scale than could place just themselves, as can be seen in column II of Table 6-2. Nonetheless, three in four respondents met these two criteria in

TABLE 6-2   Four Criteria for Issue Voting, 2004, and Comparisons with 1972–2000 Presidential Elections (in percentages)

| | Percentage of Sample Who | | | |
| | I | II | III | IV |
Issue scale	Placed self on scale	Placed both candidates on scale[a]	Saw differences between Kerry and Bush	Saw Kerry more "liberal" than Bush
Government spending/services	86	76	66	53
Defense spending	86	79	71	65
Jobs and standard of living	91	78	65	57
Aid to blacks	89	70	52	46
Jobs and the environment	83	66	52	27
Women's rights	95	77	45	35
Interventionism by diplomacy/military	93	88	85	81
Average[b]				
2004 (7)	89	76	62	52
2000 (7)	87	69	51	41
1996 (9)	89	80	65	55
1992 (3)	85	71	66	52
1988 (7)	86	66	52	43
1984 (7)	84	73	62	53
1980 (9)	82	61	51	43
1976 (9)	84	58	39	26
1972 (8)	90	65	49	41

Note: Columns II, III, and IV compare the Democratic and Republican nominees (Anderson, Perot, and Nader excluded in 1980, 1992, 1996, 2000, and 2004, respectively).

[a] Until 1996, respondents who could not place themselves on a scale were not asked to place the candidates on that issue scale. While they were asked to do so in 1996, 2000, and 2004, we have excluded them from further calculations to maintain comparability with prior surveys.

[b] Number in parentheses is the number of issue scales included in the average for each election year survey.

2004. Notice that there was relatively little variation across issues: 66 percent to 88 percent met the criteria on each issue scale. The 88 percent for the diplomacy/military scale stands out as unusually high, in comparison both to the other issues in 2004 and to issues asked about in earlier elections. The relatively consistent ability to satisfy the criteria is similar to results obtained in 1984 and thereafter, but different from the findings for earlier elections. In 1980, for instance, there were three issue scales on which fewer than half of the respondents placed themselves and both candidates. The average of 76 percent who met these two conditions in 2004 is only slightly smaller than that in 1996, and thus near its highest level. Note that it appears that the percentages meeting the two criteria seem to be increasing over time, at least on average, perhaps reflecting the greater divergence between the two parties and their leaders.

As can be seen in column III of Table 6-2, three in five met the first two criteria and also saw a difference between the positions of Bush and Kerry. The 2004 proportion is thus on a par with the other high-water-mark elections of 1984, 1992, and 1996, noticeably higher than in 1972, 1980, 1988, and 2000, and substantially greater than in 1976. What are we to conclude about these differences in the ability of the electorate to satisfy the criteria and thus be able to vote on the basis of issues? It seems highly unlikely that the ability of the public to comprehend the electoral process varies so greatly from election to election. Note that there is very little difference among elections in self-placement on the issue scales. Rather, the differences are due to perceptions of the candidates' positions. The differences between the election of 1976 and the elections of 1984, 1992, and 1996, in particular, first appear in the ability to place both candidates on the scales. Perhaps relatively few people could place both candidates in 1976 because Gerald R. Ford had not run for president before and had been the incumbent for only two years, and Jimmy Carter was a relatively unknown challenger. Perhaps other elections had higher scores because the incumbent party's candidate had served four or more years in the presidency or the vice presidency. The differences become especially pronounced, however, in the electorate's ability to characterize the candidates' positions. In 1984 the candidates adopted particularly distinctive positions on issues, and this relative clarity was perceived by the electorate. The same seems to have been true in 1992, 1996, and 2004. In 1972, 1980, 1988, and 2000 the candidates were only slightly less distinct, and the electorate saw the differences only slightly less clearly. In 1976, in contrast, Ford and Carter were generally described as moderates, albeit moderately conservative and moderately liberal, respectively. The electorate appears to have reacted to the relative lack of differences.

In sum, we agree with Morris P. Fiorina's argument that failure to satisfy the criteria for issue voting does not mean that the electorate has ill-formed preferences and perceptions.[27] Rather, the electorate's ability to perceive differences between the candidates varies because political conditions differ from election to election, and these differences result mainly from differences in the strategies that the candidates follow. Thus the "quality" of the responses to these issue questions derives in part from how clearly the candidates articulate their issue positions and how distinctly the alternative policy platforms are presented to the public.

The data in column IV reflect the ability of the electorate to discern distinctions between the candidates' policy offerings. Averaging these issues together, we see that in 2004 over half of the respondents satisfied all four issue-voting conditions, the final one being that they saw Kerry as more liberal than Bush. The 2004 data thus are indicating that the potential for issue voting was quite high, similar to the findings for 1984, 1992, and 1996 in these terms, all of which are higher than those for 1972, 1980, and 1988. In this case once again, the 1976 election stands out in very sharp contrast, as barely more than one in four voters could assess the relative positions of the two candidates.

Because the data in Table 6-2 suggest that the potential for prospective issue voting was high in 2004, we might expect these issues to be reasonably closely related to voter choice. We will examine voter choice on these issues in two ways: First, how often did people vote for the closer candidate on each issue? Second, how strongly related to the vote are all the issues, taken together?

APPARENT ISSUE VOTING IN 2004

Issue Criteria and Voting on Each Issue

The first question is, To what extent did people who were closer to a candidate on a given issue actually vote for that candidate? That is, how strong is apparent issue voting?[28] In Table 6-3 we report the proportion of major-party voters who voted for Kerry by where they placed themselves on the issue scales. We divided the seven points into the set of positions that were closer to where the average citizen placed Bush and Kerry (see Figure 6-2).[29]

As can be seen in Table 6-3, on five of the seven scales there is a clear relationship between the voters' issue positions and the candidate they supported, with the environmental issue being somewhat less clear in these terms and the women's rights issue reflecting little relationship to the vote. Those who adopted positions at the "liberal" end of each scale were very likely to vote for Kerry. If we define "liberal" as adopting position 1 or 2, Kerry received three of four votes, or even more, on six of those seven scales. Kerry rarely received three in ten votes from those at the conservative end of the scales, while those with moderate views on each issue fell in between the two extremes of support. The pattern of support we would expect from voting on the basis of these issues is particularly clear on the questions that have long defined the traditional cleavages between the two parties (the top four scales on the table and the diplomacy/military scale). Over these issues, then, there are substantial relationships between the public's opinions and their perceptions of the candidates on prospective issues.

The information on issues can be summarized, as it is in Table 6-4, to illustrate what happened when voters met the various conditions for issue voting. In the first column of Table 6-4, we report the percentage of major-party voters who placed themselves closer to the average perception of Bush or the average perception of Kerry and who voted for the closer candidate. To be more specific, the denominator is the total number of major-party voters who placed themselves closer to the electorate's perception of Bush or of Kerry. The numerator is the

TABLE 6-3 Major-Party Voters Who Voted for Kerry, by Seven-Point Issue Scales, 2004 (in percentages)

Issue scale	Closer to median perception of Kerry				Closer to median perception of Bush			(N)
	1	2	3	4	5	6	7	
Government spending/services[a] (N)[b]	79 (76)	80 (95)	58 (146)	46 (194)	27 (93)	14 (58)	7 (34)	(696)
Defense spending (N)	92 (25)	89 (39)	86 (67)	63 (190)	33 (200)	37 (120)	29 (69)	(710)
Jobs and standard of living (N)	77 (73)	79 (59)	76 (92)	60 (144)	40 (131)	24 (119)	15 (105)	(723)
Aid to blacks (N)	93 (48)	84 (41)	75 (68)	60 (177)	38 (126)	27 (130)	28 (116)	(706)
Jobs and the environment (N)	75 (64)	66 (116)	57 (130)	41 (184)	25 (104)	27 (45)	34 (31)	(674)
Women's rights (N)	56 (433)	44 (130)	33 (57)	42 (80)	33 (30)	38 (14)	46 (17)	(761)
Interventionism by diplomacy/military (N)	90 (87)	83 (104)	61 (109)	45 (161)	21 (149)	14 (78)	30 (58)	(746)

[a] Reversed from actual scoring to make a "liberal" response closer to 1 and a "conservative" response closer to 7.
[b] The numbers in parentheses are the totals on which the percentages are based. Numbers are weighted.

TABLE 6-4   Apparent Issue Voting, 2004, and Comparisons with 1972–2000 (in percentages)

Seven-point issue scale	Percentage of Voters Who Voted for Closer Candidate and		
	Placed self on issue scale	Met all four issue voting criteria	Placed self but failed to meet all three other criteria
Government spending/services	68	78	48
Defense spending	73	73	55
Jobs and standard of living	67	72	57
Aid to blacks	65	70	57
Jobs and the environment	65	68	63
Women's rights	56	79	40
Interventionism by diplomacy/military	78	82	35
Averages[a]			
2004 (7)	67	75	51
2000 (7)	60	68	40
1996 (9)	63	74	41
1992 (3)	62	70	48
1988 (7)	62	71	45
1984 (7)	65	73	46
1980 (9)	63	71	48
1976 (9)	57	70	50
1972 (8)	66	76	55

Note: An "apparent issue vote" is a vote for the candidate closer to one's position on an issue scale. The closer candidate is determined by comparing self-placement to the median placements of the two candidates on the scale as a whole. Respondents who did not place themselves, or who were equidistant from the two candidates, are excluded from the calculations.

[a] The number in parentheses is the number of seven-point issue scales included in the average for each election year survey.

total number of major-party voters who were both closer to Kerry and voted for him, plus the total number of major-party voters who were both closer to Bush and voted for him.

If voting were unrelated to issue positions, we would expect 50 percent of voters to vote for the closer candidate on average—not unlike the 56 percent on the women's rights scale, where there was essentially no difference seen between the two candidates. In 2004, 67 percent voted for the closer candidate. This is ten percentage points higher on average than in 1976, and seven points higher than in 2000, but only somewhat higher than in the remaining six elections. These figures do not tell the whole story, however, for those who placed themselves on an issue but failed to meet some other criterion were unlikely to have cast a vote based on that issue. In the second column of Table 6-4, we report the percentage of those who voted for the closer candidate on each issue among voters who met all four conditions on that issue. The third column reports the percentage that voted for the closer candidate among voters who failed to meet at least one of the three remaining conditions.

Those respondents who met all four conditions were much more likely to vote for the closer candidate on any issue. Indeed, there is relatively little difference, on average, across all nine elections. In each case, about seven of ten such voters supported the closer candidate. For those respondents who failed to meet all three of the conditions on issue voting, in contrast, voting was essentially random with respect to the issues.

The strong similarity of all nine election averages in the second and third columns suggests that issue voting seems more prevalent in some elections than others because elections differ in the number of people who clearly perceive differences between the candidates. In all elections, at least seven in ten who satisfied all four conditions voted consistently with their issue preferences; in all elections, those who did not satisfy all the conditions on perceptions of the candidates voted essentially randomly with respect to individual issues. As we saw earlier, the degree to which such perceptions vary from election to election depends more on the strategies of the candidates than on the qualities of the voters. Therefore, the relatively low percentage of apparent issue voting in 1976, for instance, results from the perception of small differences between the two, rather moderate candidates. The larger magnitude of apparent issue voting in 2004, as in most other elections, results from the greater clarity with which most people saw the positions of Kerry and Bush.

The Balance of Issues Measure

"Prospective issue voting" means that voters compare the full set of policy proposals made by the candidates. As we have noted, most issues are strongly related to the vote, and so we might expect the set of all issues to be even more strongly so. To examine the relationship, we constructed an overall assessment of the issue scales, what we call the "balance of issues measure." We did so by giving individuals a score of +1 if their positions on an issue scale were closer to the average perception of Bush, a –1 if their positions were closer to the average perception of Kerry, and a score of zero if they had no preference on an issue.[30] The scores for all seven issue scales were added together, creating a measure that ranged from –7 to +7. For instance, respondents who were closer to the average perception of Kerry's position on all seven scales received a score of –7. A negative score indicated that the respondent was, on balance, closer to the public's perception of

Kerry, while a positive score indicated the respondent was, overall, closer to the public's perception of Bush.[31] We collapsed this fifteen-point measure into seven categories, running from "strongly Democratic" through "neutral," to "strongly Republican." [32] The results are reported in Table 6-5.

As can be seen in Table 6-5A, one in ten respondents was strongly Democratic; one in seven was strongly Republican. Three in ten were moderately or slightly Democratic, somewhat fewer than the four in ten in the two comparable Republican categories. Thus the balance of issues measure tilted noticeably in the Republican direction, even though Kerry was, on average, closer to the typical respondent.[33]

The balance of issues measure was strongly related to the vote, as the findings for the individual issues would suggest (see Table 6-5B). Kerry won the vast majority of the votes of those in the strongly and moderately Democratic categories, and three of four from the slightly Democratic category. He won a bit more than four in ten votes from those in the neutral and the slightly Republican categories. His support dropped off dramatically from that point. Indeed, the decline in Democratic voting across the net balance of issues categories in 2004 is as strong as in 1984 and 1996, the two strongest cases in the past nine elections.

The Abortion Issue

We give special attention to the public policy controversy about abortion for two reasons: First, it is an especially divisive issue. The Republican national platform has taken a strong "pro-life" stand since 1980, while the Democratic Party's became increasingly "pro-choice." Abortion is one of the most contentious issues in government at all levels, between the two parties, and among the public. In addition, it is one of a complex of issues that define much of the social issue dimension, one of the two major dimensions of domestic policy (economics being the second) into which most domestic policies—and most controversial issues—fall. Whereas gay marriage was relatively new to the set of social issues (as conservatives would put it, a new addition to the set of family issues), abortion has been central to the rise of social conservatism in America, virtually back to its modern emergence in the wake of the Supreme Court decision, *Roe v. Wade* (1973), that made abortion legal throughout the United States.[34]

The second reason for examining this issue is that it is another policy question about which respondents were asked their own views as well as what they thought Bush's and Kerry's positions were, a battery that has been asked for the last several elections. It differs from (and is therefore hard to compare directly with) the seven-point issue scales, however, because respondents were given only four alternatives, but each included a specified policy option:

1. By law, abortion should never be permitted.
2. The law should permit abortion only in case of rape, incest, or when the woman's life is in danger.

TABLE 6-5 Distribution of the Electorate on the Net Balance of Issues Measure and Major-Party Vote, 2004 (in percentages)

| | Net Balance of Issues | | | | | | | |
	Strongly Democratic	Moderately Democratic	Slightly Democratic	Neutral	Slightly Republican	Moderately Republican	Strongly Republican	Total (N)
			A. Distribution of Responses					
Percent	7	14	19	9	20	18	13	100 (1,063)
			B. Major-Party Voters Who Voted for Kerry					
Percent	97	88	74	45	40	27	4	50
(N)	(70)	(103)	(137)	(47)	(159)	(153)	(116)	(785)

Note: Numbers are weighted. The numbers in parentheses for part B of the table are the totals on which the percentages are based.

3. The law should permit abortion for reasons *other than* rape, incest, or danger to the woman's life, but only after the need for the abortion has been clearly established.
4. By law, a woman should always be able to obtain an abortion as a matter of personal choice.

The electorate's responses, which can be determined from the numbers in Table 6-6, were toward the pro-choice end of the measure. Among the major-party voters who chose among the four alternatives, nearly two in five (291 of all 774 major-party voters) said that abortion should be a matter of personal choice. Eighteen percent were willing to allow abortions for reasons other than rape, incest, or danger to the woman's life, while 32 percent said abortion should be allowed only under those conditions. Only 12 percent, the same as in 2000, said that abortion should never be permitted. For all four options the percentages were similar to those in 2000. It is also noteworthy that the vast majority (98.2 percent) of the 1,066 respondents in the postelection interviews chose one of these alternatives, and another 0.8 percent chose an unspecified position.

A voter's opinion on this issue was strongly related to the way he or she voted. Table 6-6 presents the percentage of major-party voters who voted for Kerry according to their view on the abortion issue. Because the survey asked respondents what they thought Kerry's and Bush's positions were, we can see whether our issue-voting criteria apply. If they do, we can expect to find a very strong relationship between the respondents' positions and how they voted, if they met three additional conditions, beyond having an opinion on this issue themselves: First, they had to have an opinion about where the candidates stood on the issue. Second, they had to see a difference between the positions of the two major-party nominees. Third, to cast a policy-related vote reflecting the actual positions of the candidates, they had to recognize that Kerry took a more pro-choice position than Bush. In 1992, seven out of ten major-party voters met all these conditions when comparing Clinton with George H. W. Bush, and in 1996 two out of three did when they compared Clinton with Dole. In 2000, however, only half of the major-party voters met all of the conditions when comparing Gore with George W. Bush. In 2004 Bush had served as president for four years, and his conservative social policies were easier for the voters to recognize. Moreover, Kerry emphasized his commitment to a pro-choice position more than Gore had four years earlier. Seven out of ten major-party voters met all of the conditions.

Among all major-party voters there is a strong relationship between opinions on abortion and the way respondents voted, which can be seen by reading across the first row of Table 6-6. But among voters who met all of the conditions, there was a very strong relationship between policy preferences and voting. We see this relationship by reading across the second row of the table. Among the very small number of major-party voters who thought that abortions should never be allowed, only one in five supported Kerry. Among those who thought that the decision to have an abortion should be a matter of personal choice, three out of

TABLE 6-6 Percentage of Major-Party Voters Who Voted for Kerry, by Opinion about Abortion and What They Believed Bush's and Kerry's Positions Are, 2004

	Respondent's Position on Abortion							
	Abortion should never be permitted.		Abortion should be permitted only in the case of rape, incest, or health of the woman.		Abortion should be permitted for other reasons but only if a need is established.		Abortion should be a matter of personal choice.	
	%	(N)	%	(N)	%	(N)	%	(N)
All major-party voters	32	(96)	41	(249)	41	(138)	67	(291)
Major-party voters who placed both candidates, who saw a difference between them, and who saw Kerry as more "pro-choice" than Bush	19	(71)	35	(163)	46	(100)	74	(212)
Major-party voters who did not meet all three of these conditions	72	(25)	52	(86)	30	(38)	49	(80)

Note: Numbers in parentheses are the totals on which the percentages are based. Numbers are weighted.

four voted for him, with other cases falling in between. As we saw above, the percentage of voters who vote consistent with their preferences is quite similar from issue to issue and year to year, if they have met the conditions, and the most important reason why one issue varies from another seems to be the degree to which voters can see a difference between the candidates. On abortion in 2004, as in most issues this year, voters were particularly able to see the choices clearly. The final row of Table 6-6 shows the relationship of issue preferences and the vote among voters who did *not* see Kerry as more pro-choice than Bush. Among such voters, there is a much weaker relationship. In fact, voters who were pro-life (few though they were) were more likely to vote Democratic than those who held a pro-choice position. Similar results are found in 1992, 1996, and 2000.[35]

The Importance of Social and Moral Issues in 2004

We noted above that one of the surprises of the 2004 campaign was the finding in the EMR/MI exit poll that the response "moral values" was the most common choice as the most important concern in the election, even if by a small margin (22 percent, compared to 20 percent for the economy). We also note that there is likely to be at least some degree of correspondence between social issues and the set of ideas that exit-poll respondents might have had in mind when they selected moral values. In that poll, it was also true that the respondents who selected that category were far more likely to have just voted for Bush than for Kerry (80 percent reported voting for Bush, among the 22 percent who chose moral values as the most important issue). Obviously, far more chose a social issue (primarily terrorism) as most important in the NES survey than chose moral values in the exit survey (but note that Nader voters were even more likely to select moral values than Bush voters). But this correspondence may be even murkier than the results of these two polls suggest. Other credible polls yielded quite different responses. For example, a national poll conducted by Knowledge Networks for Peter D. Feaver, Christopher F. Gelpi, and Jason A. Reifler offered respondents a choice among three options for the most important concern, in polling that was conducted at several points from March through November 2004.[36] The three choices as "most important to you personally" were "foreign policy issues like Iraq and the War on Terrorism," "economic issues like jobs and taxes," and "social issues like abortion and gay marriage." The economy started out as by far the most common choice (72 percent in early March) and receded somewhat, ending as the selection of 59 percent of respondents in late October and early November. Concern over foreign policy increased, from 16 percent at the beginning to 30 percent at the end of the campaign. Social issues remained virtually unchanged over the course of the campaign, starting and ending as the choice of 10 percent of respondents. The wording of these various questions and responses is different. We suspect that the "social issues like abortion and gay marriage" response from the Feaver, Gelpi, and Reifler survey is close to what pundits had in mind when they were interpreting the "moral values" response rate from the exit poll, but that is speculation on our part. We are more confident in locating the source of these rather substantial differences in responses in the simple fact that respondents made different selections when presented with different lists of choices or, in the case of the NES survey, offered their own choice. No matter which survey results one uses, however, the potency of such social and moral issues, including abortion, is an important part of the story of 2004, but it is not clear just how large a part of the story it is in comparison to the other two major concerns, the economy and war.

While abortion and other prospective issues were particularly strongly related to the vote in 2004, these results do not prove that policy preferences shape voting decisions. Some voters may have projected the position they themselves favored onto the candidate they favored.[37] But it does appear that unless all the basic conditions for issue voting are present, issue voting does not occur. When the conditions are present, there can be a strong relationship between the positions voters hold and their choice between the major-party candidates.

CONCLUSION

The findings suggest that for major-party voters prospective issues were quite important in the 2004 election, very similar to the election in 1996, and thus at the high-water mark of the relation of prospective issues to the vote. Even so, studying prospective issues alone cannot account for Bush's narrow victory in the popular vote. Those for whom prospective issues gave a clear choice voted consistently with their views on those issues. Most people, however, were located between the candidates as the electorate saw them. Indeed, on most issues the majority of people were relatively moderate, and the candidates were seen as more liberal and more conservative, respectively.

This line of reasoning suggests that voters took prospective issues into account in 2004 but that they also considered other factors. In the next chapter, we will see that the second form of policy voting, that based on retrospective evaluations, was among those other factors, as it has been in all nine of the previous presidential elections we are considering.

Chapter 7

Presidential Performance
and Candidate Choice

On the campaign trail the candidates focused most of their attention on war and the economy, and of course, they took very different stances on them: George W. Bush argued that his policies were working, and John F. Kerry argued that they were not.[1] Voters might well have reasoned along similar lines in determining whom they would support; that is, they would choose the incumbent if they thought he was doing a good job dealing with problems and choose Kerry if they thought he would handle them better. To the extent that they considered the successes and failures of the incumbent president and his party, perhaps in comparison to what they thought his opponent and the opponent's party would have done if they had been in office, voters were casting a retrospective vote. Many voters appear to have reasoned along these lines in 2004. As we will see, international and economic issues are particularly likely to be considered retrospectively, and so, given the concerns of the electorate (see Table 6-1), we might expect a high level of retrospective voting in 2004.

In the aftermath of the very close election in 2000, many Democrats, as well as pundits, criticized Al Gore for his failure to campaign on the successes of the Clinton-Gore administration. They believed that had he done so he could have reminded voters of the positive performance of the American economy in the late 1990s.[2] These criticisms were easy to understand because there has often been a close correspondence between the performance of the economy and the electoral fortunes of the incumbent president's party, both directly and indirectly. A strong economy enhances the incumbent's approval ratings, thereby strengthening his party's support among the electorate. Indeed, in 1988 George W. Bush's father was aided in his bid to rise from vice president to president by the strong economy during the Reagan-Bush administration.[3] In 1992, in contrast, voters concluded that it was time to "throw the rascals out," voting against Bush as incumbent and electing Bill Clinton.[4]

In this chapter we will look at the evidence to see whether voters may have concluded in 2004, as they did in 1984 and 1996, that "one good term deserves another." Such appeals, based on the performance of the incumbent administration, references to the successes or failures of earlier administrations, and arguments about what previous performance indicates about the future, are attempts to benefit from retrospective evaluations. In this sort of choice, the voters in 2004 had an advantage relative to those in, say, 1996 or 2000, in that Bush and his party controlled both chambers of Congress as well as the presidency, making it easier to attribute praise or blame, whereas in those earlier elections there was divided control. Kerry hoped, of course, that the voters would decide instead to "throw the rascals out" of office in 2004, as they had done in 1980 and 1992.

Retrospective evaluations are concerns about policy, but they differ significantly from the prospective evaluations we considered in the last chapter. Retrospective evaluations are, as the name suggests, concerned with the past. While the past may be prologue, retrospective evaluations also focus on outcomes, on what actually happened rather than on the policy means for achieving outcomes, which are at the heart of prospective evaluations. For example, after his reelection Bush argued that there was a looming problem in the Social Security system and proposed private accounts as a solution. Some Democrats argued against the president on the grounds that creating private accounts would actually make the problem worse. The Democrats were focusing on the policy chosen by Bush, as in a prospective evaluation. Other Democrats argued that there really wasn't a serious problem with Social Security in the first place. Such arguments focus on outcomes of policy and thus are the basis of retrospective judgments.

WHAT IS RETROSPECTIVE VOTING?

An individual who voted for the incumbent party's candidate because the incumbent was, in the voter's opinion, a successful president is said to have cast a retrospective vote. A voter who votes for the opposition because, in the voter's opinion, the incumbent has been unsuccessful has also done so. In other words, retrospective voting decisions are based on evaluations of the course of politics over the last term of office and of how much the incumbent should be held responsible for what good or ill has occurred. V. O. Key Jr. popularized this argument by suggesting that the voter might be "a rational god of vengeance and of reward." [5]

Obviously, the more closely the candidate of one party can be tied to the actions of the incumbent, the more likely it is that voters will decide retrospectively. The incumbent president cannot escape such evaluations, and the incumbent vice president is usually identified with (and often chooses to identify himself with) the administration's performance. The electorate has often been able to play the role of Key's "rational god," because an incumbent president or vice president has stood for election in twenty-three of the twenty-seven presidential elections since 1900 (all but 1908, 1920, 1928, and 1952, and thus all of those that we consider in this chapter).

Key's thesis has three aspects. First, retrospective voters are oriented toward outcomes rather than the policy means to achieve them. Second, these voters evaluate the performance of the incumbent only, all but ignoring the opposition. Finally, they evaluate what has been done, paying little attention to what the candidates promise to do in the future.

Anthony Downs presents a different picture of retrospective voting.[6] He argues that voters look to the past to understand what the incumbent party's candidate will do in the future. According to Downs, parties are basically consistent in their goals, methods, and ideologies over time. Therefore, the past performance of both parties' candidates, but especially that of the incumbent, may prove relevant for making predictions about their future conduct. Because it takes time and effort to evaluate campaign promises and because promises are just words, voters find it faster, easier, and safer to use past performance to project the administration's actions for the next four years. Downs also emphasizes that retrospective evaluations are used in making comparisons among the alternatives presented to the voter. Key sees a retrospective referendum on the incumbent's party alone. Downs believes that retrospective evaluations are used to compare the candidates, as well as to provide a guide to the future. Even incumbents may use such Downsian retrospective claims. In 1996, for example, Clinton attempted to tie Bob Dole to the performance of congressional Republicans, since they had assumed the majority in the 1994 election (an attempt made easier by virtue of Dole's having been majority leader of the Senate throughout most of the preceding two years). Clinton pointedly referred to the 104th Congress as the "Dole-Gingrich" Congress.

Morris P. Fiorina elaborates and extends Downs's thesis. For our purposes, Fiorina's major addition to the Downsian perspective is his argument that party identification plays a central role. He argues that "citizens monitor party promises and performances over time, encapsulate their observations in a summary judgment termed 'party identification,' and rely on this core of previous experience when they assign responsibility for current societal conditions and evaluate ambiguous platforms designed to deal with uncertain futures."[7] We will return to Fiorina's views on partisanship in the following chapter.

Retrospective voting and voting according to issue positions, as analyzed in chapter 6, differ significantly. The difference lies in how concerned people are with societal outcomes and how concerned they are with the policy means to achieve desired outcomes. For example, everyone prefers economic prosperity. The disagreement among political decision makers lies in how best to achieve it. At the voters' level, however, the central question is whether people care only about achieving prosperity or whether they care, or are even able to judge, how to achieve it. Perhaps they looked at high inflation and interest rates in 1980 and said, "We tried Carter's approach, and it failed. Let's try something else—

anything else." They may have noted the long run of relative economic prosperity from 1983 to 1988 and said, "Whatever Reagan did, it worked. Let's keep it going by putting his vice president in office." In 1996 they may have agreed with Clinton that he had presided over a successful economy, and decided to remain with the incumbent. In 2004 just how these concerns would play was uncertain. Would the public judge the economy as improving sufficiently strongly, or decide that its recent improvement was too little, too late? Would Iraq be viewed as a success or a failure?

Economic policies and foreign affairs issues are especially likely to be discussed in these terms because they share several characteristics. First, the outcomes are clear, and most voters can judge whether they approve of the results. Inflation and unemployment are high or low; the economy is growing or it is not. The country is at war or at peace; the world is stable or unstable. Indeed, 2004 was unusual in that economic conditions, while improving, were still uncertain, and the outcome of the war in Iraq was also uncertain. Both the economic and foreign policy situations were unusually murky. Still, as we will see, voters could and did make assessments. Second, there is often near-consensus on the outcomes desired; no one disagrees with peace or prosperity, with world stability or low unemployment. Third, the means to achieve these ends are often very complex, and information is hard to understand; experts as well as candidates and parties disagree over the specific ways to achieve them. How should the economy be improved, and how could terrorism possibly be contained, or democracy established in a foreign land?

As issues, therefore, peace and prosperity differ sharply from policy areas such as abortion, in which there is vigorous disagreement over ends among experts, leaders, and the public. On still other issues, people value both ends *and* means. The classic cases often involve the question of whether it is appropriate for government to take action in that area at all. Ronald Reagan was fond of saying, "Government isn't the solution to our problems, government *is* the problem." For instance, should the government provide national health insurance? Few disagree with the end of better health care, but they do disagree over the appropriate means to achieve it. The choice of means involves some of the basic philosophical and ideological differences that have divided the Republicans from the Democrats for decades.[8] For example, in 1984 Democratic nominee Walter F. Mondale agreed with President Reagan that we were in a period of economic prosperity and that prosperity is a good thing; he argued that Reagan's policies were unfair to the disadvantaged. Clinton and H. Ross Perot, in 1992, also claimed that Reagan's and Bush's policies, by creating such large deficits, were sowing the seeds for future woes. Clearly these disagreements were not over ends but over the choice of means to achieve them and the consequences that would follow from those choices.

Two fundamental conditions must be met before retrospective evaluations can affect voting choices. First, individuals must connect their concerns (especially the problems they feel are the most important) with the incumbent and the actions he took in office. For example, this condition would not be present if a voter blamed earlier administrations with sowing the seeds that grew into the huge deficits of the 1980s, blamed a profligate Congress, or even believed that the problem was beyond anyone's control. Second, individuals, in the Downs-Fiorina view, must compare their evaluations of the incumbent's past performance with what they believe the nominee of the opposition party would do. For example, even if they thought Bush's performance on the economy was weak, voters might have compared that performance with Kerry's program and concluded that his efforts would not be any better, or might even make things worse.

In this second condition, a certain asymmetry exists, one that benefits the incumbent. Even if the incumbent's performance has been weak in a certain area, the challenger still has to convince voters that he could do better. It is even more difficult for a challenger to convince voters who think the incumbent's performance has been strong that he would be stronger. This asymmetry had advantaged Republican candidates in the 1980s, but it worked to Dole's disadvantage in 1996 and to Bush's in 2000.

We examine next some illustrative retrospective evaluations and study their impact on voter choice. In chapter 6 we looked at issue scales designed to measure the public's evaluations of candidates' promises. Of course, the public can evaluate not only the promises of the incumbent party but also its actions. We will compare promises with performance in this chapter, but one must remember that the distinctions are not as sharp in practice as they are in principle.[9] The Downs-Fiorina view is that past actions and projections about the future are necessarily intertwined.

EVALUATIONS OF GOVERNMENTAL PERFORMANCE ON IMPORTANT PROBLEMS

What do you consider the most important problem facing the country, and how do you feel the government in Washington has been handling the problem?[10] These questions are designed to measure retrospective judgments. Table 7-1 compares respondents' evaluations of government performance on the problem that each respondent identified as the single most important one facing the country. We are able to track such evaluations for the past nine elections.[11] The most striking findings in Table 7-1A (and Table A7-1A) are that in 2004 few thought the government was doing a very good job, but that there was a relatively close division between those who thought the government was doing a good job and those who felt it was doing a bad job or a very bad job (see also Table A7-1 in the appendix). To the extent that we can make comparisons to earlier elections, this makes 2004 look most like 2000 and not that dissimilar to 1976, 1984, and 1996—two elections that did return the incumbent party (1984 and 1996) and two that narrowly did not (1976 and 2000). By contrast, 1980 and 1992 were elections with

TABLE 7-1 Evaluation of Government Performance on Most Important Problem and Major-Party Vote, 1972–2004

Government performance[a]	1972	1976	1980	1984	1988	1992	1996	2000	2004
	A. Evaluation of Government Performance on Most Important Problem (in percentages)								
Good job	12	8	4	16	8	2	7	10	12
Only fair job	58	46	35	46	37	28	44	44	48
Poor job	30	46	61	39	56	69	48	47	40
Total	100	100	100	101	101	99	99	101	100
(N)	(993)	(2,156)[a]	(1,319)	(1,797)	(1,672)	(1,974)	(752)[b]	(856)[a]	(1,019)[a]

B. Percentage of Major-Party Vote for Incumbent Party's Nominee[c]

	Nixon	Ford	Carter	Reagan	Bush	Bush	Clinton	Gore[a]	Bush
Good job	85	72	81	89	82	70	93	70	90
(N)	(91)	(128)[b]	(43)	(214)	(93)	(27)	(38)[b]	(58)[b]	(94)[b]
Only fair job	69	53	55	65	61	45	68	60	74
(N)	(390)	(695)[b]	(289)	(579)	(429)	(352)	(238)[b]	(239)[b]	(365)[b]
Poor job	46	39	33	37	44	39	44	37	11
(N)	(209)	(684)[b]	(505)	(494)	(631)	(841)	(242)[b]	(230)[b]	(305)[b]

[a] These questions were asked of a random half sample in 1972, 1996, and 2000. In 1972 respondents were asked whether the government was being "very helpful," "somewhat helpful," or "not helpful at all" in solving this most important problem. For 1976 through 2000, they were asked whether the government was doing a "good job," an "only fair" job, or a "poor job." In 2004 respondents were asked whether the government was doing a "very good job," a "good job," a "bad job," or a "very bad job" in solving the most important issue. In this table, "very good job" is placed on the same row as "good job"; "good job" is placed in the same row as "only fair job," and "bad job" and "very bad job" are combined and placed in the same row as "poor job." For the full distribution of responses for 2004, see Table A7-1 in the appendix.

[b] The numbers are weighted.

[c] The numbers in parentheses in part B of the table are the totals on which the percentages are based.

apparently even more negative opinions and in which the incumbent party was soundly defeated.[12]

If the voter is a rational god of vengeance and reward, we can expect to find a strong relationship between the evaluation of government performance and the vote. Such is indeed the case for all elections, as can be seen in Table 7-1B (and Table A7-1B, in the appendix). From seven to nine out of ten major-party voters who thought the government was doing a good job on the most important problem voted for the incumbent party's nominee in each election. In 1996 those who thought the government was doing a good job with the most important problem supported Clinton even more strongly than they had supported incumbents in previous elections, and Bush in 2004 came very close to holding the same level of support. The half of the respondents who thought he was doing a good job (the middle category) supported him to as great a degree as his father in 1992 and Gerald R. Ford in 1976 were supported by the top category. Kerry, however, did unusually well among the two in five who thought Bush was doing a bad or very bad job, winning nine in ten such voters. This appears to be by far the strongest relationship between government handling of the most important problem and the two-party vote, although we must be cautious because the response categories in 2004 were different from those used in the previous elections.

According to Downs and Fiorina, it is important not only to know how things have been going, but also to assess how that evaluation compares with the alternative. In recent elections, respondents have been asked which party would do a better job of solving the problem they named as the most important. This question was not included in the 2004 National Election Study (NES) survey. However, the NES did include a battery of such questions for three of the most relevant and important problems: which party is seen as better on handling the nation's economy, the war on terrorism, and keeping us out of war. Recall that, as we saw in Table 6-1, these three questions measure the most important concern for a substantial majority of respondents. Table 7-2A shows the responses to these questions. The questions are clearly future oriented, but they may call for judgments about past performance, consistent with the Downs-Fiorina view. Respondents are not asked to evaluate policy alternatives, and thus their responses are most likely based on a retrospective comparison of how the incumbent party had handled things with a prediction about how the opposition would fare. We therefore consider these questions to be a measure of comparative retrospective evaluations. It is unfortunate, however, that we cannot make direct comparisons to other elections.

Table 7-2A shows that the public had different views about which party was better at handling these three important concerns. The public distinctly tilted toward the Republicans for handling the war on terrorism but toward the Democrats for keeping us out of war. The balance of opinion was closer to even on the handling of the nation's economy, but it leaned somewhat in the Democrats' favor. Over a third of the respondents, however, favored neither party on each of the problems.

TABLE 7-2 Evaluation of Party Seen as Better on Three Problems and Major-
Party Vote, 2004

A. Evaluation of Party Seen as Better on Problems (in percentages)

	Nation's economy[a]	War on terrorism	Keeping out of war
Republicans	25	41	16
About the same[a]	38	34	41
Democrats	37	25	43
Total	100	100	100
(N)	(1,177)[b]	(1,170)[b]	(1,167)[b]

B. Percentage of Major-Party Voters Who Voted Democratic for President

Republican	8	12	10
(N)[c]	(225)[b]	(350)[b]	(142)[b]
About the same[a]	41	66	39
(N)[c]	(262)[b]	(218)[b]	(273)[b]
Democrats	90	95	76
(N)[c]	(292)[b]	(205)[b]	(349)[b]

[a] For the nation's economy question, the middle response was that there "wouldn't be much [or would be no] difference between them."
[b] Numbers are weighted.
[c] The numbers in parentheses in part B of the table are the totals on which the percentages are based.

As Table 7-2B reveals, the relationship between which party is seen as better on these three important problems and the vote is very strong. Kerry won at least nine votes in ten from those who thought the Democrats were better on the economy and on the war on terrorism and three in four from those who thought the Democrats were better on keeping the United States out of war. Bush held at least seven in eight of those who thought the Republicans were better on each of those problems, and there was close to an even split among those who thought neither party would do better. It appears that one way of winning a vote is to convince the voter that your party will be better at handling issues that many feel are of major concern. If neither candidate convinces the voter that his party is better, the voter apparently looks to other factors.

The data presented in Tables 7-1 and 7-2 have an important limitation. The first survey question refers to "the government" and not to the incumbent president. (Is it the president, Congress, both—or even others, such as the bureaucracy or the courts—who are handling the job poorly?) The second question refers to the "political party" and not the candidate, whereas it is the performance of the incumbent that most directly relates to the choice between candidates. So we will look more closely at the incumbent and at people's evaluations of comparable problems where there are data to permit such comparisons.

ECONOMIC EVALUATIONS AND THE VOTE FOR THE INCUMBENT

More than any others, economic issues have received attention as suitable for studying retrospective evaluations. The impact of economic conditions on congressional and presidential elections has been studied extensively.[13] Popular evaluations of presidential effectiveness, John E. Mueller has pointed out, are strongly influenced by the economy. Edward R. Tufte suggests that because the incumbent realizes that his fate may hinge on the performance of the economy, he may attempt to manipulate it, leading to what is known as a "political business cycle." [14] A major reason for Jimmy Carter's defeat in 1980 was the perception that economic performance had been weak during his administration. Reagan's rhetorical question in the 1980 debate with Carter, "Are you better off today than you were four years ago?" indicates that politicians realize the power such arguments have with the electorate. Reagan owed his sweeping reelection victory in 1984 largely to the perception that economic performance by the end of his first term had become, after a deep recession in the middle, much stronger.

If people are concerned about economic outcomes, they might start by looking for an answer to the sort of question Reagan asked. Table 7-3A presents respondents' perceptions of whether they were financially better off than they had been one year earlier. From 1972 to 1980 about a third of the sample felt they were better off. Over that period, however, more and more of the remainder felt that they were worse off. By 1980, "Worse now" was the most common response. But in 1984 many felt the economic recovery, and more than two of five said that they were better off than in the previous year; only a little more than one in four felt worse off. Of course, 1984 was only two years after a deep recession, and so many may have seen their economic fortunes improve considerably over the prior year or so. In 1988 that recovery had been sustained, and the distribution of responses to this question in 1988 was very similar to that of 1984. By 1992 there was a return to the feelings of the earlier period, and responses were nearly evenly divided between "better," "the same," and "worse off." In 1996 the responses were like those of the 1984 and 1988 elections—and even slightly more favorable than in those years. In 2000 about a third felt better off, similar to the responses through 1980. However, far fewer felt worse off in 2000 than in any of the seven preceding elections. Over half responded in 2000 that they were about the same as a year ago. In 2004 we see a return to the pattern more typical of 1984, 1988, and 1996, with over two in five feeling better off, the most popular response. Unlike the preceding comparisons, however, nearly a third felt worse off, and a quarter felt about the same. Perhaps the recovery had hit many voters, but some still lagged, or perhaps there was a more permanent polarization of economic experiences, more consistent with the arguments of Kerry and especially of his running mate, Sen. John Edwards. In any event, the overall story is that personal economic conditions provided good news for the incumbent.

In Table 7-3B we can see that responses to this question are related to the two-party presidential vote. We can see that the findings in 2004 are different than in

TABLE 7-3 Public's Assessments of Personal Financial Situation and Major-Party Vote, 1972–2004

"Would you say that you (and your family) are better off or worse off financially than you were a year ago?"

Response	1972[a]	1976	1980	1984	1988	1992	1996	2000[a]	2004
A. Distribution of Responses (in percentages)									
Better now	36	34	33	44	42	31	46	33	43
Same	42	35	25	28	33	34	31	53	25
Worse now	23	31	42	27	25	35	24	14	32
Total	101	100	100	99	100	100	101	100	100
(N)	(955)	(2,828)[b]	(1,393)	(1,956)	(2,025)	(2,474)[b]	(1,708)[b]	(907)[b]	(1,203)[b]
B. Percentage of Major-Party Voters Who Voted for the Incumbent Party Nominee for President[c]									
Better now	69	55	46	74	63	53	66	56	65
(N)	(247)	(574)[b]	(295)	(612)	(489)	(413)[b]	(462)[b]	(164)[b]	(354)[b]
Same	70	52	46	55	50	45	52	51	50
(N)	(279)	(571)[b]	(226)	(407)	(405)	(500)[b]	(348)[b]	(291)[b]	(207)[b]
Worse now	52	38	40	33	40	27	47	45	28
(N)	(153)	(475)[b]	(351)	(338)	(283)	(453)[b]	(225)[b]	(56)[b]	(219)[b]

[a] These questions were asked of a randomly selected half sample in 1972 and 2000.
[b] Numbers are weighted.
[c] The numbers in parentheses in part B of the table are the totals on which the percentages are based.

many prior elections, with a strong relationship to the vote, especially for those who believed they were worse off, in comparison to the others. In the strength of this relationship, 2004 is most like 1984, with 1988 and 1992 not too much weaker. In other cases the relationship between the respondents' financial situations and their vote is often not particularly strong. The similarly strong findings in 1984 and 2004 suggest that personal circumstances may loom largest when there has been a recent, substantial change in conditions—in both of these cases, recent emergence from a noticeable economic decline—and thus perhaps voters are especially inclined to reward the successful incumbent who presided over a rebound or to punish the incumbent if they have not felt the recovery.

People may "vote their pocketbooks," but people are even more likely to vote retrospectively based on their judgments of how the economy as a whole has been faring. And personal and national economic experiences can be quite different. In 1980, for example, about 40 percent of the respondents thought their own financial situation was worse than the year before, but responses to the 1980 NES survey show that twice as many (83 percent) thought the national economy was worse off than the year before. In the first four columns of Table 7-4A, we see that there was quite a change in perceptions of the national economy over the past seven elections. Comparing Tables 7-3A and 7-4A, we see that in 1984 the improved status of personal finances almost matched perceptions of the status of the economy as a whole. In 1988 the personal financial situation was quite like that in 1984, but perceptions of the national economy were clearly more negative. In 1992 the public gave the nation's economy a far more negative assessment than they gave their personal financial situations. That was not the case in 1996 and 2000, when respondents gave broadly similar assessments of their personal fortunes and those of the nation—making those two elections look most like 1984. But then, in 2004, the public gave very negative views of the economy as a whole, with nearly half thinking it was worse, three in ten thinking that it had stayed the same, and only one in four thinking it was better. This makes 2004 not as bad as the two really bad years (1980 and 1992), years in which the incumbent was defeated, but not even as good as 1988, let alone the years when there was a consensus that the economy was strong.

In Table 7-4B, we show the relationship between responses to these items and the two-party vote for president. As we can see, the relationship between these measures and the vote is always strong, and 2004 the relationship is the strongest of all. Moreover, comparing Tables 7-3B and 7-4B shows that, in general, the vote is more closely associated with perceptions of the nation's economy than it is with perceptions of one's personal economic well-being. In 2004 that meant that one's personal financial situation was clearly related to the vote, but one's view of the nation's economy was very strongly related to the vote. These two reasonably strong relationships, however, tended to cancel each other out. The Bush advantage from the reasonably positive views of personal financial conditions was countered by the Kerry advantage in appealing to an electorate that held negative views of the national economy.

TABLE 7-4 Public's View of the State of the Economy and Major-Party Vote, 1980–2004

Response	1980	1984	1988	1992	1996	2000[a]	2004[a]
			"Would you say that over the past year the nation's economy has gotten . . ."				
			A. Distribution of Responses (in percentages)				
Better	4	44	19	4	40	39	24
Stayed same	13	33	50	22	44	44	31
Worse	83	23	31	73	16	17	45
Total	100	100	100	99	100	100	100
(N)	(1,580)	(1,904)	(1,956)	(2,465)[b]	(1,700)[b]	(1,787)[b]	(1,196)[b]
			B. Percentage of Major-Party Voters Who Voted for the Incumbent Party Nominee for President[c]				
Better	58	80	77	86	75	69	87
(N)	(33)	(646)	(249)	(62)[b]	(458)[b]	(408)[b]	(211)[b]
Stayed same	71	53	53	62	45	45	58
(N)	(102)	(413)	(568)	(318)[b]	(443)[b]	(487)[b]	(243)[b]
Worse	39	21	34	32	33	31	20
(N)	(732)	(282)	(348)	(981)[b]	(130)[b]	(154)[b]	(319)[b]

[a] We combined the results using standard and experimental word ordering in 2000 and 2004.

[b] Numbers are weighted.

[c] The numbers in parentheses in part B of the table are the totals on which the percentages are based.

To this point, we have looked at personal and national economic conditions and the role of the government in shaping them. We have not yet looked at the extent to which such evaluations are attributed to the incumbent. In Table 7-5 we report responses to the question of whether people approved of the incumbent's handling of the economy from the 1980 through 2004 elections. While a majority approved of Reagan's handling of the economy in both 1984 and 1988, fewer than one in five held positive views of economic performance in the Carter administration. In 1992, evaluations of Bush were also very negative. In 1996, evaluations of Clinton's handling of the economy were stronger than those of incumbents in the previous surveys. By 2000, evaluations of Clinton's handling of the economy were even stronger, with three of every four respondents approving. As one might have guessed by this point, evaluations of Bush's handling of the economy in 2004 were not nearly as negative as those of Jimmy Carter or George H. W. Bush, but also not as positive as in any of the remaining years. Bush received four positive evaluations for every six negative ones.

The bottom-line question is whether these views are related to voter choice. As the data in Table 7-5B show, the answer is yes. Those who held positive views of the incumbent's performance on the economy were very likely to vote for his party's candidate, while those who didn't were just as likely to vote against him. In 2004, for example, Bush won the votes of nine in ten who approved and lost the votes of seven in eight who disapproved. George H. W. Bush's loss to Clinton among major-party voters in 1992 is attributable primarily to the heavily negative views of his stewardship of the economy, as was Carter's loss to Reagan in 1980. In 1984 and 1996 the incumbent president benefited primarily from positive assessments of his handling of the economy, as did the senior Bush, to a lesser extent, in 1988. In 2000 Gore suffered, in relative terms, by receiving less support from those who approved—and from those who disapproved. In 2004 we had a case of an incumbent winning reelection with, at best, mixed views of his stewardship of the economy, but Bush was able to win the votes of nine out of ten who thought he had done well. His ability to hold onto a sixth of the voters with negative views is, of course, one way of pinpointing how he won, because there were more of them, and if they had defected from supporting the incumbent at the same rate as approvers backed him, Bush would have been defeated.

FOREIGN POLICY EVALUATIONS AND THE VOTE FOR THE INCUMBENT

Foreign and economic policies are, as we described above, very commonly assessed retrospectively. They share the characteristics of consensual goals (prosperity and peace, respectively, plus security in both cases), complex technology, and difficulty in ascertaining relationships between means and ends. Foreign policy differs from economic policy in one practical way, however. As Table 6-1 illustrates, economic problems are invariably of major concern, but foreign affairs are salient only sporadically. The latter are of sufficiently sporadic concern that most

TABLE 7-5   Voters' Evaluations of the Incumbent's Handling of the Economy and Major-Party Vote, 1980–2004

Response	1980[a]	Approval of Incumbent's Handling of the Economy					
		1984	1988	1992	1996	2000	2004
A. Distribution of Responses (in percentages)							
Positive view	18	58	54	20	66	77	41
Balanced view	17	—	—	—	—	—	—
Negative view	65	42	46	80	34	23	59
Total	100	100	100	100	100	100	100
(N)	(1,097)	(1,858)	(1,897)	(2,425)[b]	(1,666)[b]	(1,686)[b]	(1,173)[b]
B. Percentage of Major-Party Voters Who Voted for the Incumbent Party Nominee for President[c]							
Positive view	88	86	80	90	79	67	91
(N)	(130)	(801)	(645)	(310)[b]	(688)[b]	(768)[b]	(341)[b]
Balanced view	60	—	—	—	—	—	—
(N)	(114)						
Negative view	23	16	17	26	13	11	17
(N)	(451)	(515)	(492)	(1,039)[b]	(322)[b]	(233)[b]	(431)[b]

[a] In 1980 the questions asked whether the respondent approved or disapproved of Carter's handling of inflation and whether the respondent approved of Carter's handling of unemployment. A positive view was to approve on both; balanced responses were to approve on one and disapprove on the other; and negative responses were to disapprove on both. In 1984, 1988, 1992, 1996, 2000, and 2004, responses were whether the respondent approved of [the president's] handling of the economy.

[b] Numbers are weighted.

[c] The numbers in parentheses in part B of the table are the totals on which the percentages are based.

TABLE 7-6   Evaluations of Three Foreign Policy Issues and Major-Party Vote, 2004

A. Evaluations of Issues (in percentages)			
	U.S. standing in the world over the past year	The war in [...] was worth the cost.	
		Afghanistan	Iraq
Weaker	46	Agree	70	40
Stayed the same	28			
Stronger	26	Disagree	30	60
Total	100		100	100
(N)	(1,197)[a]		(1,186)[a]	(1,172)[a]

B. Percentage of Major-Party Voters Holding These Views Who Voted Republican for President			
Weaker	24	Agree	65	91
(N)[b]	(374)[a]		(564)[a]	(328)[a]
Stayed the same	66			
(N)[b]	(204)[a]			
Stronger	83	Disagree	12	20
(N)[b]	(204)[a]		(211)[a]	(443)[b]

[a] Numbers are weighted.
[b] The numbers in parentheses in part B of the table are the totals on which the percentages are based.

surveys, including the NES, only occasionally have many measures to judge their role in elections. Foreign concerns loomed large in 2004, and the NES survey provided an unusually large array of measures for us to consider.

In the last chapter we examined two aspects of foreign policy and its relationship to voting. One was the unusually high level of concern about it. The other was addressed by the issue scale concerning using diplomacy or the military as the primary means of solving international problems. We saw that the public perceived the candidates to be remarkably far apart on that issue, and most voters met the conditions for casting an issue vote on it. In fact, voters displayed a higher level of apparent issue voting than we discovered on any issue in the previous six elections we have studied. Earlier in this chapter we saw that people also voted consistently with their preferences for the party they deemed better on handling the two foreign policy considerations. Here we add additional insight into the public's evaluations of foreign policy in the 2004 election.

Three questions that examined evaluations of foreign affairs over the recent past were included in the 2004 NES survey. One question asked whether the United States' standing in the world had gotten stronger, weaker, or stayed the same, and thus called for a general assessment about how well things had gone for the country in the world. The other two asked for respondents' evaluations of

TABLE 7-7   Distribution of Responses on President's Handling of Three
Foreign Policy Issues and Major-Party Vote, 2004

"Do you approve or disapprove of the way [the incumbent] is handling the [...]?"

A. Distribution of Responses (in percentages)

	War on terrorism	War in Iraq	Foreign relations
Approve	54	42	44
Disapprove	46	58	56
Total	100	100	100
(N)	(1,182)[a]	(1,193)[a]	(1,172)[a]

B. Percentage of Major-Party Voters Who Voted for
the Incumbent Party's Nominee

	War on terrorism	War in Iraq	Foreign relations
Approve	81	92	93
(N)[b]	(438)[a]	(347)[a]	(354)[a]
Disapprove	10	16	14
(N)[b]	(372)[a]	(432)[a]	(414)[a]

[a] Numbers are weighted.
[b] The numbers in parentheses in part B of the table are the totals on which the percentages are based.

the two ongoing wars, specifically whether the wars in Afghanistan and Iraq were worth the cost. The responses to these questions are reported in Table 7-6.

In Table 7-6A we can see that nearly half of the respondents thought the United States had gotten weaker in the world, while about a quarter thought the nation had gotten stronger, and the rest thought that there had been little change. This was hardly good news for the incumbent: We can see that in part B of that table that Bush won seven in eight votes from those who thought the United States had strengthened, and two in three from those who saw little change, but only one vote in four from the half who felt the nation had weakened. Looking at the two wars as particular cases of that more general view, we can see quite divergent views. Most (seven in ten) thought that the war in Afghanistan was worth the cost, but only two in five thought so about Iraq. Table 7-6B shows that opinion about Iraq was quite closely related to the vote, with Bush winning support from nine in ten of those who thought the war was worth the cost but from only two in ten of those who disagreed. It is, of course, less clear whether it was opinions about Iraq that shaped voting choices, or whether those who, for example, thought Bush was a good president agreed with his assessment that Iraq was worth the cost.[15] Still, the relationship between opinion and the vote on all three of these measures belies the belief that "voting ends at water's edge," that is, that voters choose on the basis of domestic considerations and pay little attention to and care little about foreign affairs.

Table 7-7 includes data on three measures of approval of Bush's performance: how well he handled the war on terrorism, the war in Iraq, and foreign relations more generally. Table 7-7A demonstrates that Bush generally won approval for his handling of the war on terrorism but was, on average, negatively evaluated on his handling of Iraq and foreign relations generally. In each case, the split was about the same, around 55 percent to 45 percent or only a bit more one-sided. And, as Table 7-7B shows, Bush won the votes of eight or nine—or even more— in ten approvers, while winning only one or two in ten of those who disapproved.

These results present clear and strong evidence that there are at least some cases—and 2004 is one of them—when international concerns can be of great importance to the public. Furthermore, citizens provide responses that display a good bit of variation from question to question, suggesting that they, in fact, hold relatively sophisticated views (compare, for example, the differences between views on Afghanistan and Iraq). Finally, these views are often strongly related to the vote, suggesting that foreign affairs played a major role in shaping the 2004 election.

EVALUATIONS OF THE INCUMBENT

Fiorina distinguishes between "simple" and "mediated" retrospective evaluations. By "simple" Fiorina means evaluations of the direct effects of social outcomes on the person, such as one's financial status, or direct perceptions of the nation's economic well-being. "Mediated" retrospective evaluations are evaluations seen through, or mediated by, the perceptions of political actors and institutions.[16] Approval of Bush's handling of the economy or the assessment of which party would better handle the war on terrorism are examples.

As we have seen, the more politically mediated the question, the more closely responses align with voting behavior. Perhaps the ultimate in mediated evaluations is the presidential approval question: "Do you approve or disapprove of the way [the incumbent] is handling his job as president?" From a retrospective voting standpoint, this evaluation is a summary of all aspects of his service in office. Table 7-8 reports the distribution of overall evaluations and their relationship to major-party voting in the past nine elections.[17]

As can be seen in Table 7-8A, incumbents Richard M. Nixon, Gerald Ford, Ronald Reagan, and Bill Clinton enjoyed widespread approval, whereas only two respondents in five approved of Jimmy Carter's and of George H. W. Bush's handling of the job. This presented Carter in 1980 and Bush in 1992 with a problem. Conversely, highly approved incumbents, such as Reagan in 1984 and Clinton in 1996—and their vice presidents as beneficiaries in 1988 and 2000—had a major advantage. Clinton dramatically reversed any negative perceptions of his incumbency that were held in 1994, such that by 1996 he received the highest level of approval in the fall of an election year since Nixon's landslide reelection in 1972. Between 1996 and 2000 Clinton suffered through scandals that culminated in his impeachment in 1998. Such events might be expected to lead to substantial declines in his approval ratings, but instead they remained high—higher even

TABLE 7-8 Distribution of Responses on President's Handling of Job and Major-Party Vote, 1972–2004

"Do you approve or disapprove of the way [the incumbent] is handling his job as president?"[a]

	1972[a]	1976	1980	1984	1988	1992	1996	2000	2004
A. Distribution of Responses (in percentages)									
Approve	71	63	41	63	60	43	68	67	51
Disapprove	29	37	59	37	40	57	32	33	49
Total	100	100	100	100	100	100	100	100	100
(N)	(1,215)	(2,439)[b]	(1,475)	(2,091)	(1,935)	(2,419)[b]	(1,692)[b]	(1,742)[b]	(1,182)[b]
B. Percentage of Major-Party Voters Who Voted for the Incumbent Party's Nominee[c]									
Approve	83	74	81	87	79	81	84	74	91
(N)	(553)	(935)[b]	(315)	(863)	(722)	(587)[b]	(676)[b]	(662)[b]	(408)[b]
Disapprove	14	9	18	7	12	11	4	13	6
(N)	(203)	(523)[b]	(491)	(449)	(442)	(759)[b]	(350)[b]	(366)[b]	(372)[b]

[a] Question was asked of a randomly selected half sample in 1972.
[b] Numbers are weighted.
[c] The numbers in parentheses in part B of the table are the totals on which the percentages are based.

than Reagan's at the end of his presidency. As we have seen several times, 2004 presents a more variegated picture. For the first time in nine elections, the proportions approving and disapproving were almost exactly the same.

If it is true that the more mediated the evaluation, the more closely it seems to align with behavior, and if presidential approval is the most mediated evaluation of all, then we would expect a powerful relationship with the vote. As Table 7-8B illustrates, that is true. Moreover, as has been true in most cases for both prospective and retrospective evaluations, 2004 stands out as a high-water mark in this evaluation. Over nine in ten who approved supported Bush; over nine in ten who disapproved voted against him.

THE IMPACT OF RETROSPECTIVE EVALUATIONS

Our evidence strongly suggests that retrospective voting has been widespread in all recent elections. Moreover, as far as data permit us to judge, the evidence is clearly on the side of the Downs-Fiorina view. Retrospective evaluations appear to be used to make comparative judgments. Presumably, voters find it easier, less time consuming, and less risky to evaluate the incumbent party on what its president did in the most recent term or terms in office than on the nominees' promises for the future. But few people base their votes on judgments of past performance alone. Most use past judgments as a starting point for comparing the major contenders with respect to their likely future performances.

In analyzing prior elections, we constructed an overall assessment of retrospective voting and compared that overall assessment across the various elections, and then we compared that net retrospective assessment with our balance of issues measure. Our measure was constructed by combining the presidential approval measure with the evaluation of the job the government has done on the most important problem and with the assessment of which party would better handle that problem. We cannot build this measure for studying the 2004 election because the survey did not include the question about which party would better handle the most important problem. But we can construct a similar measure, incorporating presidential approval, evaluation of the job the government has done on the most important problem, and assessment of which party would do better in handling the economy, handling the war on terrorism, and keeping us out of war.[18] This creates a seven-point scale ranging from "strongly opposed" to the job the incumbent and his party have done, to "strongly supportive" of that performance. For instance, those who approved of Bush's job performance, thought the government was doing a good job, and thought the Republican Party would better handle each of the three problems are scored as strongly supportive of Bush in their retrospective evaluations in 2004.

In Table 7-9 we present the results of this measure.[19] The figures indicate that there was a wide diversity of responses, with approximately equal support and opposition (with support ahead of opposition by 48 percent to 42 percent). That

TABLE 7-9 Distribution of the Electorate on the Summary Measure of Retrospective Evaluations and Major-Party Vote, 2004 (in percentages)

	Summary Measure of Retrospective Evaluations							
	Strongly opposed	←	— Neutral —	→			Strongly supportive	Total (N)
	A. Distribution of Responses							
Percentage	16	15	11	10	6	30	12	100
								(1,034)
	B. Major-Party Voters Who Voted for Kerry							
Percentage	99	95	89	66	28	5	1	50
(N)	(141)	(111)	(83)	(62)	(32)	(230)	(112)	(772)

Note: Numbers are weighted. The numbers in parentheses in part B of the table are the totals on which the percentages are based.

diversity includes a good bit of sharply divided opinion, akin to polarization, on this as apparently on so much else in 2004. Table 7-9B presents a remarkably clear example of a very strong relationship, with 99 out of 100 in each "strong" category voting for the appropriate candidate, and 95 of 100 doing so in the two "moderate" categories as well. Kerry did better than break even in the (relatively unpopulated) neutral category. These data strongly suggest that Bush's edge in retrospective evaluations may have been crucial in providing his slim margin of victory.

Of course, we cannot compare 2004 to any other election on this measure, but we can make at least broad generalizations.[20] In prior years it was reasonable to conclude that the 1980 election was a clear and strong rejection of Carter's incumbency. In 1984 Reagan won in large part because he was seen as having performed well and because Mondale was unable to convince the public that he would do better. In 1988 George H. W. Bush won in large part because Reagan was seen as having performed well—and people thought Bush would stay the course. In 1992 Bush lost because of far more negative evaluations of his administration and his party than had been recorded in any recent election except that of 1980. In 1996 Clinton won reelection in large part for the same reasons that Reagan won in 1984: he was seen as having performed well on the job, and he was able to convince the public that his opponent would not do any better. In 2000 Gore essentially tied George W. Bush because there was a slightly pro-incumbent set of evaluations combined with a very slight asymmetry against the incumbent in translating those evaluations into voting choices. In 2004 there was a slight victory for the incumbent because, by our different measure, more thought he had performed well than poorly.

How do retrospective assessments compare to prospective judgments? As you may recall from chapter 6, prospective issues, especially our balance of issues measure, have been increasingly strongly related to the vote over the past few

TABLE 7-10 Percentage of Major-Party Voters Who Voted for Bush, by Balance of Issues Measure and Summary Retrospective Measure, 2004

| Net balance of issues | Summary Retrospective | | | | | | | |
| | Republican | | Neutral | | Democratic | | Total | |
	%	(N)	%	(N)	%	(N)	%	(N)
Republican	96	(301)	49	(30)	11	(91)	75	(422)
Neutral	100	(21)	[1]	(2)	12	(23)	53	(45)
Democratic	77	(50)	20	(31)	2	(221)	16	(302)
Total	94	(372)	34	(62)	5	(335)	50	(787)

Note: Numbers are weighted. The numbers are the total number of major-party voters on which these percentages are based. In the one instance when that included fewer than ten major-party voters, we show the total number who voted for Bush. The Republican category on the condensed measure of retrospective voting includes any voter who scores as at least slightly supportive of the incumbent party on the seven-point measure, and the Democratic category includes voters who score as at least slightly opposed to the incumbent party. The neutral score is the same as the neutral score on the seven-point measure (see Table 7-9). The Republican category on the condensed measure on the balance of issues measure includes any voter who scores at least slightly Republican on the seven-point measure, and the Democratic category includes any voter who is at least slightly Democratic. The neutral category is the same as the neutral category on the seven-point measure (see Table 6-5).

elections, peaking in 2004. Table 7-10 reports the impact of both types of policy evaluations on the major-party vote in 2004. Both policy measures were collapsed into three categories: pro-Democratic, neutral, and pro-Republican. Reading across each row, we see that retrospective evaluations are very strongly related to the vote, even when one controls for prospective issues. Reading down each column, we see that prospective issues are modestly positively related to the vote, although they do have a clear impact among the relatively small number of voters with neutral scores on our measure of retrospective evaluations. Together, the two kinds of policy measures take us a long way toward understanding voting choices. More than nineteen in twenty of those with pro-Republican stances on the two measures, for example, voted for Bush, while nearly all of those with pro-Democratic stances voted for Kerry, and this accounting of voting choices is stronger when we consider both forms of policy evaluations than when we look at either one individually. Note that the two largest cells are those with pro-Bush views on both measures and those with pro-Kerry views on both, yet another indication of just how opinions pushed the voters into clear camps, based on their assessments of the candidates.[21]

CONCLUSION

In this and the previous chapter, we have found that both retrospective and prospective evaluations have been strongly related to voting. Indeed, in 1992 dissatisfaction with George H. W. Bush's performance and with his and his party's handling of the most important problem—usually an economic concern in 1992 (see Table 6-1)—goes a long way in explaining his defeat, while satisfaction with Clinton's performance and the absence of an advantage for the Republicans in being seen as able to deal with the most important concerns of voters go a long way in explaining his 1996 victory. In 2000, prospective issues favored neither candidate because essentially the same number of major-party voters were closer to Bush as were closer to Gore. The Democrat had a modest advantage on retrospective evaluations, but Bush won greater support among those with pro-Republican evaluations than Gore did among those with pro-Democratic evaluations. The result was another even balance and, as a result, a tie. Although Kerry was favored on prospective evaluations in 2004,[22] that was offset by Bush's slight advantage based on retrospective evaluations, leading to a reelection victory with only a slight gain in the popular vote.

Our explanation remains incomplete, however. Most important, we have not accounted for *why* people hold the views they expressed on these two measures. We cannot provide a complete account of the origins of people's views, of course, but there is one important source that we can examine: Party identification, a variable we have used in previous chapters, provides a powerful means for the typical citizen to reach preliminary judgments. As we will see, partisanship is strongly related to these judgments, especially to retrospective evaluations.

Moreover, party identification plays a central role in debates about the future of American politics. Will the small Republican gains in popular support for the president between 2000 and 2004, the noticeable gains for the GOP in the Senate, and the slight advances in the House lead to a long-term Republican majority, perhaps even a partisan realignment? A dealignment? Or will the Democrats rebound and gain control of the White House in 2008, or some other part or parts of the federal government? Many political scientists believe that change of this magnitude in the political system can come only if there are changes in party loyalties in the electorate, as well as in its voting behavior. Therefore, to understand voter choice better and to assess future partisan prospects, we must examine the role of party loyalties.

Chapter 8

Party Loyalties, Policy Preferences, and the Vote

In chapter 5 we discussed the influence of social forces, such as race, ethnicity, and social class, on voting behavior. There we noted, for example, that African Americans do not vote Democratic simply because of their race. Instead, race and other social forces provide the context in which electoral politics is set and thus in which voters reach their decisions. In chapters 6 and 7, in contrast, we studied the effects of issues (and, briefly, evaluations of the candidates) on the vote. Reactions to issues and approval of George W. Bush's handling of the presidency might have caused a voter to support him, but what is missing there is why that voter, like half of the electorate, approved of Bush's performance, while half did not. The most important factor that helps connect the social setting, which stands in the background, with the more immediate assessments of issues and the candidates is partisanship. Thus, a major part of the explanation of why African Americans vote overwhelmingly Democratic lies in the various events and actions that have made the Democratic Party attractive (and the Republican Party unattractive) to African Americans, and a major part of the explanation of why some people approved of Bush's performance, while others did not, is whether they are Republicans or Democrats. But partisanship not only stands in between one's social, economic, and demographic background and evaluations of the issues and candidates in the current election. Party is the third of the triumvirate of "candidates, issues, and parties," that is, evaluations of the parties are one of three major forces that shape voting behavior.

Partisanship is not the only force that helps connect context and evaluation, but it has proved to be by far the most important for understanding elections. And its dual role in affecting voting both directly and indirectly makes it unusually critical in understanding why American citizens vote as they do.

Most Americans identify with a political party—a first reason why party is so central. Second, their identification influences their political attitudes and, ultimately, their behavior. In the 1950s and 1960s the authors of *The American Voter*, along with other scholars, began to emphasize the role of party loyalties.[1] Although today few people would deny that partisanship is central to political attitudes and behavior, many scholars question the interpretation of the evidence that has accumulated over this period. We ask two questions: What is party identification? and How does it actually structure other attitudes and behavior? We then examine the role that party identification played in the 2004 presidential election.

PARTY IDENTIFICATION: THE STANDARD VIEW

According to Angus Campbell and his colleagues, party identification is "the individual's affective orientation to an important group-object in his environment," in this case the political party.[2] In other words, an individual sees that there are two major political parties that play significant roles in elections and develops an affinity for one of them. Partisanship, therefore, represents an evaluation of the two parties, but its implications extend to a wider variety of political phenomena. Campbell and his colleagues measured partisanship by asking individuals which party they identified with and how strong that identification was.[3] If an individual did not identify with one of the parties, he or she may have either "leaned" toward a party or been a "pure" independent. Individuals who could not answer the party identification questions were classified as "apolitical."[4] Most Americans develop a preference for either the Republican or the Democratic Party. Very few identify with any third party. The remainder are mostly independents who, according to this classic view, not only are unattached to a party but also are relatively unattached to politics in general. They are less interested, less informed, and less active than those who identify with a party.

Partisan identification in this view becomes an attachment or loyalty similar to that between the individual and other groups or organizations in society, such as a religious body, a social class, or even a favorite sports team. As with loyalties to many of those groups, partisan affiliation often begins early. One of the first political attitudes children develop is partisan identification, and it develops well before they acquire policy preferences and many other political orientations. Furthermore, as with other group loyalties, once an attachment to a party develops, it tends to endure. Some people do switch parties, of course, but they usually do so only if their social situation changes dramatically, if there is an issue of overriding concern that sways their loyalties, or if the political parties themselves change substantially.

Party identification, then, stands as a base or core orientation to electoral politics. It is formed at an early age and endures for most people throughout their lives.[5] Once formed, this core orientation, predicated on a general evaluation of the two parties, affects many other specific orientations. Democratic loyalists tend to rate Democratic candidates and officeholders more highly than Republican candidates and officeholders, and vice versa. In effect, one is predisposed to evaluate the promises and performance of one's party leaders relatively more favorably. It follows, therefore, that Democrats are more likely to vote for Democratic candidates than are Republicans, and vice versa.

PARTY IDENTIFICATION: AN ALTERNATIVE VIEW

In *The Responsible Electorate,* published in 1966, V. O. Key Jr. argued that party loyalties contributed to electoral inertia and that many partisans voted as "standpatters" from election to election.[6] That is, in the absence of any information to the contrary, or if the attractions and disadvantages of the candidates are fairly evenly balanced, partisans are expected to vote for the candidate of their party. Voting for their party's candidates is their "standing decision," until and unless voters are given good reasons not to. More recently, scholars have reexamined the bases of such behavior. In this new view, citizens who consider themselves Democrats have a standing decision to vote for the Democratic nominee because of the past positions of the Democrats and the Republicans and because of the parties' comparative past performances while in office. In short, this view of partisan identification presumes that it is a "running tally" of past experiences (mostly in terms of policy and performance), a sort of summary expression of political memory, according to Morris P. Fiorina.[7]

Furthermore, when in doubt about, for example, what a Democratic candidate is likely to do on civil rights, in comparison to the Republican opponent, it is reasonable to assume that the Democrat will be more liberal than the Republican—unless the candidates indicate otherwise. Because the political parties tend to be consistent on the basic historical policy cleavages, summary judgments of parties and their typical candidates will not change radically or often.[8] As a result, a citizen's running tally serves as a good first approximation, changes rarely, and can be an excellent device for saving time and effort that would be spent gathering information in the absence of this "memory."

Many of the major findings adduced in support of the conventional interpretation of party identification are completely consistent with this more policy-oriented view. We do not have the evidence to assert that one view is superior to the other. Indeed, the two interpretations are not mutually exclusive. Moreover, they share the important conclusion that party identification plays a central role in shaping voters' decisions. These two views remain widely studied today, with adherents of each view enriching and extending the core positions on each side. For example, Robert S. Erikson, Michael B. MacKuen, and James A. Stimson have recently argued that an updated version of the Key-Downs-Fiorina view of partisanship is one of the central concepts for understanding what they call the "macro polity," that is, for explaining how political leaders, institutions, and policy respond to changes in aggregate public opinion.[9] They argue that partisanship in the electorate changes with macro-level conditions, such as inflation and unemployment rates, akin to the Key-Downs-Fiorina view. In turn, political elites react to such changes in "macro-partisanship," among other aspects of public opinion and beliefs. On the other side, Donald Green, Bradley Palmquist, and Eric Schickler have recently developed an elegant account of the affective base of partisan identification and its stability over time.[10] Their view is the modern version of the original account by Campbell et al. As recent exchanges have shown, the two sets of authors differ substantially in their interpretations of what partisanship means, although empirical differences are slighter.[11]

Both views agree that partisan identifications are long-term forces in politics. Both agree that, for most people, such identifications are formed early in life; children often develop a partisan loyalty, which they usually learn from their parents, although these loyalties are seldom explicitly taught. Both views recognize that partisan loyalties contribute to voter participation, as we demonstrated in chapter 4. Partisan identifications also are often closely associated with social forces, as discussed in chapter 5, especially when a social group is actively engaged in partisan politics. An important illustration of this point is the affiliation of many labor unions with the New Deal Democratic coalition, which often reinforced the tendency of those who were in labor unions to identify with the Democratic Party. This is similar to the affiliation of evangelical and other religious groups on the right with the Republican Party today, reinforcing the tendency of individuals who share such religious beliefs to identify with the Republican Party. Finally, both views agree that partisanship is closely associated with more immediate evaluations, including prospective and retrospective evaluations of the issues and candidates, as analyzed in chapters 6 and 7.

The two views disagree about the nature of the linkage between partisanship and other attitudes, such as those toward the candidates and issues. The standard view argues that partisanship, as a long-term loyalty, affects voters' evaluations of issues and candidates, but that it, in turn, is largely unaffected by such evaluations, except in such dramatic circumstances as realigning elections. In this sense, partisanship is a "filter" through which the concerns relevant to the particular election are viewed. In the alternative view, partisanship as a running tally may affect, but is also affected by, more immediate concerns. Fiorina's definition of partisanship makes clear that the running tally includes current as well as past assessments. Distinguishing empirically between these two views is therefore quite difficult. Although the alternative view may see partisan identification as being affected by retrospective and prospective assessments of the issues and candidates in the current election, such assessments rarely change an individual's identification because the effect of past experiences and the influence of initial socialization are strong. We shall analyze the role of partisan identification in 2004 and other recent elections in ways consistent with both major views of partisan identification.

PARTY IDENTIFICATION IN THE ELECTORATE

If partisan identification is a fundamental orientation for most citizens, then the distribution of partisan loyalties is crucial. The National Election Studies (NES) have monitored the party loyalties of the American electorate since 1952. In Table 8-1 we show the basic distributions of partisan loyalties in presidential election years from 1980 through 2004. As the table shows, most Americans identify with a political party. In 2004 about three in five claimed to think of themselves as a Democrat or as a Republican, and three in ten more, who initially said they were independent or had no partisan preference, nonetheless said they felt closer to one of the major parties than to the other.[12] One in ten was purely independent of party, and fewer than one in one hundred was classified as "apolitical." One of the largest changes in partisanship in the electorate began in the mid-1960s, when more people claimed to be independents.[13] The growth in the number of independents stopped, however, in the late 1970s and early 1980s. There was very little change in partisan loyalties between the 1984 and 1992 surveys.

There were signs in 1996 of reversal of the trend toward greater independence. All partisan groups increased slightly in 1996 compared with 1992, and the 8 percent of pure independents (that is, those with no partisan leanings) was the lowest percentage since 1968. The decline in independence stopped, however, and the percentages of independents in 2000 and 2004 were about the same as during the 1980s.

Table 8-1 also shows that more people think of themselves as Democrats than as Republicans. Over the past forty years, the balance between the two parties has favored the Democrats by about 55/45 to about 60/40. The results from the last six presidential election years fall within that range, although more often toward the narrower division. From 1984 through 2000, there was a clear shift toward the Republicans. In 1980, 35 percent of partisans were Republicans; in 1984, 42 percent were; by 1988, 44 percent were; in 1992 and in 1996, 43 percent of partisans were; and in 2000, 42 percent were Republicans. Including independents who leaned toward a party would increase the percentage of Republicans to 38 percent in 1980, 45 percent in 1984, and 47 percent in 1988. That figure dropped to 44 percent in 1992 and 1996, and then 43 percent in 2000. Thus the Democratic advantage in loyalties in the electorate narrowed. In 2004, the (strong and weak) Democrats led comparable Republicans in the NES survey, with 33 percent of the total versus 29 percent (or 54/46). The percentage of independents who leaned Democrat, however, reached a high of 17 percent, while the figure for those leaning Republican was 12 percent. Including leaners, therefore, means that the Democrats hold the loyalties of half the respondents, while Republican identifiers make up two in five respondents, keeping the partisan balance within the historical pattern of a slight Democratic lead. The Democratic advantage is made smaller in practice by the tendency of the Republicans to have higher turnout than the Democrats (see chapter 4).

TABLE 8-1 Party Identification in Presidential Election Years, Preelection Surveys, 1980–2004 (in percentages)

Party identification	1980	1984	1988	1992	1996	2000	2004
Strong Democrat	18	17	18	17	18	19	17
Weak Democrat	24	20	18	18	20	15	16
Independent, leans Democratic	12	11	12	14	14	15	17
Independent, no partisan leanings	13	11	11	12	8	12	10
Independent, leans Republican	10	13	14	13	12	13	12
Weak Republican	14	15	14	15	16	12	12
Strong Republican	9	13	14	11	13	12	17
Total	100	100	101	100	101	98	101
(N)	(1,577)	(2,198)	(1,999)	(2,450)[a]	(1,696)[a]	(1,777)[a]	(1,193)[a]
Apolitical	2	2	2	1	1	1	—[b]
(N)	(35)	(38)	(33)	(23)	(14)	(21)	(3)

[a] Numbers are weighted.
[b] Less than 1 percent.

One can also analyze the partisan loyalties of the American electorate through other surveys, and doing so reveals some differences from the 2004 NES. Among the other surveys, the most important and useful are the General Social Surveys (GSS) conducted by the National Opinion Research Council (NORC). Those surveys, usually based on about 1,500 respondents, who are interviewed in person, employ the standard party identification questions developed by the authors of *The American Voter* to measure long-term attachment to the political parties. The GSS have been conducted in most years since 1972.[14] Like the NES surveys, the GSS reveal some Republican gains: From 1972 through 1982, the percentage of party identifiers supporting the Republicans never rose above 37 percent, and even if independent leaners are included as partisans, support for the GOP never rose beyond 38 percent. The GOP made gains in 1983, and in 1984 the percentage of party identifiers who were Republican rose to 40 percent. Republican strength peaked in the 1990 GSS, which showed 48 percent of all party identifiers as Republicans, and if independents who leaned toward a party are included, 49 percent were Republicans. But the Republicans made no further gains, even in the 1991 survey conducted during and shortly after the Persian Gulf War. In the February–April 2000 survey, 43 percent of all party identifiers were Republican, and the total remains at 43 percent even when independent leaners are included. Only 25 percent were strong party identifiers, and 20 percent were independents who leaned toward neither political party. The 2004 GSS differed from the 2004 NES in two notable ways: First, the GSS found 16 percent pure independents, compared to 10 percent in the NES. Note, however, that that figure is a decline from the 20 percent that the GSS recorded in 2000, and in that way it is similar to the NES results. Second, the possible "polarization" of partisanship that we noted above is not as pronounced as in the NES—in the GSS, 29 percent were strong partisans, and 33 percent weak, compared to 34 percent strong and 28 percent weak partisans in the NES. But one similarity may be more important than any difference: both the NES and the GSS found the highest percentage of strong Republicans that either of these surveys had ever found over the entire period during which they have been conducted.

Our analysis of the NES surveys reveals that the shift toward the Republican Party is concentrated among white Americans. As we saw in chapter 5, the sharpest social division in U.S. electoral politics is race, and this division has been reflected in partisan loyalties for decades. Moreover, the racial gap appears to be widening, with a sharp increase in 2004. Although the distribution of partisanship in the electorate as a whole has changed only slightly since 1984, that stability masks a growth in Republican identification among whites and a compensating growth of already strong Democratic loyalties among African Americans. In Table 8-2 we report the party identification of whites between 1980 and 2004, and in Table 8-3 the party identification of blacks. In comparable tables in the appendix (Tables A8-2 and A8-3), we report the party identification of whites and of blacks between 1952 and 1978. As the tables show, black and white patterns in partisan loyalties have been very different throughout this period. There was a

TABLE 8-2 Party Identification among Whites, 1980–2004 (in percentages)

Party identification[a]	1980	1982	1984	1986	1988	1990	1992	1994	1996	1998	2000	2002	2004
Strong Democrat	14	16	15	14	14	17	14	12	15	15	15	12	13
Weak Democrat	23	24	18	21	16	19	17	19	19	18	14	16	12
Independent, leans Democratic	12	11	11	10	10	11	14	12	13	14	15	14	17
Independent, no partisan leaning	14	11	11	12	12	11	12	10	8	11	13	8	8
Independent, leans Republican	11	9	13	13	15	13	14	13	12	12	14	15	13
Weak Republican	16	16	17	17	15	16	16	16	17	18	14	17	15
Strong Republican	9	11	14	12	16	11	12	17	15	11	14	17	21
Apolitical	2	2	2	2	1	1	1	1	1	2	1	1	—[a]
Total	101	100	101	101	99	99	100	100	100	101	100	100	99
(N)	(1,405)	(1,248)	(1,931)	(1,798)	(1,693)	(1,663)	(2,702)[b]	(1,510)[b]	(1,451)[b]	(1,091)[b]	(1,404)[b]	(1,129)[b]	(859)[b]

[a] The percentage supporting another party has not been presented; it usually totals less than 1 percent and never totals more than 1 percent.
[b] Numbers are weighted.

TABLE 8-3 Party Identification among Blacks, 1980–2004 (in percentages)

Party identification[a]	1980	1982	1984	1986	1988	1990	1992	1994	1996	1998	2000	2002	2004
Strong Democrat	45	53	32	42	39	40	40	38	43	48	47	53	30
Weak Democrat	27	26	31	30	24	23	24	23	22	23	21	16	30
Independent, leans democratic	9	12	14	12	18	16	14	20	16	12	14	17	20
Independent, no partisan leaning	7	5	11	7	6	8	12	8	10	7	10	6	12
Independent, leans Republican	3	1	6	2	5	7	3	4	5	3	4	2	5
Weak Republican	2	2	1	2	5	3	3	2	3	3	3	4	2
Strong Republican	3	0	2	2	1	2	2	3	1	1	0	2	1
Apolitical	4	1	2	2	3	2	2	3	0	2	1	—[b]	—[b]
Total	100	100	99	99	101	101	100	101	100	99	100	100	100
(N)	(187)	(148)	(247)	(322)	(267)	(270)	(317)[c]	(203)[c]	(200)[c]	(149)[c]	(225)[c]	(161)[c]	(193)[c]

[a] The percentage supporting another party has not been presented; it usually totals less than 1 percent and never totals more than 1 percent.
[b] Empty cells indicate less than 1 percent.
[c] Numbers are weighted.

sharp shift in black loyalties in the mid-1960s. Before then, about 50 percent of African Americans were strong or weak Democrats; since that time, 60 percent to 70 percent—and even more—of blacks have considered themselves Democrats.

The party loyalties of whites have changed more slowly. Still, the percentage of self-professed Democrats among whites declined over the Reagan years, while the percentage of Republicans increased. In the past five elections partisanship by race has changed, with shifts among whites. If independents who lean Republican are included, there was close to an even balance between the two parties among whites in 1984. By 1988 the numbers of strong and weak Democrats and strong and weak Republicans were virtually the same, with more strong Republicans than strong Democrats for the first time. Adding in the two groups of independent leaners gives Republicans a clear advantage in identification among whites. In 1992, however, that advantage disappeared. There were slightly more strong and weak Democrats than strong and weak Republicans. In 1996 all four of the partisan categories were larger, by one to three points, than in 1992. The result was that the balance of Republicans to Democrats changed very slightly, and the near-parity of identifiers with the two parties among whites remained. By 2000 the parity was even more striking. But 2002 revealed a substantial increase in Republican identification among whites, one that was constant in terms of the three Republican groups in 2004. Democratic identification declined slightly, such that by 2004 there was a four-point decrease of strong and weak Democrats compared to 2000, partially balanced by a two-point gain among independent leaners. Pure independents among whites declined sharply to 8 percent in both 2002 and 2004, a decline of five percentage points from 2000 (Table 8-2). Although that was a figure reached in 1996 as well, 8 percent is more typical of the 1950s and early 1960s. Weak and leaning Republican responses were essentially the same in 2004 as in 2000, but the dramatic change was the four-point increase in strong Republicans, to 21 percent, for the first time the largest category of response among whites (although it had been tied with weak Republicans for that lead in 2002). The decline in pure independents and growth in strong Republicans is one possible sign that, perhaps, the white electorate is polarizing somewhat by party. As a result, the three Republican groups constitute very nearly one-half of the white electorate and lead Democrats by a 49/42 margin.

Although the increased Republicanism of the white electorate is partly the result of long-term forces, such as generational replacement, the actual movement between 1964 and 1988 appears to be the result of two shorter-term increases in Republican identification. There was a five-percentage-point movement toward the GOP from 1964 through 1968, and a ten-point movement toward the GOP occurred between 1982 and 1988. This movement waned modestly in the 1990s, as we saw. In 2000 the Republican categories, like the Democratic categories, had declined about equally, while the pure independent category had increased from 8 percent to 13 percent of the white electorate between 1996 and 2000. The increase in Republican identification from 2000 to 2002 and 2004 constitutes a third short-term change.

Party identification among blacks is very different, as Table 8-3 shows. In 2004 there were very few black Republicans. Indeed, only 8 percent of blacks chose any of the three Republican identification categories, and 3 percent were strong or weak Republicans. John F. Kerry was occasionally criticized for not making sufficiently strenuous or effective appeals to the minority communities. Perhaps as a result, although blacks remained loyal to the Democratic Party, the strength of their attachment waned noticeably, with growth among weak and independent-leaning Democrats offsetting the sharp decline among strong Democrats.

These racial differences in partisanship are long-standing, and over time, changes have increased the division. Between 1952 and 1962, blacks were primarily Democratic, but about one in seven supported the Republicans (see Table A8-3 in the appendix). Black partisanship shifted massively and abruptly even further toward the Democratic Party in 1964. In that year, over half of all black voters considered themselves *strong* Democrats. Since then, well over half have identified with the Democratic Party. Black Republican identification fell to barely a trace in 1964 and has edged up only slightly since then.

The abrupt change in black loyalties in 1964 reflects the two presidential nominees of that year. President Lyndon B. Johnson's advocacy of civil rights legislation appealed directly to black voters, and his Great Society and War on Poverty programs in general made an only slightly less direct appeal. Sen. Barry M. Goldwater, Ariz., the Republican nominee, voted against the 1964 Civil Rights Act, a vote criticized even by many of his Republican peers. Party stances have not changed appreciably since then, although the proportion of blacks who were strong Democrats declined somewhat after 1968.[15]

Also in 1964, the proportion of blacks considered apolitical dropped from the teens to a very small proportion, similar to that among whites. This shift resulted from the civil rights movement, the contest between Johnson and Goldwater, and the passage of the Civil Rights Act. The civil rights movement stimulated many blacks, especially in the South, to become politically active. Furthermore, the 1965 Voting Rights Act enabled many of them to vote for the first time.

PARTY IDENTIFICATION AND THE VOTE

As we saw in chapter 4, partisanship is related to turnout. Strong supporters of either party are more likely to vote than weak supporters, and independents who lean toward a party are more likely to vote than independents without partisan leanings. Republicans are somewhat more likely to vote than Democrats. Although partisanship influences whether people vote, it is more strongly related to *how* people vote.

Table 8-4 reports the percentage of white major-party voters who voted for the Democratic candidate, across all categories of partisanship, since 1952.[16] Clearly, there is a strong relationship between partisan identification and choice of candidate. In every election except 1972 the Democratic nominee has received more

TABLE 8-4 Percentage of White Major-Party Voters Who Voted Democratic for President, by Party Identification, 1952–2004

Party identification	1952	1956	1960	1964	1968	1972	1976	1980	1984	1988	1992	1996	2000	2004
Strong Democrat	82	85	91	94	89	66	88	87	88	93	96	98	96	97
Weak Democrat	61	63	70	81	66	44	72	59	63	68	80	88	81	78
Independent, leans Democratic	60	65	89	89	62	58	73	57	77	86	92	91	72	88
Independent, no partisan leanings	18	15	50	75	28	26	41	23	21	35	63	58	44	54
Independent, leans Republican	7	6	13	25	5	11	15	13	5	13	14	26	15	13
Weak Republican	4	7	11	40	10	9	22	5	6	16	18	21	16	10
Strong Republican	2	—[a]	2	9	3	2	3	4	2	2	2	3	1	3

Note: To approximate the numbers on which these percentages are based, see Tables 8-2 and A8-2 (appendix). Actual *N*s will be smaller than those that can be derived from these tables because respondents who did not vote (or voted for a non-major-party candidate) have been excluded from the calculations. Numbers also will be lower since the voting report is provided in the postelection interviews, which usually contain about 10 percent fewer respondents than the preelection interviews in which party identification is measured.

[a] Less than 1 percent.

than 80 percent of the votes of strong Democrats and majority support from both weak Democratic partisans and independent Democratic leaners. In 1996 these figures were higher than in any other election in the period. Although they fell somewhat in 2000, especially for independents leaning Democratic, that reversed in 2004, with Kerry holding onto very large majorities of those who identified with the Democratic Party, including nearly nine of ten independents who leaned Democratic. Since 1952, strong Republicans have given the Democratic candidate less than one vote in ten. In 1988 more of the weak Republicans and independents who leaned Republican voted for Michael S. Dukakis than had voted for Walter F. Mondale, but, even so, only about one in seven voted Democratic. In 1992 Clinton won an even larger percentage of the two-party vote from these Republicans, and he increased his support among Republicans again in 1996. In 2000 George W. Bush held essentially the same level of support in the three white Republican categories as his father had in 1988 and 1992. But in 2004 Kerry won virtually no support from strong Republicans, and Bush won about nine in ten votes in the other two Republican categories. The pure independent vote, which fluctuates substantially, has tended to be Republican. John F. Kennedy won 50 percent of that vote in 1960, and Bill Clinton won nearly two-thirds of the pure independents' two-party votes in 1992 and nearly three-fifths of the white independent vote in 1996. Gore was able to carry only two in five such votes in 2000, but Kerry was able to win 54 percent of the pure independent vote. Thus, at least among major-party voters, Bush won the popular vote by a tiny margin because he held his own white party identifiers just a little more strongly than Kerry held white Democrats. Kerry's slight edge among pure independents was offset by Bush's ability to hold onto his weak partisan supporters better than Kerry did, even though Kerry did better among white Democrats than most of his party's nominees have in recent elections.

Nearly all blacks vote Democratic, regardless of their partisan affiliation. Even the handful of black Republicans are likely to vote Democratic. As a result, there is no relationship between party identification and the vote among African Americans.

Between 1964 and 1980 the relationship between party identification and the vote was declining among whites, but in 1984 it was higher than in any of the five elections from 1964 through 1980. The relationship remained strong in 1988 and continued to be quite strong in the two Clinton elections and the Gore-Bush contest, at least among major-party voters. The question of whether the parties are gathering new strength at the presidential level could not be answered definitively from the 2000 election data, but the 2004 data now make it clear that these growing signs have become a strong trend, such that party identification is as strongly related to the presidential vote as it has been since the NES surveys began. The relationship between party identification and voting in general will be reconsidered in chapter 10, when we assess its relationship to the congressional vote.[17]

Partisanship is related to the way people vote. The question, therefore, is, Why do partisans support their party's candidates? As we shall see, party identification affects behavior because it helps structure (and, according to Fiorina, is structured by) the way voters view both policies and performance.

POLICY PREFERENCES AND PERFORMANCE EVALUATIONS

In their study of voting in the 1948 election, Bernard R. Berelson, Paul F. Lazarsfeld, and William N. McPhee discovered that Democratic voters attributed to their nominee, incumbent Harry S. Truman, positions on key issues that were consistent with their beliefs—whether those beliefs were liberal, moderate, or conservative.[18] Similarly, Republicans tended to see their nominee, Gov. Thomas E. Dewey of New York, as taking whatever positions they preferred. Research since then has emphasized the role of party identification not only in the projection onto the preferred candidate of positions similar to the voter's own views, but in shaping the policy preferences of the public as well.[19] We use four examples to illustrate the strong relationship between partisan affiliation and perceptions, preferences, and evaluations of candidates.

First, most partisans evaluate the job done by a president of their party more positively than do independents and, especially, more positively than those who identify with the other party. Figure 8-1 shows the percentage of each of the seven partisan groups that approved of the way the incumbent had handled his job as president (as a proportion of those approving or disapproving) in the past eight presidential elections, and Table A8-1 in the appendix presents the percentages who approved of the president according to party identification. Strong partisans of the incumbent's party typically give overwhelming approval to that incumbent. It is not invariably guaranteed, however. In 1980, "only" three strong Democrats in four approved of Jimmy Carter, but even in 2000, shortly after Bill Clinton's impeachment and despite the various scandals in which he was enmeshed, all Democratic categories gave Clinton very high marks. In all but 1980 and 1992, independents have approved of the incumbent. In 1972, 1976, and 1984 through 1992, that meant that they approved of a Republican incumbent, but in 1996 and 2000, they approved of a Democratic incumbent. In both 1996 and 2000, about half of the independents who leaned Republican and the weak Republicans approved of Clinton, which is not unlike the percentages that popular Republican incumbents received from weak Democrats and Democratic-leaning independents in 1972, 1984, 1988, and even 1976. Strong partisans, however, rarely approve of an incumbent of the other party, as the data in Figure 8-1 illustrate. And, as those data also illustrate, 2004 was no exception. Virtually all strong Republicans, and a very high percentage of weak Republicans, approved of Bush, and more than three in four independents who lean Republican did as well. The Democrats, for their part, disapproved to nearly the same degree, and only two in five pure independents approved. Overall, the relationship between partisan identification and approval of the incumbent was stronger than in any election between 1972 and 2000.

FIGURE 8-1   Approval of Incumbent's Handling of Job, by Party Identification, 1972–2004

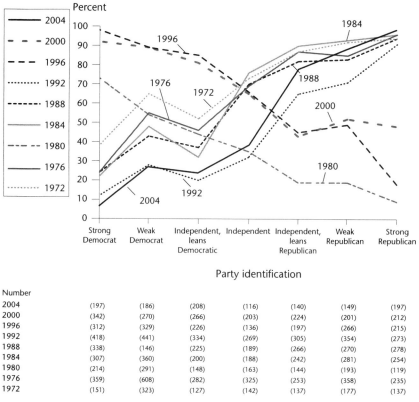

Number							
2004	(197)	(186)	(208)	(116)	(140)	(149)	(197)
2000	(342)	(270)	(266)	(203)	(224)	(201)	(212)
1996	(312)	(329)	(226)	(136)	(197)	(266)	(215)
1992	(418)	(441)	(334)	(269)	(305)	(354)	(273)
1988	(338)	(146)	(225)	(189)	(266)	(270)	(278)
1984	(307)	(360)	(200)	(188)	(242)	(281)	(254)
1980	(214)	(291)	(148)	(163)	(144)	(193)	(119)
1976	(359)	(608)	(282)	(325)	(253)	(358)	(235)
1972	(151)	(323)	(127)	(142)	(137)	(177)	(137)

Our second illustration extends the connection we have drawn between partisanship and approval of the incumbent. In this case we examine the relationship between partisanship and approval of the incumbent's handling of the economy. Table 8-5 shows the relationship among all seven partisan categories and approval of the handling of the economy by Ronald Reagan in 1984 and 1988, George H. W. Bush in 1992, Clinton in 1996 and 2000, and George W. Bush in 2004.[20]

In 1984 and 1988 more than three-quarters of each of the three Republican groups approved of Reagan's handling of the economy, and more than half—often more than two-thirds—of the three Democratic groups disapproved. Independents generally approved of Reagan's economic efforts, albeit more strongly in 1984 than in 1988. The 1992 election was dramatically different, with overwhelming disapproval of Bush's handling of the economy among the three Democratic groups and the pure independents. Even two-thirds of the weak Republicans and Republican-leaning independents disapproved. Only strong Republicans typically approved, and even then, one in three did not. The relationship in 1996

TABLE 8-5 Approval of Incumbent's Handling of the Economy among Partisan Groups, 1984–2004 (in percentages)

Year	Attitude toward handling of the economy	Strong Democrat	Weak Democrat	Independent, leans Democrat	Independent	Independent, leans Republican	Weak Republican	Strong Republican	Total
					Party Identification				
1984	Approve	17	41	32	68	84	86	95	58
	Disapprove	83	59	68	32	16	14	5	42
	Total	100	100	100	100	100	100	100	100
	(N)	(309)	(367)	(207)	(179)	(245)	(277)	(249)	(1,833)
1988	Approve	19	35	32	57	76	79	92	54
	Disapprove	81	65	68	43	24	21	8	46
	Total	100	100	100	100	100	100	100	100
	(N)	(337)	(332)	(229)	(185)	(262)	(262)	(269)	(1,876)
1992[a]	Approve	3	9	6	9	31	34	66	20
	Disapprove	97	91	94	91	69	66	34	80
	Total	100	100	100	100	100	100	100	100
	(N)	(425)	(445)	(340)	(267)	(310)	(347)	(266)	(2,401)
1996[a]	Approve	96	82	76	58	46	49	30	66
	Disapprove	4	18	24	42	54	50	70	34
	Total	100	100	100	100	100	100	100	100
	(N)	(310)	(325)	(228)	(131)	(188)	(263)	(209)	(1,655)
2000[a]	Approve	95	90	84	73	60	70	47	77
	Disapprove	5	10	16	27	40	30	53	23
	Total	100	100	100	100	100	100	100	100
	(N)	(342)	(265)	(264)	(198)	(206)	(184)	(200)	(1,659)
2004[a]	Approve	5	18	10	34	68	72	89	40
	Disapprove	95	82	90	66	32	28	11	60
	Total	100	100	100	100	100	100	100	100
	(N)	(197)	(176)	(204)	(107)	(139)	(141)	(194)	(1,158)

[a] Numbers are weighted.

is most like that of 1984. In 2000 Clinton received even higher approval levels for his handling of the economy. As a result, the vast majority of Democrats, and even three in four of the pure independents, approved of his economic performance. That represented by far the highest level of economic-approval that independents have given. But then, most Republicans also approved. In 2004 the weak but improving economy meant that Bush was approved by "only" nine in ten strong and about seven in ten weak Republicans and independents leaning Republican. Democratic disapproval reached very high levels, and once again pure independents did not favor Bush, only one in three approving of his handling of the economy. Thus, while showing some differences from election to election (typically related to changes in the economy), the relationship between partisanship and approval of the incumbent's economic performance is clear and strong.

The third example of the impact of partisanship on attitudes and beliefs is its relationship to positions on policy issues. In Table 8-6, we report the relationship between the seven partisan categories and our balance of issues measure, developed in chapter 6, collapsed into a threefold grouping of pro-Republican, neutral, and pro-Democratic.[21] As we saw in chapter 6, these issues favored the Republicans in 1972, 1976, and 1980, worked slightly to the Democrats' advantage in 1984, 1988, and 1992, and then once again favored the Republicans in 1996, 2000, and 2004. In all cases, the balance of issues measure has only moderately favored one party over the other.

As the table shows, there has regularly been a clear and moderately strong relationship between partisanship and the balance of issues measure, but the relationship is one that, by 2000 and 2004, had strengthened considerably. Until 1984 the relationship had been stronger among Republicans than among Democrats. In 1984 and 1988 (and also 1992, but that measure depends upon only three issues and is therefore less useful) the relationship was, if anything, stronger among Democrats than Republicans. That change very likely was due to the changing political context. In 1980, for example, more people, Democrats as well as Republicans, were closer to Reagan's median position than to Carter's on such important issues as defense spending and cutting income taxes. Reagan pushed increases in defense spending and cuts in income taxes through Congress in his first term, and he slowed increases in spending for many domestic programs as well. By 1984, therefore, the electorate no longer favored as great an increase in defense spending and was more amenable to increased spending on some domestic programs. Thus, in the next three elections issues tended to divide the electorate along party lines, with Democrats closer to their party's nominee. The result was a sharper and more balanced relationship between partisanship and the balance of issues measure. The increased polarization of the parties in Congress and among candidates generally accelerated in the 1994 congressional elections. The division between the two parties appears to have translated into partisan affiliation in the public as well. In 1996, while the balance of issues measure favored the Republicans, its relationship to party identification was stronger.

TABLE 8-6 Balance of Issues Positions among Partisan Groups, 1976–2004 (in percentages)

| | Party Identification | | | | | | | |
Issue positions closer to[a]	Strong Democrat	Weak Democrat	Independent, leans Democrat	Independent	Independent, leans Republican	Weak Republican	Strong Republican	Total
1976								
Democratic candidate	28	27	22	15	12	9	3	18
Neutral[b]	32	26	37	29	27	23	27	29
Republican candidate	39	47	40	55	61	67	69	53
Total	99	100	99	99	100	99	99	100
(N)	(422)	(655)	(336)	(416)	(277)	(408)	(254)	(2,778)
1980								
Democratic candidate	26	23	27	20	12	10	9	19
Neutral	34	37	33	43	40	43	31	37
Republican candidate	40	40	40	37	48	48	60	43
Total	100	100	100	100	100	101	100	99
(N)	(245)	(317)	(161)	(176)	(150)	(202)	(127)	(1,378)
1984								
Democratic candidate	57	49	59	35	23	29	14	39
Neutral	32	37	28	48	46	40	39	38
Republican candidate	11	14	13	17	32	32	47	23
Total	100	100	100	100	101	101	100	100
(N)	(331)	(390)	(215)	(213)	(248)	(295)	(256)	(1,948)
1988								
Democratic candidate	49	36	50	33	21	21	11	32
Neutral	34	40	38	48	46	43	35	40
Republican candidate	17	24	12	19	33	36	53	29
Total	100	100	100	100	100	100	99	101
(N)	(355)	(359)	(240)	(215)	(270)	(281)	(279)	(1,999)

(Table continues on next page)

TABLE 8-6 Balance of Issues Positions among Partisan Groups, 1976–2004 (in percentages) *(continued)*

Issue positions closer to[a]	Strong Democrat	Weak Democrat	Independent, leans Democrat	Independent	Independent, leans Republican	Weak Republican	Strong Republican	Total
1992[b]								
Democratic candidate	40	36	30	26	13	13	9	25
Neutral	55	57	65	70	74	77	74	67
Republican candidate	5	7	4	5	13	11	17	9
Total	100	100	99	101	100	101	100	101
(N)	(380)	(389)	(313)	(235)	(283)	(335)	(238)	(2,192)
1996[b]								
Democratic candidate	44	27	35	17	13	9	1	22
Neutral	27	36	34	43	27	23	14	29
Republican candidate	30	37	31	40	60	68	85	49
Total	101	100	100	100	100	100	100	100
(N)	(313)	(333)	(229)	(140)	(195)	(268)	(217)	(1,696)
2000[b]								
Democratic candidate	30	26	25	20	8	10	2	19
Neutral	47	48	46	49	40	33	25	43
Republican candidate	23	25	29	31	51	57	73	38
Total	100	99	100	100	99	100	100	100
(N)	(188)	(161)	(157)	(113)	(134)	(101)	(99)	(953)
2004[b]								
Democratic candidate	71	55	57	40	19	21	9	40
Neutral	8	11	9	10	9	6	5	8
Republican candidate	21	33	34	50	73	73	86	52
Total	100	99	100	100	101	100	100	100
(N)	(168)	(157)	(181)	(101)	(124)	(136)	(179)	(1,046)

[a] The Democratic category on the condensed balance of issues measure includes any respondent who is at least slightly Democratic; the Republican category includes any respondent who is at least slightly Republican. The neutral category is the same as the neutral category on the seven-point issue measure (see Table 6-5).
[b] Numbers are weighted.

It was almost as strong in 2000 and was moderately strong on both sides of the competition. Prospective issues appear to be increasingly polarized by party, strikingly so by 2000. The data for 2004 are just like those for 2000, but more so. That is, the relationship is stronger. These relationships are even more polarized by party in 2004, and are markedly stronger than in any of the previous elections. Partisan polarization characterizes not only prospective issues but also most other factors we have examined. In the case of our balance of issues measure, "polarization" really means "consistency"; that is, partisans find that their party's candidate is closer to them than is the opposing party's nominee on more and more issues. This seems to align with increased ability to see differences between the candidates and to see that the Democratic candidate is the more liberal (see chapter 6). It suggests that, on these measures, what we observe as growing polarization is due as much to the increased differentiation and consistency of the candidates' positions as it is to changes in the issue positions of the public.

Finally, we find a strong relationship between party identification and our measure of retrospective evaluations in 2004. We cannot directly compare this measure in 2004 with earlier elections because the questions that made up the summary retrospective measure in the past seven presidential elections differ from those in 2004.[22] Still, it is worth noting that this measure was very strongly related to partisanship in those earlier elections. Table 8-7 shows the relationship in 2004, collapsing the summary retrospective measure into the three categories of pro-Democratic, neutral, and pro-Republican. The relationship is overwhelming in 2004. Almost all strong Republicans had positive retrospective evaluations, and nearly nine in ten weak Republicans and eight in ten independents who lean Republican were likewise positive. The extent of negative assessments is only slightly less among Democrats. Unlike the balance of issues measure, in which pure independents were more on the Democratic side, there is a close balance of retrospective assessments among pure independents in 2004, with a slight edge giving positive assessments. This advantage may have been just the slight edge Bush needed to win his close reelection. Although we cannot directly compare 2004 to prior elections, we can conclude that retrospective evaluations are invariably strongly related to partisanship and that 2004 is no exception. If anything, the relationship is stronger in 2004 than in most, perhaps all, of the seven preceding elections.[23]

We have seen that both party identification and retrospective evaluations have been consistently and strongly related to the vote, but these two measures are also strongly related to each other in every election. Do they both still contribute independently to the vote? The answer, as we found for the preceding seven elections, and as can be seen for 2004 in Table 8-8, is yes.[24] In that table, we have examined the combined impact of party identification and retrospective evaluations on voting choices. To simplify the presentation, we have used the threefold grouping of the summary retrospective evaluations measure, and we have also regrouped party identification into the three groups of strong and weak Republicans, all three independent categories, and strong and weak Democrats.

TABLE 8-7 Retrospective Evaluations among Partisan Groups, 2004 (in percentages)

Summary measure of retrospective evaluations[a]	Party Identification							
	Strong Democrat	Weak Democrat	Independent, leans Democrat	Independent	Independent, leans Republican	Weak Republican	Strong Republican	Total
Democratic	93	65	71	35	14	6	1	42
Neutral	5	14	12	26	9	7	3	10
Republican	2	21	17	39	77	88	96	48
Total	100	100	100	100	100	101	100	100
(N)[b]	(158)	(148)	(176)	(97)	(123)	(136)	(179)	(1,017)

[a] The Democratic category on the condensed measure of retrospective evaluations includes any respondent who is at least slightly opposed to the incumbent party; the Republican category includes any respondent who at least slightly supports the incumbent party. The neutral category is the same as the neutral score on the seven-point measure (see Table 7-9).
[b] Numbers are weighted.

TABLE 8-8 Percentage of Major-Party Voters Who Voted for Bush, by Party Identification and Summary Retrospective Measures, 2004

Party identification[a]	Summary Retrospective[b]							
	Republican		Neutral		Democratic		Total	
	%	(N)[c]	%	(N)[c]	%	(N)[c]	%	(N)[c]
Republican	98	(260)	49	(15)	[4]	(8)	94	(282)
Independent	89	(92)	32	(30)	8	(121)	42	(243)
Democratic	54	(18)	25	(17)	1	(205)	7	(240)
Total	94	(369)	34	(62)	4	(333)	50	(786)

[a] Democratic identifiers include "strong" and "weak" Democrats; Republican identifiers include "strong" and "weak" Republicans. Independents include those who leaned toward either the Republican or the Democratic Party, as well as those who did not feel closer to either party.
[b] The Republican category on the condensed measure of retrospective evaluations includes any voter who is at least slightly supportive of the incumbent party; the Democratic category includes any voter who is at least slightly opposed to the incumbent party. The neutral category is the same as the neutral category on the seven-point measure.
[c] The numbers in parentheses are the numbers of major-party voters on which these percentages are based. In the one instance that included fewer than ten major-party voters, we show the total number who voted for Bush.

Table 8-8 shows the percentage of major-party voters who voted Republican, by both party identification and retrospective evaluations. Reading across the rows reveals that retrospective evaluations are strongly related to the vote, regardless of the voter's party identification, a pattern found in all seven previous elections. Reading down each column shows that in all elections, party identification is related to the vote, regardless of the voter's retrospective evaluations, once again a pattern discovered in all seven earlier elections, although in 2004 the relationship was weak among voters with negative evaluations. Moreover, as in all seven elections between 1976 and 2000, party identification and retrospective evaluations have a combined impact on how people voted. For example, in 2004 among Republicans with pro-Republican evaluations, 98 percent voted for Bush; among Democrats with pro-Democratic evaluations, only 1 percent did. Finally, partisanship and retrospective assessments appear to have roughly equal effects on the vote, and certainly both are strongly related to the vote, even when we examine both variables together. Thus, for example, the effect of retrospective evaluations on the vote is not—or at least not only—the result of partisans' having positive retrospective assessments of their party's presidents and negative assessments when the opposition holds the White House. Republicans who hold pro-Republican retrospective judgments were much more likely to vote for Bush than other Republicans, while Democratic partisans with pro-Democratic retrospective assessments were much more likely to vote for Kerry than other Democrats. Therefore, we can conclude that partisanship is key for understanding the evaluations of the public and their votes, but the large changes in outcomes over time must be traced to retrospective and prospective evaluations, simply because partisanship does not change substantially over time.

In sum, partisanship appears to affect the way voters evaluate incumbents and their performance. Positions on issues have been a bit different. Although partisans in the 1970s and early 1980s were likely to be closer to their party's nominee on policy, the connection was less clear than that between partisanship and retrospective evaluations. It is only recently that prospective evaluations have emerged as nearly as important a set of influences on candidate choice as retrospective evaluations. It may well be that the strengthening of this relationship is a reflection of the increasingly sharp cleavages between the parties among candidates and officeholders.[25] Still, policy-related evaluations are influenced partly by history and political memory and partly by the candidates' campaign strategies. Partisan attachments, then, limit the ability of a candidate to control his or her fate with the electorate, but such attachments are not entirely rigid. Candidates have some flexibility in the support they receive from partisans, especially depending on the candidates' or their predecessors' performance in office and on the policy promises they make in the campaign.

CONCLUSION

Party loyalties affect how people vote, how they evaluate issues, and how they judge the performance of the incumbent president and his party. In recent years, research has suggested that party loyalties not only affect issue preferences, perceptions, and evaluations, but also may affect partisanship itself. There is good reason to believe that the relationship between partisanship and these factors is more complex than suggested by any model that assumes only a one-way relationship. Doubtless, evaluations of the incumbent's performance may also affect party loyalties.[26]

As we saw in this chapter, there was a substantial shift toward Republican loyalties over the 1980s; among whites, the clear advantage that the Democrats enjoyed over the past four decades appears to be gone. To some extent, this shift in party loyalties must have reflected Reagan's appeal and his successful performance in office, as judged by the electorate. It also appears that he was able to shift some of that appeal in Bush's direction in 1988, directly, by the connection between performance judgments and the vote, and also indirectly, through shifts in party loyalties among white Americans. Bush lost much of the appeal he inherited, primarily because of negative assessments of his performance in office with respect to the economy, and he was also not able to hold onto the high approval ratings that he attained in 1991 after the success of the Persian Gulf War. In 1996 Clinton demonstrated that a president could rebound from a weak early performance, as judged by the electorate, and benefit from a growing economy.

The 1996 election stands as one comparable to the reelection campaigns of other recent, successful incumbents. Clinton received marks as high as or higher than Nixon's in 1972 and Reagan's in 1984 for his overall performance and for his handling of the economy. With strong retrospective judgments, the electorate basically decided that one good term deserved another.

The political landscape was dramatically different after the 1996 election, compared to the time just before the 1992 elections. While the proportion of Democrats to Republicans in the electorate had been quite close for over a decade, the general impression was that Republicans had a "lock" on the White House, while the Democrats' forty-year majority in the U.S. House was thought to be unbreakable. The 1992 election demonstrated that a party has a lock on the presidency only when the public believes that party's candidate will handle the office better than the opposition. The 1994 elections so reversed conventional thinking that some then judged Congress a stronghold for the Republican Party. Conventional wisdom, a lengthy history of such outcomes, and the apparent strength of the Republican delegation seemed to ensure that the GOP would gain seats in the 1998 congressional elections. But not only did Republicans fail to gain any congressional seats in 1998, they actually lost five House seats. This loss so shocked politicians that Speaker Newt Gingrich of Georgia resigned his office and his seat. A Democratic resurgence seemed to be in the making. The Republicans' handling of the impeachment and Senate trial of Clinton seemed to further set the stage for Democratic gains. Perhaps the single most surprising fact, leading into the 2000 presidential race, was the high approval ratings that an impeached, but not convicted, Clinton held.

The question for the 2000 campaign was why Gore was unable to do better than essentially tie Bush in the election (whether one counts popular or electoral votes). We must remember, however, how closely balanced all other key indicators were. Partisanship among whites was essentially evenly split between the two parties, with a Republican advantage in turnout at least partially offsetting the Democratic partisanship of blacks. Prospective issues, as in most election years, only modestly favored one side or the other. Retrospective evaluations, however, provided Gore with a solid edge, as did approval ratings of Clinton on the economy.

The failure, then, was in Gore's inability to translate that edge in retrospective assessments into a more substantial edge in the voting booth. Retrospective evaluations were an important factor in voters' choices, and it appears that such evaluations were almost as strongly related to the vote in 2000 as in other recent elections. But Gore failed to push that edge to turn a virtual tie into an outright win.

In 2004 it appeared that Bush may well have learned some lessons from 2000. He faced an electorate that, as before, was close to an even partisan balance, with the slight Democratic edge in number of identifiers balanced by their lower propensity to turn out than Republican identifiers. And with a continuing decline in the proportion of pure independents, there were fewer opportunities to win over those not already predisposed to support one party or the other. Furthermore, neither Bush nor Kerry held a clear edge in prospective evaluations. Bush held a small advantage on retrospective assessments. (In chapter 7, we showed that Bush held an edge. Who holds the edge in prospective evaluations depends on whether one uses the distance from the median candidate placements or the balance of issues measure.) Thus, with fewer independents to woo and such an even balance, the battle becomes a contest for the remaining independents and the weak partisans, as well as one of "strengthening the base," that is, appealing to those already predisposed to be supporters to motivate them to turn out. Perhaps for this reason we observed a strengthening of the affective component of partisan attachments, that is, a growth in strong partisanship at the expense of weak attachment, at least during the campaign itself.

Despite the shifts in partisan identification during the past half-century, we should not exaggerate the change. The same two parties hold the loyalties of three-fifths of the electorate, and since at least some professed independents may be actual partisans, the share is probably higher. Moreover, the Democrats still hold an edge, although it may be offset by their somewhat lower turnout. The share of strong party identifiers, who form the most reliable core of supporters for each party, has grown from a low of only about one in five in 1978, to about one in three in 2004. And the relationship between party identification and the vote was very strong in both 2000 and 2004. Although none of these changes demonstrates that the Republicans have won the "hearts and minds" of the electorate, they do call into question the thesis that a partisan dealignment has occurred.

No assessment of whether a realignment has occurred can be complete on the basis of presidential voting alone. After all, in the years from January 1953 to January 1993, during which the Republicans controlled the White House for twenty-eight of forty years, few scholars considered the GOP to be the dominant party, because it controlled the U.S. House of Representatives for only two of those years. In fact, between 1954 and 1992, the Democrats won a majority in the House in twenty straight elections. That winning streak ended in 1994. We must now turn to a study of congressional elections to evaluate the prospects for partisan change.

PART 3

The 2004 Congressional Election

So far we have discussed the presidential election, the main event of the 2004 elections. But the president shares responsibility with Congress, which must enact a legislative program and approve major appointments. Having concluded our discussion of George W. Bush's election, we now turn to the election of the Congress that governs with him. In part 3, we consider the selection of the 109th Congress.

There were many elections in 2004, including 11 gubernatorial elections, 34 Senate contests, and elections for all 435 members of the U.S. House of Representatives.[1] In addition to other statewide offices, 5,809 state legislative seats were at stake. There were also more than 150 initiatives and referendums on the ballot. On election day, eleven states voted on ballot proposals to ban same-sex marriages, many of them also banning civil unions between same-sex couples. (Two states had already passed bans on same-sex marriages earlier in the year.) The proposals passed in every state, and in every state except for Michigan and Oregon they passed with over 60 percent of the vote.[2]

The 2004 congressional election must be seen in the historical context of the 1994 midterm election, which set the stage for all five subsequent congressional contests. In 1994 the Democrats lost control of the U.S. House of Representatives, which they had held over the course of twenty consecutive elections since 1954.[3] They also lost control of the Senate, although that was not as remarkable, inasmuch as they had lost the Senate in the 1980, 1982, and 1984 elections. Granted, the Democrats expected to lose seats in 1994. After all, the party holding the White House had lost strength in the House in thirty-seven of the thirty-eight midterm elections between 1842 and 1990. Although the magnitude of the Democratic loss was not unprecedented, it was the second-largest midterm loss since World War II, surpassed only by the losses the Democrats suffered in the first midterm after FDR's death. The Republicans have continued to hold the House since 1994, sometimes suffering modest losses and sometimes making modest gains. In 2004, they gained three seats and held 232 seats to the Democrats' 202, with one independent. Thus, the GOP has now held the House for six consecutive elections, equaling their record between 1918 and 1928.[4] The Republicans' hold on the Senate has been more tenuous, and they actually lost control between June 2001 and January 2003. In 2004 they gained four Senate seats, holding a fifty-five to forty-four edge, again with one independent.

By reelecting Bush and maintaining the Republican majorities in both the House and Senate, voters continued united government. The Republicans held a comfortable majority in both chambers. But despite George W. Bush's exuberant claim two days after his reelection that he had earned political capital, a year later he was burdened by low approval ratings, as well as a Congress reluctant to support his proposed reform of the Social Security system. Some Republican Senate leaders were willing to transform the Senate by eliminating the filibuster against nominations to the judiciary, a proposal that some called the "nuclear option" because of its potential to grind Senate business to a halt. Despite growing polarization within Congress, in May 2005 a group of seven moderate Republicans and seven moderate Democrats ("the Gang of Fourteen") prevented a vote on this option from reaching the floor.

As we will see, the 2004 congressional elections closely resembled the elections of 2000. The major difference was that in 2004 the Republicans had a clear, if not filibuster-proof, majority in the Senate, while in 2000 the Senate was tied and Republican control depended upon Vice President Dick Cheney's tie-breaking vote. Why were these elections so similar? As we shall see, one of the main reasons was the overwhelming success of incumbents of both parties. We examine the regional bases of partisan support, showing that there has been a transformation in voting for Congress that is similar to, although not as dramatic as, regional change in presidential voting. We look at the campaign process for congressional races showing how the national parties are actively engaged in recruiting candidates and providing money. We also discuss redistricting, the process of redrawing the boundaries of congressional districts. Redistricting used to take place once every ten years, and it affected every state that had more than one representative, even if it neither gained nor lost representation in Congress. Congressional districts must have as close to the same number of residents as possible after a Census, and disparities can grow between a redistricting and the next Census. In several states party leaders have attempted to draw new district lines even after new boundaries have been drawn and used. The congressional district boundaries drawn in Texas after the 2000 Census, and used in the 2002 midterm, were redrawn in 2003 after Republicans gained control of the state legislature. Chapter 9 also examines factors contributing to the success of candidates in congressional elections, the most important of which are campaign spending and the quality of the candidates. We discuss alternative explanations for the growing margins by which incumbents are being reelected and the reasons why those margins narrowed in the 1990s. We turn to the role of campaign spending and show why we conclude that, although having adequate money to run a campaign is essential, elections cannot be bought.

Chapter 9 discusses the impact of the 2004 election on Congress. Partisan conflict became especially intense in the Senate where, as mentioned, the Republican leadership threatened to remove the Democrats' right to attempt to block court nominations with a filibuster. We discuss the reasons why, despite Republican majorities in the House and Senate, Bush has had relatively little success with his domestic agenda. We then turn to the 2006 midterm elections, using the information currently at hand to speculate about their outcome. We examine academic models that political scientists have developed to predict and explain the results of midterm elections in the House. We also briefly discuss prospects for the 2006 Senate elections. Finally, we speculate about congressional elections after 2006, asking whether there will be a solidified Republican majority or continued uncertainty.

Chapter 10 examines how voters make decisions in choosing how to vote for Congress—one of the most exciting and rapidly growing areas of research since the National Election Studies introduced new questions in 1978. Because only one-third of Senate seats are contested in each election, our analysis focuses mainly on the House. The chapter examines how social forces influence voters' choices and compares these factors with presidential voting. The effects of party identification on voting choices in all twenty-seven elections between 1952 and 2004 are examined. We ask whether congressional voting can be seen as a referendum on the performance of particular members of Congress, and whether it is partly a referendum on President George W. Bush's performance. We also attempt to discover whether Bush had "coattails," that is, whether he drew votes for other Republicans. In past elections, the Democrats were able to capitalize on their incumbency advantage to win votes. The Republicans have only a narrow incumbency edge, but they may be able to use it to retain congressional power.

Chapter 9

Candidates and Outcomes in 2004

In 1994 the Republicans unexpectedly won control of both chambers of Congress, the first time the GOP had won the House of Representatives since 1952. The electoral earthquake of 1994 shaped all subsequent congressional contests. In the 1996 election the Republicans held the House for a second election in a row (something they had not done since 1928), and they successfully defended their majority again in 1998 and in 2000, although the Democrats gained ground. In the Senate, the Republicans added to their majority in 1996, broke even in 1998, and then lost ground in 2000. Then in 2002 the GOP made small gains in both the House and Senate, to get a little breathing room. Thus, going into the elections of 2004, the GOP still had control of Congress, but that control was again potentially on the line. As it turned out, the Republicans succeeded in both House and Senate races, gaining three seats in the House and four in the Senate. In the House, they won 232 seats to the Democrats' 202, with one independent.[1] In the Senate, the result was a 55–44 division in favor of the GOP, again with one independent.[2]

In this chapter, we examine the pattern of congressional outcomes for 2004 and see how it compares to those in previous years. We explain why the 2004 results took the shape they did—what factors affected the success of incumbents seeking to return and what permitted some challengers to run better than others. We also discuss the likely impact of the election results on the politics of the 109th Congress. Finally, we consider the implications of the 2004 results for the 2006 midterm elections and for other upcoming elections.

ELECTION OUTCOMES IN 2004

Patterns of Incumbency Success

Most races involve incumbents and most incumbents are reelected. This generalization has been true for every set of congressional elections since World War II, although the degree to which it has held has varied somewhat from one election to another. Table 9-1 presents information on election outcomes for House and Senate races involving incumbents between 1954 and 2004.[3] During that period, an average of 93 percent of House incumbents and 84 percent of Senate incumbents who sought reelection were successful.

In 2004 the proportion of representatives reelected (98 percent) was noticeably above the twenty-six-election average (nearly identical to 1998 and 2000), and the success rate for senators was nearly the same as for the members of the House (96 percent), well above the Senate average since 1954. The results for the House contrasted markedly with some elections in the previous decade. Incumbent success was depressed in 1992 by higher-than-usual defeat rates in both primary and general elections. The large number of losses occurred partly because it was the election after a Census (when redistricting changed many district lines and forced a number of representatives to face one another in the same district) and partly because of a major scandal involving many House incumbents.[4] In 1994 the lower rate of reelection was due almost entirely to the general election defeat of an unusually large number of Democrats, causing the turnover of partisan control of the House. In contrast, 2004 saw very few primary defeats (two Democrats, both from Texas), and the proportion that lost in the general election was only a little higher (1.7 percent). In the 2004 Senate races, not a single incumbent lost in a primary, and only one, Senate Minority Leader Tom Daschle, S.D., was defeated in the general election.

During the period covered by Table 9-1, House and Senate outcomes have sometimes been similar and sometimes exhibited different patterns. For example, in most years between 1968 and 1988, House incumbents were substantially more successful than their Senate counterparts. In the three elections between 1976 and 1980, House incumbents' success averaged over 93 percent, whereas senators averaged only 62 percent. In contrast, their success rates in the last five elections before 2000 were fairly similar. Then in 2000, and to a lesser degree in 2002, we again saw divergence in the two chambers' results.

These differences between the two bodies stem from at least two factors. The first is primarily statistical: House elections routinely involve around 400 incumbents, whereas Senate contests usually have fewer than 30. A smaller number of cases is more likely to produce volatile results over time, and thus, the proportion of successful incumbents tends to vary more for the Senate than for the House. Second, Senate races are more likely to be vigorously contested than House races, making Senate incumbents more vulnerable. In many years a substantial number of representatives have had no opponent at all, or had one who was inexperienced, underfunded, or both. Senators, on the other hand, often had strong, well-financed opponents. Thus representatives were advantaged relative to senators. In the early 1990s, the competitiveness of House elections increased, reducing the relative advantage for representatives, although the last four cycles have seen competition confined to a more narrow range of districts. We will consider this issue in more detail later in the chapter.

TABLE 9-1   House and Senate Incumbents and Election Outcomes, 1954–2004

Year	Incumbents running (N)	Primary defeats (N)	%	General election defeats (N)	%	Reelected (N)*	%
House
1954	(407)	(6)	1.5	(22)	5.4	(379)	93.1
1956	(410)	(6)	1.5	(15)	3.7	(389)	94.9
1958	(394)	(3)	0.8	(37)	9.4	(354)	89.8
1960	(405)	(5)	1.2	(25)	6.2	(375)	92.6
1962	(402)	(12)	3.0	(22)	5.5	(368)	91.5
1964	(397)	(8)	2.0	(45)	11.3	(344)	86.6
1966	(411)	(8)	1.9	(41)	10.0	(362)	88.1
1968	(409)	(4)	1.0	(9)	2.2	(396)	96.8
1970	(401)	(10)	2.5	(12)	3.0	(379)	94.5
1972	(392)	(13)	3.3	(13)	3.3	(366)	93.4
1974	(391)	(8)	2.0	(40)	10.2	(343)	87.7
1976	(383)	(3)	0.8	(12)	3.1	(368)	96.1
1978	(382)	(5)	1.3	(19)	5.0	(358)	93.7
1980	(398)	(6)	1.5	(31)	7.8	(361)	90.7
1982	(393)	(10)	2.5	(29)	7.4	(354)	90.1
1984	(411)	(3)	0.7	(16)	3.9	(392)	95.4
1986	(393)	(2)	0.5	(6)	1.5	(385)	98.0
1988	(409)	(1)	0.2	(6)	1.5	(402)	98.3
1990	(407)	(1)	0.2	(15)	3.7	(391)	96.1
1992	(368)	(20)	5.4	(23)	6.3	(325)	88.3
1994	(387)	(4)	1.0	(34)	8.8	(349)	90.2
1996	(384)	(2)	0.5	(21)	5.5	(361)	94.0
1998	(401)	(1)	0.2	(6)	1.5	(394)	98.3
2000	(403)	(3)	0.7	(6)	1.5	(394)	97.8
2002	(398)	(8)	2.0	(7)	1.8	(383)	96.2
2004	(404)	(2)	0.5	(7)	1.7	(395)	97.8
Senate
1954	(27)	(0)	—	(4)	15	(23)	85
1956	(30)	(0)	—	(4)	13	(26)	87
1958	(26)	(0)	—	(9)	35	(17)	65
1960	(28)	(0)	—	(1)	4	(27)	96
1962	(30)	(0)	—	(3)	10	(27)	90
1964	(30)	(0)	—	(2)	7	(28)	93
1966	(29)	(2)	7	(1)	3	(26)	90
1968	(28)	(4)	14	(4)	14	(20)	71
1970	(28)	(1)	4	(3)	11	(24)	86
1972	(26)	(1)	4	(5)	19	(20)	77

TABLE 9-1   (continued)

Year	Incumbents running (N)	Primary defeats (N)	Primary defeats %	General election defeats (N)	General election defeats %	Reelected (N)	Reelected %
1974	(26)	(1)	4	(2)	8	(23)	88
1976	(25)	(0)	—	(9)	36	(16)	64
1978	(22)	(1)	5	(6)	27	(15)	68
1980	(29)	(4)	14	(9)	31	(16)	55
1982	(30)	(0)	—	(2)	7	(28)	93
1984	(29)	(0)	—	(3)	10	(26)	90
1986	(27)	(0)	—	(6)	22	(21)	78
1988	(26)	(0)	—	(3)	12	(23)	88
1990	(30)	(0)	—	(1)	3	(29)	97
1992	(27)	(1)	4	(3)	11	(23)	85
1994	(26)	(0)	—	(2)	8	(24)	92
1996	(20)	(0)	—	(1)	5	(19)	95
1998	(29)	(0)	—	(3)	10	(26)	90
2000	(27)	(0)	—	(6)	22	(21)	78
2002	(26)	(1)	4	(2)	8	(23)	88
2004	(25)	(0)	—	(1)	5	(24)	96

Having considered incumbency, we now consider political parties. Figure 9-1 shows the percentage of seats in the House and Senate held by the Democrats after each election since 1952. It graphically demonstrates how large a departure from the past the elections of 1994 through 2004 were. In House elections before 1994, the high percentage of incumbents running and the high rate of incumbent success led to fairly stable partisan control. Most important, the Democrats won a majority in the House in every election since 1954, twenty consecutive national elections. That was by far the longest period of dominance of the House by the same party in American history.[5] This winning streak was ended by the upheaval of 1994, when the GOP made a net gain of fifty-two representatives, winning 53 percent of the total seats. They held their majority in each subsequent election, although there were small shifts back to the Democrats in 1996, 1998, and 2000.

In the Senate, previous control by the Republicans was much more recent. They had taken the Senate in the Reagan victory of 1980 and retained it in 1982 and 1984. When the class of 1980 faced the voters again in 1986, however, the Democrats won back the majority. They held it until the GOP regained control in 1994; then the Republicans expanded their margin in 1996. In fact, the 55 percent of the seats they achieved that year (and repeated in 1998) was the highest Republican percentage in either House during this fifty-two-year period. Then in 2000, fortune turned against them, and the chamber reverted to a fifty-fifty division. (This was followed a few months later by the decision of Sen. James Jeffords

FIGURE 9-1 Democratic Share of Seats in the House and Senate, 1953–2005
(in percentages)

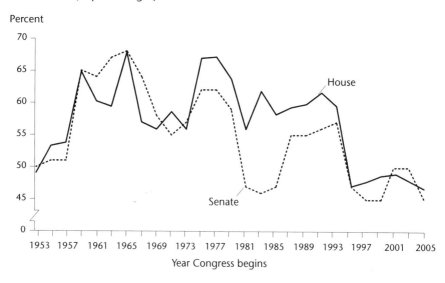

of Vermont to become an independent and to vote with the Democrats on organizing the chamber, shifting majority control to them until after the 2002 elections.) In 2004 the GOP gained four seats and returned to its high-water mark of
55 percent.

The combined effect of party and incumbency in the general election of 2004
is shown in Table 9-2. Overall the Republicans won 53 percent of the races for
House seats and 56 percent of the Senate contests. Despite the sharp partisanship
of the presidential and the congressional races, incumbents of both parties did
very well in House races. Ninety-nine percent of House Republican incumbents
in the general election won reelection, and 98 percent of House Democrats were
successful (two Democrats in Texas lost to Republican incumbents in redrawn
districts). In Senate races, 93 percent of Democratic incumbents won, as did 100
percent of GOP incumbents. One cause of the Democrats' failure to gain ground
in the House was their relatively poor success rate in open-seat contests. Those
races had created opportunities for the Democrats because the Republicans were
defending more open seats, but the Democrats lost a higher proportion of their
open seats than the GOP did. In open Senate contests, the Democrats' performance was also disappointing. Although they won half of the available GOP
seats, they lost every one of theirs, all of which were in the South.

The important points from these results are (1) that in 2004 House races, the
GOP was able to improve its margin slightly and (2) that this was the fifth consecutive election in which the GOP had successfully defended its majority. Perhaps more important, the Republicans were able to expand their hold on the Sen-

TABLE 9-2   House and Senate General Election Outcomes, by Party and Incumbency, 2004 (in percentages)

| | Democratic incumbent | No Incumbent | | Republican incumbent | Total |
		Democratic seat	Republican seat		
House					
Democrats	98	69	16	1	47
Republicans	2	31	84	99	53
Total	100	100	100	100	100
(N)	(190)[a]	(16)	(19)	(210)	(435)
Senate					
Democrats	93	0	50	0	44
Republicans	7	100	50	100	56
Total	100	100	100	100	100
(N)	(14)	(5)	(4)	(11)	(34)

[a] Excludes two Democratic incumbents who were defeated by Republican incumbents.

ate significantly. We will explore below the implications of this election series for future Democratic prospects.

Regional Bases of Power

The geographic pattern of 2004 outcomes in the House and Senate can be seen in the partisan breakdown by region in Table 9-3.[6] For comparison we present the corresponding data for 1981 (after the Republicans took control of the Senate in Reagan's first election) and 1953 (the last Congress before 1995 in which the Republicans controlled both chambers). Comparing 2005 to 1981, we see that in the House the GOP share was similar in the East, Midwest, and West, with no more than a seven-point difference in any of those regions. The big shift, compared with 1981, was the substantial Republican gains in the South and the border states. Overall, the Republicans won a majority of House seats in all regions but the East and West in 2004. The pattern is roughly similar in the Senate. Between 1981 and 2005, GOP gains were limited to two regions (the South and the border states), while they lost ground in the West, Midwest, and East.

The 2005 results are more interesting when viewed from the longer historical perspective. In 1953 there were sharp regional differences in party representation in both houses. Those differences have greatly diminished. The most obvious changes occurred in the South. The percentage of southern House seats held by Democrats declined from 94 percent in 1953 to 37 percent in 2005. In 1953 the Democrats held all twenty-two southern Senate seats, but in 2005 they controlled only four. The regional shift was less dramatic in congressional elections than in

TABLE 9-3   Party Shares of Regional Delegations in the House and Senate, 1953, 1981, and 2005

	1953			1981			2005		
Region	Demo-crats %	Repub-licans %	(N)	Demo-crats %	Repub-licans %	(N)	Demo-crats %	Repub-licans %	(N)
House									
East	35	65	(116)	56	44	(105)	61	39	(84)
Midwest	23	76	(118)[a]	47	53	(111)	40	60	(91)
West	33	67	(57)	51	49	(76)	54	46	(98)
South	94	6	(106)	64	36	(108)	37	63	(131)
Border	68	32	(38)	69	31	(35)	45	55	(31)
Total	49	51	(435)	56	44	(435)	47	53	(435)
Senate									
East	25	75	(20)	50	50	(20)	60	35	(20)[a]
Midwest	14	86	(22)	41	59	(22)	59	41	(22)
West	45	55	(22)	35	65	(26)	42	58	(26)
South	100	0	(22)	55	45	(22)	18	82	(22)
Border	70	30	(10)	70	30	(10)	40	60	(10)
Total	49	51	(96)	47	53	(100)	44	55	(100)

[a] Includes one independent.

presidential elections (see chapter 3), but in both instances there has been a change away from Democratic dominance to solid Republican control.

This change in the partisan shares of the South's seats in Congress has had an important impact on that region's influence within the two parties. The South used to be the backbone of Democratic congressional representation. This, and the tendency of southern members to build seniority, gave southerners disproportionate power within the Democratic Party in Congress. Because of declining Democratic electoral success in the region, the numerical strength of southern Democrats in Congress has waned. In 1953, with the Republicans in control of both chambers, southerners accounted for around 45 percent of Democratic seats in the House and Senate. By the 1970s, southern strength had declined, to stabilize at between 25 percent and 30 percent of Democratic seats. In 2005 southerners accounted for 24 percent of Democratic House seats and only 9 percent of Democratic senators.

The South's share of Republican congressional representation presents the reverse picture. Minuscule at the end of World War II, it steadily grew, reaching about 20 percent in the House after the 1980 elections and 35 percent after 2004. As a consequence of these changes, southern influence has declined in the Democratic Party and grown in the GOP, to the point that southerners have recently held a disproportionate share of the Republican leadership positions in both houses of Congress.[7] Because southerners of both parties tend to be more conservative than their colleagues from other regions, these shifts in regional strength have tended to make the Democratic Party in Congress more liberal and the Republican Party more conservative.[8]

Other regional changes since 1953, although not as striking as those in the South, are also significant. In the 1953 House, the Republicans controlled the East and West by two-to-one margins and the Midwest by three to one; in 2005 they held a substantially reduced advantage in the Midwest, and the Democrats had a majority of eastern and western seats. The Senate also exhibited shifts away from substantial Republican dominance of the East and Midwest. On the other hand, with the increased Republican dominance of the South, regional differences in party shares are somewhat more prominent in 2005 than they were in the 1990s. Still, partisan representation is more homogeneous across regions in the Congress of 2005 than it was in the Congress of 1953. Thus, it may be appropriate to call the change in the regional bases of partisan support "deregionalization."

National Forces in the Congressional Elections

The patterns of outcomes discussed above were shaped by a variety of influences. As with most congressional elections, the most important were the resources available to individual candidates and how those resources were distributed between the parties in specific races. We will discuss those matters shortly, but first we consider potential and actual national-level influences particular to 2004.

The first national force to assess is whether there was a pattern in public opinion that advantaged one party or the other. Such "national tides" occur in presidential years as well as midterms, and they can have a profound impact on the outcomes of congressional elections. Often these tides flow from reaction to presidents or presidential candidates. For example, in 1964 the presidential landslide victory of Lyndon B. Johnson over Barry M. Goldwater carried over to major Democratic gains in both congressional chambers, and Ronald Reagan's ten-point margin over Jimmy Carter in 1980 helped Republicans achieve an unexpected majority in the Senate and major gains in the House. Similarly, negative public reactions to events in the first two years of Bill Clinton's presidency played a major part in the Republicans' congressional victories in 1994.

Clearly 2004 was not an election with a significant national tide. Although the results didn't exhibit the remarkably even balance between the parties, across all three national races—president, House, and Senate—that the 2000 results did, the Republican edge in 2004 was minimal. The narrow popular-vote margin in favor of George W. Bush indicates that neither of the presidential candidates had a strong popular advantage that significantly influenced the balance of the congressional vote. Nor did the electorate exhibit a desire for revenge against the incumbent's party. We will examine the direct link between presidential approval and the congressional vote in the next chapter. We can note here that Bush's approval ratings were mixed throughout 2004, and respondents to the

Edison Media Research/Mitofsky International (EMR/MI) exit poll gave him a narrow positive approval of 53 percent to 46 percent,[9] while in the National Election Study (NES) survey 51 percent approved and 49 percent disapproved (see Table 7-8).

Another potential national influence is public reaction to the performance of Congress. In the 1996 presidential race, Clinton and the Democrats tried to focus public attention on what they claimed were the extremism and excesses of the new GOP congressional majority, with very limited success.[10] In 2004 public opinion toward Congress had turned somewhat negative. For example, in Gallup polls between February and November 2004, the number of those disapproving of the way Congress was handling its job exceeded the number who approved by eight to thirteen percentage points. Supporting these data, a CBS/*New York Times* poll in October showed disapproval outweighing approval by 46 percent to 38 percent.[11] According to the NES survey, opinion was somewhat more favorable, with 45 percent approving of the job Congress was doing, while 41 percent disapproved. But even though both Congress and the presidency were in Republican hands, these generally negative feelings about Congress were neither extreme enough nor salient enough to influence the aggregate outcomes.

Efforts of National Parties and Their Allies

The efforts of congressional party leaders and their allies to influence the races have been growing in importance. Before the 1980s, the activities of national parties in congressional elections were very limited. Individual candidates were mostly self-starters who were largely on their own in raising money and planning strategy. More recently, that has changed substantially, and party leaders and organizations are now heavily involved in recruiting and funding their candidates.[12] As we will see, the quality of candidates and how much money they can raise are two of the central determinants of election outcomes. Moreover, because party control of the House, and perhaps the Senate, was seen to be in doubt in 2004, both parties had particularly strong incentives to be active.

Candidates and Money. National party organizations are now almost continuously active in candidate recruiting and fund-raising. As soon as the voting in one election ends, activity for the next begins. House Democrats' main concern after their disappointing showing in 2002 was that many senior Democrats would become frustrated by their minority status (and the expectation that it would continue) and retire. National campaign leaders and their staffs were active in 2003 trying to stave off possible retirements and to promote candidacies for higher office. The plans of individual candidates were monitored, and strategies for taking back the majority were discussed at the Democrats' party retreat. The perceived likelihood of success was a key element of members' strategic calculations. As one Democratic campaign aide said, "You've got to demonstrate that there's a plan and get members to buy into it. . . . You've got to show them the way." [13]

In the end the Democrats were quite successful in this respect. Only six of their representatives decided to retire, although eight others sought higher office. They were initially less successful in their efforts to attract candidates to oppose Republican incumbents or to run in open seats. To increase their chances to retake the majority, Democrats needed to "expand the playing field"—that is, to make more races competitive than had been the case in 2002. However, given the poor track record of challengers in recent decades, it is not easy to make a convincing case to ambitious politicians that they should buck the odds.[14] Ultimately, however, House Democrats fielded a relatively strong set of candidates, certainly much stronger than their lineup in 2002. We will have more to say below about candidate quality in the 2004 House races.

Both parties were also active in Senate recruitment. In particular, the Bush administration badly wanted to increase the GOP margin in that chamber, and it sought to influence the choice of candidates to advance that goal. In January 2003 White House officials pressured two Republican House members who were contemplating Senate candidacies (Bill Janklow, S.D., and George Nethercutt, Wash.) to delay their ambitions until others favored by the administration reached their decisions.[15] In the end the desired candidate in South Dakota, John Thune, ran and defeated Sen. Tom Daschle, while in Washington, Rep. Jennifer Dunn declined to run. Nethercutt became the GOP candidate against Democratic incumbent Patty Murray and lost. The White House's efforts also demonstrate that sometimes there are competing interests within a party. Administration officials tried to persuade Rep. Bob Beauprez of Colorado to run to succeed retiring Republican senator Ben Nighthorse Campbell, while House campaign leaders pressed Beauprez to seek reelection to improve their chances of holding his seat.[16] In the end Beauprez won reelection comfortably, but the GOP lost the Senate seat.

In addition to recruitment, party leaders have grown increasingly active in fund-raising, pursuing many different strategies. For example, top party leaders solicit donations to congressional campaign committees, such as the National Republican Congressional Committee (NRCC) and the Democratic Congressional Campaign Committee (DCCC), and appear at fund-raisers for individual candidates in their districts. Majority Leader Tom DeLay organized a fund-raising effort for the most vulnerable GOP representatives called "Retain Our Majority Program," or ROMP. This highly successful effort raised $21 million for the 2000 election cycle and $24 million for 2002.[17] DeLay continued the program in 2004. The Republican leadership launched another effort, called "Battleground 2004," that targeted GOP representatives for donations. It assessed members particular amounts depending on their status, from $500,000 from each of the top four leaders to $10,000 for a vulnerable incumbent.[18]

Raising campaign funds for the party has become a prominent obligation for members who want leadership posts and committee chairmanships. During the 2004 campaign three senior Republicans on the Appropriations Committee who wanted to fill the prospective vacancy in the chairmanship contributed several hundred thousand dollars each to candidates and party committees.[19] Democrats assessed members of the most desirable committees higher party dues than other members, mostly in the range of $100,000 to $150,000.[20]

Party leaders are able to do more to help candidates' reelection efforts than just raise money, at least for the House majority. Because the majority has greater influence over the floor agenda and the content of bills, they can add or remove legislative provisions that will enhance their members' reelection chances; they can permit vulnerable colleagues to bring popular bills to the floor. In May 2004 the GOP leadership put on the agenda a bill sponsored by a first-termer from Pennsylvania to end the "marriage penalty" in the income tax. In the next two weeks they scheduled bills dealing with the alternative minimum tax and the child tax credit, both sponsored by Republican incumbents in tough races.[21] This gave their party an advantage over the Democrats because the minority leadership had no comparable ability to influence the legislative schedule.

The Continuing Redistricting Battle. Another area in which the national parties have been active is House redistricting. The parties have always recognized that the way districts are drawn can affect their political fortunes, but until recently efforts to influence the process have been largely a concern of the state parties. As with other matters that have partisan consequences, however, the national parties are becoming increasingly involved in this process.[22] In addition, partly as a result of increasing polarization between the parties, the battle over redistricting is no longer restricted to the period after the decennial Census results are announced.

The first major redistricting struggle after the 2002 election occurred when the U.S. Supreme Court resolved a dispute over the interpretation of the Voting Rights Act.[23] The Justice Department had interpreted the act to prohibit reducing the number of minority voters below a majority of a district. This interpretation helped the Republican strategy of concentrating the maximum number of minority voters in as few districts as possible. That increased the chances of minority representatives being elected, but it usually also led to the defeat of white Democrats in neighboring districts. The Supreme Court ruled, however, that redistricting plans could legally consider a variety of factors when drawing district lines, not just the number of minority voters.[24] This would permit minority voters to be spread across a number of districts and increase the number of Democrats who could be elected.

The day after that case was decided, the Court agreed to hear another districting case initiated by some Pennsylvania Democrats. The plaintiffs claimed that their constitutional rights were violated by the state's congressional districting plan, which was drawn to increase the number of Republican representatives. The Court had ruled previously that a plan could be so extreme in its pursuit of partisan interests that the right to equal protection under the law, guaranteed by the Fourteenth Amendment, would be violated, but the Court had not subsequently found such a plan in practice. And it didn't find one here. A majority ruled that the Pennsylvania plan did not reach the high threshold of proof necessary to justify a ruling that a constitutional violation had occurred. Four members of the five-justice majority wanted to go further. They wanted to overturn the earlier ruling and say that such constitutional challenges would no longer be considered, but the other five justices agreed to maintain the possibility.[25]

Beyond the Supreme Court contests, the most important redistricting contest between 2002 and 2004 came about because of a Republican plan to redraw the Texas district lines. Despite growing GOP strength in Texas, after the 2000 Census the party had been unable to achieve a redistricting strongly tilted in its direction. After taking control of both houses of the state legislature in 2002, the Republicans—led by House Majority Leader DeLay—decided to try again. Democrats resisted the effort, but eventually a new set of lines was agreed on for 2004. The Democrats tried legal challenges to the GOP plan, but in April 2004 the Supreme Court ruled against their claims.[26] The Republican efforts yielded immediate dividends when Rep. Ralph M. Hall, elected as a Democrat since 1980, switched to the GOP after many Republican voters were added to his district. Then in November, four Democratic incumbents were defeated, two by GOP representatives and the others by nonincumbent challengers. In all, the Republicans netted six seats from the redistricting. In fact, without this help the party would have lost seats nationally in 2004. Republicans also tried to redraw Colorado's districts before the 2004 elections, but the state's supreme court blocked the effort.[27] We will return to the ongoing battle over districting later in the chapter.

CANDIDATES' RESOURCES AND ELECTION OUTCOMES

Seats in the House and Senate are highly valued, and candidates compete for them vigorously. In contests for these offices, candidates draw on every resource they have, and to explain the results of congressional elections we must consider the candidates' comparative advantages and disadvantages. In this section we will discuss the most significant resources available to candidates and their impact on congressional election outcomes.

Candidate Quality

Personal abilities that foster electoral success can be a major political asset. Few constituencies today offer certain victory to one of the two major parties, and so election outcomes usually depend heavily on candidate quality. A strong, capable candidate is a significant asset for a party; a weak, inept one is a liability that is difficult to overcome. In his study of the activities of House members in their districts, Richard F. Fenno Jr. described how members try to build support within their constituencies, establishing bonds of trust between themselves and their constituents.[28] Members attempt to convey to their constituents a sense that they are qualified for their job, that they identify with their constituents, and that they empathize with constituents and their problems. Challengers of incumbents and candidates for open seats must engage in similar activities to win support. The winner of a contested congressional election will usually be the candidate who is better able to establish such bonds of support among constituents and convince them that he or she is the person for the job.

One indicator of candidate quality is previous success at winning elective office. The more important the office a candidate has held, the more likely it is that he or she has overcome significant competition to obtain it. Moreover, the visibility and reputation for performance that usually accompany public office can also be a significant electoral asset. For example, state legislators running for House seats can claim that they have experience that has prepared them for congressional service. State legislators may also have built successful organizations that are useful in conducting congressional campaigns. Finally, previous success in an electoral arena suggests that experienced candidates are more likely than candidates without previous success or experience to be able to run strong campaigns. Less-adept candidates are likely to have been screened out at lower levels of office competition. For these and other reasons, an experienced candidate tends to have an electoral advantage over one who has held no previous elected office.[29] The higher the office previously held, the stronger the candidate will tend to be in the congressional contest.

In Table 9-4 we present data showing which candidates were successful in 2004, controlling for office background, party, and incumbency.[30] The vast majority of candidates who challenged incumbents lost, regardless of their office background or party. Indeed, in this election cycle so few incumbents lost that there is little variation possible across categories of experience. The impact of candidate quality is more visible in races without incumbents. Here candidates who had been state legislators were overwhelmingly successful, and those with other elective experience won at a much higher rate than those without any elective office experience. In Senate races, the pattern was similar. Only one incumbent was defeated (by a former congressman, who had once represented the entire state), and in Senate open-seat races, seven of the eight winners had top office experience.

Given the importance of candidate quality, it is worth noting that there has been substantial variation in the proportion of experienced challengers over time. During the 1980s the proportion of House incumbents facing challengers who had previously won elective office declined. This decline was reversed in 1992 and to some degree in 1996. In 1980, 17.6 percent of incumbents faced such challengers; in 1984, 14.7 percent did; in 1988, only 10.5 percent did. In 1992, largely because of perceptions of incumbent vulnerability due to redistricting and scandal, the proportion rose to 23.5 percent, but in 1996 it was back down to 16.5 percent, and it remained at that level in 2000.[31] In 2004, however, there was a substantial resurgence in the number of experienced candidates in both parties, with 22.4 percent of the challengers having previously held elective office.[32]

Whether experienced politicians actually run for the House or Senate is not an accident. These are significant strategic decisions, made by politicians who have much to lose if they make the wrong choice. Their choices will be governed by

TABLE 9-4   Success in House and Senate Elections, Controlling for Office Background, Party, and Incumbency, 2004

Candidate's last office	Candidate Is Opponent of				No Incumbent in District			
	Democratic incumbent		Republican incumbent		Democratic candidate		Republican candidate	
	%	(*N*)	%	(*N*)	%	(*N*)	%	(*N*)
House								
State legislature or U.S. House	0	(13)	0	(10)	83	(12)	92	(12)
Other elective office	7	(31)	3	(36)	60	(5)	86	(7)
No elective office	3	(116)	1	(128)	6	(16)	29	(14)
Senate								
U.S. House	100	(1)	0	(1)	0	(2)	100	(4)
Statewide elective office	0	(4)	0	(5)	50	(4)	100	(1)
Other elective office	0	(3)	0	(1)	0	(1)	—	(0)
No elective office	0	(6)	0	(5)	0	(3)	33	(3)

Note: Percentages show the proportions of candidates in each category who won; numbers in parentheses are the totals on which percentages are based. The 19th and 32nd Texas districts are excluded from the incumbent races because both major-party candidates were incumbents. The Georgia 6th and Texas 10th district House races are not included in the "no incumbent" races because the Republican candidates did not face major-party opponents.

factors related to the perceived chance of success, the potential value of the new office compared to what will be lost if the candidate fails, and the costs of running.[33] The chances of success of the two major parties vary from election to election, both locally and nationally. Therefore, each election offers a different mix of experienced and inexperienced candidates from the two parties for the House and Senate.

The most influential factor in whether a potential candidate will run is whether there is an incumbent in the race. High reelection rates tend to discourage potentially strong challengers from running, which in turn makes it more likely that the incumbents will win. In addition to the general difficulty of challenging incumbents, factors related to specific election years (both nationally and in a particular district) will affect decisions to run. For example, the Republican Party had particular difficulty recruiting strong candidates in 1986 because of fears about a potential backlash from the Iran-Contra scandals. On the other hand, recent research indicates that potential House candidates are most strongly influenced in their decision by their perceived chances of winning their party's nomination.[34] Moreover, the actions of incumbents may influence the decisions of potential challengers. For example, if an incumbent builds up a large reserve of campaign funds between elections, it may dissuade some possible opponents, although analysis of Senate contests (which usually involve experienced challengers) indicates that this factor does not have a systematic impact in those races.[35]

As we have seen, most congressional races do not involve challengers who have previous experience in office. Given their slight chance of winning, why do challengers without experience run at all? As Jeffrey S. Banks and D. Roderick Kiewiet have pointed out, although the chances of success against incumbents may be small, such a race may be an individual's best chance of ever winning a seat in Congress.[36] If inexperienced challengers put off their candidacies until a time when there is no incumbent, their opposition is likely to include several experienced candidates from both parties. Moreover, as David Canon demonstrated, previous experience in office is an imperfect indicator of candidate quality because some candidates without such experience can still have significant political assets and be formidable challengers.[37] For example, four former television journalists who had never previously held office won House seats in 1992, and three of them defeated incumbents. They were able to build on their substantial name recognition among voters to win nomination and election.[38] For more recent examples, consider two 2000 contests, one from each chamber: The Republican candidate for the House in Nebraska's third district was Tom Osborne, the extremely popular former head coach of the University of Nebraska's football team. Osborne was elected to an open seat with a phenomenal 82 percent of the vote. In the New York Senate race, the very visible (and ultimately successful) Democratic candidate was then first lady, Hillary Rodham Clinton.

Incumbency

One reason most incumbents win is that incumbency itself is a significant resource. Actually, incumbency is not a single resource but a status that usually gives a candidate a variety of benefits. In some respects, incumbency works to a candidate's advantage automatically. For example, incumbents tend to be more visible to voters than their challengers.[39] Less automatic, but very important, incumbents tend to be viewed more favorably than challengers. Moreover, at least a plurality of the electorate in most districts will identify with the incumbent's political party. Incumbents can also use their status to gain advantages. Incumbents usually raise and spend more money than challengers, and they usually have a better-developed and more-experienced campaign organization. They also have assets provided at public expense, such as a staff and franking privileges (free postage for mail to their constituents), that both help them perform their jobs and provide electoral benefits.

Increasing Electoral Margins. From the mid-1960s through the late 1980s, the margins by which incumbents were reelected increased (the pattern was less clear and more erratic in Senate elections than in House elections).[40] These changing patterns have interested analysts primarily because they believe that the disappearance of marginal incumbents means less congressional turnover and leads to a House that is less responsive to the electorate.

Edward R. Tufte offered an early explanation for the increased incumbency margins by arguing that redistricting had protected incumbents of both parties.[41] This argument seemed plausible because the increase in margins occurred at about the same time as the massive redistrictings required by Supreme Court decisions of the mid-1960s. But other analysts showed that incumbents had won by larger margins both in states that had redistricted and in those that had not, as well as in Senate contests.[42] Thus redistricting could not be the major reason for the change.

Another explanation for the increase in incumbents' margins was the growth in the perquisites of members and the greater complexity of government. Morris P. Fiorina noted that in the post–New Deal period both federal services and the bureaucracy that administers them have grown tremendously.[43] More complex government means that many people will encounter problems in receiving services, and people who have problems frequently contact their representative to complain and seek help. Fiorina contended that in the mid-1960s new members of Congress emphasized such constituency problem solving more than their predecessors. This expanded constituency service developed into a reservoir of electoral support. Although analyses of the impact of constituency services have produced mixed conclusions, it is likely that the growth of these services offers a partial explanation for changing incumbent vote margins and for the incumbency advantage generally.[44]

The declining impact of party loyalties offered a third explanation for the growth in incumbent vote margins, either alone or in interaction with other factors. Until the mid-1960s there was a very strong linkage between party identification and congressional voting behavior. Most Americans identified with a political party, many identified strongly, and most voters supported the candidate of their chosen party. Subsequently, however, the impact of party identification decreased (as we will see in chapter 10). John A. Ferejohn, drawing on data from the National Election Studies (NES), showed that the strength of party ties weakened, and that within any given category of party identification the tendency to support the candidate of one's party declined.[45] An analysis by Albert D. Cover showed that between 1958 and 1974 voters who did not identify with the party of a congressional incumbent were increasingly likely to defect from their party and support the incumbent, whereas there had been no increase in defections from party identification by voters of the same party as incumbents.[46] Thus, weakened party ties produced a substantial net benefit for incumbents,[47] although, as we saw in chapter 8, party loyalties among the electorate may have grown stronger in 2004.

The Trend Reversed. Whatever the relative importance of these factors, and the others we will discuss, the increase in incumbents' victory margins continued through the 1980s, as the data in Table 9-5 show. The average share of the vote for all incumbents was 61.7 percent in 1974; in 1980 it was 65.5 percent. The

TABLE 9-5 Average Vote Percentages of House Incumbents, Selected Years, 1974–2004

Year	Democrats	Republicans	All incumbents
1974	68.5	55.2	61.7
1980	64.0	67.9	65.5
1982	67.9	59.9	64.1
1984	64.2	68.2	65.9
1986	70.2	65.6	68.2
1988	68.8	67.5	68.2
1990	65.8	59.8	63.5
1992	63.3	62.9	63.1
1994	60.0	67.6	62.8
1996	66.6	60.7	63.3
1998	65.0	61.6	63.3
2000	67.2	62.9	65.1
2002	66.4	66.1	66.3
2004	67.8	63.9	65.4

Note: These figures only include races where both major parties ran candidates.

share then continued to grow, peaking at 68.2 percent in 1986 and 1988.[48] These data are only for races in which both parties ran candidates; they exclude contests in which an incumbent ran unopposed. Because such races were also increasing in number over this period, the data actually understate the growth in incumbents' margins.

Then, in 1990, something changed. The average share of the vote for incumbents declined by nearly five percentage points. The decline was, moreover, not a result of a shift of voters toward one party, such as occurred from 1980 to 1982; both parties' incumbents suffered. Rather, the shift in incumbents' electoral fortunes was apparently the result of what was called "the anti-incumbent mood" among the voters. Early in 1990 pollsters and commentators began to perceive stronger anti-Congress sentiments in the electorate.[49] For the first time, analysts began to question whether incumbency was still the asset it used to be.

There was, of course, nothing new about Congress being unpopular; Congress had long suffered ups and downs in approval, just as the president had. Indeed, Fenno had noted long before that candidates for Congress often sought election by running against Congress—they sought to convince voters that while most members of Congress were untrustworthy, they were different and deserved the voters' support.[50] What changed in 1990 was that Congress's unpopularity appeared to be undermining the approval of individual members by their own constituents. Yet as the data presented in Table 9-1 showed, even though there was a drop in the average percentage of the vote that incumbents received in 1990, the rate of reelection still reached 96 percent. The decline in vote margins was not great enough to produce a rash of defeats. Many observers wondered, however, whether 1990 was the beginning of a new trend: Would incumbents' electoral drawing power continue to decline?

In 1992, scandals damaged many representatives of both parties, and the public's evaluation of Congress was very low. Opponents of incumbents emphasized that they were "outsiders" and not "professional politicians" (even when they had substantial political experience). The results from 1992 show that incumbents' share of the vote dropped a bit more. Republicans rebounded a little from their bad 1990 showing, while Democrats fell more than two percentage points. Again, however, the casualty rate among incumbents who ran in the general election was lower than many expected: 93 percent were reelected. (It is important to note that a substantial number of incumbents had already been defeated in the primaries). Then in 1994, although there was only a slight additional drop in incumbents' share of the vote overall, the drop was greater (and concentrated) among Democrats, and their casualty rate was high. The result was the loss of their majority. Next, in 1996, there was a slight rebound in incumbents' vote share, with Democrats' increasing sharply while the GOP's fell. That vote shift translated into the defeat of eighteen Republican incumbents but only three Democrats. Finally, the results from 2000 through 2004—with the continuing Democratic effort to whittle away at the GOP majority—fall in between the highs of the mid-1980s and the lows of 1994 and 1996.[51] It is also important to note that Democratic incumbents averaged a substantially higher share of the vote than Republicans in 2004. This likely reflects the fact that redistricting by Republicans created a greater number of safer Democratic districts, in which Democratic votes are wasted.

This discussion illustrates that incumbents' vote margins and incumbents' reelection success are related but distinct phenomena. When—as was true in the 1980s—the average share of the vote received by incumbents is very high, they can lose a lot of ground before a large number of defeats occur. What appears to have occurred in 1990 is that many incumbents were subjected to vigorous competition for the first time in many years. Such challenges were then repeated or extended to additional incumbents in 1992, 1994, and 1996. Potential candidates apparently looked at the political situation and concluded that incumbents who had previously looked unbeatable could now potentially be defeated, and there was a substantial increase in the number of candidates for Congress. These vigorous contests, by challengers who were stronger than usual, resulted in a decrease in the share of the vote received by many incumbents. In most cases in 1990, the decrease was not large enough to bring the challenger victory. In later years, however, the increased competition caught up with a greater number of incumbents. Now, in the twenty-first century, competition is again at a low point, largely due to the deliberate crafting of safe districts for both parties' incumbents.

Campaign Spending

A third resource that strongly affects congressional elections is campaign spending. Campaign spending has received a great deal of attention in the last three decades because researchers gained access to more dependable data than had previously been available.[52] The data on spending have consistently shown that incumbents generally outspend their challengers, often by large margins, and that through the early 1990s, the disparity had increased.[53] In 1990 incumbent spending averaged about $401,000, while challengers spent approximately $116,000—a ratio of 3.45 to 1. In 1992 challenger spending increased to an average of $160,000, but the stronger challenges of that year also stimulated the incumbents to keep pace, and their spending rose to $560,000. This was a ratio of 3.50 to 1, which left challengers and incumbents in about the same relative positions as they had been in two years earlier.[54] (As we will see shortly, more recent data show significant changes.)

Disparities in campaign spending are linked to the increase in incumbents' election margins. In the 1960s congressional campaigns began relying more heavily on campaign techniques that cost money—for example, media time, campaign consulting, and direct mail—and these have become more and more expensive. At the same time, candidates were progressively less likely to have available pools of campaign workers from established party organizations or from interest groups. This has made using expensive media and direct mail strategies relatively more important. Most challengers are unable to raise significant campaign funds. Neither individuals nor groups interested in the outcomes of congressional elections like to throw money away; before making contributions they usually need to be convinced that the candidate has a chance. Yet we have seen that few incumbents have been beaten. Thus it is often difficult to convince potential contributors that their money will produce results, and contributions are often not forthcoming. Most challengers are thus at a strategic disadvantage, and they are unable to raise enough money to wage a competitive campaign.[55]

It is the ability to compete, rather than the simple question of relative amounts of spending, that is at the core of the issue. We have noted that incumbents have many inherent advantages that a challenger must overcome if he or she hopes to win, but often the money is not there to overcome them. In 2004, for example, more than 38 percent of challengers spent $25,000 or less, and 58 percent spent $75,000 or less. With so little money available, challengers are unable to make themselves visible to the electorate or to convey a convincing message. Under such circumstances, most voters—being unaware of the positions, or perhaps even the existence, of the challenger—vote for the incumbent.

Data on 2004 campaign spending and election outcomes seem consistent with this argument, but they also show changes in the political landscape.[56] The increased competitiveness during the 1990s that was shown by the data on incumbents' vote share is reflected in the spending figures. Challenger spending was up sharply, compared to the 1990–1992 figures presented above, and averaged about $269,000. Incumbent spending was also up enormously (averaging a little over $1 million), and that yielded an increased incumbent-to-challenger ratio of 3.85 to 1.[57] (This ratio is up substantially more from the 2.57 to 1 of 1996, when a strong effort by organized labor targeted thirty-two Republican incum-

TABLE 9-6   Incumbents' Share of the Vote in the 2004 House Elections, by Challenger Campaign Spending (in percentages)

Challenger spending[a]	Incumbents' Share of the Two-Party Vote					
	70% or more	60%–69%	55%–59%	Less than 55%	Total	(N)
0–25	41.5	56.9	0.8	0.8	100.0	(130)
26–75	20.6	71.4	6.3	1.6	99.9	(63)
76–199	15.6	71.1	13.3	0.0	100.0	(45)
200–399	12.5	53.1	25.0	9.4	100.0	(32)
400–799	0.0	50.0	33.3	16.7	100.0	(24)
800 or more	0.0	34.1	17.1	48.8	100.0	(41)
All	23.3	57.9	10.1	8.7	100.0	(335)

Note: Challenger campaign spending that was unavailable was coded in the 0–25,000 row.

[a] In thousands of dollars.

bents, providing direct contributions to challengers as well as to independent anti-incumbent advertising.)[58]

Yet this increase in incumbent dominance may be less than meets the eye, because 2004 involved a major change in campaign finance laws. The Bipartisan Campaign Reform Act (or BRCA) made a number of significant changes in financing rules. Among the most important were a ban on "soft money" (unlimited donations from corporations, unions, and wealthy individuals supposedly for party-building activities and not directly linked to the election of individual candidates), an increase in the size of allowable hard money donations by individuals to a candidate, and limits on political advertising around election time. In December 2003, the Supreme Court ruled that these major revisions of the law were constitutional, and they governed the 2004 campaign. With the rules changes it is difficult to be sure whether the 2004 numbers reflect real increases in incumbents' campaign resources or just a change in how similar distributions of resources are counted.

Linking spending to outcomes, Table 9-6 shows the relationship between incumbents' share of the vote in the 2004 House elections and the amount of money their challenger spent. Clearly, there is a strong negative relationship between how much challengers spend and how well incumbents do. In races where challengers spent less than $26,000, 98 percent of the incumbents received 60 percent or more of the vote. At the other end of the spectrum, in races where challengers spent $800,000 or more, 66 percent of the incumbents received less than 60 percent of the vote, and almost half received less than 55 percent. These results are consistent with those in earlier House elections for which comparable data are available.[59]

These findings are reinforced by other research that shows that challenger spending has a greater influence on election outcomes than does incumbent spending.[60] This generalization has been questioned on methodological grounds,[61] but further research by Gary C. Jacobson reinforced his earlier findings. Using both aggregate and survey data, Jacobson found that "the amount spent by the challenger is far more important in accounting for voters' decisions than is the amount of spending by the incumbent." [62] Analysis of Senate elections has also resulted in conflicting conclusions.[63]

Of course, challengers who appear to have good prospects will find it easier to raise money than those whose chances seem slim. Thus one might wonder whether these data simply reflect the fulfillment of expectations, in which money flows to challengers who would have done well regardless of spending. But other research indicates that that is probably not the case. In an analysis of the 1972 and 1974 congressional elections, Jacobson concluded, "Our evidence is that campaign spending helps candidates, particularly non-incumbents, by bringing them to the attention of the voters; it is not the case that well-known candidates simply attract more money; rather money buys attention." [64]

From this perspective, adequate funding is a necessary but not a sufficient condition for a closely fought election contest, a perspective consistent with the data in Table 9-6. Heavily outspending one's opponent is not a guarantee of victory; the evidence does not support the conclusion that elections can be bought. If an incumbent outspends the challenger, the incumbent can still lose if the challenger is adequately funded and runs a campaign that persuades the voters. The 1996 elections, for example, offer clear evidence of this. In eleven of the twenty-one races that year in which incumbents lost, the loser outspent the winner. In those contests, incumbents outspent challengers by 60 percent to 40 percent, on average, and in three instances the loser spent more than twice as much. Most important, however, no victorious challenger spent less than $600,000. That may be a rough estimate of the amount needed to have a chance to win against an incumbent.

On the other hand, a spending advantage is not a guarantee to a challenger. In an extreme example from 2000, Republican challenger Phil Sudan spent $3.247 million running against incumbent Ken Bentsen of Texas, who spent $1.354 million. Despite being outspent more than two to one, Bentsen won more than 60 percent of the vote.

Based on this analysis, our view can be summarized as follows: If a challenger is to attain visibility and get his or her message across to the voters—neutralizing the incumbent's advantages in name recognition and perquisites of office—the challenger needs to be adequately funded. If both sides in a race are adequately funded, the outcome will tend to turn on factors other than money, and the relative spending of the two candidates will not control the outcome.

This argument carries us full circle back to our earlier discussion and leads us to bring together the three kinds of resources that we have considered—candidate experience, incumbency, and campaign spending. Table 9-7 presents data showing the impact of these three factors in the 2004 House elections. We categorized challenger experience as strong or weak depending on previous elective office experience; challenger spending was classified as low or high depending on whether it was below or above $200,000.[65] The data show that each element exerts some independent effect, but the impact of spending seems to be more consequential in 2004, perhaps reflecting the growing attractiveness of "outsider" candidates. When challengers had weak experience and low spending (almost 60 percent of the races), all incumbents won, and 95 percent won with more than 60 percent of the vote. In the opposite situation, when the challenger both had strong experience and spent substantially, almost 60 percent of the races were relatively close. The combined results for the two intermediate categories fall between the extremes. In addition, three of the five incumbent defeats occurred in situations where the challenger was experienced and spent more than $200,000. Yet note how few such races there were in 2004. Table 9-7 also reveals that about half the challengers with strong experience were able to raise substantial funds, whereas only about one out of five challengers with little experience were able to do so.

This combination of factors also helps to explain the greater volatility of outcomes in Senate races. Previous analysis has shown that the effects of campaign spending in Senate contests are consistent with what we have found for House races: If challenger spending is above some threshold, the election is likely to be quite close; if it is below that level, the incumbent is likely to win by a large margin.[66] In Senate races, however, the mix of well-funded and poorly funded challengers is different. Senate challengers are more likely to be able to raise significant amounts of money than their House counterparts. Indeed, in recent elections a number of challengers (and open-seat candidates) have been wealthy individuals who could provide a large share of their funding from their own resources. The most extreme example comes from 2000, when Jon Corzine, the Democratic candidate for the open New Jersey Senate seat, spent more than $60 million of his own money to defeat his opponent by 50 percent to 47 percent. Corzine spent a total of $63 million; the Republican spent $6.4 million.[67]

Senate challengers are also more likely to possess significant experience in office. In Senate contests incumbents often face well-funded and experienced challengers, and the stage is then set for their defeat if other circumstances work against them. The lesson from the evidence presented here is captured by the words of David Johnson, the director of the Democratic Senatorial Campaign Committee, to Rep. Richard C. Shelby of Alabama, who was challenging Republican senator Jeremiah Denton in 1986. Shelby, who eventually won, was concerned that he did not have enough campaign funds because Denton was outspending him two to one. Johnson responded: "You don't have as much money, but you're going to have enough—and enough is all it takes to win." [68]

THE 2004 ELECTIONS: THE IMPACT ON CONGRESS

Because the electoral politics of recent years has revolved around efforts to reinforce or reverse the massive shift to the Republicans in 1994, subsequent elections have naturally been viewed in relation to the consequences of that upheaval. By

TABLE 9-7 Incumbents' Share of the Vote in the 2004 House Elections, by Challenger Spending and Office Background (in percentages)

Challenger experience/ spending	70% or more	60%–69%	55%–59%	Less than 55%	Total	(N)	Incumbents defeated (%)
Weak/low	32.6	62.2	3.6	1.6	100.0	(193)	0.0
Strong/low	23.9	67.4	8.7	0.0	100.0	(46)	0.0
Weak/high	7.7	48.1	25.0	19.2	100.0	(52)	3.8
Strong/high	0.0	40.9	22.7	36.4	100.0	(44)	6.8

Note: Percentages read across. Strong challengers have held a significant elective office (see note 65). High-spending challengers spent more than $200,000.

that standard the elections of 2004 had modest immediate effects, although they did have consequences for congressional policymaking. In terms of membership change, 2004 (like 2000) yielded considerably smaller shifts than elections in the early 1990s. The "class of 2004" included forty new representatives (9 percent of that body) and nine new senators (also 9 percent). Moreover, the 1992, 1994, and 1996 elections produced significant membership change, so their cumulative effect was profound. After 1996, nearly two-thirds of the Republicans in the House and almost half of the Democrats had come to that body in the previous three elections. In the Senate, twenty-seven of the fifty-five GOP members and thirteen of the forty-five Democrats had less than six years' service. With high House reelection rates from 1998 through 2004, the membership has become a little less "bottom-heavy," with 37 percent of Republicans and 25 percent of Democrats arriving in the 2000 election or later. The proportions were similar in the Senate, with nineteen of fifty-five Republicans and twelve of forty-four Democrats having less than six years' service.

The relatively small membership change yielded a narrow Republican majority in the House and a slightly larger one in the Senate, but it did give the GOP leadership a little more breathing room compared to the previous Congress. The situation, however, maintained the importance of moderate members of both bodies. This occurred in the context of a long-term decline of such members in Congress and an increase in the number of conservative Republicans and liberal Democrats. Twenty-five or thirty years ago, there was considerable ideological overlap between the parties. The Democrats had a substantial conservative contingent, mostly from the South, that was as conservative as the right wing of the Republican Party. Similarly, the GOP had a contingent (primarily northeasterners) who were as liberal as northern Democrats. In addition, each party had moderate members. During the intervening years, however, because of changes in the electorate and in Congress, this overlap between the parties began to disappear.[69] By the mid-1980s both parties in both houses of Congress had become more politically homogeneous, and in each chamber there was little departure from a complete ideological separation of the two parties.[70] Thus in the 109th Congress that convened after the 2004 elections, substantial majorities of each party had sharply different policy preferences from those in the other party, with the balance of power being held by a small group of members in the middle. This created a difficult situation for leaders of both parties in both chambers.

The House: Reinforcing Majority-Party Control

In 1995 the new Republican majorities instituted major institutional changes, especially in the House.[71] By comparison, the changes in House organization for the 109th Congress were modest, although still important. The most controversial action by House Republicans occurred shortly after the election: In November 2004, while organizing for the new Congress, the GOP removed a requirement that a party leader who was indicted for a crime must step down from his or her position. The Republicans were concerned about the possibility that Majority Leader DeLay might be indicted in Texas as part of a campaign finance investigation. The change caused a substantial uproar and produced a great deal of criticism from Democrats and more-neutral observers. GOP members, fearing that they might suffer electoral damage, pressured the leadership to reverse the change, and they complied in January 2005.[72]

The January rules package, however, contained other ethics changes that produced further controversy. The principal sticking point was a new rule that said that an Ethics Committee investigation of a complaint would only proceed if a majority of the committee voted to do so. The Ethics Committee membership was evenly divided between the two parties, and under the previous Congress's rules an investigation would begin if the vote was tied. The change meant that no inquiry into a Republican's conduct could begin without Republican support. This revision also produced great criticism and led to a stalemate in the Ethics Committee that blocked it from conducting business. Eventually the GOP leadership relented, and at the end of April 2005 the House reversed the changes in Ethics Committee procedures.[73] One change that was not undone, however, was a wholesale revision of the Republican membership of the committee. During the previous Congress, Ethics had three times rebuked DeLay for his behavior, causing him and the party much embarrassment. In January, Speaker J. Dennis Hastert removed the chairman and two other Republicans from the committee and replaced them with members who were more responsive to the leadership (including two who had made donations to DeLay's legal defense fund).[74]

Other actions taken at the beginning of the 109th Congress further reinforced the dominance of the majority leadership. The party's steering committee picked Jerry Lewis of California over two other candidates to chair the Appropriations Committee, partly because of his commitment to restrain government spending. "All three candidates, a GOP aide said, were required to 'jump through hoops' to prove they would cooperate closely with the White House and the speaker's office to stave off spending pressures from colleagues in both parties." [75] The Lewis selection was followed up by a plan, proposed by DeLay, to revise the subcommittee structure of the Appropriations Committee. "A Republican leadership aide said DeLay explained his plan to his colleagues by arguing that the current Appropriations structure was designed by Democrats to fund Democratic priorities. . . . DeLay argued that the new system would make it easier to hold the line on spending." [76] A month later the reorganization, which eliminated three of the thirteen subcommittees and redistributed the jurisdictions of the remaining subcommittees, was adopted by Appropriations. The Senate Appropriations Committee, after much resistance, eventually adopted most of the House's changes.

Perhaps the most striking of the House GOP's personnel actions involved the chairman of the Veterans' Affairs Committee, Christopher H. Smith of New Jersey. Smith had been a thorn in the side of the party leadership in the 108th Congress, frequently opposing efforts to cut back on expenditures for veterans. He had been warned that his activities could endanger his position, but he persisted, and in January 2005 the Republican leadership responded by removing Smith from his position as chair, the first chair that had been removed since the Republicans regained the majority after the 1994 elections. This put the final nail into the coffin of the old seniority system, which had exerted declining influence since the 1970s. Before that, committee chairmanships were guaranteed to go to the most senior member of the majority, whether or not that person was loyal to the party. Today in the House, the majority leadership can decide who will chair each committee, without regard to seniority.

The majority leadership's efforts to strengthen their party's hold on the levers of power have reinforced the partisan divisions in the chamber. Indeed, Speaker Hastert has made clear that he will try to prevent the Democrats from influencing the content of legislation. For example, in November, after the elections, Hastert stated that he would permit a piece of legislation to come to the House floor only if "the majority of the majority" supported it.[77] As we mentioned above, the ideological gulf within each chamber is huge, and there are fewer moderates to bridge the gap than in the past. This situation is reinforced because more members than ever have constituencies that support their party's agenda. In 2004 only fifty-nine representatives were elected from districts won by the opposition party's presidential candidate. By comparison, there were eighty-six such districts in 2000 and over one hundred in the Clinton years.[78]

The lack of ideological overlap between the parties and the absence of constituency pressure for centrist policies have fostered an atmosphere of personal dislike and conflict among members, most of whom play to their party's core supporters. One GOP member, Ray LaHood of Illinois, remarked: "We have deteriorated to a level of negativity and nastiness that I haven't seen in my ten years." [79] There have been efforts to counteract the situation, both in the 109th Congress and earlier. For example, representatives from each party announced in February 2005 that they were forming a "civility caucus" (formally called the Center Aisle Caucus) to find ways to improve decorum.[80] The bitterness, however, has clearly continued. In May 2005 the chairman of the House Judiciary Committee was pressured by party leaders to agree to change the language in a committee report contending that Democratic amendments to an abortion bill could benefit sexual predators.[81] Then in June, House business was brought to a halt when an Indiana Republican spoke during debate on a Democratic amendment to an appropriations bill that would have required the Air Force Academy to develop a plan to prevent "coercive and abusive religious proselytizing." (The amendment was in response to reports that non-Christian students had been discriminated against by conservative Christian students.) John Hostettler of Indiana argued, "Like a moth to a flame, Democrats can't help themselves when it comes to denigrating and demonizing Christians. . . ." [82] Despite the calls for civility, there is little prospect of significant reduction in the personal animosities and conflicts as long as the underlying electoral forces continue to produce political divisions such as we have seen for the last decade.

The Senate: Historical Traditions Unraveling

The four-seat Republican gain in the Senate strengthened the party's hold on the chamber and reinforced the polarization in it. As observed with the House's membership, the states' choices for president and senator exhibited closer alignment. In 1987, fifty-six senators—more than half the membership—had been elected from states carried by the other party's presidential candidate; in 2005 there were only twenty-five such senators.[83] Also as in the House, moderate senators, and those atypical of their parties, continue to be replaced by new members with more extreme views. Commenting on the trend, GOP senator Olympia J. Snowe, Maine, said, "Regrettably, we have seen an erosion in the Senate of centrists on both sides of the aisle." [84]

The change in membership has helped to reinforce the power of the Republican Party's leadership and of the conservative majority of the GOP. The most striking formal change was the adoption by the Republican Conference of a new rule that gave their party leader, Bill Frist, Tenn., additional influence over initial committee assignments. Until 2005, Republican committee vacancies were filled strictly by seniority. When a slot was open, each GOP senator had the chance, in order of seniority, to take it. The process, however, gave the leadership no influence over the allocation of this most valuable resource. So a number of more conservative members proposed an alternative: that the party leader would be able to appoint half of the Republican vacancies on the top twelve Senate committees. The proposal was adopted by a margin of one vote on a secret ballot, and a party aide indicated that the votes of the seven GOP freshmen provided the difference.[85] Nor was there any doubt among Republican moderates about the purpose of the new rule. Senator Snowe said, "There is only one reason for that change, and it is to punish people. . . . It is a punitive instrument to suppress diverse views." [86]

Other changes in the 109th Congress revolved around the effects of Republican rules on term limits for committee chairmen. During the 1990s the GOP set a limit of six years' service as chair of an individual committee, and a number of chairmen were affected by this rule at the beginning of the Congress in 2005. Most visible among the changes was the prospective replacement of Orrin G. Hatch of Utah, a solid conservative, by Arlen Specter of Pennsylvania, a moderate, as chairman of the Senate Judiciary Committee. This committee was particularly important to conservatives because it has jurisdiction over nominations to federal courts, including vacancies on the Supreme Court.

Immediately after the election, Specter had created a firestorm with remarks that the press interpreted as a warning to President Bush against choosing a nominee for the Supreme Court who would seek to overturn existing Court rulings on abortion. Specter denied that he had warned the president and noted that he had supported all of Bush's judicial nominees, but conservative groups around the country tried to marshal supporters to block his approval as chair.[87] Specter drafted a formal statement guaranteeing that Bush nominees would get quick hearings and early committee votes; it also said that he had no reason to believe that he couldn't support any nominee the president chose.[88] This was sufficient to secure the support of other Republicans on the Judiciary Committee, but conservatives in the country were not persuaded, and negative reactions continued in January when Specter chose two lawyers identified with Democratic causes as staff members for his committee.[89]

The controversy over Specter, however, merely set the stage for a bigger fight over Senate rules for considering Bush's judicial nominees. During the previous Congress, Senate Democrats had found some of the president's choices (approximately ten of more than two hundred nominees) too "extreme," and they used the filibuster to block a vote on confirming them. A filibuster involves continuing debate so that a vote cannot take place. The only way to stop a filibuster is to secure the votes of sixty senators to terminate debate, a procedure called "cloture." The filibuster had been used to block controversial legislation throughout the Senate's history, and it had been used with increasing frequency in the last two decades. Republicans, however, claimed that filibustering judicial nominations violated the Senate's constitutional obligation to "advise and consent" to presidential nominees. Given this constitutional interpretation, they also argued that a filibuster in this context could be terminated by a majority vote of the Senate. Moreover, they argued that such a change in Senate procedures could be implemented by a majority vote.

Democrats, and many outside observers, saw this possibility as a violation of Senate norms and the tradition of minority rights in the institution. The proposal was termed "the nuclear option" because using it, some argued, would bring mutual destruction to the contending parties and to the Senate's business. (Republicans preferred the term "constitutional option" and argued that they would restore the intended constitutional balance.) Democratic Leader Harry Reid of Nevada wrote a letter to Bill Frist in March warning that if the option was invoked, Democrats would stop working with the Republicans on most legislative business, excepting only bills to support U.S. troops and continuing government operations. "Beyond that," Reid said, "we will be reluctant to enter into any consent agreement that facilitates Senate activities, even on routine matters."[90]

Sparring over the nuclear option continued until May, when Frist made clear that he intended to bring one of the blocked nominations to the floor and use a ruling that fifty-one votes would be sufficient to terminate debate. The impending move and its possible consequences led a group of fourteen senior and moderate senators (seven from each party) to try to negotiate a compromise that would stave off potential disaster. At the last minute, the negotiators found sufficient common ground. The agreement committed the Democratic signers to refrain from a filibuster of future judicial nominees except in "extraordinary" circumstances, while the Republicans agreed not to support the nuclear option (as long as the Democrats abided by their commitment). The pact divided the controversial judicial nominees into three groups: three nominees were specifically cleared for a vote, two were specifically excluded from the agreement, and five others were not mentioned at all.[91] For the time being, a potential Senate meltdown was averted. Because John G. Roberts Jr., first nominated to fill the vacancy created by the planned resignation of Associate Justice Sandra Day O'Connor and then to be chief justice after the death of William H. Rehnquist, had such widespread support no filibuster was plausible. Yet O'Connor's position remained unfilled, and other vacancies are possible. It remained to be seen whether the agreement would persist or whether the nuclear option would confront the chamber again, especially given that the agreement did not define what "extraordinary" circumstances were.

The Bush Administration and Congress: Mandate or Lame Duck?

Other immediate consequences of the 2004 elections relate to their potential effects on governance in the next two years. One issue is whether President Bush has received a mandate from the electorate for the policies he argued for in the campaign. Obviously it is in the interest of every winning presidential candidate to claim a mandate, to increase the chances that his initiatives will be adopted. It is also clear that mandates are interpreted events—whether they exist is not a matter of meeting some clear standard, but rather a function of whether the media and other observers say they exist. To Bush's advantage, the day after the voting a number of media outlets discussed the White House's claim of a Bush mandate, a claim enhanced by the GOP gains in Congress. If a mandate implies that the public had endorsed the president's policy positions, however, there is plenty of evidence that 2004 did not provide one.

For example, a *Los Angeles Times* poll released October 25 asked respondents if they thought "the country is better off because of George W. Bush's policies and should proceed in the direction he set out, or do you think the country is not better off and needs to move in a new direction?" Forty-three percent chose the first option, and 55 percent chose the second.[92] Similarly, after the election, Gallup offered respondents two choices: "Because the election was so close, Bush should emphasize programs that both parties support," or "Because he won a majority of the votes, George W. Bush has a mandate to advance the Republican Party's agenda." Sixty-three percent selected the former statement, while only 29 percent agreed with the latter.[93] Lyn Nofziger, a former Reagan staffer, wrote, "The president and his people are deluding themselves if they think his victory signified general approval of his record, even within the Republican party." [94]

Mandate or not, Bush became president for four more years and will have the right to exercise presidential powers to secure his policy priorities. The additional seats won by the GOP in Congress will surely be an asset, especially in the Senate, but neither that nor this president's majority win guarantees smooth sailing, or even congressional support. Victory did not bring an end to political division. Postelection Gallup polls show that the partisan difference in Bush's approval ratings (seventy-six points) was the greatest for any second-term president since 1956.[95] And, as we saw in chapter 8 (see Figure 8-1 and also Table A8-1 in the appendix), the relationship between party identification and presidential approval was stronger in 2004 than in any of the previous eight National Election Study (NES) presidential election year surveys between 1972 and 2000. This political polarization in the public, and its reflection in Congress, will continue to offer challenges to the president's efforts to advance his agenda and thus to his party's ability to build a record of success for the future.

Moreover, now that Bush has been reelected, his incentives and those of his administration will continue to diverge from those of Republicans in Congress, because they will have to face the electorate in 2006, whereas he never will again. Bush claimed that he had secured political capital from the election and said that he intended to spend it to achieve his preferred policies. Chief among his domestic priorities was his plan to transform Social Security. Public support for his proposal was not very great, and even some Republicans expressed doubts, so the president and members of his administration spent two months traveling the country to try to persuade the voters. At the end of the effort, public support was lower than before.

We will discuss attitudes in the next chapter, but it is worth noting here that the president's declining approval ratings, which had reached approximately 40 percent in most polls by fall 2005, undermine efforts to rally congressional support for his initiatives. This is particularly true among the more moderate GOP members in both houses whose districts contain a smaller proportion of core Republican voters. They will not want to be perceived as linked with more extreme party positions and may be more inclined to defect and vote with Democrats than in the past. By fall 2005 this context had already produced a number of Republican defeats in the House during the 109th Congress, including adoption of a restriction on the FBI's use of a controversial provision of the Patriot Act related to access to library and bookstore records and the defeat of an effort to slash funding for public television.[96] Another example was the adoption of a bill authorizing the use of federal funding for additional stem cell research, beyond the limits that President Bush approved in 2001, which threatened to bring the first veto of the Bush presidency.[97]

THE 2006 ELECTIONS AND BEYOND

The Elections of 2006

Expectations about midterm elections are usually shaped by a strong historical pattern: The party of the president has lost strength in the House in twenty-three of the twenty-six midterm elections since the beginning of the twentieth century. The first column in Table 9-8 shows the magnitude of midterm losses since World War II. They average 23.1 seats for the president's party. There is, however, considerable variation, from the fifty-five-seat loss by the Democrats in 1946 to the six-seat Republican gain in 2002. Another consideration related to the president, however, clarifies the context for analysis: During the first midterm election

TABLE 9-8   House Seat Losses by the President's Party in Midterm Elections, 1946–2002

All elections			First term of administration			Later term of administration		
1946:	55	Democrats	1954:	18	Republicans	1946:	55	Democrats
1950:	29	Democrats	1962:	4	Democrats	1950:	29	Democrats
1954:	18	Republicans	1970:	12	Republicans	1958:	47	Republicans
1958:	47	Republicans	1978:	11	Democrats	1966:	47	Democrats
1962:	4	Democrats	1982:	26	Republicans	1974:	43	Republicans
1966:	47	Democrats	1990:	9	Republicans	1986:	5	Republicans
1970:	12	Republicans	1994:	52	Democrats	1998:	(+5)	Democrats
1974:	43	Republicans	2002:	(+6)	Republicans			
1978:	11	Democrats				Average: 31.6		
1982:	26	Republicans	Average: 15.8					
1986:	5	Republicans						
1990:	9	Republicans						
1994:	52	Democrats						
1998:	(+5)	Democrats						
2002:	(+6)	Republicans						
Average: 23.1								

of his presidency, the president may be able to make a plausible appeal that he has not had enough time to bring about substantial change or to solidify many achievements. Even if things are not going very well, voters may not be inclined to blame a president who has served for such a short time. But four years later (if the president is fortunate enough to face a second midterm), appeals of too little time are unlikely to be persuasive. After six years, if the economy or foreign policy is not going well, voters may seek a policy change by reducing the number of the president's partisans in Congress.

The second and third columns in Table 9-8 indicate that this is what has usually happened in the past. Losses by the president's party in the first midterm election of a presidency have tended to be much smaller than losses in subsequent midterms.[98] Indeed, with the exception of the results in 1986, 1994, 1998, and 2002, the two categories yield outcomes that are sharply different from one another. In the six midterm elections besides 1994 and 2002 that took place during a first term, the president's party lost between four and twenty-six seats, with an average loss of thirteen. In the five elections after the first term (excluding 1986 and 1998), the range of losses was between twenty-nine and fifty-five seats, with an average loss of forty-four. (We will discuss the atypical years later.)

Models of House Elections. In the last three decades, a number of scholars have constructed and tested models of congressional election outcomes, focusing especially on midterms, seeking to isolate the factors that most strongly influence the results. The earliest models, constructed by Tufte and by Jacobson and Samuel Kernell, focused on two variables: presidential approval and a measure of the state of the economy.[99] Tufte hypothesized a direct influence by these forces on voter choice and election outcomes. The theory was that an unpopular president or a poor economy would cause the president's party to lose votes and, therefore, seats in the House. In essence, the midterm elections were viewed as a referendum on the performance of the president and his party. Jacobson and Kernell, on the other hand, saw more indirect effects of presidential approval and the economy. They argued that these forces affected election results by influencing the decisions of potential congressional candidates. If the president is unpopular and the economy is in bad shape, potential candidates will expect the president's party to perform poorly. As a consequence, strong potential candidates of the president's party will be more inclined to forgo running until a better year, and strong candidates from the opposition party will be more inclined to run because they foresee good prospects for success. According to Jacobson and Kernell, this mix of weak candidates from the president's party and strong opposition candidates will lead to a poor election performance by the party occupying the White House. To measure this predicted relationship, their model related the partisan division of the vote to presidential approval and the economic situation early in the election year. This, they argued, is when decisions to run for office are being made, not at the time of the election, so it is not appropriate to focus on approval and the economy at that time. This view has come to be called the "strategic politicians hypothesis." [100]

More recent research has built from this base. One model, developed by Alan I. Abramowitz, Albert D. Cover, and Helmut Norpoth, considered a new variable: short-term party evaluations.[101] They argued that voters' attitudes about the economic competence of the political parties affect the impact of presidential approval and economic conditions on voting decisions: If the electorate judges that the party holding the presidency is better able to deal with the problems they regard as most serious, the negative impact of an unpopular president or a weak economy will be reduced. These authors concluded from their analysis of both aggregate votes and responses to surveys in midterm elections that there is evidence for their "party competence" hypothesis.

All of these models used the division of the popular vote as the variable to be predicted, and they focused only on midterm elections. More recent work has merged midterm results with those from presidential years, contending that there should be no conceptual distinction between them. These efforts have sought to predict changes in seats, without reference to the division of the vote. For example, a study by Bruce I. Oppenheimer, James A. Stimson, and Richard W. Waterman argued that the missing piece in the congressional election puzzle is the degree of "exposure," or "the excess or deficit number of seats a party holds measured against its long-term norm." [102] If a party wins more House seats than normal, those extra seats will be vulnerable in the next election, and the party is likely to suffer losses. Thus the party that wins a presidential election does not automatically benefit in House elections. But if the president's party does well in the House races, it will be more vulnerable in the subsequent midterm elections. Indeed, the May 1986 article by Oppenheimer and his colleagues predicted only small Republican losses for 1986 because Reagan's large 1984 victory was not accompanied by substantial congressional gains for his party. The actual result in 1986 was consistent with that prediction, for the GOP lost only five seats.

Another model of House elections was constructed by Robin F. Marra and Charles W. Ostrom Jr.[103] They developed a "comprehensive referendum voting model" of both presidential year and midterm elections and included factors such as foreign policy crises, scandals, unresolved policy disputes, party identification, and changes in the level of presidential approval. The model also incorporated measures reflecting hypothesized relationships in the models we discussed earlier: the level of presidential approval, the state of the economy, the strategic politicians hypothesis, exposure, and party competence. The model was tested on data from all congressional elections from 1950 through 1986.

The Marra-Ostrom analysis showed significant support for most of the predicted relationships. The results indicated that the most powerful influences affecting congressional seat changes were presidential approval (directly and through various events) and exposure. The model was striking in its statistical accuracy: the average error in the predicted change was only four seats. The average error varied little whether presidential or midterm years were predicted, and the analysis demonstrated that the usually greater losses for the president's party in second-midterm years resulted from negative shifts in presidential approval, exposure, and scandals.

Drawing on the insights of the various models, we can see how these factors may influence outcomes in the 2006 House elections. How well the economy is doing and what proportion of the voters approve of Bush's performance early in the year may encourage or discourage high-quality potential challengers. The same variables close to election time may lead voters to support or oppose Republican candidates, based on their judgments of the job the Bush administration is doing. The usual midterm losses happen for reasons; they are not part of the laws of nature. Therefore, if the usual reasons for such losses (such as a recession or an unpopular president) are not present in 2006, we should not expect the consequent losses to occur.[104] If those reasons are present, the context will be quite different.

In fall 2005 Bush's approval was about 40 percent, the lowest level of his presidency. Moreover, the economy continued to lag, compared with the sustained growth of the Clinton years, and the public was concerned about high gasoline prices and the flat stock market. If Bush's popularity stays at low levels and the economy does not improve, Republicans could be in danger of suffering losses, as in previous second midterms. The models indicate that other considerations are also important. Republican exposure is not as low as it was in 2002 (because of the loss of the most marginal districts in the 1996, 1998, and 2000 elections), but it is not high, either. The data on vote margins in 2004 that we examined above indicate that there are relatively few vulnerable GOP seats for the Democrats to target. Moreover, the analysis of short-term party evaluations reminds us that highly salient issues may offset the negative effects of poor economic conditions. Survey data in May 2005 showed that although Bush had negative ratings on the handling of every other issue, on terrorism his rating remained positive by 55 percent to 40 percent.[105] Finally, the impact of events such as crises and scandals, in the Marra-Ostrom model, reminds us that many unforeseeable events could influence the 2006 congressional election results.

The Redistricting Battle Continues. Earlier in this chapter we noted that Republican efforts to gain advantage through districting continued during the period before the 2004 elections and further efforts related to 2006. The 2004 election gave the GOP control over both the governorship and the legislature in Georgia, one of the few states that the Democrats had completely controlled after the 2000 Census and in which they thus could draft a set of districts tilted their way. After it gained political control, the GOP wanted to replace the Democratic plan, and in May 2005 the governor signed a redistricting bill that improved GOP chances in a number of districts. The position of a Republican incumbent was strengthened, and one Democratic representative saw more Republicans added to his district. Another Democrat had his residence removed from the district he represented. Some Democrats threatened a lawsuit against the new plan, on the grounds that it diluted minority voting strength in violation of the Voting Rights Act, but it was not clear that they would have the financial resources to make good on the threat.[106]

The Texas redistricting in 2003 and Georgia's in 2005 motivated Democrats to look for opportunities to retaliate in kind. The party gained control of the governor's office and the legislature in three states after the 2004 elections: Illinois, Louisiana, and New Mexico. So far, however, none of those states has been willing to redraw its district lines. In Illinois, for example, most of the Democratic representatives resisted the idea of the mid-decade redistricting. As one of them, Rep. Jerry F. Costello, said, "We have more of a concern for the institution than we do our partisan concerns. . . . Just because this was done in Texas doesn't make it right." [107] Of course it must also be noted that the political fortunes of the current members could be affected if the lines were changed.

Because of partisan conflict over redistricting in various states, some people have proposed new ways of dealing with this contentious issue. One of the most prominent efforts involved California and its new governor, Republican Arnold Schwarzenegger. The governor contended that leaving districting in the hands of the legislature undermined competition, noting that of the 153 seats in the state legislature and the California congressional delegation that were on the ballot in 2004, none changed party hands.[108] He proposed that the task of drawing district lines be given to a panel of retired judges and that the plan take effect before the 2006 elections. Schwarzenegger encountered significant resistance to his proposal, and not just from Democrats. Rep. David Dreier, the Republican chairman of the House Rules Committee, who had drawn the current map with Democratic Rep. Howard L. Berman, opposed the proposal, indicating that he thought any change should wait until after the 2010 Census.[109] Unable to get the state legislature to adopt his proposal, Schwarzenegger called a special election for November 2005 to vote on the redistricting proposal and three other reform proposals, but in July a state judge ruled that the districting proposal should be removed from the November ballot.[110] Then in August, the California Supreme Court reversed the lower court ruling and reinstated the districting proposal on the ballot for November. On November 8, the proposal was defeated.

Finally, the matter of the Texas redistricting is not yet completely settled. In October 2004, the Supreme Court overturned a ruling by a federal district court that had rejected the Democrats' argument that the districting plan was an unconstitutional partisan gerrymander. The Court returned the case to the district court for reconsideration in light of the decision in the Pennsylvania case we discussed earlier in this chapter. Although a majority in that case did not regard the Pennsylvania legislature's actions as unconstitutional, a different majority maintained that some other plan might violate constitutional restrictions. Some observers think that the Court's action is a signal that the swing vote on the issue, Justice Anthony M. Kennedy, may think that the Texas legislature went too far.[111] It is important to note that the departing Justice O'Connor voted against finding the Pennsylvania districting illegal.

Some Additional Considerations. A few further points related to the previous discussion are necessary to complete our analysis of the prospects for 2006 House races. The vulnerability of individual members varies between parties and across other attributes, and we should not expect those distributions to be similar from election to election. For example, in one year a party may have a relatively high percentage of freshmen or of members who won by narrow margins in the preceding election, whereas in another year the party's proportion of such potentially vulnerable members may be low. As Table 9-9 shows, both parties have a similar (and relatively small) number of members who won with less than 55 percent of the vote. Twenty-seven Republicans and sixteen Democrats fall into that category. This is fewer close races for each party than the number that resulted from the 2000 elections, and it is substantially fewer than the total of ninety-five after 1996. It is in this type of district that strong challengers are most likely to come forward and where the challengers who do run are most able to raise adequate campaign funds. Thus this aspect of the electoral landscape does not present a very attractive prospect for challengers of either party.

As our earlier analysis indicates, the parties' success in recruiting strong candidates for open seats and in opposing the other party's incumbents can be expected to play a significant role in shaping outcomes in 2006. Both Democratic and Republican campaign organizations were actively pursuing recruits during 2005. However, the personal and financial costs of candidacy and the difficulty of

TABLE 9-9   Percentage of the Vote Received by Winning House Candidates, by Party and Type of Race, 2004

Percentage of the vote	Republicans			Democrats		
	Reelected incumbent	Successful challenger	Open seat	Reelected incumbent	Successful challenger	Open seat
55 or less	18	2	7	8	2	6
55.1–60.0	22	0	3	13	0	2
60.1–70.0	111	1	6	82	0	4
70.1–100	57	0	5	84	0	2
Total	208	3	21	187	2	14

defeating an incumbent make recruitment difficult. For example, Diane Farrell was the Democratic candidate for the House in 2004 against Republican Rep. Christopher Shays of Connecticut. She lost, but she held him to 52 percent, the lowest vote share of his career. Yet as of early 2005 Farrell was reluctant to commit to another race against Shays because of doubts about her chances of improving on her previous showing.[112] Similarly on the Republican side, it has been difficult to recruit a challenger to Democratic Rep. Stephanie Herseth of South Dakota, even though Bush beat Kerry in the state by more than twenty points and the GOP defeated Tom Daschle in the Senate race.[113]

Of particular note here is the continuing impact of term limits in the states. Although the term limits movement failed to impose restrictions on members of Congress, it succeeded in imposing them on state legislators in more than twenty states, and those limits have been taking effect. One potential course for a state legislator who cannot run for reelection is to seek a congressional seat. This may lead to a greater number of strong challengers in House races than would otherwise be the case.

Also related to the questions of candidate recruitment and district vulnerability is the potential number of open seats. We have seen that open seats are more likely to switch parties than are those with incumbents and that both parties are more likely to field strong candidates for them. As of fall 2005, it was not clear how many vacancies there were likely to be. Only a few members have announced their retirement, but both parties are concerned about the prospects. Of particular concern is the likelihood that a number of representatives will leave the House to seek Senate seats or governorships.

A final factor is adequate campaign funding. Our earlier analysis indicates that the ability of 2006 challengers to raise campaign money will strongly affect the results in competitive districts. Given the potential impact that the 2006 results could have on the parties' political fates and the Bush administration's policies, campaign committees of both parties started working actively in 2005 to raise money. As has often been the case in recent election cycles, the Republicans had better results in the early going. The parties' April 2005 filings with the Federal

Election Commission showed that the NRCC had three times as much cash on hand as its Democratic counterpart ($9.6 million to $3.1 million). But the Democrats' Senate committee had 50 percent more funds available than the GOP committee.[114] Of course these early results may not be indicative of the final party totals. The only thing we can be fairly sure of is that the amounts of money raised and spent by both parties will be huge.

Senate Races in 2006. Because there are few Senate races and they are relatively independent of one another, we have focused our discussion of 2006 on the House to this point. We will now close with a few comments about the upper body's contests. Because of the Senate's six-year terms, and because the terms are staggered, the number of seats to be defended by each party varies from election to election. Even though the Republicans hold fifty-five seats in the entire Senate, more Democratic seats are at risk in 2006—seventeen to the Republicans' fifteen, plus the Vermont seat being vacated by independent James M. Jeffords. The number of potentially vulnerable seats appears to be about the same for both parties. Thus, as of now, the probability of a Democratic takeover of the Senate appears low. Because the numerical balance is so important for the fate of the parties' legislative agendas, however, many seats will be hotly contested, and each party is investing great efforts to recruit candidates. As we write, there are four definitely open seats because of the retirements of Jeffords, Democrat Mark Dayton of Minnesota, Democrat Paul S. Sarbanes of Maryland, and Majority Leader Bill Frist (the only Republican so far, who may be retiring to have more time to pursue a presidential candidacy). Hoping to stave off other Democratic departures, the chairman of the Democratic Senatorial Campaign Committee sought to induce potentially wavering Democrats to run again, and he received pledges to do so from all those who seemed doubtful.[115]

Given that there may not be any additional open seats, the recruitment of strong challengers against incumbents becomes even more salient. Of course, some candidates take little or no persuasion to run. For example, Sen. Rick Santorum, Pa., was generally recognized as one of the most vulnerable Republicans up for reelection, given his conservative record in a "blue" state. A number of Democrats considered entering the race, but others cleared the way when moderate state treasurer Bob Casey Jr. (the son of a former governor) decided to run. A number of polls in spring 2005 confirmed Santorum's precarious situation. One showed Casey with a fourteen-point lead.[116] To moderate his image, Santorum has taken a number of visible positions on issues such as the minimum wage and Amtrak, designed to appeal to moderate and liberal voters.[117] Another potentially vulnerable Republican is Lincoln Chafee, R.I., the most liberal GOP senator, in a very Democratic state. On the Democratic side, the incumbent who is likely to face the strongest challenge is Bill Nelson, Fla.

To summarize, then, House results are likely to depend heavily on the political context that exists both late in 2005 (when many candidates' decisions will be made) and in November 2006. The context will probably determine whether the historical pattern of losses by the president's party holds or is broken, as it was in the last two midterms. If there are few open Senate seats, the results probably depend on individual races fought independently of one another.

Beyond 2006: Solidifying the GOP Majority or Continued Uncertainty?

Just as every election has implications for those that follow, the elections of 2006 will have an impact on subsequent contests. We do not know those results, so we cannot yet describe the effects, but a few general considerations are likely to have an impact on future congressional contests.

As our discussion of redistricting indicates, the demographic shifts over the past decade that the Census revealed have political implications. Estimates from the Census Bureau indicate that rapid population growth continues in many states of the South and West, particularly Arizona, Florida, and Nevada. After the 2010 census, House seats will again be redistributed based on population shifts. Projections indicate that midwestern and Mid-Atlantic states, such as Ohio, New York, and Pennsylvania, will again lose seats to fast-growth states.[118] Some observers argue that because the gainers are mostly "red" states, this trend will automatically benefit the Republicans. We disagree. The situation is potentially more complex. After all, California experienced its most explosive population growth when it was a dependable GOP bastion in presidential voting. Subsequently it became a solidly Democratic state across the board. Population shifts also relate to ongoing conflicts over redistricting. In Ohio, a bipartisan citizens' group proposed a reform, similar to the plan proposed in California, that would have created an independent commission to redraw the state's congressional districts, although the plan would probably not have been implemented until after the next Census. But the proposal was also defeated on November 8, 2005. In Florida, a similar ballot proposal will face a referendum in 2006.[119] Finally, if the Democrats win complete control of New York in the next election, they may attempt to redraw the state's districts before the 2008 elections.[120]

One of the most important developments in recent decades has been the substantial growth of the Latino share of the electorate, from 3 percent to 7 percent between 1988 and 2000;[121] the growth kept pace with the expanded turnout in 2004. This growth is likely to continue, offering both opportunities and concerns to the two parties. Exit poll data for 2000 showed that Gore beat Bush among Hispanics by 67 percent to 31 percent, even though the Republican had run well among that ethnic group in Texas in both his gubernatorial and presidential races. The division of the Latino vote in 2004 is a matter of some controversy because, as we saw in chapter 5, there were substantial differences among the three exit polls that measured voting among Hispanics. GOP analysts hope that as Latinos make economic gains, they will shift more to the Republican Party, but they worry about the consequences if that shift does not happen. Alex Castellanos, a Republican media consultant, said, "The left side of the spectrum is growing. Our side is shrinking. . . . The Reagan coalition is not enough to win any more." [122] Thus it is important for the GOP to improve its competitive position among Latino voters or to compensate for the prospective population shifts in other ways. How this tug-of-war for Latino political support comes out will have significant consequences through the rest of this decade and in the future.

Finally, the issue of campaign finance reform remains in flux, and how it is resolved could have a significant impact on congressional elections. We noted in chapter 2 that the independent "527" groups, such as the Swift Boat Veterans for Truth, played a substantial role in the presidential election, especially financially. Campaign strategists in both parties expect such organizations to remain active, and the groups' public statements indicate that they have that intention. For example, Americans Coming Together, a pro-Democratic 527 group, has stated that it raised nearly $6 million between January and June 2005 and that it plans to spend about $30 million in a few battleground states in 2005 and 2006.[123] The Republican-controlled House is seeking to pass new legislation to reduce the role of the 527s. One bill, supported by the GOP leadership, would repeal the sections of the campaign finance law that place limits on the total amount individuals can contribute to candidates and party committees in each election cycle. It would also impose on 527s the same disclosure rules as currently apply to parties, PACs, and candidates and remove spending limits on political parties.[124] If such legislation passed, it could substantially alter the campaign finance environment. The Supreme Court may also face the campaign finance issue again. Vermont has placed limits on the amounts that campaigns can spend in state races, and the limits are being challenged in federal court.[125] This creates the possibility that the Supreme Court could revisit its previous ruling in *Buckley v. Valeo* (1976), which dealt with the post-Watergate campaign reforms. In that case the Court ruled that no spending limits could be imposed on congressional elections. If that ruling were revised or reversed, it could set the stage for even more consequential efforts at reform.

Chapter 10

The Congressional Electorate in 2004

In the preceding chapter we viewed congressional elections at the district and state levels and saw how they formed a national result. In this chapter we consider congressional elections from the point of view of the individual voter, using the same National Election Studies (NES) surveys we employed to study presidential voting. We discuss how social forces, issues, partisan loyalties, incumbency, and evaluations of congressional and presidential performance influence the decisions of voters in congressional elections. We also try to determine the existence and extent of presidential coattails.

SOCIAL FORCES AND THE CONGRESSIONAL VOTE

In general, social forces relate to the congressional vote the same way they do to the presidential vote (Table 10-1).[1] This has been true in our previous analyses of national elections, but the relationship is somewhat closer in 2004 than it was in the 1980s and 1990s. The vote for Democratic House candidates and the vote for Kerry are similar, both in the aggregate and in virtually all the categories we used in the presidential vote analysis (see Table 5-1).[2] This may reflect the closer relationship between party identification and the vote, in recent elections for both the president and Congress, that Larry M. Bartels has demonstrated in his analyses.[3]

Consider, for example, the relationship between voting and gender. In the total electorate, George W. Bush received 49 percent of the vote and House Republicans received 47 percent. Republicans ran one point better for the presidency than for the House among white female voters and three points better among white males. (Except for the discussion of voting and race, the analysis here, as in chapter 5, focuses on white voters.) The gender results are interesting when compared with the past. In 1988 there was a small gender gap in the presidential vote (about three points), with women more likely to vote Democratic than men, but there was no gap in the House vote. By 2000, however, the gender gap was more

TABLE 10-1 How Social Groups Voted for Congress, 2004 (in percentages)

Social group	Democratic	Republican	Total	(N)[a]
Total electorate	53	47	100	(689)
Electorate, by race				
African American	94	6	100	(94)
White	44	56	100	(769)
Hispanic (of any race)	73	27	100	(41)
Whites, by gender				
Female	46	54	100	(279)
Male	43	57	100	(245)
Whites, by region				
New England and Mid-Atlantic	51	49	100	(107)
North Central	37	63	100	(167)
South	37	63	100	(105)
Border	59	41	100	(29)
Mountain and Pacific	51	49	100	(116)
Whites, by urbanicity				
Inner city or large city	56	44	100	(105)
Suburb	41	59	100	(152)
Small town	45	55	100	(136)
Rural	36	64	100	(100)
Whites, by birth cohort				
Before 1939	47	53	100	(107)
1940–1954	42	58	100	(151)
1955–1962	42	58	100	(104)
1963–1970	32	68	100	(69)
1971–1978	52	48	100	(52)
1979–1986	63	37	100	(41)
Whites, by social class				
Working class	44	56	100	(132)
Middle class	46	54	100	(338)
Whites, by occupation				
Unskilled manual	51	49	100	(47)
Skilled manual	41	59	100	(86)
Clerical, sales, other white collar	40	60	100	(130)
Managerial	45	55	100	(71)
Professional and semi-professional	52	48	100	(137)

TABLE 10-1   (continued)

Social group	Democratic	Republican	Total	(N)[a]
Whites, by level of education				
Not high school graduate	49	51	100	(39)
High school graduate	48	52	100	(154)
Some college	39	61	100	(153)
College graduate	39	61	100	(105)
Advanced degree	52	48	100	(73)
Whites, by annual family income				
Less than $15,000	47	53	100	(36)
$15,000–$24,999	59	41	100	(48)
$25,000–$34,999	46	54	100	(54)
$35,000–$49,999	52	48	100	(73)
$50,000–$69,999	29	71	100	(83)
$70,000–$89,999	45	55	100	(84)
$90,000–$119,999	49	51	100	(63)
$120,000 and over	35	65	100	(66)
Whites, by union membership[b]				
Member	50	50	100	(116)
Nonmember	43	57	100	(407)
Whites, by religion				
Jewish	73	27	100	(22)
Catholic	51	49	100	(147)
Protestant	32	68	100	(269)
No preference	64	36	100	(78)
White Protestants, by religious commitment				
Medium to low	43	57	100	(90)
High	25	75	100	(80)
Very high	17	83	100	(48)
White Protestants, by religious tradition				
Mainline	43	57	100	(88)
Evangelical	23	77	100	(116)
Whites, by social class and religion				
Working-class Catholics	62	38	100	(34)
Middle-class Catholics	53	47	100	(98)
Working-class Protestants	26	74	100	(69)
Middle-class Protestants	35	65	100	(165)

[a] Numbers are weighted. The fifteen respondents who said they did not know how they voted and six voters who voted for other candidates have been excluded from the analysis.

[b] Respondent or a family member in a union.

pronounced in the votes both for president and for representatives; women who voted for a major-party candidate voted nine points more Democratic for president and ten points more Democratic for representatives. In 2004, gender differences were substantially reduced in both types of races, with the Democratic advantage among women down to seven points for president and three points in House contests.

The presidential and congressional voting patterns are similar within many other social categories, including race, social class, education, income, and religion. In both the presidential and the congressional votes, African Americans were much more likely to vote Democratic than whites. The difference was forty-seven points for the presidential race and fifty points in House contests. Working-class voters were two points *less* Democratic than middle-class voters in the House vote, but they were three points more Democratic for president. Catholics were nineteen points more likely to vote Democratic for representative than Protestants, and among Protestants, those we classified as Evangelical were twenty points more Republican than those we classified as mainline. Religious commitment was also related to congressional voting preferences, with the relationship not quite as strong as we found between religious commitment and presidential voting choices. Forty-three percent of the white Protestants who had medium or low levels of religious commitment voted Democratic, while Protestants who scored very high gave the Democrats only 17 percent. This is still an impressive relationship when one bears in mind that we are examining the impact of religious commitment only among white Protestants, a group that is predisposed to voting Republican by both race and religion.

There are some differences in the ways the presidential and congressional votes relate to income categories. It may be that the differences reflect the smaller number of cases in those categories, but overall patterns are similar and consistent: the propensity to vote Democratic is greater in lower-income categories. There is, however, one systematic difference. The Democratic presidential and House votes differ by only a single percentage point in all of the lowest five income categories, but the difference in the top three categories is four to eleven points higher for the House. Thus higher-income voters found the party's candidates for representative more attractive than its presidential candidate.

There are a few additional differences worth noting in the way social forces relate to the two types of votes. One is union membership. Union voters were only seven points more likely to vote Democratic for the House than nonunion voters, but they were nineteen points more likely to vote Democratic for the presidency. The relationship in 2000 was reversed, with the Democrats doing relatively better among union voters in House contests. Finally, with respect to education, the Democrats' support among those with advanced degrees was somewhat better for president than for representative. This also was a reversal from 2000. It should be noted, however, that all of these differences involve categories with relatively small numbers of respondents, so the results may simply be due to sampling variation.

The bottom line is that, overall, presidential and congressional voting among social groups was strikingly similar in 2004.

ISSUES AND THE CONGRESSIONAL VOTE

In chapter 6 we analyzed the impact of issues on the presidential vote in 2004. Any attempt to conduct a parallel analysis for congressional elections is hampered by limited data. One interesting perspective on issues in the congressional vote is gained by asking whether voters are affected by their perceptions of where candidates stand on the issues. Previous analysis has demonstrated a relationship between a voter's perception of House candidates' positions on a liberal-conservative issue scale and the voter's choice,[4] and we found similar relationships in 2004. For example, among self-identified liberals in the NES survey who viewed the Democratic House candidate as more liberal than the Republican candidate ($N = 92$), 90 percent voted Democratic; among self-identified conservatives who saw the Republican House candidate as more conservative than the Democrat ($N = 113$), 86 percent voted Republican.[5]

Research by Alan I. Abramowitz sheds additional light on this question. Abramowitz used NES surveys to demonstrate a relationship between candidate ideology and voter choice in both House and Senate elections, presenting his findings in two articles.[6] For the 1978 Senate election, Abramowitz classified the contests according to the clarity of the ideological choice that the two major-party candidates offered to voters. He found that the higher the ideological clarity of the race, the more likely voters were to perceive some difference between the candidates on a liberalism-conservatism scale and the stronger the relationship was between voters' positions on that scale and the vote. Indeed, in races with a very clear choice, ideology had approximately the same impact on the vote as party identification. In an analysis of House races in 1980 and 1982, Abramowitz found that the more liberal the voter was, the more likely the voter was to vote Democratic; but the relationship was statistically significant only in 1982.

Another perspective was offered in an analysis by Robert S. Erikson and Gerald C. Wright.[7] They examined the positions of 1982 House candidates on a variety of issues (expressed in response to a CBS News/*New York Times* poll) and found that, on most issues, most districts had the choice between a liberal Democrat and a conservative Republican. They also found that moderate candidates did better in attracting votes than more extreme candidates. In a more recent study, involving the 1994 House elections, Erikson and Wright show that both the issue stands of incumbents (measured by roll call votes) and the district's ideology (measured by the district's propensity to vote for Michael S. Dukakis in the previous presidential election) are strongly related to the congressional vote.[8] The same authors, in a study of the 1998 elections, employed a measure of candidate ideology that was derived from candidates' responses to questions about issues,

TABLE 10-2   Percentage of White Major-Party Voters Who Voted Democratic for the House, by Party Identification, 1952–2004

Party identification	1952	1954	1956	1958	1960	1962	1964	1966	1968	1970	1972	1974
Strong Democrat	90	97	94	96	92	96	92	92	88	91	91	89
Weak Democrat	76	77	86	88	85	83	84	81	72	76	79	81
Independent, leans Democrat	63	70	82	75	86	74	78	54	60	74	78	87
Independent, no partisan leanings	25	41	35	46	52	61	70	49	48	48	54	54
Independent, leans Republican	18	6	17	26	26	28	28	31	18	35	27	38
Weak Republican	10	6	11	22	14	14	34	22	21	17	24	31
Strong Republican	5	5	5	6	8	6	8	12	8	4	15	14

Note: To approximate the numbers on which these percentages are based, see Tables A8-2 (in appendix) and 8-2. Actual *N*s will be smaller than those that can be derived from these tables because respondents who did not vote (or who voted for a minor party) have been excluded from these calculations. Numbers also will be lower for the presidential election years because the voting report is provided in the postelection interviews, which usually

rather than from roll calls. That analysis confirms that incumbent ideology has a substantial effect on vote share, with moderates gaining more votes relative to more extreme members. Challengers' ideology does not have a consistent effect, reflecting the lesser visibility of their positions to the electorate.[9]

We examined the relationships between issues and congressional voting choices in 2004, analyzing the issues we studied in chapter 6. For the most part, the relationship between issue preferences and congressional vote choices was weak and inconsistent, and it was even weaker when we controlled for the tendencies of Democratic identifiers to have liberal positions on the issues and of Republicans to have conservative positions. However, partisan loyalties clearly affect congressional voting, even when we take issue preferences into account. Therefore, before considering the effects of other factors, we will provide more information about the effects of party identification on House voting.

PARTY IDENTIFICATION AND THE CONGRESSIONAL VOTE

As our previous discussion demonstrates, party identification has a significant effect on voters' decisions. Table 10-2 (corresponding to Table 8-4 on the presidential vote) reports the percentage of whites voting Democratic for the House across all categories of partisanship from 1952 through 2004.[10] The data reveal that the proportion of voters who cast ballots in accordance with their party identification declined substantially over time through the 1980s. During the 1990s, however, there was some resurgence of party voting for the House, especially among Republican identifiers.

1976	1978	1980	1982	1984	1986	1988	1990	1992	1994	1996	1998	2000	2002	2004
86	83	82	90	87	91	86	91	87	87	87	88	88	93	92
76	79	66	73	66	71	80	80	81	73	70	60	69	73	74
76	60	69	84	76	71	86	79	73	65	70	62	71	75	74
55	56	57	31	59	59	66	60	53	55	42	45	50	42	46
32	36	32	36	39	37	37	33	36	26	19	23	27	28	30
28	34	26	20	33	34	29	39	35	21	19	25	15	26	19
15	19	22	12	15	20	23	17	16	6	2	8	11	6	8

contain about 10 percent fewer respondents than the preelection interviews in which party identification was measured. The 1954 survey measured voting intention shortly before the election. Except for 1954, the off-year election surveys are based on a postelection interview.

Consider first the "strong" identifier categories. In every election from 1952 through 1964, at least nine out of ten strong party identifiers supported the candidate of their party. After that, the percentage dropped, falling to four out of five in 1980, and then fluctuated through 1992. But in the last six elections, strong identifiers have showed levels of loyalty similar to those in the late 1960s. The relationship between party and voting among weak party identifiers shows a more erratic pattern, although defection rates tend to be higher in most years between 1970 and 1992 than earlier. (Because we present the percentage of major-party voters who voted Democratic, the defection rate for Democrats is the reported percentage subtracted from 100 percent.) Note that during this period the tendency to defect was stronger among Republicans, which reflected the Democrats' greater number of incumbents, as discussed in chapter 9. Probably reflecting the effects of the Republicans' majority status and the corresponding increase in the number of Republican incumbents, from 1992 through 2000 the tendency of Democrats to defect rose, whereas among Republicans it fell. In the last two elections, however, the Democratic defection rate was lower in all three Democratic categories (and the GOP defection rate was lower among strong Republicans) compared to the previous two elections. We consider these matters further in the next section.

Despite the increase in defections from party identification since the mid-1960s, strong party identifiers continue to be notably more likely to vote in accord with their party than weak identifiers. In most years, weak Republicans were more likely to vote Republican than independents who leaned toward the Republican Party, although in 1996 and 1998 these groups were about equally likely to vote Republican. Weak Democrats were more likely to vote Democratic than independents who leaned Democratic in most of the elections from 1952 through 1978, but in a number of elections since then, the pattern has been reversed, and in 2004 the two groups were equally likely to vote Democratic. In general, then, the relationship between party identification and the vote was strongest in the 1950s and early 1960s, less strong thereafter, and shows a substantial recent rebound.

If party identifiers were defecting more frequently in House elections over recent decades, to whom have they been defecting? As one might expect from the last chapter, the answer is, to incumbents.

INCUMBENCY AND THE CONGRESSIONAL VOTE

In chapter 9 we mentioned Albert D. Cover's analysis of congressional voting behavior from 1958 through 1974.[11] Cover compared the rates of defection from party identification among voters who were of the same party as the incumbent and those who were of the same party as the challenger. The analysis showed no systematic increase over time in defections among voters who shared identification with incumbents; the proportions defecting varied between 5 percent and 14 percent. Among voters who identified with the same party as challengers, however, the rate of defection—that is, the proportion voting for the incumbent instead of the candidate of their own party—increased steadily, from 16 percent in 1958 to 56 percent in 1972, then dropped to 49 percent in 1974. Thus the declining relationship between party identification and House voting results largely from increased support for incumbents. Because there were more Democratic incumbents, this tendency was consistent with the higher defection rates among Republican identifiers, as seen in Table 10-2.

Controlling for party identification and incumbency, in Table 10-3 we present data on the percentage of respondents who voted Democratic for the House and Senate in 2004 that confirm this view. In voting for both House and Senate we found the same relationship as Cover did. As we have based the table on the percentage of major-party voters who voted Democratic, the defection rate for Democrats is the reported percentage subtracted from 100 percent. Among Republicans, the percentage reported in the table is the defection rate. (By definition, independents cannot defect.) For the House, the proportion of voters defecting from their party identification is low when that identification is shared by the incumbent: 3 percent among both Democrats and Republicans.[12] When, however, the incumbent belongs to the other party, the rates are much higher: 24 percent among Democrats and 27 percent among Republicans. It is worth noting that these pro-incumbent defection rates are both somewhat smaller than they were in 2000. This may reflect the strengthening of the relationship between party and voting behavior that we discussed above. Note also that the support of the independents is skewed sharply in favor of the incumbent: When there was an incumbent Democrat running, 87 percent of the independents voted Demo-

TABLE 10-3　Percentage Who Voted Democratic for the House and Senate, by Party Identification and Incumbency, 2004

	Party Identification					
	Democrat		Independent		Republican	
Incumbency	%	(*N*)	%	(*N*)	%	(*N*)
House						
Democrat	97	(106)	87	(85)	27	(63)
None	90	(30)	56	(25)	20	(41)
Republican	76	(55)	35	(83)	3	(117)
Senate						
Democrat	94	(89)	73	(92)	17	(102)
None	87	(38)	61	(23)	16	(37)
Republican	79	(42)	36	(28)	7	(44)

Note: Numbers in parentheses are the totals on which the percentages are based. Numbers are weighted. In this table and in subsequent tables in this chapter, we combine strong and weak Democrats and strong and weak Republicans. Independents include those who lean toward either party and "pure" independents.

cratic; when there was an incumbent Republican, 65 percent of the independents voted Republican.

The analogous pattern is somewhat weaker in the data on Senate voting (although it is stronger than in some of our previous analyses of Senate data). When given the opportunity to support a Republican House incumbent, 24 percent of the Democratic identifiers defected. Faced with the opportunity to support an incumbent Republican senator, 21 percent defected. Similarly, 27 percent of Republicans supported a Democratic House incumbent, but only 17 percent backed an incumbent Democratic senator. Because the proportion of the electorate that has the chance to vote for Democratic and Republican senatorial candidates will vary greatly from election to election, it is difficult to generalize about the overall effects of incumbency in Senate contests from data of this type. In the remainder of this chapter we continue to explore this relationship among party identification, incumbency, and congressional voting.

THE CONGRESSIONAL VOTE AS REFERENDUM

In chapter 7 we analyzed the effect on the vote for president in 2004 of perceptions of presidential performance, more or less viewing that election as a referendum on Bush's job performance. A similar approach can be applied here, employing different perspectives. On the one hand, a congressional election can be considered as a referendum on the performance of a particular member of Congress; on the other hand, it can be viewed as a referendum on the president's performance. We will consider both possibilities here.

TABLE 10-4   Percentage of Voters Who Supported Incumbents in House Voting, by Party Identification and Evaluation of Incumbent's Performance, 2004

	Voters' Evaluation of Incumbent's Job Performance			
	Approve		Disapprove	
	%	(N)	%	(N)
Incumbent is of same party as voter	99	(214)	[6]	(7)
Incumbent is of opposite party	57	(53)	0	(39)

Note: Numbers in parentheses are the totals on which the percentages are based. Numbers are weighted. The total number of cases is markedly lower than for previous tables because we have excluded respondents who did not evaluate the performance of the incumbent and those who live in a district that had no incumbent running. The number in brackets is the total number voting for the incumbent when there are fewer than ten total voters.

As we noted in chapter 9, for some time public opinion surveys have shown that the approval ratings that their constituents give to congressional incumbents are very high, even when judgments on the performance of Congress as an institution are not. While traveling with House incumbents in their districts, Richard F. Fenno Jr. noted that the people he met overwhelmingly approved of the performance of their own representative, although at the time the public generally disapproved of the job the institution was doing.[13] Data in the 2004 NES survey again indicate widespread approval of House incumbents: among respondents who had an opinion, 85 percent endorsed their member's job performance. Approval was widespread regardless of the party identification of the voter or the party of the incumbent. Indeed, as Table 10-4 shows, approval is above 50 percent even among identifiers of the party opposing that of the incumbent (53 respondents approved, and only 39 disapproved).

Further evidence indicates, moreover, that the level of approval has electoral consequences. Table 10-4 presents the level of pro-incumbent voting among voters who share the incumbent's party and among those who are of the opposite party, controlling for whether they approved or disapproved of the incumbent's job performance. If voters approved of the member's performance and shared his or her party identification, support was nearly 100 percent. At the opposite pole, among voters from the opposite party who disapproved, support is zero. In the mixed categories, the incumbents received intermediate levels of support. Because approval rates are very high even among voters of the opposite party, most incumbents are reelected by large margins, even in a difficult year for the Democrats such as 1994.

In chapter 9 we pointed out that midterm congressional elections are influenced by public evaluations of the president's job performance. Voters who think the president is doing a good job are more likely to support the congressional candidate of the president's party. Less scholarly attention has been given to this

TABLE 10-5   Percentage Who Voted Democratic for the House, by Evaluation of Bush's Performance, Party Identification, and Incumbency, 2004

	Evaluation of Bush's job							
	Incumbent Is Republican				Incumbent Is Democrat			
	Approve		Disapprove		Approve		Disapprove	
Party identification	%	(N)	%	(N)	%	(N)	%	(N)
Democrat	[2]	(7)	75	(52)	88	(16)	99	(107)
Independent	20	(56)	49	(37)	74	(31)	97	(68)
Republican	2	(126)	10	(10)	30	(64)	[0]	(1)

Note: Numbers in parentheses are the totals on which the percentages are based. Numbers are weighted. The number in brackets is the total number voting for the incumbent when there are fewer than ten total voters.

phenomenon in presidential election years, but the 2004 NES survey provides us with the data needed to explore the question.

On the surface at least, there would appear to be a strong relationship. Among voters who approved of Bush's job performance, only 24 percent voted Democratic for the House; among those who disapproved of the president's performance, 82 percent supported Democrats. In 1980 there was a similar relationship between the two variables, but when controls were introduced for party identification and incumbency, the relationship all but disappeared.[14] Approval of Carter increased the Democratic House vote by a small amount among Democrats but had virtually no effect among independents and Republicans. In 2004, however, the results are somewhat different. Table 10-5 presents the relevant data on House voting, controlling for party identification, incumbency, and evaluation of Bush's job performance. They show that even with these controls, evaluations of the president's job had an impact on House voting by all groups of identifiers. To be sure, Republicans were still more likely both to approve of Bush and to vote Republican than were Democrats. Yet even after controlling for the pull of incumbency, within the Democratic and independent party identification categories those who disapproved of Bush's job performance were more likely to vote Democratic for the House than were those who approved. (There are so few Republicans who disapproved of Bush that there is little room for an effect in that category.)

PRESIDENTIAL COATTAILS AND THE CONGRESSIONAL VOTE

Another perspective on the congressional vote, somewhat related to the presidential referendum concept we just considered, is the impact of the voter's presidential vote decision, or the length of a presidential candidate's "coattails." That is, does a voter's decision to support a presidential candidate make him or her more likely to support a congressional candidate of the same party, so that the congressional candidate, as the saying goes, rides into office on the president's coattails?

Expectations about presidential coattails have been shaped in substantial measure by the period of the New Deal realignment. Franklin D. Roosevelt won by landslide margins in 1932 and 1936 and swept enormous congressional majorities into office with him. Research has indicated, however, that such strong pulling power by a presidential candidate may have been a historical aberration, and that in any event, that candidates' pulling power has declined in recent decades.[15] In an analysis of the coattail effect since 1868, John A. Ferejohn and Randall L. Calvert pointed out that the effect is a combination of two factors: how many voters a presidential candidate can pull to congressional candidates of his party and how many congressional seats can be shifted between the parties by the addition of that number of voters.[16] (The second aspect is called the "seats/votes relationship," or the "swing ratio.")

Ferejohn and Calvert discovered that the relationship between presidential and congressional voting from 1932 through 1948 was virtually the same as it was from 1896 through 1928 and that the impact of coattails was strengthened by an increase in the swing ratio. In other words, the same proportion of votes pulled in by a presidential candidate produced more congressional seats in the New Deal era than it had previously. After 1948, they argue, the coattail effect declined because the relationship between presidential and congressional voting waned. Analyzing data from presidential elections from 1956 through 1980, Calvert and Ferejohn reached similar conclusions about the length of presidential coattails.[17] They found that although every election during the period exhibited significant coattail voting, over time the extent of such voting probably declined. More recently, James E. Campbell and Joe A. Sumners concluded from an analysis of Senate elections that presidential coattails exert a modest but significant influence on the Senate vote.[18]

Data on the percentage of survey respondents who voted Democratic for the House and Senate in 2004, controlling for their presidential vote and their party identification, are presented in Table 10-6. For both houses the expected relationship is apparent, although it is somewhat weaker than in 2000. Within each party identification category, the proportion of Bush voters who supported Democratic congressional candidates is lower than the proportion of Kerry voters who supported Democratic candidates. There were only two Nader voters in the survey, and we omitted them from the table.

Because we know that this apparent relationship could be just an accidental consequence of the distribution of different types of voters among Democratic and Republican districts, in Table 10-7 we present the same data on House voting in 2004, but this time controlling for the party of the House incumbent. When we made this comparison in 1996, we found that despite this additional

TABLE 10-6   Percentage Who Voted Democratic for the House and Senate, by Party Identification and Presidential Vote, 2004

| Presidential vote | Party Identification | | | | | |
| | Democrat | | Independent | | Republican | |
	%	(N)	%	(N)	%	(N)
House						
Bush	67	(12)	31	(72)	12	(209)
Kerry	92	(178)	81	(111)	39	(13)
Senate						
Bush	39	(13)	28	(58)	14	(175)
Kerry	92	(158)	92	(77)	25	(12)

Note: Numbers in parentheses are the totals on which the percentages are based. Numbers are weighted.

TABLE 10-7   Percentage Who Voted Democratic for the House, by Presidential Vote, Party Identification, and Incumbency, 2004

| Party identification | Voted for Bush | | Voted for Kerry | |
	%	(N)	%	(N)
Incumbent Is Democrat				
Democrat	[1]	(6)	98	(99)
Independent	63	(24)	98	(57)
Republican	25	(60)	[2]	(3)
Incumbent Is Republican				
Democrat	[3]	(5)	80	(50)
Independent	13	(40)	62	(37)
Republican	2	(109)	[2]	(8)

Note: Numbers in parentheses are the totals on which the percentages are based. Numbers are weighted. The number in brackets is the total number voting for either Bush or Kerry when there are fewer than ten total voters.

control, the relationship held up very well. Within every category for which comparisons were possible, Dole voters supported Democratic candidates at substantially lower rates than did Clinton voters. In 2004 (as well as in 2000), however, there are so few defectors in the two major parties that the comparisons are largely limited to independents, where the effect remains substantial. These limited data are consistent with the interpretation that the presidential vote exerted some small influence on the congressional vote, although not as strong an influence as partisanship and congressional incumbency.

CONCLUSION

In this chapter we have considered a variety of possible influences on voters' decisions in congressional elections. We found that social forces have some impact on their choices. There is evidence from the work of other researchers that issues also have an effect. Incumbency has a major and consistent impact on voters' choices. It solidifies the support of the incumbent's partisans, attracts independents, and leads to defections by voters who identify with the challenger's party. Incumbent support is linked to a positive evaluation of the representative's job by the voters. The tendency to favor incumbents currently appears to benefit the Republican Party in House races. Within the context of this incumbency effect, voters' choices also seem to be affected by their evaluations of the job the president is doing and by their vote for president. Partisanship has some direct impact on the vote, even after controlling for incumbency. The total effect of partisanship, however, is augmented because most incumbents represent districts that have more partisans of their party than of the opposition. Thus, the long-term advantage of Democrats in congressional elections was built on a three-part base: there were more Democrats than Republicans in the electorate; most incumbents of both parties achieved high levels of approval in their constituencies; and the incumbents had resources that made it possible for them to create direct contacts with voters. With the GOP now in the majority in Congress, their members may continue to benefit from the last two factors while they try to reduce their weakness on the first.

PART 4

The 2004 Elections in Perspective

A careful analysis of voting patterns provides evidence for speculating about future elections. Political leaders have always wanted advice about the future, and there were usually people willing to oblige them. Few have fared as well as the Greek commander Themistocles, who was rewarded by correctly interpreting the cryptic advice of the oracle at Delphi, going on to defeat the Persians at the decisive naval Battle of Salamis (480 B.C.) because he relied on her prophecy that the Greeks would be saved by a "wooden wall." Few fared as badly as King Saul who, even after the woman at En-dor raised the prophet Samuel from his grave, was told that he faced certain defeat (I Samuel 28:7–20).

We do not have the powers attributed to the Delphic oracle, nor are we prophets like Samuel.[1] But we recognize that there is a great deal of uncertainty in politics, making any projections risky. As Nicolò Machiavelli reminded us more than four centuries ago, "Fortune is arbiter of half of our actions, but she ... leaves the other half, or close to it, for us to govern."[2]

Anyone who attempts to discern the implications of the 2004 elections for the future of American party politics must recognize that those elections were in large part a reaction to the terrorist attacks against the United States on the morning of Tuesday, September 11, 2001. On that morning American Airlines Flight 11, which took off from Boston heading to Los Angeles at 7:59 a.m. (EDT), was hijacked, and at 8:46:40 a.m. crashed into the North Tower of the World Trade Center; at 8:14 a.m. United Airlines Flight 175 took off from Boston headed to Los Angeles, was hijacked, and at 9:03:11 a.m. crashed into the South Tower; at 8:20 a.m. American Airlines Flight 77 took off from Dulles International Airport near Washington, D.C., bound for Los Angeles, was hijacked, and at 9:37:46 a.m. crashed into the Pentagon; finally, at 8:42 a.m. United Airlines Flight 93 took off from Newark, New Jersey, bound for San Francisco and was hijacked. By now many passengers had heard on their cell phones about the earlier hijackings that morning, and they revolted against the hijackers to prevent them from crashing the aircraft into an important target. The airplane crashed into a field near Shanksville, Pennsylvania, at 10:03:11 a.m.[3] These hijackings were clearly the work of the al Qaeda terrorist organization. Nearly three thousand people died, the largest loss of life from an enemy attack on U.S. soil.[4]

The 9/11 attacks quickly became the basis for the war in Afghanistan, Operation Enduring Freedom, which began on October 7, 2001. George W. Bush justified this war on the widely accepted premise that the Taliban, the extremist Moslem leaders in Afghanistan, were harboring al Qaeda training bases, and this justification was accepted by many countries. On March 20, 2003, the United States, and a more limited coalition, launched Operation Iraqi Freedom against Saddam Hussein's regime in Iraq. For this operation, the links to the 9/11 terrorist attacks were much more tenuous, and subsequent research suggests that there was very little direct relationship between Hussein's regime and al Qaeda. In addition, Bush argued that Saddam was developing weapons of mass destruction (WMDs). It was well known that he had used poison gas against both the Iranians in the Iraq-Iran war (1980–1988) and against the Kurdish minority in his own country. But after Saddam was ousted no WMDs were found, nor was there any evidence that Iraq had a program that could have produced nuclear weapons.

This setting made the 2004 election unusual because, unlike most elections, there were serious arguments about terrorism and foreign policy issues. Of course Americans want to be protected from terrorists. But two questions still exist: Who would do a better job of protecting them? What, if any, civil liberties should we be willing to sacrifice to be more secure? These are arguments that go back to the Alien and Sedition Acts of 1798–1801. Most Americans were also willing to fight to prevent terrorism overseas, and most agreed that the Taliban regime in Afghanistan had harbored terrorists. But the connection between Iraq and terrorism was much less clear. Once again, two questions were raised: How should the war on terrorism be fought? Who would do a better job of fighting it? And despite the importance of terrorism and war, voters still had economic concerns. So their votes would still be affected by their answers to two additional questions: What was the condition of the national economy? Who would do a better job of taking care of the economy?

Voters were also influenced by their positions on specific issues, as well as their partisan loyalties, both directly and in conjunction with the way those loyalties shaped their retrospective evaluations and policy preferences. We have presented a good deal of the evidence about evaluations of the government and attitudes toward the issues in our previous chapters, and in chapter 11 we attempt a summary assessment of its implications.

Just as no one could have predicted the impact of 9/11, even several years after the attack, no one can predict the specific events that may shape the 2006 midterm and the 2008 presidential elections, let alone later elections of this century. All the same, the U.S. government has certain constitutional features that make it more predictable than most other democracies. Writing in 1984, Arend Lijphart classified the United States as the only established democracy with a presidential system.[5] Unlike parliamentary democracies, in which no one can predict when elections will be held, American congressional and presidential elections are held at fixed intervals. Even if the president must be replaced, no special election is held to replace him.[6] The U.S. election schedule is so fixed that presidential and congressional elections were held in 1864, during the Civil War,[7] and in 1944, when World War II was still being heavily fought in both Europe and Asia.[8]

Given our constitutional system, we know that all 435 seats in the U.S. House of Representatives will be filled in 2006 and again in 2008.[9] In each of these years, about a third of the Senate seats will be filled. Moreover, we know that George W. Bush's second term will end on January 20, 2009. Although election dates are not constitutionally fixed, we can be confident that a midterm election will be held on November 7, 2006, and that a presidential election will be held on November 4, 2008.

We have already discussed prospects for the 2006 midterm elections, but even there we encountered problems. One of the most regular patterns in American elections is that the party holding the White House loses strength in the House of Representatives during midterm elections. This had been true, with but a single exception (1934), in thirty-eight of the thirty-nine midterm elections between 1842 and 1994. The one exception occurred during Franklin D. Roosevelt's first presidential term, when the Democrats, who gained seats, were emerging as the majority party. But this pattern failed to hold in both 1998 and 2002. Because there are so few Senate contests during each election year, it is easier to look at the contests on a case-by-case basis, but in all elections there are surprises. As we have seen, however, it is difficult to envision how the Democrats can overcome the current five-seat GOP margin.

We do see a potentially tight race for the presidency, although whether a pattern of highly competitive races will prevail past 2008 is far more difficult to assess. We can examine four broad possibilities. First, we consider the prospects of the Democrats' becoming the majority party again. Second, we explore prospects for the Republicans, noting that divisions within the GOP may complicate its efforts to hold political power. Of course, both parties will need to choose nominees for 2008, since George W. Bush cannot run because of the Twenty-second Amendment. Although it seems clear that Hillary Rodham Clinton would be the Democratic front-runner if she decides to run, the Republican contest appears to be far more wide open. Third, we discuss the prospects for a new political party, discussing the demise of the Reform Party and showing why new parties find it so difficult to break the duopoly held by the Republicans and the Democrats. Lastly, we examine the prospects for electoral volatility, the pattern that has prevailed in postwar American politics.

Chapter 11

The 2004 Elections and the Future of American Politics

In his classic study of political parties, Maurice Duverger argued that in some democracies there is a clearly dominant party. Despite competitive elections, a single party is consistently at the center of political power. A party, Duverger wrote, "is dominant when it holds the majority over a long period of political development." Although a dominant party may occasionally lose an election, it remains dominant because "it is identified with an epoch" and because "its doctrines, ideas, methods, its style, so to speak, coincide with those of the epoch." One reason a party dominates is that it is believed to be dominant. "Even the enemies of the dominant party, even citizens who refuse to give it their vote," Duverger wrote, "acknowledge its superior status and its influence; they deplore it but admit it." [1]

Duverger's concept of the dominant party provides insights about the decline of the Democratic Party after 1964. Scholars of comparative politics provide at least four clear examples of dominant parties: Mapai in Israel (now the Labor Party);[2] the Christian Democrats (DC) in Italy; the Social Democratic Party in Sweden; and the Liberal Democratic Party (LDP) in Japan.[3] But Duverger argued that if a country has free elections, a dominant party is always in peril. "The dominant party wears itself out in office, it loses its vigour, its arteries harden." And, he concluded, "every domination bears within itself the seeds of its own destruction." [4]

Duverger appears to have been prophetic.[5]

Mapai was the dominant party in Israel even before Israel attained statehood in 1948. Asher Arian writes:

In the years immediately following independence, Mapai was presented with an opportunity shared by few parties in democratic polities—that of presiding over the creation of a constitutional and political order. As a consequence, it was closely identified with the new state, and it was the party of those segments of Israeli society most involved with those heroic years. It was able to translate this identification into an organizational net-work that complemented and amplified the advantages conveyed by its image. Furthermore, most of this network consisted of channels main-tained largely at the expense of the state, with the result that the party and government tended to merge in the popular mind.[6]

Mapai remained dominant until 1977, when an electoral "upheaval" drove the Alignment (the successor to Mapai) from office. Although the Alignment was the largest party in the Knesset after the 1996 election, the Israeli electorate also voted directly for prime minister, and Labor again lost power. Labor, running an elec-toral list named "One Israel," was the largest party in 1999, and its leader, Ehud Barak, was elected prime minister. But One Israel won only twenty-nine of the 120 Knesset seats. Moreover, two years later it lost power again, when Ariel Sharon, the leader of the opposition Likud, won a landslide election for prime minister.[7] And in the Knesset election held in January 2003, Labor won only nineteen seats.

In Italy, the Christian Democrats, with United States support, won nearly half the vote in 1948. They lost power more gradually than Mapai, but they suffered a major loss in 1983, which brought to power Italy's first socialist prime minis-ter.[8] By 1994, with revelations of widespread corruption, the DC lost two-thirds of its remaining support, and a new coalition, headed by media magnate Silvio Berlusconi, came to power. In 1996, the remnants of the DC lost even more sup-port, and a coalition of new political parties, the Olive Tree coalition, came to power, only to be replaced by a more leftist coalition in 1998. In the 2001 election the Casa delle Libertà (House of Freedom) won. The main party in that coalition, Forza Italia (Forward Italy) was Berlusconi's party, and he once again became prime minister. By 2001 the Christian Democrats were splintered and won only a negligible percentage of the vote.

The Swedish Social Democratic Party came to power in 1932. Although it was forced into opposition in 1976 and 1979, it returned to power in 1982. But in 1991 the nonsocialists won an absolute majority of the vote. The Social Demo-crats regained power in 1994, and despite winning only 36 percent of the vote, the party narrowly held power in 1998. Although four parties made a major effort to defeat the Social Democrats in 2002, the party gained ground, winning 40 percent of the vote. Clearly, it remains an important political force, but it is not the markedly dominant party it was before 1976.

Since its formation in 1955, Japan's Liberal Democratic Party has consistently been the largest party in the country's House of Representatives, but in 1993, in the face of mounting scandals, the LDP split and the prime minister dissolved the House of Representatives and called new elections. Although it was still the largest party, the LDP was excluded from the coalition formed after the election.

The LDP won nearly half the seats in the House of Representatives in 1996 and formed a government supported by several parties. The LDP suffered major losses in the Upper House elections in 1998, forcing the resignation of the prime minister. In the 2000 elections for the House of Representatives, the LDP did not win enough seats to reestablish its past dominance, but it continued to rule in coalition with smaller parties. The LDP was initially expected to do poorly in the summer 2001 Upper House elections, but it chose a dynamic new leader, Junichiro Koizumi, and surpassed expectations, providing its coalition with a majority of the seats. In fall 2003 the LDP won the election for the House of Representatives, but with a reduced majority. Most observers thought that the real winner was the Democratic Party (DPJ), which had strong support among the young and in urban areas. It actually won a plurality of the popular vote and gained seats. And in the Upper House elections in summer 2004, the DPJ again did well, outpolling the LDP and gaining seats. Commentators began to argue that Japan could be close to developing a two-party system. However, in summer 2005 Koizumi declared a snap election for the House, in which he made the privatization of the Japanese postal system, which also is the world's largest bank, the major issue. Throwing its opponents on the defensive, the LDP and its allies made major gains in the September 2005 election, while the Democratic Party lost over a third of its seats. This victory may not end the LDP's long-term decline, but for the moment, it clearly diminishes the prospects for Japan to develop a two-party system.

Writing in 1958, Duverger argued that the Democrats were the dominant party in the United States, even though Dwight D. Eisenhower, running as a Republican, had been elected president in both 1952 and 1956. Duverger viewed Eisenhower's election as a personal victory that did not change the balance of partisan power.[9] Scholars writing in 1964 might have seen the Democrats as even more dominant. The Democrats won the White House under Franklin D. Roosevelt in 1932 and then went on to win six of the next eight elections. In 1964, under Lyndon B. Johnson, the Democrats had won by a landslide over Republican Barry M. Goldwater and gained thirty-eight seats in the House. The only Republican victories between 1932 and 1964 had come under a former general, Eisenhower, who had been courted by both the Democratic and the Republican parties. The Republicans, much like the Whigs, who ran William Henry Harrison in 1840 and Zachary Taylor in 1848, defeated the Democrats by choosing a war hero as their standard-bearer. Both generals elected by the Whigs died shortly after taking office, whereas Eisenhower served two full terms. Between the 73rd Congress, elected in 1932, and the 89th, elected in 1964, the Republicans had held a majority for only four years (the 80th Congress, elected in 1946, and the 83rd Congress, elected in 1952).

In retrospect, it is easy to see that Democratic dominance had within it "the seeds of its own destruction," and they were in the composition of the coalition that supported it. The Democratic Party drew support from northern blacks and southern whites. That coalition was sustainable only as long as discrimination against African Americans in the South was not a major issue. After the civil rights movement began in the mid-1950s, ignoring racial injustice in the South became untenable. By backing the Civil Rights Act of 1964 and the Voting Rights Act of 1965, Lyndon Johnson chose a position that was morally correct, and he may have had strategic goals in mind as well. In hindsight, the seeds of future Democratic defeats can be seen in Johnson's landslide victory over Goldwater, for in addition to winning his home state of Arizona, Goldwater carried Alabama, Georgia, Louisiana, Mississippi, and South Carolina. By the end of the 1960s, African Americans in those states could vote, and as Johnson expected, they voted heavily Democratic. Even so, in most subsequent elections, these and the remaining southern states, have voted Republican. Virginia has voted Republican in all ten presidential elections between 1968 and 2004.

From 1968 to 1988 the Republicans won five of six presidential elections, and the only Democratic victory came in 1976, when Jimmy Carter narrowly defeated Gerald R. Ford, the president who had pardoned Richard M. Nixon after he was forced out of office because of the Watergate scandal. Several political scientists, writing in 1988, argued that the Republicans had become the dominant party in presidential elections.[10]

Yet after the 1988 election it appeared that the coalition that had supported Ronald Reagan and his successor, George H. W. Bush, might also have within it the seeds of its own destruction. Reagan had created a coalition of social conservatives, for whom the battles against abortion and for the right to hold prayers in public schools were important issues, and economic conservatives, who believed that reducing the power of the government was the key to economic growth. Although both Reagan and Bush paid mainly lip service to conservative values, they provided tangible benefits to social conservatives by a series of court appointments, especially appointments to the Supreme Court, that put *Roe v. Wade* in jeopardy. In 1992, when Republican economic policies no longer appeared to provide economic growth, many economic conservatives and some social conservatives deserted Bush, although many turned to H. Ross Perot instead of to Bill Clinton. In 1994 two-thirds of the Perot voters who went to the polls voted Republican, contributing to the party's legislative landslide.

Despite Clinton's reelection in 1996, the Democrats did not return to electoral dominance, for they failed to regain control of Congress. Between 1828 and 1996, the Democrats had won the presidency twenty times in forty-three elections, but 1996 was the first time they won the White House without winning control of the U.S. House of Representatives. Although the Democrats unexpectedly gained five House seats in 1998, the Republicans retained control of both chambers. In 2000 the Democrats gained another two seats in the House, but they were still short of control. Moreover, despite their popular-vote victory, they lost the presidency as well.

When George W. Bush became president in January 2001 the Republicans held the presidency, the House, and the Senate for the first time since the 83rd Congress ended in January 1955. But the Republicans had won with a minority of the popular vote and had won just 271 electoral votes, only one more than the 270-vote majority required. They held only a 221-to-212 edge in the House and controlled the Senate only because Vice President Dick Cheney could cast a tie-breaking vote in a chamber divided between fifty Republicans and fifty Democrats. And after Republican senator James M. Jeffords, Vt., left the Republican Party to become an independent in May 2001, the Democrats regained control of the Senate.

The Republicans gained six House seats in the 2002 midterm elections, and they gained two seats in the Senate. Even though the net distribution of seats between the parties changed very little, the Republicans once again controlled the presidency, the House, and the Senate.

The Republicans did better in 2004 than in 2000, but we should not exaggerate their success. George W. Bush did win a majority of the popular vote, but he held only a 2.4 percentage point margin over John F. Kerry, the narrowest popular-vote margin of all seventeen incumbent victories since 1832.[11] His margin of thirty-five electoral votes was second lowest among all twenty-one elections in which an incumbent was elected.[12] The Republicans gained three seats in the House, extending their margin to 232 to 202, with one independent, Bernard Sanders, Vt., who votes with the Democrats. But, according to Gary C. Jacobson, had it not been for the extraordinary redistricting in Texas in 2003, the GOP would have lost several House seats.[13] The Republicans, as we saw in chapter 9, did best in the 2004 Senate contests: By winning five open Democratic seats in the South, they gained a net of four Senate seats, resulting in a total of fifty-five to the Democrats' forty-four, with Jeffords, an independent, voting with the Democrats.

Although the Republicans' majority is tenuous, it is difficult to deny that they hold an edge over the Democrats. But the Republicans have not become dominant, and they still have obstacles to face before they can cement their majority. We will do our best to avoid specific predictions, but we will apply what we have learned to address alternative possibilities. First, we discuss the likelihood of a resurgent Democratic Party. Second, we examine Republican prospects for the future. Third, we explore prospects for a new political party, paying particular attention to the reasons the Reform Party failed to effectively challenge the major parties. Finally, we discuss prospects for continued electoral volatility, the condition that has prevailed in postwar American politics.

PROSPECTS FOR THE DEMOCRATS

When Clinton assumed the presidency in January 1993, the Democratic Party had control of the House and the Senate, and twelve years of divided government came to an end. Although Clinton had won only 43 percent of the popular vote, he had, in principle, the opportunity to provide a policy agenda that would transform the Democrats into the majority party for decades to come. Despite some early policy successes, the second year of his administration was marked by pol-

icy failures. The ambitious health care reforms that Clinton proposed received little legislative support, and Clinton abandoned his own reforms to back a proposal by Senate majority leader George J. Mitchell, D-Maine. Ultimately, neither
the House nor the Senate passed a health care reform bill. Clinton also failed to
achieve significant welfare reform, another important policy goal.

Whatever prospects the Democrats had to seize the policy agenda disappeared
with the Republican midterm victory of 1994. After the Democrats' defeat, Clinton moved to the policy center. In 1996 he signed legislation substantially changing the welfare system, transferring authority to the states, and ending "welfare as
we know it." But he did not entirely abandon liberal Democratic goals. Indeed, in
1996 the electorate saw substantial policy differences between Clinton and Bob
Dole on policy issues. The main reason for Clinton's reelection was the good condition of the economy and favorable retrospective evaluations by the electorate.

In 2000 Al Gore, responding to the need to minimize defections to the Green
Party candidate, Ralph Nader, made some populist appeals. Even so, although the
electorate saw clear policy differences between Al Gore and George W. Bush, they
had seen sharper differences between Clinton and Dole four years earlier. The
issue preferences of the electorate did not clearly favor either Gore or Bush. However, the retrospective evaluations of the electorate favored the Democrats, and
that should have worked more to Gore's advantage. Perhaps Gore lost the election because he did not emphasize the successes of the Clinton presidency.

After the 2000 election the Democrats had the solace of having won the plurality of the popular vote and having broken even with the Republicans in the
Senate. Indeed, the 2000 election was so close that James W. Ceaser and Andrew
E. Busch refer to it as "the politics of the perfect tie." [14] The 2004 election was not
as close, but the Democrats have some reason for optimism, especially with
respect to regaining the presidency. As we saw in chapter 6, the issue preferences
of the electorate may have been somewhat closer to where Bush was perceived to
stand, but they were not as clearly pro-Republican as they had been four years
earlier. As we saw in chapter 8, both the 2004 National Election Study (NES) survey and the 2004 General Social Survey (GSS) show that the Democrats still held
a small majority in the party loyalties of the electorate, although, given that
Republicans are somewhat more likely to vote than Democrats, there is for all
intents and purposes an equal distribution of partisan support. [15] The Democrats
can hope that Bush's success was due to retrospective evaluations on issues, such
as terrorism and domestic security, that may not provide a long-term advantage
for the Republican Party.

It is possible to write an optimistic scenario for the Democrats. The most
extensive thesis arguing that the Democrats will regain their majority was
advanced by John B. Judis and Ruy Teixeira in their widely discussed book *The
Emerging Democratic Majority.* [16] They argue that the demographic groups that
tend to support the Democrats are growing as a percentage of the electorate,
especially African Americans, Hispanics, and Asian Americans. Women are also
more likely to support the Democratic Party (although, as we saw, gender differ-

ences were small in 2004). Moreover, professionals, who used to support the Republican Party, are increasingly supporting the Democrats. Democratic strength, they argue, will be based in urban areas that specialize in the production of ideas, which Judis and Teixeira call "ideopolies." But they are not claiming that a Democratic majority is a certainty. "This survey is not intended to show that a Democratic majority is inevitable," they write. "What it shows is that over the next decade the Democrats will enter elections at an advantage over the Republicans in securing a majority. Whether Democrats actually succeed will depend, in any given race, on the quality of the candidates they nominate and on the ability of candidates and their strategists to weld what is merely a potential majority into a real one." [17] As we pointed out in the introduction to part 1, the 2004 election results have not led Teixeira to abandon his thesis. He currently edits an online newsletter, *Donkey Rising*, which publishes research showing favorable prospects for the Democrats.[18]

Finally, the Democrats will need to choose a presidential nominee for 2008 in a process that may be even more frontloaded than the 2004 nomination contest. It is difficult to imagine that the Democratic nomination will be uncontested, but as of this writing, Hillary Rodham Clinton seems to be a formidable front-runner, if she chooses to run. Although she was seen as a liberal, since becoming the junior senator from New York in January 2001 she has become more moderate and developed a reputation as a pragmatic legislator.[19] Granted, she would need to be reelected to her Senate seat in November 2006, but she has already raised a huge war chest, and few credible Republicans seem ready to challenge her. Whether she would make a strong general election candidate might very well depend on whom the Republicans nominate, a question we discuss in the next section.

PROSPECTS FOR THE REPUBLICANS

After the 2004 elections many Republicans viewed their victory as a triumph and many Democrats viewed the future with despair. We saw at the beginning of the book that several political scientists viewed the election as a crucial event signaling a Republican majority. It is clear that Democratic dominance has been shattered. But in our opinion the Republicans have not yet attained a dominant position. Rather, there is still a close balance between the political parties.

We hold this view mainly because Bush's win was not accompanied by a sizable shift in party identification toward the GOP, although there was some shift in a Republican direction. It is true that the NES party identification time series of twenty-seven surveys since 1952 and the GSS series of twenty-five surveys between 1972 and 2004 show that the percentage of strong Republicans was higher in 2004 than in any previous survey conducted by these organizations. Even so, the NES found only one in six respondents to be a strong Republican, and the GSS found only one in seven. Granted, some groups that used to support the Democrats now strongly support the Republicans, most notably southern whites. And there are other social groups, such as white Catholics and the white working class, that no longer provide reliable support for the Democratic Party. For a Methodist to win a majority of the Catholic vote against a Catholic was a major achievement.

Although the Republicans have won the last two elections, that does not mean that the Democrats face dismal prospects. They have won two of the last four elections, measured by electoral votes, and they won the popular vote in three of the last four. Even viewing 2004 by itself, one must recall that Bush was an incumbent president in the middle of an ongoing war, with an improving economy. What is more surprising—that he won reelection, or that his opponent came as close as he did? Many analysts (and Republican strategists) have pointed out that Bush won the greatest number of votes for president in the history of the United States—certainly an impressive achievement. What few have recognized is that Kerry received the second-largest number of votes in history, over 4.5 million more than Reagan received in his historic 1984 landslide.[20] Despite Bush's claim to have earned political capital, we saw in chapter 9 that there is substantial evidence that the 2004 election did not provide a mandate for his policies. Since his reelection Bush has had considerable difficulty launching new policy initiatives. Despite his extensive efforts to promote Social Security reforms, including private accounts, neither the public nor Congress has been receptive. By October 2005, in the wake of the poor handling of the Hurricane Katrina disaster, the growing number of U.S. deaths in Iraq, which reached 2,000 in October, the failed attempt to nominate Harriet E. Miers to the Supreme Court, and the indictment of I. Lewis Libby Jr., Dick Cheney's chief of staff, for obstruction of justice and perjury, had created a sense of political crisis. Of course, Bush may recover from his current difficulties, as Ronald Reagan did after the Iran-Contra scandals during his second term. In any event, Bush does not have to face the electorate himself, although if his second term is viewed as a failure that will hurt Republican congressional candidates, as well as the GOP standard-bearer in 2008. Some Democrats were already gloating that Bush's difficulties had severely damaged Republican prospects. "If there was a realignment going on," according to John Podesta, a White House chief of staff for Bill Clinton, "it has crashed and burned." [21]

Bush's failure to achieve much success may result largely from his reelection's resting mainly on positive retrospective evaluations concerning the war on terrorism. We saw in chapter 7 that when the public was asked which party would do best in handling the economy, keeping the country out of war, and the war on terrorism, the Republicans held a lead on fighting terrorism. As we also saw, the Edison Media Research/Mitofsky International (EMR/MI) poll showed that Bush held a substantial lead over Kerry on the question of who could best be trusted to handle terrorism. We grant that the Republicans benefited for over four decades from the perception that they were the better party to fight the cold war, but the war against terrorism may not continue to yield a partisan advantage. We agree with the assessment that the struggle against terrorism will last for decades. But given the randomness of terrorist acts, it seems difficult to see how the struggle to contain it will provide a long-term advantage to either party. All mainstream political leaders want to combat terrorism, so the only arguments are what strategies are the most effective for fighting it and the extent to which Americans may need to surrender some personal freedoms to contain it. Moreover, although Bush may have benefited by being a wartime president, it is difficult to see how the GOP nominee in 2008 will benefit if U.S. forces are still suffering substantial casualties. The GOP could benefit, however, if the war in Iraq is viewed as successful.

Meanwhile, the Republicans hold a minority position on some social issues. Granted, most Americans do not favor unrestricted access to abortion, for example, but very few want to make it illegal. A majority of Americans do not favor same-sex marriages, but most do not want to amend the U.S. Constitution to outlaw them. Most do not favor euthanasia, but most do not favor politicians intervening to prevent courts from removing feeding tubes from patients in a persistent vegetative state, as when Congress, the Florida legislature, and Republican governor Jeb Bush tried to have feeding tubes reinserted to prolong the life of Terri Schiavo in spring 2005. Most Americans probably would not prefer liberals on the Supreme Court, but most do not want ideological conservatives, either. And most Americans, including many Republicans in Congress, favor embryonic stem cell research, which Bush severely limited by executive order in summer 2001.

These social issues are important because they are the main concern of Evangelical Christians, a key component of the Republican coalition. Many believe that it would be difficult for any Republican to win the 2008 presidential nomination without their support. Perhaps this belief encouraged Senate majority leader Bill Frist, Tenn., to declare, based on viewing a videotape, that Schiavo was not brain-dead, or led Gov. Jeb Bush to attempt to have feeding tubes reinserted. Even after Schiavo's death, and after an autopsy showed she had no chance of recovery, Bush ordered the Florida attorney general to investigate her husband, Michael Schiavo, for failing to call 911 promptly when she first collapsed; but the governor was so heavily criticized that this order was canceled.

The greatest test of social conservative influence may come in conflicts about filling vacancies on the U.S. Supreme Court. When Chief Justice William H. Rehnquist died on September 3, 2005, Bush nominated John G. Roberts Jr., who had already been nominated to replace retiring Associate Justice Sandra Day O'Connor, to be chief justice. After Roberts was confirmed, Bush nominated his own White House counsel, Miers, to replace O'Connor. The main opposition to Miers came from conservatives, who were not convinced she had appropriate conservative credentials. On October 31, Bush nominated Samuel A. Alito Jr., a Third Circuit appeals judge, who has served as a judge for fifteen years, to replace O'Connor. Alito is viewed as a favorite of conservatives, although his nomination may face strong opposition from Senate Democrats.

Thus, although the Republicans may be able to recover from their current problems, their prospects do not seem as bright as they seemed in the first months after the election. In our view, the electorate is still very evenly balanced between the two major parties.

PROSPECTS FOR A NEW POLITICAL PARTY

For more than 150 years the Democrats and Republicans have held a duopoly in American politics. Ever since the election of Democrat Franklin Pierce in 1852, either a Republican or a Democrat has won the presidency. And of the thirty-six elections between 1864 (when Abraham Lincoln was reelected) and 2004, there have only been six elections in which a third-party or independent candidate won the electoral votes of even a single state. Moreover, the Republicans and the Democrats have dominated Congress. The last Congress in which more than one out of ten members was from a third party was the 55th (1897–1899). From the 76th Congress (1939–1941) to the present, there has never been a single House in which more than two members did not affiliate with one of the major parties. In his study of twenty-seven democracies, Arend Lijphart classifies the United States as having the lowest number of "effective electoral parties" and the second-lowest number of "effective parliamentary parties." [22]

Third parties in the United States face many obstacles, the most important of which are the rules by which candidates win office. With the exception of Maine and Nebraska, all states and the District of Columbia have winner-take-all rules for allocating presidential electors. To win the electoral votes of these states, a presidential candidate (or to be more precise, a slate of electors pledged to a presidential candidate) must win a plurality of the popular votes in the state. Despite winning nearly a fifth of the popular vote in 1992, Ross Perot did not win a single electoral vote. The only third-party candidates to win electoral votes since World War II were the States' Rights Democrats in 1948 and the American Independent Party in 1968, and all of their votes came from the states of the old Confederacy. Despite some regional variation in Perot's vote in 1992, he had no regional base, and there was very little regional variation in his support in 1996.

Third parties have a difficult time getting on the ballot, although in recent years court decisions have made it somewhat easier than it was before George C. Wallace's 1968 candidacy. Independent or third-party candidates also have financial problems, and federal election laws place limits on their ability to raise money. Democratic and Republican candidates are guaranteed federal funding, whereas third-party candidates can receive funding only if they win 5 percent of the vote, and then only after the election. In 1992 Perot spent $65 million of his own money. In 1996, he accepted $29 million in federal funding (which he was entitled to on the basis of his 1992 vote). Based on Perot's 1996 vote, the Reform Party was entitled to $12.6 million in federal funding in 2000, one of the reasons its nomination was attractive.

In 1992 Perot ran as an independent, but in 1995 he announced that he would help fund efforts to create a new political party, the Reform Party. One of his claims was that Americans wanted a new political party. This new party, he predicted, would be "the largest party in the country" and would replace either the Republican or the Democratic Party.[23] But Perot's share of the popular vote fell from 18.9 percent to 8.4 percent. By summer 2000 the Reform Party was badly split. Two conventions were held, one nominating Pat Buchanan, the other selecting John Hagelin, who had run as the Natural Law Party candidate in 1992 and 1996. The Federal Election Commission was forced to decide who the party nominee was because it had the authority to determine who would receive federal funding. It ruled in favor of Buchanan. But Buchanan won only .4 percent of the vote. The Green Party, with Ralph Nader as its candidate, was more successful drawing 2.7 percent of the vote, but it fell short of its goal of winning 5 percent and did not qualify for federal funding in 2004. In 2004 David Cobb, the Green Party candidate, won only .1 percent of the vote, and Nader, running as an independent, won .4 percent. The Reform Party did not field a candidate.

In 2004, only the Democrats and Republicans qualified for federal funding. Although both the Bush and Kerry campaigns had declined federal funding for the nomination contest, each campaign received nearly $75 million for the 2004 general election campaign.[24]

One may ask whether the Reform Party or the Green Party is, or ever was, a political party. In effect, the Reform Party was never much more than a vehicle for Perot's presidential candidacy. The Green Party was willing to nominate Nader, even though he was not a member of the party, because it needed someone to give it visibility and credibility. But it seems ill-positioned to challenge the major parties. Environmentalist parties usually win only a small percentage of the vote and are heavily disadvantaged by the plurality-vote rules used in American elections.[25]

As Joseph A. Schlesinger reminds us, a political party in a democracy is an organized attempt to gain political office by winning elections.[26] When the Republican Party emerged in 1854, it ran candidates for office at every level in the nonslave states. Politically ambitious Whigs, as well as members of the Free Soil Party and the Know-Nothing Party, could become Republicans and seek election to state legislatures, Congress, and governorships. In the 34th Congress, the first elected after the Republican Party was founded, 108 of the 234 House members were Republicans. The Republican Party provided the collective benefit of limiting slavery, but it also provided selective incentives for individuals seeking political office. Politically ambitious citizens today may want selective benefits, such as office for themselves, as well as collective goods, such as electing Perot and protecting the environment.[27]

Third parties face another fundamental problem: they find it difficult to recruit attractive presidential candidates. The very openness of the major-party nomination contests encourages strong candidates to seek either the Republican or the Democratic presidential nomination. There are no constraints on entering the primaries, and a major-party nomination will probably continue to attract far more votes than it repels. Strong candidates who actually have a chance of winning the presidency are likely to seek one of the major-party nominations.[28]

PROSPECTS FOR CONTINUED ELECTORAL VOLATILITY

Although many are predicting a period of Republican dominance, we see solid reasons for predicting continued electoral volatility. Perot's appeal in 1992 is the main reason for this prediction. More than nineteen million Americans voted for Perot in 1992, even though he had a negligible chance of winning and even though Clinton's margin in the preelection polls was not large enough for confidence that he would be elected. Even in 1996, Perot won eight million votes; and a total of 10 percent of the electorate voted for Perot and other minor-party candidates. The 1992 and 1996 elections mark the first time since the Civil War that the two major parties together failed to win 90 percent of the vote in two consecutive elections.

In both 1992 and 1996 Perot's success resulted partly from the weak partisan loyalties of the electorate. But party loyalties have grown somewhat stronger since 1996, and as we saw in the 2004 NES survey, 34 percent were strong partisans, the same level as during the "steady-state" period between 1952 and 1964 that Philip E. Converse has described.[29] On the other hand, the 2004 GSS survey showed that only 29 percent were strong party identifiers. Weak partisans, and independents with no party leanings, are more likely to be volatile in their voting choices than are those with strong party ties.

As we saw in chapters 5 and 10, with the exception of race, social forces have a relatively weak relationship to voting behavior, and that may also contribute to electoral volatility. Today few voters feel bound to a party by social class, religion, or ethnicity. This absence of affiliation increases the share of the electorate that is likely to switch its vote from one election to the next.

Finally, the relatively low turnout in the United States may also contribute to future volatility. Even though many observers have emphasized the four-percentage-point increase in turnout in 2004, compared with other democracies, turnout in the United States remains very low (see Table 4-1). The 80 million Americans who did not vote in 2004 could easily have overcome the three-million-vote margin of Bush over Kerry. On the other hand, there was clearly a substantial increase in turnout, and the mobilization of new groups into the electorate has been viewed as one of the key indicators of a partisan realignment. So however much we believe that continued electoral volatility is likely, we would readily concede that both the increase in partisan loyalties and the increase in turnout in 2004 weaken the thesis that there has been a partisan dealignment.

In our view, it is too soon to conclude that 2004 was a "defining moment," as William Crotty and his colleagues argue.[30] Our best guess is that the 2008 presidential election will be hotly contested, with two strong parties nominating contenders with good chances of victory—and of defeat. And despite recent strength by independent and third-party candidates in 1992 and 1996, we see little evidence that the duopoly of the Republicans and Democrats is threatened. The U.S. electoral system, like that in Britain, provides considerable protection for the two major parties. Ultimately, however, the people can displace a major party, although that has not happened in the United States since the 1850s or in Britain since the 1930s. But the ability of the Republicans and the Democrats to retain their duopoly depends on the ability of their leaders to solve the nation's problems.

Appendix

TABLE A7-1   Evaluation of How Well the Government Has
Done on the Most Important Issue and Major-
Party Vote, 2004

Rating	Percentage
A. Evaluation of Governmental Performance on Most Important Issue (in percentages)	
Very good job	12
Good job	48
Bad job	24
Very bad job	15
Total	99
(N)	(1,019)[a]
B. Percentage of Major-Party Vote for Incumbent Party's Nominee (Bush)[b]	
Very good job	90
(N)	(94)[a]
Good job	74
(N)	(365)[a]
Bad job	14
(N)	(179)[a]
Very bad job	6
(N)	(126)

[a] Numbers are weighted.
[b] The numbers in parentheses in part B of the table are the total number of cases on
which the percentages are based.

TABLE A8-1   Approval of Incumbent's Handling of Job, by Party Identification, 1972–2004 (in percentages)[a]

Approve of incumbent	Party Identification						
	Strong Democrat	Weak Democrat	Independent, leans Democrat	Independent	Independent, leans Republican	Weak Republican	Strong Republican
2004	6	26	23	39	78	89	98
2000	92	88	81	65	49	52	49
1996	98	89	85	66	45	49	18
1992	12	28	20	32	65	71	91
1988	24	43	37	70	82	83	94
1984	22	48	32	76	90	93	96
1980	73	54	44	35	19	19	9
1976	24	55	46	69	87	85	96
1972	38	65	52	73	87	92	94

[a] For the numbers on which these percentages are based, see Figure 8-1.

TABLE A8-2 Party Identification among Whites, 1952–1978 (in percentages)

Party identification[a]	1952	1954	1956	1958	1960	1962	1964	1966	1968	1970	1972	1974	1976	1978
Strong Democrat	21	22	20	26	20	22	24	17	16	17	12	15	13	12
Weak Democrat	25	25	23	22	25	23	25	27	25	22	25	20	23	24
Independent, leans Democratic	10	9	6	7	6	8	9	9	10	11	12	13	11	14
Independent, no partisan leaning	6	7	9	8	9	8	8	12	11	13	13	15	15	14
Independent, leans Republican	7	6	9	5	7	7	6	8	10	9	11	9	11	11
Weak Republican	14	15	14	17	14	17	14	16	16	16	14	15	16	14
Strong Republican	14	13	16	12	17	13	12	11	11	10	11	9	10	9
Apolitical	2	2	2	3	1	3	1	1	1	1	1	3	1	3
Total	99	99	99	100	99	101	99	101	100	99	99	99	100	101
(N)	(1,615)	(1,015)	(1,610)	(1,638)[b]	(1,739)[b]	(1,168)	(1,394)	(1,131)	(1,387)	(1,395)	(2,397)	(2,246)[b]	(2,490)[b]	(2,006)

[a] The percentage supporting another party has not been presented; it usually totals less than 1 percent and never totals more than 1 percent.
[b] Numbers are weighted.

TABLE A8-3   Party Identification among Blacks, 1952–1978 (in percentages)

Party identification[a]	1952	1954	1956	1958	1960	1962	1964	1966	1968	1970	1972	1974	1976	1978
Strong Democrat	30	24	27	32	25	35	52	30	56	41	36	40	34	37
Weak Democrat	22	29	23	19	19	25	22	31	29	34	31	26	36	29
Independent, leans Democratic	10	6	5	7	7	4	8	11	7	7	8	15	14	15
Independent, no partisan leaning	4	5	7	4	16	6	6	14	3	12	12	12	8	9
Independent, leans Republican	4	6	1	4	4	2	1	2	1	1	3	—[b]	1	2
Weak Republican	8	5	12	11	9	7	5	7	1	4	4	—[b]	2	3
Strong Republican	5	11	7	7	7	6	2	2	1	0	4	3	2	3
Apolitical	17	15	18	16	14	15	4	3	3	1	2	4	1	2
Total	100	101	100	100	101	100	100	100	101	100	100	100	99	100
(N)	(171)	(101)	(146)	(161)[c]	(171)[c]	(110)	(156)	(132)	(149)	(157)	(267)	(224)[c]	(290)[c]	(230)

[a] The percentage supporting another party has not been presented; it usually totals less than 1 percent and never totals more than 1 percent.
[b] Empty cells indicate less than 1 percent.
[c] Numbers are weighted.

Notes

INTRODUCTION TO PART 1

1. For an analysis of strategies in this election, see John H. Kessel, *The Goldwater Coalition: Republican Strategies in 1964* (Indianapolis: Bobbs-Merrill, 1968).

2. See, for example, Benjamin Ginsberg and Martin Shefter, *Politics by Other Means: The Declining Importance of Elections in America* (New York: Basic Books, 1990); and Matthew A. Crenson and Benjamin Ginsberg, *Downsizing Democracy: How America Sidelined Its Citizens and Privatized Its Public* (Baltimore: Johns Hopkins University Press, 2002).

3. William Crotty, "The Bush Presidency: Establishing the Agenda for the Campaign," in *A Defining Moment: The Presidential Election of 2004*, ed. William Crotty (Armonk, N.Y.: M. E. Sharpe, 2005), 3.

4. Ibid., 14.

5. Michael Nelson, "The Setting: George W. Bush: Majority President," in *The Elections of 2004*, ed. Michael Nelson (Washington, D.C.: CQ Press, 2005), 11.

6. Patricia Conley, "The Presidential Race of 2004: Strategy, Outcome, and Mandate," in *A Defining Moment: The Presidential Election of 2004*, ed. William Crotty (Armonk, N.Y.: M. E. Sharpe, 2005), 116.

7. Ibid.

8. Robert Toner, "Voters Are Very Settled, Intense, and Partisan, and It's Only July," *New York Times*, July 24, 2004, A1.

9. Richard W. Stevenson, "Focus on Social Security and Tax Code," *New York Times*, November 4, 2004, A1.

10. Robert Toner and Richard W. Stevenson, "Bush Pledges a Broad Push toward Market-Based Policies," *New York Times*, November 4, 2004, P1.

11. David D. Kirkpatrick, "Some Backers of Bush Say They Anticipate a 'Revolution,' " *New York Times*, November 4, 2004, P1.

12. Ibid., P1, P11.

13. Adam Nagourney, "Bush's Court Strategy," *New York Times*, July 20, 2005, A1.

14. Elisabeth Bumiller, "White House Tries to Quell a Rebellion on the Right," *New York Times,* October 7, 2005, A14.

15. William Crotty, "Armageddon, Just Another Campaign, or Something In-Between? The Meaning and Consequences of the 2004 Election," in *A Defining Moment: The Presidential Election of 2004,* ed. William Crotty (Armonk, N.Y.: M. E. Sharpe, 2005), 236.

16. Nelson, "The Setting," 2.

17. James W. Ceaser and Andrew E. Busch, *Red over Blue: The 2004 Elections and American Politics* (Lanham, Md.: Rowman and Littlefield, 2005), 2.

18. For a discussion of the history of this concept, see Theodore Rosenof, *Realignment: The Theory That Changed the Way We Think about American Politics* (Lanham, Md.: Rowman and Littlefield, 2003).

19. Ceaser and Busch, *Red over Blue,* 22.

20. Fred Barnes, "Realignment, Now More Than Ever: The Next Best Thing to a Permanent Majority," *The Weekly Standard,* November 22, 2004.

21. For Burnham's discussion of the implications of the Republican House victories of 1994 and 1996, see Walter Dean Burnham, "Bill Clinton: Riding the Tiger," in *The Election of 1996: Reports and Interpretations,* ed. Gerald M. Pomper (Chatham, N.J.: Chatham House, 1997), 7–8.

22. Quoted in Barnes, "Realignment, Now More than Ever."

23. Kevin P. Phillips, *The Emerging Republican Majority* (New Rochelle, N.Y.: Arlington House, 1969).

24. Phil Gailey, "Republicans Start to Worry about Signs of Slippage," *New York Times,* August 25, 1985, E5.

25. V. O. Key Jr., "A Theory of Critical Elections," *Journal of Politics* 17 (February 1955): 4.

26. V. O. Key Jr., "Secular Realignment and the Party System," *Journal of Politics* 21 (May 1959): 198.

27. These states were, and still are, the most heavily Catholic states. Both voted Republican in seventeen of the eighteen presidential elections from 1856 through 1924, voting Democratic only when the Republican Party was split in 1912 by Theodore Roosevelt's Progressive Party candidacy. For a discussion of partisan change in New England since World War II, see chapter 3.

28. V. O. Key Jr., *Parties, Politics, and Pressure Groups,* 5th ed. (New York: Thomas Y. Crowell, 1964), 186.

29. James L. Sundquist, *Dynamics of the Party System: Alignment and Re-alignment of Political Parties in the United States,* rev. ed. (Washington, D.C.: Brookings Institution Press, 1983), 4.

30. Lawrence G. McMichael and Richard J. Trilling, "The Structure and Meaning of Critical Realignment: The Case of Pennsylvania, 1928–1932," in *Realignment in American Politics: Toward a Theory,* ed. Bruce A. Campbell and Richard J. Trilling (Austin: University of Texas Press, 1980), 25.

31. Byron E. Shafer, ed., *The End of Realignment? Interpreting American Electoral Eras* (Madison: University of Wisconsin Press, 1991). See, for example, Joel

H. Silbey, "Beyond Realignment and Realignment Theory: American Political Eras, 1789–1989," 3–23; Everett Carll Ladd, "Like Waiting for Godot: The Uselessness of 'Realignment' for Studying Change in Contemporary American Politics," 24–36; and Byron E. Shafer, "The Notion of an Electoral Order: The Structure of Electoral Politics at the Accession of George Bush," 37–84. Shafer's book also contains an excellent bibliographic essay: Harold F. Bass Jr., "Background to Debate: A Reader's Guide and Bibliography," 141–178.

32. David R. Mayhew, *Electoral Realignments: A Critique of an American Genre* (New Haven: Yale University Press, 2002).

33. We maintain that in past realignments there have been increases in turnout and that new issues have divided the electorate. Mayhew writes that the thesis that turnout increases when there are realignments is a basic claim of students of realignment (*Electoral Realignments*, 20). Regarding issues, he argues that the main thesis is that "at least as regards the U.S. House, realigning elections hinge on national issues, nonrealigning elections on local ones" (24).

34. For recent evidence based on an analysis of congressional and presidential election results between 1868 and 2004 that supports this conclusion, see James E. Campbell, "Party Systems and Realignments in the United States: 1868–2004," *Social Science History,* forthcoming.

35. David W. Brady, *Critical Elections and Congressional Policy Making* (Stanford: Stanford University Press, 1988) presents important evidence on changes during the 1890s. See also Peter F. Nardulli, "The Concept of a Critical Realignment, Electoral Behavior, and Political Change," *American Political Science Review* 89 (March 1995): 10–22; and Gary Miller and Norman Schofield, "Activists and Partisan Realignment in the United States," *American Political Science Review* 97 (May 2003): 245–260. In *Electoral Realignments,* Mayhew comments on Brady's and Nardulli's work. (The Miller and Schofield article appeared a year after his book was published.) For a more extensive presentation of Nardulli's thesis, see his *Popular Efficacy in the Democratic Era: A Reexamination of Electoral Accountability in the United States, 1828–2000* (Princeton: Princeton University Press, 2005).

36. In addition to the eleven states that formed the Confederacy (Alabama, Arkansas, Florida, Georgia, Louisiana, Mississippi, North Carolina, South Carolina, Tennessee, Texas, and Virginia), Delaware, Kentucky, Maryland, and Missouri were slave states. The fifteen free states in 1848 were Connecticut, Illinois, Indiana, Iowa, Maine, Massachusetts, Michigan, New Hampshire, New Jersey, New York, Ohio, Pennsylvania, Rhode Island, Vermont, and Wisconsin. By 1860 three additional free states, California, Minnesota, and Oregon, had been admitted into the Union.

37. James M. McPherson, *Battle Cry of Freedom: The Civil War Era* (New York: Oxford University Press, 1988), 223.

38. Michael Nelson, "Constitutional Aspects of the Election," in *The Elections of 1988,* ed. Michael Nelson (Washington, D.C.: CQ Press, 1989), 198.

39. Byron E. Shafer, "The Election of 1988 and the Structure of American Politics: Interpreting an Electoral Order," *Electoral Studies* 8 (April 1989): 11.

40. This electronic newsletter is published by the Emerging Democratic Majority: The Election Strategy Center for Building a New Majority. It is available online at www.emergingdemocraticmajorityweblog.com/donkeyrising/. Although this newsletter obviously has a partisan viewpoint, it also publishes interesting research results.

41. Ronald Inglehart and Avram Hochstein, "Alignment and Dealignment of the Electorate in France and the United States," *Comparative Political Studies* 5 (October 1972): 343–372.

42. Russell J. Dalton, Paul Allen Beck, and Scott C. Flanagan, "Electoral Change in Advanced Industrialized Democracies," in *Electoral Change in Advanced Industrial Democracies: Realignment or Dealignment?* ed. Russell J. Dalton, Scott C. Flanagan, and Paul Allen Beck (Princeton: Princeton University Press), 14.

43. Russell J. Dalton and Martin P. Wattenberg, "The Not So Simple Act of Voting," in *Political Science: The State of the Discipline II,* ed. Ada W. Finifter (Washington, D.C.: American Political Science Association, 1993), 202.

44. Bo Särlvik and Ivor Crewe, *Decade of Dealignment: The Conservative Victory of 1979 and Electoral Trends in the 1970s* (Cambridge: Cambridge University Press, 1983).

45. Harold D. Clarke et al., *Absent Mandate: Canadian Electoral Politics in an Era of Restructuring* (Toronto: Gage Educational Publishing, 1996), 183.

46. These figures are based on our analysis of the 2004 National Election Study survey.

47. The second-longest period of dominance by one political party was between 1884 and 1908, when the Republicans won control of the House in eight consecutive elections.

48. As in all of the presidential election year surveys, not all of the respondents interviewed before the election were reinterviewed after the election. The number of respondents in the postelection survey was 1,066. Except for the 2000 and 2004 National Election Study (NES) surveys, all of the other studies were also based on in-person interviews. In 2000, 44 percent of the surveys were conducted as telephone interviews, and in 2002 all of the interviews were conducted by telephone. In order to go back to in-person interviews in 2004, the NES reduced both its sample size and the length of its interviews.

49. For a brief, nontechnical introduction to polling, see Herbert Asher, *Polling and the Public: What Every Citizen Should Know,* 6th ed. (Washington, D.C.: CQ Press, 2004).

50. For a brief discussion of the procedures used by the Survey Research Center to carry out its sampling for in-person interviews, see Paul R. Abramson, *Political Attitudes in America: Formation and Change* (San Francisco: W. H. Freeman, 1983), 18–23. For a more detailed description, see Survey Research Center, *Interviewer's Manual,* rev. ed. (Ann Arbor: Institute for Social Research, 1976).

51. The magnitude of sampling error is greater for proportions near 50 percent and diminishes somewhat for proportions above 70 percent or below 30

percent. The magnitude of error diminishes markedly for proportions above 90 percent or below 10 percent.

52. For an excellent table that allows us to evaluate differences between two groups, see Leslie Kish, *Survey Sampling* (New York: Wiley, 1965), 580. Kish defines differences between two groups to be significant if the results are more than two standard errors apart.

53. In 2004—as well as in 1958, 1960, 1974, 1976, 1992, 1994, 1996, 1998, 2000, and 2002—a weighting procedure is necessary to obtain a representative result, and we report the "weighted" number of cases. For 2004, we weight by V040101 when we are presenting results that do not include the postelection interview. (For example, we use this weight when we report the distribution of party identification among whites and among blacks.) Whenever we present results that include the postelection interview results (for example, whether people said they voted, how they voted for president, or how they voted for Congress) we weight by V040102.

1. THE NOMINATION STRUGGLE

1. For more on these nomination contests, see Paul R. Abramson, John H. Aldrich, and David W. Rohde, *Change and Continuity in the 1984 Elections*, rev. ed. (Washington, D.C.: CQ Press, 1987), esp. chap. 1.

2. See Paul R. Abramson, John H. Aldrich, and David W. Rohde, "Will Changing the Rules Change the Game? Front-Loading and the 2004 Democratic Presidential Nomination," *The Forum* 1, no. 3, article 2, www.bepress.com/forum/vol1/iss3/art2/.

3. See Paul R. Abramson, John H. Aldrich, and David W. Rohde, *Change and Continuity in the 1992 Elections*, rev. ed. (Washington, D.C.: CQ Press, 1995), 26–30.

4. In 1912 the incumbent Republican president, William Howard Taft, faced two strong challengers, former president Theodore Roosevelt and Sen. Robert M. La Follette, Wis. There were twelve presidential primaries, and Roosevelt won nine, La Follette won two, and Taft won only one. But too few delegates were chosen by primaries to deny Taft the Republican nomination. Roosevelt launched a third-party candidacy that outpolled Taft. Splitting the Republican Party led to the election of the Democratic candidate, Woodrow Wilson. For an interesting account, see James Chace, *1912: Wilson, Roosevelt, Taft and Debs—The Election That Changed the Country* (New York: Simon and Schuster, 2004).

5. Sen. Bob Graham, D-Fla., announced his candidacy but then withdrew in October 2003.

6. See Paul R. Abramson, John H. Aldrich, and David W. Rohde, *Change and Continuity in the 2000 and 2002 Elections* (Washington, D.C.: CQ Press, 2003), chap. 1.

7. Graham and Gephardt had good (Gephardt very, very good) chances of reelection, had they decided to run again. Edwards's chances were less clear, with

some observers believing that his decision to run for the presidential nomination was aided by the uncertainty over his senatorial reelection prospects.

8. For a discussion see Joseph A. Schlesinger, *Ambition and Politics: Political Careers in the United States* (Chicago: Rand McNally, 1966); and Schlesinger, *Political Parties and the Winning of Office* (Ann Arbor: University of Michigan Press, 1991).

9. Since World War II, the U.S. Senate has been a major source of presidential candidates. However, only two sitting senators have ever been elected president, Warren G. Harding in 1920 and John F. Kennedy in 1960. For a discussion of the factors that influence whether or not senators seek the presidency, see Paul R. Abramson, John H. Aldrich, and David W. Rohde, "Progressive Ambition among United States Senators: 1972–1988," *Journal of Politics* 49 (February 1987): 3–35.

10. Not all the prominent Democrats who could have run in 2004 chose to compete. Al Gore is the most obvious example. Three other cases in point are senators Joseph R. Biden Jr., Del., Hillary Rodham Clinton, N.Y., and Tom Daschle, S.D. For a discussion of their reasons for not running see James W. Ceaser and Andrew E. Busch, *Red over Blue: The 2004 Elections and American Politics* (Lanham, Md.: Rowman and Littlefield, 2005), 88.

11. The one exception was in 1836, when the Whigs ran three separate candidates to oppose the sitting vice president, Martin van Buren. The Republican Party has always used majority rule to select its nominees. The Democratic Party required that the nominee be selected by a two-thirds majority in every convention from its founding (except 1840) until 1936, when the requirement changed to a majority.

12. Because some states object to this feature, or object to registration with a party at all, any Democratic delegates so chosen would not be recognized as properly selected. Parties in those states use other procedures for choosing their delegates.

13. The importance of "momentum" and related dynamics is developed in John H. Aldrich, *Before the Convention: Strategies and Choices in Presidential Nomination Campaigns* (Chicago: University of Chicago Press, 1980). See also Larry M. Bartels, *Presidential Primaries and the Dynamics of Public Choice* (Princeton: Princeton University Press, 1988).

14. Quoted in Theodore H. White, *The Making of the President, 1968* (New York: Pocket Books, 1970), 153.

15. He was aided because one-third of the delegates had been chosen in 1967, before Johnson's renomination faced serious opposition.

16. The Republican Party does not require that its delegates be bound. Many states (especially those that hold primaries and follow Democratic Party rules) do bind Republican delegates.

17. This account of the importance of pre-primary campaigning is developed in Phil Paolino, "Candidate Name Recognition and the Dynamics of the Pre-Primary Period of the Presidential Nomination Process" (PhD diss., Duke University, 1995).

18. See Abramson, Aldrich, and Rohde, *Change and Continuity in the 2000 and 2002 Elections*, chap. 1, for more details on the nomination campaigns in 2000.

19. EMILY's List, a group that supports female candidates, draws its name from an acronym of this phrase.

20. The most important adaptation politicians have made to campaign finance requirements is the acquisition and use of "soft money," that is, money that can be raised and spent without limit for party-building and turnout efforts. Soft money became controversial in 1996 because of the increasingly vast sums raised, the sources of the contributions, and alleged misuse of soft money for promoting the election of candidates. Soft money is not, however, a major factor in intraparty competition, including presidential nomination campaigns.

21. Available at www.zogby.com/news/ReadNews.dbm?ID=732.

22. For example, www.sfgate.com/cgi-bin/article.cgi?f=/c/a/2004/01/21/MNG4F4E5N51.DTL, which is a *San Francisco Chronicle* Web log. The quote in the text, reported on the blog, was from " 'Iowa yell' Stirring Doubts about Dean." See also Carla Marinucci, "Battle Cry to Troops Strikes Some Critics as Over the Top," *San Francisco Chronicle*, January 21, 2004, 1.

23. The presidential nominee does not have to make the choice. In 1956, Adlai E. Stevenson, the Democratic nominee, turned the decision over to the convention, which chose Sen. Estes Kefauver, Tenn., over John F. Kennedy, Mass. In an earlier era, the choice of the vice president was made by party bosses to create a "balanced" ticket or to provide a running mate who might help win a swing state.

24. In 1996 the Democrats held their convention in late August (26–29), but the Republican convention was also held in August (12–15).

2. THE GENERAL ELECTION CAMPAIGN

1. The district system is not the only alternative to the statewide selection of presidential electors. For example, in 2004 a ballot proposal in Colorado would have allocated its electors according to proportional representation. For a discussion, see chapter 3.

2. Hawaii, Iowa, Massachusetts, New York, Oregon, Rhode Island, Washington, and Wisconsin.

3. The eighteen states were Arizona, Arkansas, Florida, Iowa, Maine, Michigan, Minnesota, Missouri, Nevada, New Hampshire, New Mexico, Ohio, Oregon, Pennsylvania, Tennessee, Washington, West Virginia, and Wisconsin. See the *Washington Post*, March 15, 2004, A11.

4. For a discussion of electoral-vote strategies in 1988–1996, see Daron R. Shaw, "The Methods behind the Madness: Presidential Electoral College Strategies, 1988–1996," *Journal of Politics* 61 (November 1999): 893–913. There were methodological mistakes in Shaw's analysis. A reanalysis of Shaw's data by Andrew Reeves, Lanhee Chen, and Tiffany Nagano concludes that none of Shaw's substantive conclusions are supported by their study. See "A Reassessment of 'The Methods behind the Madness: Presidential Electoral College Strategies,

1988–1996,' " *Journal of Politics* 66 (May 2004): 616–620. Shaw acknowledges errors in his analysis but maintains that correcting for these errors leads to few changes in his conclusions. See "Erratum for 'The Methods behind the Madness: Presidential Electoral College Strategies, 1988–1996,' " *Journal of Politics* 66 (May 2004): 611–615.

5. The five successful incumbents (and their average approval in Gallup surveys conducted in March, April and May) were as follows: Eisenhower 1956 (70), Johnson 1964 (76), Nixon 1972 (56), Reagan 1984 (54), and Clinton 1996 (54). The unsuccessful candidates were Johnson 1968 (36), Ford 1976 (48), Carter 1980 (40), and Bush 1992 (40). (Johnson's approval is only for March because he withdrew from consideration at the end of that month.) The approval data are from Gallup polls, and for presidents through Reagan they were obtained from *Presidential Approval: A Source Book,* ed. George C. Edwards III, with Alec M. Gallup (Baltimore: Johns Hopkins University Press, 1990). For Bush and Clinton, the data were taken respectively from the August 1992 and the May 1996 issues of the *Gallup Poll Monthly.*

6. Data reported at www.pollingreport.com (accessed June 9, 2005).

7. *USA Today,* March 10, 2004, 4A.

8. *USA Today,* March 9, 2004, 1A.

9. *USA Today,* March 12, 2004, 4A.

10. *Newsweek,* November 15, 2004, 61.

11. Ibid., 70.

12. *USA Today,* March 30, 2004, 4A.

13. *Newsweek,* November 15, 2004, 73.

14. *Washington Post,* June 17, 2004, A1.

15. *The Hill,* April 20, 2004, 10.

16. *The 9/11 Commission Report: Final Report of the National Commission on Terrorist Attacks upon the United States* (New York: Norton, 2004).

17. *Washington Post,* June 22, 2004, A1.

18. *USA Today,* June 25, 2004, 1A.

19. *Washington Post,* August 3, 2004, A1.

20. See, for example, the analysis by the *Detroit Free Press,* August 21, 2004, 4A.

21. *Newsweek,* November 15, 2004, 92.

22. Ibid., 84.

23. *Washington Post,* August 31, 2004, A12.

24. *USA Today,* September 7, 2004, 10A.

25. *Washington Post,* September 8, 2004, A1.

26. *Washington Post,* September 9, 2004, A6.

27. Data reported at www.pollingreport.com (accessed September 30, 2004).

28. *USA Today,* September 21, 2004, 19A.

29. *Newsweek,* November 15, 2004, 108.

30. Dana Milbank, *Washington Post,* October 2, 2004, A10.

31. Newsweek, November 15, 2004,108.

32. Ibid., 113.

33. Ibid.

34. Ibid.

35. Data on this survey were downloaded from www.latimes.com, on October 2, 2004.

36. *National Journal,* October 16, 2004, 3144.

37. Ibid., 3143.

38. *USA Today,* October 14, 2004, 4A.

39. *Washington Post,* October 15, 2004, A8.

40. John F. Harris and Richard Morin, "Debate Helps to Sway Undecided," *Washington Post,* October 15, 2004, A6.

41. *New York Times,* October 19, 2004, A1.

42. See Shanto Iyengar and Donald R. Kinder, *News That Matters: Television and American Opinion* (Chicago: University of Chicago Press, 1987).

43. These data were collected by students in Duke University's Political Science 101AS course for a study in preparation by John Aldrich, John Griffin, and Jill Rickershauser. We are grateful to these students for sharing their data with us.

44. Gerald M. Pomper, "The Presidential Election: The Ills of American Politics after 9/11," in *The Elections of 2004,* ed. Michael Nelson (Washington, D.C.: CQ Press, 2005), 54–56. We are grateful to Pomper for providing us with information about his analysis.

45. *New York Times,* November 11, 2004, A1.

46. Ibid.

47. *Washington Post,* November 1, 2004, A1.

48. *Washington Post,* October 23, 2004, A8.

49. Glenn Justice, "Advocacy Groups Reflect on Their Role in the Election," *New York Times,* November 5, 2004, A18.

50. Ibid.

51. See William Schneider, "The Label That Sank Kerry," *National Journal,* November 11, 2004, 3500.

52. Elisabeth Bumiller, "Tireless Push to Raise Turnout Was Crucial in G.O.P. Victory," *New York Times,* November 4, 2004, A1, P6.

53. There has been much interesting research in recent years on the impact of presidential campaigns on outcomes. See, for example, Thomas H. Holbrook, *Do Campaigns Matter?* (Thousand Oaks, Calif.: Sage Publications, 1996); James E. Campbell, *The American Campaign* (College Station: Texas A&M University Press, 2000); and Daron R. Shaw, "A Study of Presidential Campaign Effects from 1956 to 1992," *Journal of Politics* 61 (May 1999): 387–422.

54. For a discussion of the concept of party identification, see chapter 8. For the questions used to measure party identification, see chapter 4, note 68. The question used to measure the point at which the respondent decided how to vote was asked in the postelection interview and read as follows: "How long before the election did you decide that you were going to vote the way you did?"

55. The four wartime presidents who were reelected were James Madison in 1812, Abraham Lincoln in 1864, Franklin D. Roosevelt in 1944, and Richard M.

Nixon in 1972. Lyndon B. Johnson, in 1964, is difficult to classify. He was elected to a full term three months after the Gulf of Tonkin Resolution, which granted him considerable discretion in using military force in Vietnam, but the first U.S. combat forces did not arrive in Vietnam until three months after his election. We cannot conclude that all wartime presidents would have been reelected. Harry S. Truman chose not to run for reelection in 1952, and Johnson did not run in 1968 (see chapter 1). Both would have faced significant opposition, especially Truman if he had faced Dwight D. Eisenhower.

56. All exit poll results reported here were taken from the CNN Web site, www.cnn.com/ELECTION/2004/pages/results/states/US/P/00/epolls.0.html (accessed June 16, 2005).

57. From an AP report by Deb Riechmann, "Kerry's Votes Key to Bush Win, Rove Says," retrieved from story.news.yahoo.com, on November 7, 2004.

58. Matt Bai, "Who Lost Ohio?" *New York Times Magazine*, November 21, 2004, 66–74.

3. THE ELECTION RESULTS

1. Political Forecasting Special Interest Group, http://morris.upenn.edu/forecast/ (accessed November 1, 2004).

2. Ibid.

3. James E. Campbell, "Introduction—The 2004 Presidential Election Forecasts," *PS: Political Science and Politics* 37 (October 2004): 733–735. The forecasts are on p. 734.

4. Political Forecasting Special Interest Group, http://morris.upenn.edu/forecast (accessed November 1, 2004).

5. David Bauder, "TV Cautious on Calling Election Results," Associated Press, http://news.yahoo.com/news?tmpl=story&u=a[2004/ (accessed November 8, 2004).

6. Ibid.

7. James W. Ceaser and Andrew E. Busch, *Red over Blue: The 2004 Elections and American Politics* (Lanham, Md.: Rowman and Littlefield, 2005), 6. Woodrow Wilson's popular-vote win over Charles Evans Hughes in 1916 was the second closest (3.1 percentage points), although Wilson won by an even narrower electoral vote margin, 277 to 254.

8. Richard V. Scammon, Alice M. McGillivray, and Rhodes Cook, *America Votes 26, 2003–2004: Election Returns by State* (Washington, D.C.: CQ Press, 2006), 9.

9. One faithless elector from Minnesota cast his or her vote for John Edwards.

10. In the disputed election of 1876, records suggest that Samuel J. Tilden, the Democrat, won 51.0 percent of the popular vote and that Rutherford B. Hayes, the Republican, won 48.0 percent. In 1888 Grover Cleveland, the incumbent Democratic president, won 48.6 percent of the vote, and Benjamin Harrison, the Republican, won 47.8 percent. In the disputed election of 2000, Gore won 48.4 percent of the vote, and Bush won 47.9 percent.

11. The fourteen winners were James K. Polk (Democrat) in 1844, with 49.5 percent of the popular vote; Zachary Taylor (Whig) in 1848, with 47.3 percent; James Buchanan (Democrat) in 1856, with 45.3 percent; Abraham Lincoln (Republican) in 1860, with 39.9 percent; James A. Garfield (Republican) in 1880, with 48.3 percent; Grover Cleveland (Democrat) in 1884, with 48.5 percent; Cleveland in 1892, with 46.1 percent; Woodrow Wilson (Democrat) in 1912, with 41.8 percent; Wilson in 1916, with 49.2 percent; Harry S. Truman (Democrat) in 1948, with 49.6 percent; John F. Kennedy (Democrat) in 1960, with 49.7 percent; Richard M. Nixon (Republican) in 1968, with 43.4 percent; Bill Clinton (Democrat) in 1992, with 43.0 percent; and Clinton in 1996, with 49.2 percent. The results for Kennedy can be questioned, however, mainly because voters in Alabama voted for individual electors, and one can argue that Nixon won more popular votes than Kennedy.

12. Britain provides an excellent example of the effects of plurality-vote-win systems on third parties. In Britain, as in the United States, candidates for the national legislature run in single-member districts, and in all British parliamentary districts the plurality-vote winner is elected. In all seventeen general elections since World War II ended in Europe, the Liberal Party (and more recently the Alliance and the Liberal Democratic Party) has received a smaller percentage of the seats in the House of Commons than it won of the popular vote. For example, in the May 2005 election the Liberal Democrats won 22 percent of the popular vote but won only 10 percent of the seats in the House of Commons.

13. The New England states include Connecticut, Maine, Massachusetts, New Hampshire, Rhode Island, and Vermont. Although the U.S. Bureau of the Census classifies several border states and the District of Columbia as southern, we use an explicitly political division, the eleven states that made up the old Confederacy, which are Alabama, Arkansas, Florida, Georgia, Louisiana, Mississippi, North Carolina, South Carolina, Tennessee, Texas, and Virginia.

14. These states include Arizona, Colorado, Idaho, Montana, Nevada, New Mexico, Utah, and Wyoming.

15. For a comparison of Wallace's regional strength in 1968, Anderson's regional strength in 1980, and Perot's regional strength in 1992, see Paul R. Abramson, John H. Aldrich, and David W. Rohde, *Change and Continuity in the 1992 Elections*, rev. ed. (Washington, D.C.: CQ Press, 1995), 73–76.

16. Third party candidates are not always underrepresented in the Electoral College. In 1948 J. Strom Thurmond, the States-Rights Democrat, won only 2.4 percent of the popular vote but won 7.3 percent of the electoral vote. Thurmond won 55 percent of the popular votes he received in the four states he carried (Alabama, Louisiana, Mississippi, and South Carolina), all of which had low turnout. He received no popular votes at all in thirty-one of the forty-eight states.

17. Maurice Duverger, *Political Parties: Their Organization and Activity in the Modern State*, trans. Barbara North and Robert North (New York: Wiley, 1963), 217. In the original, Duverger's formula is, "le scrutin majoritaire à un seul tour tend au dualisme des partis." Duverger, *Les Partis Politiques* (Paris: Armand Colin, 1958), 247. For a discussion of Duverger's law, see William H. Riker, "The Two-

Party System and Duverger's Law: An Essay on the History of Political Science," *American Political Science Review* 76 (December 1982): 753–766. For a more recent statement by Duverger, see "Duverger's Law Forty Years Later," in *Electoral Laws and Their Political Consequences*, ed. Bernard Grofman and Arend Lijphart (New York: Agathan Press, 1986), 69–84. For discussions of the effects of electoral laws, see Rein Taagepera and Matthew Soberg Shugart, *Seats and Votes: The Effects and Determinants of Electoral Systems* (New Haven: Yale University Press, 1989); and Gary W. Cox, *Making Votes Count: Strategic Coordination on the World's Electoral Systems* (New York: Cambridge University Press, 1997).

18. Duverger's inclusion of "a single ballot" in his formulation is redundant since with a plurality-vote-win system there will be no need for a second ballot unless they are necessary to break ties. With a large electorate ties will be extremely rare.

19. Duverger, *Political Parties*, 218.

20. William H. Riker, *The Art of Political Manipulation* (New Haven: Yale University Press, 1986), 79.

21. See Paul R. Abramson et al., "Third-Party and Independent Candidates in American Politics: Wallace, Anderson, and Perot," *Political Science Quarterly* 110 (Fall 1995): 349–367; Paul R. Abramson, John H. Aldrich, and David W. Rohde, *Change and Continuity in the 1996 and 1998 Elections* (Washington, D.C.: CQ Press, 1999), 118–120; Paul R. Abramson, John H. Aldrich, and David W. Rohde, *Change and Continuity in the 2000 and 2002 Elections* (Washington, D.C.: CQ Press, 2003), 124–126.

22. See George C. Edwards III, *Why the Electoral College Is Bad for America* (New Haven: Yale University Press, 2004).

23. The only other elections in which incumbent presidents were defeated in two straight elections were in 1888, when Grover Cleveland was defeated by Benjamin Harrison, and in 1892, when Cleveland defeated Harrison.

24. For a discussion of agenda setting during this period, see William H. Riker, *Liberalism against Populism: A Confrontation Between the Theory of Democracy and the Theory of Social Choice* (San Francisco: W. H. Freeman, 1982), 213–232; and John H. Aldrich, *Why Parties? The Origin and Transformation of Political Parties in America* (Chicago: University of Chicago Press, 1995), 126–156.

25. As we saw in the introduction to part 1, not all scholars agree with this assessment. The most important dissent is found in David R. Mayhew, *Electoral Realignments: A Critique of an American Genre* (New Haven: Yale University Press, 2002).

26. Michael Nelson, "The Presidential Election," in *The Elections of 1988*, ed. Michael Nelson (Washington, D.C.: CQ Press, 1989), 195–196.

27. After the 2000 elections, the Republicans and Democrats each had fifty senators, and the Republicans held control by virtue of Dick Cheney's tie-breaking vote. When James M. Jeffords of Vermont left the Republican Party to become an Independent, and to vote with the Democrats on the organization of the Senate, the Democrats took control of the Senate from June 2001 until January 2003.

28. As the result of the Twenty-third Amendment (ratified in 1961) the District of Columbia has had three electoral votes since the 1964 election.

29. See Abramson, Aldrich, and Rohde, *Change and Continuity in the 2000 and 2002 Elections,* 56.

30. According to the U.S. Bureau of the Census, the West includes thirteen states: Alaska, Arizona, California, Colorado, Hawaii, Idaho, Montana, Nevada, New Mexico, Oregon, Utah, Washington, and Wyoming. But as Walter Dean Burnham points out, for presidential elections the ninety-sixth meridian of longitude provides a dividing line. See Burnham, "The 1980 Earthquake," in *The Hidden Election: Politics and Economics in the 1980 Presidential Campaign,* ed. Thomas Ferguson and Joel Rogers (New York: Pantheon, 1981), 111. For this chapter, we will consider Kansas, Nebraska, North Dakota, Oklahoma, and South Dakota to be western. Even though Texas lies mainly to the west of this meridian, we have classified it as southern, since it was a Confederate state.

31. U.S. Department of Commerce, U.S. Bureau of the Census, *Statistical Abstract of the United States,* 101st ed. (Washington, D.C.: U.S. Government Printing Office, 1980), 514.

32. Ironically, the "red" states are those usually won by the Republicans, while the "blue" states are those usually won by the Democrats. Red was the color often associated with revolution and with socialism, as demonstrated by the song, "The Red Flag," composed by James Connell in 1889, which became the official song of the British Labour Party. It became one of the three colors of the French tricolor, and, aside from the hammer and sickle, the flag of the Soviet Union was red.

33. See Abramson, Aldrich, and Rohde, *Change and Continuity in the 1992 Elections,* 82–85; Abramson, Aldrich, and Rohde, *Change and Continuity in the 1996 and 1998 Elections,* 53; and Abramson, Aldrich, and Rohde, *Change and Continuity in the 2000 and 2002 Elections,* 58.

34. See Joseph A. Schlesinger, *Political Parties and the Winning of Office* (Ann Arbor: University of Michigan Press, 1991), Figure 5-1, 112. Schlesinger does not present the exact values, but he has provided them to us in a personal communication. Including the District of Columbia, which has voted since 1964, increases the standard deviation, since it always votes more Democratic than the most Democratic state. We have reported Schlesinger's results for states, not the alternative results he presents that include the District of Columbia. Likewise, our updated results are for the fifty states.

35. V. O. Key Jr., *Southern Politics in State and Nation* (New York: Alfred A. Knopf, 1949), 5.

36. There have been many excellent studies of the postwar South. For one that presents state-by-state results, see Alexander P. Lamis, *The Two-Party South,* 2nd exp. ed. (New York: Oxford University Press, 1990). For three other studies, see Earl Black and Merle Black, *Politics and Society in the Postwar South* (Cambridge: Harvard University Press, 1987); Black and Black, *The Vital South: How Presidents Are Elected* (Cambridge: Harvard University Press, 1991); and Black and Black, *The Rise of Southern Republicans* (Cambridge: Harvard University Press, 2002).

37. Alabama, Georgia, Louisiana, Mississippi, and South Carolina are generally considered the five Deep South states. They are also the five states with the highest percentages of African Americans.

38. Southern Democrats suffered additional defeats at the 1948 Democratic presidential nominating convention. Their attempts to weaken the civil rights platform were defeated. In addition, Hubert H. Humphrey, then mayor of Minneapolis, argued that the proposed civil rights platform was too weak and offered an amendment for a stronger statement. Humphrey's amendment was passed by a vote of 651½ to 582½.

39. Kennedy made a symbolic gesture that may have helped him with African Americans. Three weeks before the election, Martin Luther King Jr. was arrested in Atlanta for taking part in a sit-in demonstration. Although all the other demonstrators were released, King was held on a technicality and sent to the Georgia State Penitentiary. Kennedy telephoned King's wife to express his concern, and his brother Robert F. Kennedy made a direct appeal to a Georgia judge that led to King's release on bail. This incident received little notice in the press, but it had a great effect in the African American community. See Theodore H. White, *The Making of the President, 1960* (New York: Athenaeum, 1961), 321–323.

40. Eric R. A. N. Smith and Peverill Squire, "State and National Politics in the Mountain West," in *The Politics of Realignment: Party Change in the Mountain West,* ed. Peter F. Galderisi et al. (Boulder, Colo.: Westview, 1987), 34.

41. For a discussion of the reasons for this lack of attention, see Peter F. Galderisi and Michael S. Lyons, "Realignment Past and Present," in *The Politics of Realignment,* ed. Galderisi et al., 12.

42. Arthur H. Miller, "Political Opinion and Regional Political Realignment," in *The Politics of Realignment,* ed. Galderisi et al., 98.

43. Ibid., 100.

44. Nichol C. Rae, *The Decline and Fall of the Liberal Republicans* (New York: Oxford University Press, 1989), 145.

45. We count Nixon as a Californian in 1968, even though he officially ran as a resident of New York.

46. If one includes only major-party voters in 1968, Nixon received 51.7 percent of the vote in California and 50.4 percent in the nation as a whole.

47. Mark Baldassare, *California in the New Millennium: The Changing Social and Political Landscape* (Berkeley: University of California Press, 2000), 101; Baldassare, *A California State of Mind: The Conflicted Voter in a Changing World* (Berkeley: University of California Press, 2002), 152.

48. Baldassare, *A California State of Mind,* 159.

49. MSNBC, "California, Exit polls—president," www.msnbc.msn.com/id/5297147/ (accessed May 13, 2005). It seems highly implausible that the Hispanic share of the vote could have increased from 14 percent in 2000 to 21 percent in 2005. We know that the actual relative size of the Hispanic population did not increase dramatically during this four-year period, and a change of this magnitude could occur only if there were massive increases in Hispanic turnout and/or

massive decreases in non-Hispanic turnout, neither of which occurred. So it seems far more likely that these results occur due either to sampling error or to differences between the Voter News Service poll used in 2000 and the Edison Media Research/Mitofsky International poll used in 2004.

50. Baldassare, *A California State of Mind,* 224.

51. See Abramson, Aldrich, and Rohde, *Change and Continuity in the 1992 Elections,* Figure 2-1, 47.

52. Marjorie Randon Hershey, "The Campaign and the Media," in *The Election of 1988: Reports and Interpretations,* ed. Gerald M. Pomper (Chatham, N.J.: Chatham House), 74.

53. Michael Nelson, "Constitutional Aspects of the Elections," in *The Elections of 1988,* 193–195; James C. Garand and T. Wayne Parent, "Representation, Swing, and Bias in U.S. Presidential Elections, 1872–1988," *American Journal of Political Science* 35 (November 1991): 1001–1031.

54. I. M. Destler, "The Myth of the 'Electoral Lock,' " *PS: Political Science and Politics* 29 (September 1996): 494. Although Destler's analyses are sound, his conclusion is overstated. After all, candidates do have electoral vote strategies, and we cannot reach strong conclusions about whether candidates who ignored these strategies would win.

55. Andrew Gelman, Jonathan N. Katz, and Gary King, "Empirically Evaluating the Electoral College," in *Rethinking the Vote: The Politics and Prospects of American Election Reform,* ed. Ann N. Crigler, Marion R. Just, and Edward J. McCaffrey (New York: Oxford University Press, 2004), 75–88.

56. Abramson, Aldrich, and Rohde, *Change and Continuity in the 2000 and 2002 Elections,* 63. Our conclusions about the 1992 election are similar to Destler's.

57. For an interesting, if alarmist, discussion of the possibility, see David W. Abbott and James P. Levine, *Wrong Winner: The Coming Debacle in the Electoral College* (New York: Praeger, 1991).

INTRODUCTION TO PART 2

1. This estimate of the total number of Americans eligible to vote comes from two sources. Walter Dean Burnham, of the University of Texas, estimates that 201,541,000 Americans were eligible to participate in the 2004 elections (personal communication, May 31, 2005); and Michael P. McDonald, of George Mason University, estimates the voting-eligible population to have been 202,674,771. See United States Election Project, "2004 Voting-Age and Voting-Eligible Population and Voter Turnout," updated as of June 7, 2005, www.elections.gmu.edu/Voter_ Turnout_2004.html (accessed July 25, 2005). We are grateful to Professors Burnham and McDonald for providing this information.

2. For an excellent set of articles dealing with some of the major controversies, see Richard G. Niemi and Herbert F. Weisberg, eds., *Controversies in Voting Behavior,* 4th ed. (Washington, D.C.: C.Q. Press, 2001). For two excellent sum-

maries of research about voting behavior, see Russell J. Dalton and Martin P. Wattenberg, "The Not So Simple Act of Voting," in *Political Science: The State of the Discipline II*, ed. Ada W. Finifter (Washington, D.C.: American Political Science Association, 1993), 193–218; and Morris P. Fiorina, "Parties, Participation, and Representation in Amerca: Old Theories Face New Realities," in *Political Science: The State of the Discipline*, ed. Ira Katznelson and Helen V. Milner (New York: Norton, 2002), 511–541.

3. For an excellent summary of alternative theoretical approaches to the study of political behavior, see Edward G. Carmines and Robert Huckfeldt, "Political Behavior: An Overview," in *A New Handbook of Political Science*, ed. Robert E. Goodin and Hans-Dieter Klingemann (New York: Oxford University Press, 1996), 223–254.

4. Paul F. Lazarsfeld, Bernard Berelson, and Hazel Gaudet, *The People's Choice: How the Voter Makes Up His Mind in a Presidential Campaign*, 2nd ed. (New York: Columbia University Press, 1948), 27. See also Bernard R. Berelson, Paul F. Lazarsfeld, and William N. McPhee, *Voting: A Study of Opinion Formation in a Presidential Campaign* (Chicago: University of Chicago Press, 1954).

5. See Robert R. Alford, *Party and Society: The Anglo-American Democracies* (Chicago: Rand McNally, 1963); Richard F. Hamilton, *Class and Politics in the United States* (New York: Wiley, 1972); and Seymour Martin Lipset, *Political Man: The Social Bases of Politics*, exp. ed. (Baltimore: Johns Hopkins University Press, 1981). For a more recent book that uses this perspective, see Jeff Manza and Clem Brooks, *Social Cleavages and Political Change: Voter Alignments and U.S. Party Coalitions* (Oxford: Oxford University Press, 1999).

6. Angus Campbell et al., *The American Voter* (New York: Wiley, 1960).

7. The most important single work by Converse, and one that draws heavily on a social-psychological perspective is Philip E. Converse, "The Nature of Belief Systems in Mass Publics," in *Ideology and Discontent*, ed. David E. Apter (New York: Free Press, 1964), 206–261. For the best single summary of Converse's views on voting behavior, see Converse, "Public Opinion and Voting Behavior," in *Nongovernmental Politics*, ed. Fred I. Greenstein and Nelson W. Polsby, vol. 4 of *Handbook of Political Science* (Reading, Mass.: Addison-Wesley, 1975), 75–169. For an excellent summary of research on political psychology see Donald R. Kinder, "Opinion and Action in the Realm of Politics," in *The Handbook of Social Psychology*, 4th ed., vol. 3, ed. Daniel T. Gilbert, Susan T. Fiske, and Gardner Lindzey (Boston: McGraw Hill, 1998), 778–867. For an alternative approach to the study of political psychology, see Paul M. Sniderman, Richard A. Brody, and Philip E. Tetlock, with others, *Reasoning and Choice: Explorations in Political Psychology* (Cambridge: Cambridge University Press, 1991). See also Sniderman, "The New Look in Public Opinion Research," in *Political Science: The State of the Discipline, II*. For another perspective, see John R. Zaller, *The Nature and Origins of Mass Opinion* (Cambridge: Cambridge University Press, 1992).

8. Warren E. Miller and J. Merrill Shanks, *The New American Voter* (Cambridge: Harvard University Press, 1996). Although reemphasizing the importance

of party identification, this book also demonstrates a shift away from the social-psychological tradition employed by Miller and his colleagues in *The American Voter.*

9. Anthony Downs, *An Economic Theory of Democracy* (New York: Harper and Row, 1957); William H. Riker, *A Theory of Political Coalitions* (New York: Yale University Press, 1962).

10. See, for example, William H. Riker and Peter C. Ordeshook, "A Theory of the Calculus of Voting," *American Political Science Review* 62 (March 1968): 25–32; John A. Ferejohn and Morris P. Fiorina, "The Paradox of Not Voting: A Decision Theoretical Analysis," *American Political Science Review* 68 (June 1974): 525–536; and Morris P. Fiorina, *Retrospective Voting in American National Elections* (New Haven: Yale University Press, 1981). For summaries of much of this research see Melvin J. Hinich and Michael Munger, *Analytical Politics* (Cambridge: Cambridge University Press, 1977); and Kenneth A. Shepsle and Mark S. Bonchek, *Analyzing Politics: Rationality, Behavior, and Institutions* (New York: Norton, 1997). For an interesting perspective that combines rational choice and psychological approaches, see Samuel L. Popkin, *The Reasoning Voter: Communication and Persuasion in Presidential Campaigns* (Chicago: University of Chicago Press, 1991).

11. The most important exception, at least in the study of elections, is Fiorina's, *Retrospective Voting,* to which we refer extensively. The most widely known critique of the rational choice perspective is Donald P. Green and Ian Shapiro, *Pathologies of Rational Choice Theory: A Critique of Applications in Political Science* (New Haven: Yale University Press, 1994). For critiques of Green and Shapiro, see Jeffrey Friedman, ed., *The Rational Choice Controversy: Economic Models of Politics Reconsidered* (New Haven: Yale University Press, 1996).

12. We are grateful to Peter D. Feaver of Duke University, Christopher F. Gelpi of Duke University, and Jason A. Reifler of Loyola University of Chicago for providing these results.

13. We are grateful to Tom Smith of the National Opinion Research Center for providing us with the results of the 2004 GSS.

4. WHO VOTED?

1. Turnout in the fourteen congressional elections held during presidential election years was 51.8 percent.

2. For a discussion of turnout change in comparative perspective, see Mark N. Franklin, *Voter Turnout and the Dynamics of Electoral Competition in Established Democracies Since 1945* (Cambridge: Cambridge University Press, 2004).

3. According to Walter Dean Burnham there were 201,541,000 politically eligible Americans in 2004 (personal communication, May 31, 2005), and his results suggest there were 79 million nonvoters. Michael P. McDonald estimates that the voting-eligible population in 2004 was 202,674,771. See Michael P.

McDonald, "2004 Voting-Age and Voting-Eligible Population Estimates and Voter Turnout," at http://elections.gmu.edu/Voter_Turnout_2004.htm (accessed July 25, 2005). Using his numbers, we would conclude that there were 82 million nonvoters.

4. This chapter focuses on only one form of political participation, voting. For an excellent study of other forms of political participation in the United States, as well as a different perspective on electoral participation, see M. Margaret Conway, *Political Participation in the United States*, 3rd ed. (Washington, D.C.: CQ Press, 2000). For a major study of many forms of political participation, see Sidney Verba, Kay Lehman Scholzman, and Henry E. Brady, *Voice and Equality: Civic Voluntarism in American Politics* (Cambridge: Harvard University Press, 1995).

5. It is difficult to calculate the total number of voters, but in most elections more people vote for president than for any other office.

6. In 1916 women had full voting rights only in Arizona, California, Colorado, Idaho, Kansas, Montana, Nevada, Oregon, Utah, Washington, and Wyoming. Only 10 percent of the U.S. population lived in these states. For a provocative discussion of the struggle for women's suffrage, see Alan P. Grimes, *The Puritan Ethic and Women's Suffrage* (New York: Oxford University Press, 1967). For another interesting discussion, see Holly J. McCammon et al., "How Movements Win: Gendered Opportunity Structures and the U.S. Women's Suffrage Movements, 1866–1919," *American Sociological Review* 66 (February 2001): 49–70.

7. See Martin J. Kousser, *The Shaping of Southern Politics: Suffrage Restrictions and the Establishment of the One-Party South, 1880–1910* (New Haven: Yale University Press, 1974). For a more general discussion of the decline of turnout in the nineteenth century, see Paul Kleppner, *Who Voted? The Dynamics of Electoral Turnout, 1870–1980* (New York: Praeger, 1982), 55–82.

8. There has been a great deal of disagreement about the reasons for and the consequences of registration requirements. For some of the more interesting arguments, see Walter Dean Burnham, "The Changing Shape of the American Political Universe," *American Political Science Review* 59 (March 1965): 7–28; Philip E. Converse, "Change in the American Electorate," in *The Human Meaning of Social Change*, ed. Angus Campbell and Philip E. Converse (New York: Russell Sage, 1972), 266–301; and Walter Dean Burnham, "Theory and Voting Research: Some Reflections on Converse's 'Change in the American Electorate,' " *American Political Science Review* 68 (September 1974): 1002–1023. For two other perspectives, see Frances Fox Piven and Richard A. Cloward, *Why Americans Still Don't Vote: And Why Politicians Want It That Way* (Boston: Beacon Press, 2000); and Matthew A. Crenson and Benjamin Ginsberg, *Downsizing Democracy: How America Sidelined Its Citizens and Privatized Its Public* (Baltimore: Johns Hopkins University Press, 2002).

9. For a rich source of information about the introduction of the Australian ballot and its effects, see Jerrold G. Rusk, "The Effect of the Australian Ballot on

Split-Ticket Voting, 1876–1908," *American Political Science Review* 64 (December 1970): 1220–1238.

10. Burnham's estimates of turnout among the politically eligible population, which include results from 1789 through 1984, are presented in Walter Dean Burnham, "The Turnout Problem," in *Elections American Style,* ed. A. James Reichley (Washington, D.C.: Brookings Institution Press, 1987), 113–114. According to Burnham's estimates, turnout was 52.7 percent in 1988, 56.9 percent in 1992, 50.8 percent in 1996, 54.9 percent in 2000, and 60.7 percent in 2004 (based on personal communications, June 21, 1993; July 1, 1997; and May 31, 2005). McDonald and Popkin's estimates of turnout among the voting-eligible population between 1948 and 2000 are in Michael P. McDonald and Samuel L. Popkin, "The Myth of the Vanishing Voter," *American Political Science Review* 95 (December 2001): 966. According to McDonald, there were 122,294,978 votes cast for president in 2004, and the voting-eligible population was 202,674,771. Turnout, according to his estimate, was 60.3 percent. See "2004 Voting-Age and Voting-Eligible Population Estimates and Voter Turnout," http://elections.gmu.edu/Voter_Turnout_2004.htm (accessed July 25, 2005). For Burnham's procedures for calculating the size of the politically eligible population, see Burnham, "The Turnout Problem," 114; for McDonald and Popkin's procedures for calculating the size of the voting eligible population, see McDonald and Popkin, "The Myth of the Vanishing Voter," 966.

11. Thomas E. Patterson, *The Vanishing Voter: Public Involvement in an Age of Uncertainty* (New York: Alfred A. Knopf, 2002), 8. See also, Pippa Norris, *Count Every Vote: Democratic Participation Worldwide* (New York: Cambridge University Press, 2002).

12. As Table 4-3 shows, this was also an election in which a very small share of the voting-age population voted for third-party or independent candidates.

13. According to Burnham's estimate, turnout was 64.5 percent, while according to the McDonald and Popkin estimate it was 63.8 percent. See Burnham, "The Turnout Problem," 114; and McDonald and Popkin, "The Myth of the Vanishing Voter," 966.

14. See Glenn Firebaugh and Kevin Chen, "Vote Turnout among Nineteenth Amendment Women: The Enduring Effects of Disfranchisement," *American Journal of Sociology* 100 (January 1995): 972–996.

15. Robert Toner, "Parties Pressing to Raise Turnout as Election Nears," *New York Times,* October 20, 1996, Y1, Y4. For estimates of the effect of this reform on turnout, see Raymond E. Wolfinger and Jonathan Hoffman, "Registering and Voting with Motor Voter," *PS: Political Science and Politics* 34 (March 2001): 85–92.

16. McDonald and Popkin argue that when one studies the voting-eligible population, the decline of turnout ended in 1972. Although they present many important insights about factors that have eroded turnout, especially the growth of the noncitizen population, we argue that it is preferable to study change among the voting-age population.

17. For our analysis of the reasons for the increase in turnout in 1992, see Paul R. Abramson, John H. Aldrich, and David W. Rohde, *Change and Continuity in the 1992 Elections,* rev. ed. (Washington, D.C.: CQ Press, 1995), 120–123. As we point out, it is difficult to demonstrate empirically that Perot's candidacy made an important contribution to the increase in turnout. For additional analyses, see Stephen M. Nichols and Paul Allen Beck, "Reversing the Decline: Voter Turnout in 1992," in *Democracy's Feast: Elections in America,* ed. Herbert F. Weisberg (Chatham, N.J.: Chatham House, 1995), 62–65; and Steven J. Rosenstone, Roy L. Behr, and Edward H. Lazarus, *Third Parties in America: Citizen Response to Major Party Failure,* 2nd ed. (Princeton: Princeton University Press), 254–257.

18. In our analyses of the 1980, 1984, 1988, and 1992 elections, we made extensive use of published reports using the Current Population Surveys conducted by the U.S. Bureau of the Census. In our analysis of the 1996 election, only a preliminary report was available, but we used it where we could to compare these findings with those of the NES survey. However, in our analysis of turnout in 2000, not even a preliminary version of the Current Population Survey report was available. Fortunately, the Census Bureau published a detailed report of the 2004 CPS in May 2005. See *Voting and Registration in the Election of November 2004* (U.S. Department of Commerce, U.S. Bureau of the Census, 2005), available at www.census.gov/population/www/socdemo/voting/cps2004.html (accessed June 21, 2005).

19. We classified one respondent who said that she voted, but who said she did not vote for president, as a nonvoter.

20. In 2004, as part of a question-wording experiment, half the respondents were asked the standard question on voter participation that had been used between 1952 and 1996, and the other half were asked a question employed in 2000. The standard question reads as follows:

"In talking to people about the elections, we often find that a lot of people were not able to vote because they weren't registered, they were sick, or they just didn't have time. How about you—did you vote in the elections this November?"

The other half of the sample was asked:

"In talking to people about elections, we often find that a lot of people were not able to vote because they weren't registered, they were sick, or they just didn't have time. Which of the following statements best describes you? One, I did not vote (in the elections this November); two, I thought about voting this time, but didn't; three, I usually vote, but this time I didn't; or four, I am sure that I voted."

Respondents were more likely to say that they voted when the standard question was used. Among the 536 respondents asked the standard version of the question, 80 percent said that they voted; among the 525 asked the experimental version of the question, 73 percent said that they voted.

21. Vote validation studies were conducted after the 1964, 1976, 1980, 1984, and 1988 presidential elections and after the 1978, 1986, and 1990 midterm elections. Mainly for reasons of cost they were discontinued after 1990. Fortunately, even though validation studies were not conducted in the most recent elections,

these past studies provide considerable information about the sources of bias in overreporting.

Most analyses that compare results of reported voting with those as measured by the validation studies suggest that *relative* levels of turnout among most social groups can be compared using reported turnout. However, these studies suggest that blacks are more likely to overreport voting than whites. As a result, differences between the races are always greater when turnout is measured by the vote validation studies. For results between 1964 and 1988, see Paul R. Abramson and William Claggett, "Racial Differences in Self-Reported and Validated Turnout in the 1988 Presidential Election," *Journal of Politics* 53 (February 1991): 186–187. For results for 1990, see Abramson, Aldrich, and Rohde, *Change and Continuity in the 1992 Elections*, 382. For a discussion of the factors that contribute to false reports of voting, see Brian D. Silver, Barbara A. Anderson, and Paul R. Abramson, "Who Overreports Voting?" *American Political Science Review* 80 (June 1986): 613–624. For a more recent study that argues that biases in reported turnout are more severe, see Robert Bernstein, Anita Chada, and Robert Montjoy, "Overreporting Voting: Why It Happens and Why It Matters," *Public Opinion Quarterly* 65 (Spring 2001): 22–44.

22. See Michael W. Traugott and John P. Katosh, "Response Validity in Surveys of Voting Behavior," *Public Opinion Quarterly* 43 (Fall 1979): 359–377; and Barbara A. Anderson, Brian D. Silver, and Paul R. Abramson, "The Effects of Race of the Interviewer on Measures of Electoral Participation by Blacks in SRC National Election Surveys," *Public Opinion Quarterly* 52 (Spring 1988): 53–83.

23. In 2004 race was classified according to the respondent's response to the following question: "Which racial or ethnic group best describes you?" In our analysis, we classify respondents who answered "Black," "Black and Asian," "Black and Native American," and "Black and White" as black. Respondents who answered "White" and mentioned no other race were classified as white.

Relying upon the respondent's self-classification differs from previous procedures in which people interviewed in person were classified by the interviewer. As noted in the introduction to part 1, the 2004 survey relied on in-person interviews, but the survey does not report any interviewer classification of the respondents' race.

24. The vote validation studies are not free from error, for some true voters may be classified as validated nonvoters if no record can be found of their registration or if the records inaccurately fail to show that they voted. The voting records where African Americans live are not as well maintained as the records where whites are likely to live. Still, it seems unlikely that the finding that blacks are more likely to falsely report voting results from the poorer quality of black voting records. See Paul R. Abramson and William Claggett, "The Quality of Record-Keeping and Racial Differences in Validated Turnout," *Journal of Politics* 54 (August 1992): 871–880. See also, Carol A. Cassel, "Voting Records and Validated Voting Studies," *Public Opinion Quarterly* 68 (Spring 2004): 102–108.

25. The Current Population Surveys are much larger than the NES surveys and report information about registration and voting for over 60,000 people. About two out of five of these reports are proxy reports provided by the respondent about other members of his or her household. A recent study by Benjamin Highton suggests that relying on these proxy reports does not create significant biases in analyzing the correlates of turnout. See Benjamin Highton, "Self-Reported Versus Proxy-Reported Voter Turnout in the Current Population Surveys," *Public Opinion Quarterly* 69 (Spring 2005): 113–123.

26. See Katherine Tate, "Black Political Participation in the 1984 and 1988 Presidential Election," *American Political Science Review* 85 (December 1991): 1159–1176. For a more extensive discussion, see Katherine Tate, *From Protest to Politics: The New Black Voters in American Elections,* enl. ed. (Cambridge: Harvard University Press, 1994).

27. U.S. Bureau of the Census, *Voting and Registration in the Election of November 2004.*

28. As we explain in chapter 3, we consider the South to include the eleven states of the old Confederacy. In our analysis of NES surveys, however, we do not classify residents of Tennessee as southern because the University of Michigan Survey Research Center conducts samples in Tennessee to represent the border states. In this analysis, as well as analyses of NES surveys later in this book, we classify the following ten states as southern: Alabama, Arkansas, Florida, Georgia, Louisiana, Mississippi, North Carolina, South Carolina, Texas, and Virginia.

29. Our classification was based on the same question used to classify the respondent's race: "What racial or ethnic group best describes you?" The following categories were classified as Hispanic: "Black and Hispanic," "Asian and Hispanic," "Native American and Hispanic," "Hispanic," and "Hispanic and White."

30. U.S. Bureau of the Census, *Voting and Registration in the Election of November 2004.*

31. Ibid.

32. Based on McDonald, "2004 Voting-Age and Voting-Eligible Population Estimates and Voter Turnout." Turnout among the voting-eligible population in these states was 49.0 percent and 76.8 percent, respectively. Of course, for a state that has a large noncitizen population, differences between these alternative measures of turnout will be substantial. For example, McDonald estimates that 20 percent of California's voting-age population is made up of noncitizens. In 2004, turnout among California's voting-age population was only 47.1 percent; among its voting-eligible population it was 59.3 percent.

33. Based on our calculations, using statistics compiled by McDonald. Among the voting-eligible population, these percentages are 56.0 percent and 62.3 percent, respectively. According to Burnham, turnout among the politically eligible population was 56.4 percent in the South, and 62.6 percent outside the South.

34. See Raymond E. Wolfinger and Steven J. Rosenstone, *Who Votes?* (New Haven: Yale University Press, 1980), 93–94.

35. This variable is based on the interviewer's classification. As there were only 22 whites in the inner-cities, we combined them with the 155 whites living in urban areas.

36. Wolfinger and Rosenstone, *Who Votes?* 46–50.

37. See Benjamin Highton and Raymond E. Wolfinger, "The First Seven Years of the Political Life Cycle," *American Journal of Political Science* 45 (January 2001): 202–209.

38. We use this distinction because it allows us to make comparisons over time and is especially interesting for studying change over the entire postwar period. Nonetheless, there were changes in the way occupation was measured between 1984 and 1988, and once again between 1996 and 2000. We discuss the changes between 1984 and 1988 in Paul R. Abramson, John H. Aldrich, and David W. Rohde, *Change and Continuity in the 1988 Elections,* rev. ed. (Washington, D.C.: CQ Press, 1991), chap. 4, note 26, 116; we discuss changes between 1996 and 2000 in Paul R. Abramson, John H. Aldrich, and David W. Rohde, *Change and Continuity in the 2000 and 2002 Elections* (Washington, D.C.: CQ Press, 2003), chap. 4, note 26, 313.

In 2004 there were additional changes, mainly because the number of available occupational categories was reduced from 75 in 2000 to 25 in 2004. We did our best to maintain comparability with the 2000 survey, but in some cases the categories employed in 2004 seemed to include respondents in differing occupational grades. For those who wish to replicate our 2004 results, we used the following procedures. Codes 14 through 16 and 24 were classified as unskilled manual; 13, and 20 through 23 were classified as skilled manual; 17 and 18 were classified as clerical, sales, or other white-collar; 1 through 3 were classified as managerial; and codes 4 through 12 were classified as professional and semi-professional.

39. Our measure of family income is based upon the respondent's estimate of his or her family income in 2003 before taxes. For those cases where the respondent refused to reveal his or her family income or where the interviewer thought the respondent was answering dishonestly, we relied on the interviewer's assessment.

40. See Wolfinger and Rosenstone, *Who Votes?* 13–36.

41. A question asking Christians whether they were a "born-again Christian" was not included in the 2004 NES survey.

42. David C. Leege, Lyman A. Kellstedt, and others, *Rediscovering the Religious Factor in American Politics* (Armonk, N.Y.: M. E. Sharpe, 1993).

43. We are grateful to David C. Leege for providing us with the detailed information used to construct this measure. We constructed the measure as follows: Respondents who prayed several times a day received 2 points, those who prayed less often received 1 point, and those who never prayed received 0 points; those who attended religious services at least once a week received 2 points, those who attended less frequently received 1 point, and those who never attended received 0 points; those who said that religion provided "a good deal" of guidance in their

lives received 2 points, those who said it provided "quite a bit" received 1 point, and those who said it provided "some" or no guidance received 0 points. Respondents who said the Bible was literally true or the "word of God" received 2 points; those who said it "was written by men and is not the word of God" received 0 points. Respondents received a score of 1 for each ambiguous, "don't know," or "not ascertained" response, but respondents with more than two such responses were excluded from the analysis. Scores ranged from 0 to 8. In regrouping the scores into three categories, we classified respondents with 8 points as "very high," those with 6 or 7 points as "high," and those with a score below 6 as "medium or low" on religious commitment.

44. Kenneth D. Wald, *Religion and Politics in the United States,* 4th ed. (Lanham, Md.: Rowman and Littlefield, 2003), 161.

45. R. Stephen Warner, *New Wine in Old Wineskins: Evangelicals and Liberals in a Small-Town Church* (Berkeley: University of California Press, 1977), 173.

46. We are grateful to David Leege for providing us with the specific NES codes used to classify Protestants according to their religious tradition. These codes are based upon the religious denomination variable in the NES codebook. Categories 50, 60, 70, 100–109, 120–149, 160–219, 221–223, 240, 250–269, 271–275, 280, 282, 289, 292, and 293 were classified as evangelicals; categories 80, 90, 110, 150–159, 220, 229, 230, 249, 270, 276, 279, 281, and 290–291 were classified as mainline.

47. Wolfinger and Rosenstone, *Who Votes?* 13–36.

48. Because there were only 31 whites who had not attended high school, we combined whites with eight grades of education or less with whites who had not graduated from high school.

49. Silver, Anderson, and Abramson's analysis of the 1964, 1968, and 1968 vote validation studies shows that respondents with higher levels of education do have very high levels of turnout. However, their analysis also shows that persons with high levels of formal education who do not vote are more likely to claim falsely to have voted than nonvoters with lower levels of formal education. See Silver, Anderson, and Abramson, "Who Overreports Voting?" Our analysis shows a similar pattern with the 1978, 1984, 1986, 1988, and 1990 vote validation studies. We do not know if a similar pattern would be found in 2004, but if it were, the results in Table 4-4 may somewhat exaggerate the relationship between formal education and turnout.

50. See McDonald and Popkin, "The Myth of the Vanishing Voter," 966; McDonald, "2004 Voting-Age Population and Voting-Eligible Population Estimates and Voter Turnout."

51. Ibid. According to estimates by Jeff Manza and Christopher Uggen, a total of approximately 4.7 million Americans were disfranchised in 2004 because they were in prison, parolees, on probation, ex-felons, or in jail on election day. See Manza and Uggen, "Punishment and Democracy: Disenfranchisement of Nonincarcerated Felons in the United States," *Perspectives on Politics* 2 (September 2004): 491–505.

52. U.S. Bureau of the Census, *Statistical Abstract of the United States, 2004–2005,* 124th ed. (Washington, D.C.: U.S. Government Printing Office, 2004), Table 213, 141. The *Statistical Abstract* is also available online at www.census.gov.statab/www/.

53. Richard A. Brody, "The Puzzle of Political Participation in America," in *The New American Political System,* ed. Anthony King (Washington, D.C.: American Enterprise Institute, 1978), 287–324.

54. Walter Dean Burnham, "The 1976 Election: Has the Crisis Been Adjourned?" in *American Politics and Public Policy,* ed. Walter Dean Burnham and Martha Wagner Weinberg (Cambridge: MIT Press, 1978), 24; Thomas E. Cavanagh, "Changes in American Voter Turnout, 1964–1976," *Political Science Quarterly* 96 (Spring 1981): 53–65.

55. Ruy A. Teixeira, *The Disappearing American Voter* (Washington, D.C.: American Enterprise Institute, 1992), 66–67. Teixeira is skeptical about the finding from NES surveys showing that turnout did not decline among college graduates.

56. Jan E. Leighley and Jonathan Nagler, "Socioeconomic Bias in Turnout, 1964–1988: The Voters Remain the Same," *American Political Science Review* 86 (September 1992): 725–736. For an analysis of congressional elections that supports Leighley and Nagler's conclusions, see Todd G. Shields and Robert K. Goidel, "Participation Rates, Socioeconomic Class Biases, and Congressional Elections: A Crossvalidation," *American Journal of Political Science* 41 (April 1997): 683–691.

57. This procedure assumes that education levels were the same in 2004 as they were in 1960, but that reported levels of turnout in each education level were the same as those observed in the 2004 survey.

58. Teixeira, *The Disappearing American Voter,* 47.

59. Steven J. Rosenstone and John Mark Hansen, *Mobilization, Participation, and Democracy in America* (New York: Macmillan, 1993), 214–215.

60. Teixeira, *The Disappearing American Voter,* 47.

61. Rosenstone and Hansen, *Mobilization, Participation, and Democracy,* 215.

62. Warren E. Miller, "The Puzzle Transformed: Explaining Declining Turnout," *Political Behavior* 14, no. 1 (1992): 1–43. See also Warren E. Miller and J. Merrill Shanks, *The New American Voter* (Cambridge: Harvard University Press, 1976), 95–114.

63. Robert D. Putnam, *Bowling Alone: The Collapse and Revival of American Community* (New York: Simon and Schuster, 2000), 265.

64. George I. Balch, "Multiple Indicators in Survey Research: The Concept 'Sense of Political Efficacy,' " *Political Methodology* 1 (Spring 1974): 1–43. For an extensive discussion of feelings of political efficacy, see Paul R. Abramson, *Political Attitudes in America* (San Francisco: W. H. Freeman, 1983), 135–189.

65. Ruy A. Teixeira, *Why Americans Don't Vote: Turnout Decline in the United States, 1960–1984* (New York: Greenwood Press, 1987). In his more recent study, *The Disappearing American Voter,* Teixeira develops a measure of party-related

characteristics that includes strength of identification, concern about the electoral outcome, perceived differences between the parties, and knowledge about the parties and candidates.

66. Our first analysis studied the decline of turnout between 1960 and 1980. See Paul R. Abramson, John H. Aldrich, and David W. Rohde, *Change and Continuity in the 1980 Elections*, rev. ed. (Washington, D.C.: CQ Press, 1983), 85–87. For a more detailed analysis using probability procedures, see Paul R. Abramson and John H. Aldrich, "The Decline of Electoral Participation in America," *American Political Science Review* 76 (September 1982): 502–521.

67. See Paul R. Abramson, John H. Aldrich, and David W. Rohde, *Change and Continuity in the 1984 Elections* rev. ed. (Washington, D.C.: CQ Press, 1987), 115–118; Abramson, Aldrich, and Rohde, *Change and Continuity in the 1988 Elections*, 103–106; Paul R. Abramson, John H. Aldrich, and David W. Rohde, *Change and Continuity in the 1996 and 1998 Elections* (Washington, D.C.: CQ Press, 1999), 81–84; Abramson, Aldrich, and Rohde, *Change and Continuity in the 2000 and 2002 Elections*, 86–89.

68. Respondents were asked, "Generally speaking, do you usually think of yourself as a Republican, a Democrat, an Independent, or what?" Persons who called themselves Republicans or Democrats were asked, "Would you call yourself a strong Republican (Democrat) or a not very strong Republican (Democrat)?" Those who called themselves independents, named another party, or who had no preference were asked, "Do you think of yourself as closer to the Republican party or to the Democratic party?" Respondents with no preference are usually classified as independents. They are classified as "apoliticals" only if they have low levels of political interest and involvement.

69. Angus Campbell et al., *The American Voter* (New York: Wiley, 1960), 120–167.

70. This expectation follows from the rational choice perspective. For the most extensive discussion of party identification from this view, see Morris P. Fiorina, *Retrospective Voting in American National Elections* (New Haven: Yale University Press, 1980), 84–105. For a more recent discussion, see John H. Aldrich, "Rational Choice and Turnout," *American Journal of Political Science* 37 (February 1993): 246–278. For a comment on Aldrich's essay, see Robert W. Jackman, "Rationality and Political Participation," *American Journal of Political Science* 37 (February 1993): 279–290. For an extensive critique of the rational choice approach to the study of electoral participation, see Donald P. Green and Ian Shapiro, *Pathologies of Rational Choice: A Critique of Applications in Political Science* (New Haven: Yale University Press, 1994), 41–71.

71. Respondents who disagreed with both of these statements were scored as high in their feelings of political effectiveness; those who agreed with one statement and disagreed with the other were scored as medium; and those who agreed with both statements were scored as low. Respondents who scored "don't know" or "not ascertained" to one statement were scored either high or low according to their answer on the remaining statement, but those with "don't know" or "not

ascertained" responses to both statements were excluded from the analysis. In 1988, 1992, 1996, 2000, and 2004 respondents were asked whether they "strongly agreed," "agreed," "disagreed," or "strongly disagreed" with each statement. For all five years, we classified respondents who "neither agreed nor disagreed" with both statements as medium on this measure. This scoring decision has little effect on the results, since only 3 percent of the respondents in 1988, 2 percent in 1992, 3 percent in 1996, 4 percent in 2000, and 5 percent in 2004 answered "neither agree nor disagree" to both of the statements.

72. This is consistent with the findings of Bruce E. Keith and his colleagues that independents who feel closer to one of the parties are as politically involved as weak partisans. See Bruce E. Keith et al., *The Myth of the Independent Voter* (Berkeley: University of California Press, 1992), 38–59. However, as we will see, this was not the case in 2004.

73. This calculation is based on the assumption that each partisan strength and sense of political efficacy category was the same size as we observed in 1960, but that reported turnout for each category was the same as that observed in 2000. For a full explanation of this technique, see Abramson, *Political Attitudes in America*, 296.

74. Our analysis was based upon an algebraic standardization procedure. To simplify our analysis we combined whites with an eighth grade education or less with whites who had not graduated from high school, and we combined weak partisans with independents who leaned toward a party.

75. For a discussion of political trust, see Abramson, *Political Attitudes in America*, 193–238. For a more recent discussion, see Marc J. Hetherington, *Why Trust Matters: Declining Political Trust and the Demise of American Liberalism* (Princeton: Princeton University Press, 2005).

76. Russell J. Dalton reports a decline of confidence in politicians and government in fifteen of sixteen democracies. Although many of the trends are not statistically significant, the overall pattern of decline is impressive. Dalton's report includes results from the U.S. NES surveys, where the trend toward declining confidence is unlikely to occur by chance on two of the three questions Dalton employs. See Russell J. Dalton, *Democratic Challenges, Democratic Choices: The Erosion of Political Support in Advanced Industrial Democracies* (Oxford: Oxford University Press, 2004), 28–31.

77. Respondents were asked, "How much of the time do you think you can trust the government in Washington to do what is right—just about always, most of the time, or only some of the time?"

78. Respondents were asked, "Would you say the government is pretty much run for a few big interests looking out for themselves, or that it is run for the benefit of all the people?"

79. Personal communication, May 31, 2005. These different estimates of increases in turnout result from using different denominators to calculate the percentage who voted.

80. The two large previous surges were the 8.1 percent increase between 1924 and 1928 and the 10.0 percent increase between 1948 and 1952 (Ibid.). Using the voting-age population as the turnout denominator, we also found that the increase was the third largest during this 84-year period (see Table 4-3 and Figure 4-1).

81. See Paul R. Abramson, John H. Aldrich, and David W. Rohde, "The 2004 Presidential Election: The Emergence of a Permanent Majority?" *Political Science Quarterly* 120 (Spring 2005): 42–43.

82. Respondents were asked, "The political parties try to talk to as many people as they can to get them to vote for their candidate. Did anyone from the political parties call you up or come around to talk with you about the campaign this year?"

83. As Paul R. Abramson and William Claggett show, the effects of elite recruitment on increasing turnout persist even when one takes into account that political elites are more likely to recruit people who have participated in the past. See Paul R. Abramson and William Claggett, "Recruitment and Political Participation," *Political Research Quarterly* 54 (December 2001): 905–916.

84. In the SRC survey, respondents were asked who they thought would be elected president. Those who named a candidate were asked, "Do you think the election will be close or do you think that [the candidate named] will win by quite a bit?" Those who said they did not know who would win were asked, "Do you think the presidential race will be close, or will one candidate win by quite a bit?"

85. Orley Ashenfelter and Stanley Kelley Jr., "Determinants of Participation in Presidential Elections," *Journal of Law and Economics* 18 (December 1975): 721.

86. James DeNardo, "Turnout and the Vote: The Joke's on the Democrats," *American Political Science Review* 74 (June 1980): 406–420.

87. Abramson, Aldrich, and Rohde, *Change and Continuity in the 1980 Elections*, 88–92; Abramson, Aldrich, and Rohde, *Change and Continuity in the 1984 Elections*, 119–124; Abramson, Aldrich, and Rohde, *Change and Continuity in the 1988 Elections*, 406–420.

88. Abramson, Aldrich, and Rohde, *Change and Continuity in the 1992 Elections*, 124–128.

89. Abramson, Aldrich, and Rohde, *Change and Continuity in the 1996 and 1998 Elections*, 86–89.

90. Gerald M. Pomper, "The Presidential Election," in *The Election of 2000: Reports and Interpretations*, ed. Gerald M. Pomper (New York: Chatham House, 2001), 114.

91. The results for 1980, 1984, and 1988 are based on the responses of people whose voting was verified by checking the voting and registration records. However, the Republican advantage was also found when we studied reported electoral participation.

92. Among Republicans, 49 percent said they had been contacted by a political party, while among Democrats 44 percent said they had been contacted. The

NES question asks only about contact by a political party, and it is possible that Republicans were more likely to be mobilized by groups supporting Bush and other Republican candidates.

93. Abramson, Aldrich, and Rohde, *Change and Continuity in the 2000 and 2002 Elections*, 92–93; 143.

94. In our analysis of retrospective evaluations and turnout in 1980, we used a different measure as well. See Abramson, Aldrich, and Rohde, *Change and Continuity in the 1980 Elections*, 90. However, the measure we developed to analyze the 1984 NES survey, and which we used in all subsequent studies, can be built with the 1980 NES survey. The Republican turnout advantage we discovered in analyzing the 1980 data is also found when the summary measure of retrospective evaluations we developed in 1984 is used.

95. See Wolfinger and Rosenstone, *Who Votes?* 108–114.

96. Frances Fox Piven and Richard A. Cloward, *Why Americans Don't Vote* (New York: Pantheon Books, 1988), 21. For a more recent formulation, see Piven and Cloward, *Why Americans Still Don't Vote*.

97. See Seymour Martin Lipset, *Political Man: The Social Bases of Politics*, enl. ed. (Baltimore: Johns Hopkins University Press, 1981), 226–229. Lipset emphasizes the dangers of sudden increases in political participation.

98. Gerald M. Pomper, "The Presidential Election," in *The Election of 1980: Reports and Interpretations*, ed. Gerald M. Pomper (Chatham, N.J.: Chatham House, 1981), 86.

99. "When People Vote," *The Rhodes Cook Letter*, March 2005, 7. Clearly, Cook resorts to hyperbole when he refers to "sky high turnout." U.S. turnout is not "sky high" by either comparative or U.S. historical standards (see Tables 4-1 through 4-3 and Figure 4-1).

5. SOCIAL FORCES AND THE VOTE

1. The social characteristics used in this chapter are the same as those used in chapter 4. The variables are described in the notes to that chapter. For similar tables showing the results for elections between 1980 and 2000, see Paul R. Abramson, John H. Aldrich, and David W. Rohde, *Change and Continuity in the 1980 Elections*, rev. ed. (Washington, D.C.: CQ Press, 1983), 98–99; Paul R. Abramson, John H. Aldrich, and David W. Rohde, *Change and Continuity in the 1984 Elections*, rev. ed. (Washington, D.C.: CQ Press, 1987), 136–137; Paul R. Abramson, John H. Aldrich, and David W. Rohde, *Change and Continuity in the 1988 Elections*, rev. ed. (Washington, D.C.: CQ Press, 1991), 124–125; Paul R. Abramson, John H. Aldrich, and David W. Rohde, *Change and Continuity in the 1992 Elections*, rev. ed. (Washington, D.C.: CQ Press, 1995), 133–135; Paul R. Abramson, John H. Aldrich, and David W. Rohde, *Change and Continuity in the 1996 and 1998 Elections* (Washington, D.C.: CQ Press, 1999), 93–95; and Paul R. Abramson, John H. Aldrich, and David W. Rohde, *Change and Continuity in the 2000 and 2002 Elections* (Washington, D.C.: CQ Press, 2003), 98–100.

2. In the elections we studied between 1980 and 2000, the smallest number of reported voters in an NES survey was 972 in 1980. In the other years, the numbers of reported voters were 1,389 in 1984; 1,227 in 1988; 1,685 in 1992; 1,120 in 1996; and 1,087 in 2000.

3. This poll was conducted by Edison Media Research/Mitofsky International and is based on questionnaires completed by 13,110 voters as they left 250 polling places throughout the United States on election day, and 500 telephone polls of early voters. It was sponsored by a consortium of newspapers and television networks. The results we report are from three sources: Marjorie Connelly, "Election 2004: How America Voted," *New York Times,* November 7, 2004, WW4; MSNBC, "Decision 2004," www.msnbc.com/id/5297138 (accessed November 10, 2004); and CNN.com, "Election Results," www.cnn.ELECTION/2004/pages/results/states/US/P/00/epolls.0.html (accessed June 16, 2005). Four questionnaire formats were used, so the number of cases will vary with both the size of the subgroup and the number of formats for which the group affiliation was collected. Most of these relationships are presented in Paul R. Abramson, John H. Aldrich, and David W. Rohde, "The 2004 Presidential Election: The Emergence of a Permanent Majority?" *Political Science Quarterly* 120 (Spring 2005): 33–57.

4. The *Los Angeles Times* poll was based on voters as they left 136 polling places throughout the United States. Sixty-five percent of the respondents were sampled as they left fifty polling places within California.

5. Exit polls have three main advantages: First, they are less expensive to conduct than the multistage probability samples conducted by the Survey Research Center of the University of Michigan. Second, because of their lower cost, a large number of people can be sampled. Third, because persons are selected to be interviewed as they leave the polling stations, the vast majority have actually voted for president. But these surveys also have four disadvantages: First, exit polls usually do not sample the growing number of voters who use absentee ballots, although the EMR/MI poll did sample early voters. Second, the self-administered questionnaires must be relatively brief. Third, it is difficult to supervise the fieldwork to be sure that the interviewers are using proper procedures to select respondents. Last, these studies are of little use in studying turnout, since persons who do not vote are not sampled. For a discussion of the procedures used to conduct exit polls, as well as some of their limitations, see Albert H. Cantril, *The Opinion Connection: Polling, Politics, and the Press* (Washington, D.C.: CQ Press, 1991).

6. This brief discussion cannot do justice to the complexities of black electoral participation. For an important study based on the black NES survey, see Patricia Gurin, Shirley Hatchett, and James S. Jackson, *Hope and Independence: Blacks' Response to Electoral and Party Politics* (New York: Russell Sage Foundation, 1989). For two important studies that use the 1984 black NES and the 1988 follow-up survey, see Michael C. Dawson, *Behind the Mule: Race and Class in African American Politics* (Princeton: Princeton University Press, 1994); and Katherine Tate, *From Politics to Protest: The New Black Voters in American Elections,* enl. ed. (Cambridge: Harvard University Press, 1994). For a summary of

recent research on race and politics, see Michael C. Dawson and Cathy Cohen, "Problems in the Politics of Race," in *Political Science: The State of the Discipline,* ed. Ira Katznelson and Helen V. Milner (New York: Norton, 2002), 488–510.

7. Although we have examined the results for blacks for all the categories in Table 5-1, we do not present them. Given that we have a sample of only 114 black voters, the number of blacks in these subgroups is too small to present meaningful results.

8. See Darryl Fears, "Pollsters Debate Hispanics' Presidential Voting," *Washington Post,* November 27, 2004, www.washingtonpost.com (accessed November 27, 2004). Gerald M. Pomper argues that sampling problems may lead exit polls to make unreliable estimates of the Hispanic vote. See Gerald M. Pomper, "The Presidential Election: The Ills of American Politics After 9/11," in *The Elections of 2004,* ed. Michael Nelson (Washington, D.C.: CQ Press, 2005), chap. 3, note 14, 66.

9. These results are reported in David L. Leal et al., "The Latino Vote in 2004," *PS: Political Science and Politics* 38 (January 2005): 42. The poll is based upon 957 Latino voters sampled in forty-one precincts in eleven states. We are grateful to David L. Leal of the University of Texas at Austin for providing information about the sample.

10. Ibid.

11. For a review of research on Hispanics, as well as African Americans, see Paula D. McClain and John D. Garcia, "Expanding Disciplinary Boundaries: Black, Latino, and Racial Minority Groups in Political Science," in *Political Science: The State of the Discipline II,* ed. Ada W. Finifter (Washington, D.C.: American Political Science Association, 1993), 274–279. For analyses of Hispanic voting behavior in the 1996 elections, see Rudolfo O. de la Garza and Louis DeSipio, eds., *Awash in the Mainstream: Latino Politics in the 1996 Election* (Boulder: Westview Press, 1999).

12. For two reviews of research on women and politics, see Susan J. Carroll and Linda M. G. Zerelli, "Feminist Challenges to Political Science," in *Political Science: The State of the Discipline II,* ed. Ada W. Finifter, 55–76; and Nancy Burns, "Gender: Public Opinion and Political Action," in *Political Science: The State of the Discipline,* ed. Katznelson and Milner, 462–487. For a global comparison, see Barbara J. Nelson and Najma Chowdhury, eds., *Women and Politics Worldwide* (New Haven: Yale University Press, 1994).

13. See Abramson, Aldrich, and Rohde, *Change and Continuity in the 1980 Elections,* 290.

14. The 2000 VNS exit poll was based on 13,279 voters sampled as they left 300 polling places on election day. For a description of the sampling and for the results of this survey, see Marjorie Connelly, "The Election: A Portrait of American Politics, 1976–2000," *New York Times,* November 12, 2000, WK 4.

15. The NES survey reports six types of marital status: married and living with spouse, never married, divorced, separated, widowed, and partners who are not married. In this paragraph, we discuss the first two of these groups.

16. In the "secret ballot" used by this survey, respondents were asked, "Are you gay, lesbian, or bisexual?"

17. According to the *LA Times* poll, voters between the ages of eighteen and twenty-nine made up 20 percent of the electorate.

18. See, for example, Walter Dean Burnham, *Critical Elections and the Mainsprings of American Politics* (New York: Norton, 1970); Everett Carll Ladd Jr., with Charles D. Hadley Jr., *Transformations of the American Party System: Political Coalitions from the New Deal to the 1970s*, 2nd ed. (New York: Norton, 1978).

19. According to our analyses of NES surveys, voters who themselves belong to unions are more likely to vote Democratic than those who are members of union households but do not themselves belong to a union. For example, in 2004, among whites who belonged to a union ($N = 76$), 62 percent voted for Kerry; among those who were in a union household but did not themselves belong to a union ($N = 55$), 53 percent did. According to the EMR/MI poll, 61 percent of union members voted for Kerry, whereas of voters who lived in a union household but were not themselves union members, 57 percent did.

20. For the best single summary, see Kenneth D. Wald, *Religion and Politics in the United States*, 4th ed. (Lanham, Md.: Rowman and Littlefield, 2003). For a discussion of religion and politics in a comparative context, see Pippa Norris and Ronald Inglehart, *Sacred and Secular: Religion and Politics Worldwide* (Cambridge: Cambridge University Press, 2004).

21. As we note in chapter 4, Alfred E. Smith, the Democratic presidential candidate in 1928, was a Catholic.

22. For an analysis of that election using the NES surveys, see Philip E. Converse et al., "Stability and Change: A Reinstating Election," *American Political Science Review* (June 1961): 269–280. For a discussion of variation in voting among Catholics, see Theodore H. White, *The Making of the President, 1960* (New York: Atheneum, 1961), 355–357.

23. As we noted above, past NES surveys asked Christians whether they were "born-again Christians." In the past, responses to this question were strongly related to the vote. For example, in 2000, among white Protestants who said they were "born again," 69 percent voted for Bush; among those who said they were not born again, 49 percent did. This question was not asked in the 2004 NES survey.

24. David C. Leege and Lyman A. Kellstedt, with others, *Rediscovering the Religious Factor in American Politics* (Armonk, N.Y.: M. E. Sharpe, 1993).

25. Stanley B. Greenberg, *The Two Americas: Our Current Political Deadlock and How to Break It* (New York: St. Martin's, 2004), 97.

26. As we have already used the respondent's report of his or her church attendance in our measure of religious commitment, we do not want to focus on these results separately. For those who want to compare the NES results with the exit poll results, however, we will report the following: Among whites who attended church every week ($N = 151$), 70 percent voted for Bush; among those who attended almost every week ($N = 73$), 64 percent did; among those who attended once a month ($N = 84$) 67 percent did; among those who attended only a few

times a year (N = 90), 48 percent voted for Bush. While church attendance is clearly related to voting for Bush, the relationship is obviously substantially weaker than the relationship with our four-item index.

27. Morris P. Fiorina, with Samuel J. Abrams and Jeremy C. Pope, *Culture War? The Myth of a Polarized America* (New York: Pearson/Longman, 2005), 69.

28. Robert Axelrod, "Where the Votes Come From: An Analysis of Electoral Coalitions, 1952–1968," *American Political Science Review* 66 (March 1972): 11–20. Axelrod continued to update his results through the 1984 elections. For his most recent estimate, which includes results from 1952 through 1980, see Axelrod, "Presidential Election Coalitions in 1984," *American Political Science Review* 80 (March 1986): 281–284. Using Axelrod's categories, Nelson W. Polsby provides estimates of the social composition of the Democratic and Republican presidential coalition between 1952 and 2000. See Nelson W. Polsby and Aaron Wildavsky, *Presidential Elections: Strategies and Structures of American Politics,* 11th ed. (Lanham, Md.: Rowman and Littlefield, 2004), 32.

29. John R. Petrocik, *Party Coalitions: Realignment and the Decline of the New Deal Party System* (Chicago: University of Chicago Press, 1981).

30. Harold W. Stanley, William T. Bianco, and Richard G. Niemi, "Partisanship and Group Support over Time: A Multivariate Analysis," *American Political Science Review* 80 (September 1986): 969–976. Stanley and his colleagues assess the independent contribution that group membership makes toward Democratic loyalties after controls are introduced for membership in other pro-Democratic groups. For an update and extension through 2000, see Stanley and Niemi, "Partisanship, Party Coalitions, and Group Support," in *Models of Voting in Presidential Elections: The 2000 U.S. Election,* ed. Herbert F. Weisberg and Clyde Wilcox (Stanford: Stanford University Press, 2004), 123–140. For an alternative approach, see Robert S. Erikson, Thomas D. Lancaster, and David W. Romero, "Group Components of the Presidential Vote, 1952–1984," *Journal of Politics* 51 (May 1989): 337–346.

31. For a discussion of the contribution of the working class to the Democratic presidential coalition, see Paul R. Abramson, *Generational Change in American Politics* (Lexington, Mass.: D. C. Heath, 1975).

32. See Axelrod, "Where the Votes Come From."

33. The NORC survey, based on 2,564 civilians, used a quota sample that does not follow the probability procedures used by the University of Michigan Survey Research Center. Following the procedures used at the time, southern blacks were not sampled. Because the NORC survey overrepresented upper-income groups and the middle and upper classes, it cannot be used to estimate the contribution of social groups to the Democratic and Republican presidential coalitions.

34. Abramson, *Generational Change,* 65–68.

35. As Figure 5-1 shows, Clinton did win a majority of the white major-party vote in 1992 and 1996.

36. Racial voting, as well as our other measures of social cleavage, is affected by including Wallace voters with Nixon voters in 1968, Anderson voters with Rea-

gan voters in 1980, Perot voters with Bush voters in 1992, and Perot voters with Dole voters in 1996. For reports on the effects of including these independent or third-party candidates, see Abramson, Aldrich, and Rohde, *Change and Continuity in the 1996 and 1998 Elections,* 102, 104–106, 108, and 111.

37. As we explain in chapter 3, we consider the South to include the eleven states of the old Confederacy, although with our analysis of NES surveys we classify Tennessee as a border state. Because we cannot use this definition with either the 1944 NORC survey or the 1948 University of Michigan Survey Research Center survey, we have not included these years in our analysis of regional differences among the white electorate.

38. See, for example, chapter 3, where we compare Kennedy's black support in the South in 1960 with Carter's black support in 1976.

39. Officially known as the Labor-Management Relations Act, this legislation, passed in 1947, qualified or amended much of the National Labor Relations Act of 1935 (popularly known as the Wagner Act). Union leaders argued that the Taft-Hartley Act placed unwarranted restrictions on organized labor. The act was passed by the Republican-controlled 80th Congress, vetoed by Truman, and passed over his veto.

40. Kerry's share of the vote coming from union households is higher with both of the exit polls. According to our calculations, the EMR/MI poll shows that 30 percent of Kerry's vote came from members of a union household; according to the *LA Times* poll, 33 percent came from union households.

41. See Robert R. Alford, *Party and Society: The Anglo-American Democracies* (Chicago: Rand McNally, 1963); Seymour Martin Lipset, *Political Man: The Social Bases of Politics,* exp. ed. (Baltimore: Johns Hopkins University Press, 1981); and Ronald Inglehart, *Modernization and Postmodernization: Cultural, Economic, and Political Change in 43 Societies* (Princeton: Princeton University Press, 1997).

42. The variation in class voting is smaller if one focuses on class differences in the congressional vote, but the data clearly show a decline in class voting between 1952 and 2004. See Russell J. Dalton, *Citizen Politics: Public Opinion and Political Parties in Advanced Industrial Democracies,* 4th ed. (Washington, D.C.: CQ Press, 2006), 153.

43. Readers should bear in mind that in 2000 (and 2004) there was no measure of the head of household's occupation or of the spouse's occupation, but our analysis of the 1996 data suggests that this limitation probably does not account for the negative level of class voting in the 2000 contest.

44. As we point out in *Change and Continuity in the 2000 and 2002 Elections,* when we define social class according to the respondent's own occupation, the overall size of the working class falls and the overall size of the middle class grows. As the relatively small size of the working class in 2000 and 2004 results largely from a redefinition in the way our measure of class is constructed, we will assume that the sizes of the working class and the middle class in 2000 and 2004 were the same as they were in the 1996 NES. See Abramson, Aldrich, and Rohde, *Change and Continuity in the 2000 and 2002 Elections,* chap. 4, note 26, 313.

45. See Mark N. Franklin, "The Decline of Cleavage Politics," in *Electoral Change: Responses to Evolving Social and Attitudinal Structures in Western Countries*, ed. Mark N. Franklin, Thomas T. Mackie, and Henry Valen, with others (Cambridge: Cambridge University Press, 1992), 383–405. See also Inglehart, *Modernization and Postmodernization*, 237–266.

46. Jeff Manza and Clem Brooks, *Social Cleavages and Political Change: Voter Alignments and U.S. Party Coalitions* (New York: Oxford University Press, 1999).

47. U.S. Bureau of the Census, *Statistical Abstract of the United States 2004–2005*, 124th ed. (Washington, D.C.: U.S. Government Printing Office, 2004), Table 69, 56. We list these states in descending order by their estimated number of Jews. The estimates of the number of Jews in each state are based on information provided by local Jewish organizations.

48. Since 1860 the Democrats have won the presidency only twice without winning New York: 1916, when Woodrow Wilson narrowly defeated Charles Evans Hughes by a margin of 23 electoral votes, and 1948, when Harry S. Truman defeated the incumbent governor of New York, Thomas E. Dewey. Dewey won 46.0 percent of the popular vote in New York, while Truman won 45.0 percent. Henry A. Wallace, the Progressive candidate, won 8.2 percent of the New York vote, substantially better than his share in any other state.

49. The published results of the *LA Times* poll do not show how white Catholics voted. Based upon our calculations, these polls suggest that 23 percent of Kerry's support came from Catholics (of any race). The NES surveys and the EMR/MI both show that 26 percent of Kerry's vote came from Catholics of all races.

50. Wilson Carey McWilliams, "The Meaning of the Election: Ownership and Citizenship in American Life," in *The Elections of 2004*, ed. Michael Nelson (Washington, D.C.: CQ Press, 2005), 200–201. Although defections by white Catholics played a crucial role in weakening the New Deal coalition, we do not agree that these defections were more crucial than Bush's support among white evangelicals. The NES survey shows that Bush received more of his total vote from white evangelicals than from white Catholics.

51. Robert Huckfeldt and Carol Weitzel Kohfeld, *Race and the Decline of Class in American Politics* (Urbana: University of Illinois Press, 1989).

52. For evidence on this point, see Paul R. Abramson, *Political Attitudes in America: Formation and Change* (San Francisco: W. H. Freeman, 1983), 65–68.

53. Edward G. Carmines and James A. Stimson, *Issue Evolution: Race and the Transformation of American Politics* (Princeton: Princeton University Press, 1989). For a critique of their thesis, see Alan I. Abramowitz, "Issue Evolution Reconsidered: Racial Attitudes and Partisanship among the U.S. Electorate," *American Journal of Political Science* 38 (February 1994): 1–24.

54. This is not to argue that abortion is necessarily an issue that works against the Democrats. For example, in a study of the 1992 presidential election, Alan I. Abramowitz argues that abortion was the most important issue influencing voting choices and that Clinton was the beneficiary. See Alan I. Abramowitz, "It's

Abortion Stupid: Policy Voting in the 1992 Presidential Election," *Journal of Politics* 57 (February 1995): 176–186.

55. James W. Ceaser and Andrew E. Busch, *Upside Down and Inside Out: The 1992 Elections and American Politics* (Lanham, Md.: Rowman and Littlefield, 1993), 168–171.

6. CANDIDATES, ISSUES, AND THE VOTE

1. This set of attitudes was first formulated and tested extensively in Angus Campbell et al., *The American Voter* (New York: Wiley, 1960), using data from what are now called the National Election Studies (NES) surveys. The authors based their conclusions primarily on data from a survey of the 1956 presidential election, a rematch between the Democrat Adlai E. Stevenson and the Republican (and this time incumbent) Dwight D. Eisenhower.

2. See, for example, Wendy M. Rahn et al., "A Social-Cognitive Model of Candidate Appraisal," in *Information and Democratic Processes,* ed. John A. Ferejohn and James H. Kuklinski (Urbana: University of Illinois Press, 1990), 136–159, and sources cited therein. Ronald Reagan was generally perceived to be especially attractive on personal grounds, while Bill Clinton was the extreme version of the exact opposite. These considerations about Clinton helped shape Gore's campaign strategy, downplaying administration successes for fear of making Clinton's personal scandals more prominent as well.

3. For the most extensive explication of the theory and tests in various electoral settings, see Gary W. Cox, *Making Votes Count: Strategic Coordination in the World's Electoral Systems* (New York: Cambridge University Press, 1997). For an examination in the American context see Paul R. Abramson et al., "Third-Party and Independent Candidates in American Politics: Wallace, Anderson, and Perot," *Political Science Quarterly* 110 (Fall 1995):349–367.

4. These elections are discussed in Paul R. Abramson, John H. Aldrich, and David W. Rohde, *Change and Continuity in the 1980 Elections,* rev. ed. (Washington, D.C.: CQ Press, 1983); Paul R. Abramson, John H. Aldrich, and David W. Rohde, *Change and Continuity in the 1992 Elections,* rev. ed. (Washington, D.C.: CQ Press, 1995); Paul R. Abramson, John H. Aldrich, and David W. Rohde, *Change and Continuity in the 1996 and 1998 Elections* (Washington, D.C.: CQ Press, 1999); and Paul R. Abramson, John H. Aldrich, and David W. Rohde, *Change and Continuity in the 2000 and 2002 Elections* (Washington, D.C.: CQ Press, 2003).

5. We reproduce the feeling thermometer in Abramson, Aldrich, and Rohde, *Change and Continuity in the 1992 Elections,* rev. ed., 166; *Change and Continuity in the 1996 and 1998 Elections,* 117; and *Change and Continuity in the 2000 and 2002 Elections,* 123.

6. See Abramson et al., "Third-Party and Independent Candidates."

7. Abramson, Aldrich, and Rohde, *Change and Continuity in the 2000 and 2002 Elections*, Table 6-1, 125–126.

8. The Marquis de Condorcet (1743–1794) was a French philosopher best known for his theories of human progress. For a discussion of his theories of social choice, see Duncan Black, *The Theory of Committees and Elections* (Cambridge: Cambridge University Press, 1958).

9. William H. Riker, *Liberalism against Populism: A Confrontation between the Theory of Democracy and the Theory of Social Choice* (San Francisco: W. H. Freeman, 1982), 85–88.

10. For evidence on 1968, 1980, and 2002, see Abramson et al., "Third-Party and Independent Candidates"; and for evidence on 1996, see Abramson, Aldrich, and Rohde, *Change and Continuity in the 1996 and 1998 Elections*, 120–121.

11. Abramson, Aldrich, and Rohde, *Change and Continuity in the 2000 and 2002 Elections*, 127–128.

12. For an analysis of how the candidates' campaign strategies in 1996, 2000, and 2004 shaped the voters' decisions, and in turn were shaped by the concerns of the voters, see John H. Aldrich and Thomas Weko, "The Presidency and the Election Campaign: Framing the Choice in 1996," in *The Presidency and the Political System*, 6th ed., ed. Michael Nelson (Washington, D.C.: CQ Press, 2000); John H. Aldrich and John D. Griffin, "The Presidency and the Campaign: Creating Voter Priorities in the 2000 Election, in *The Presidency and the Political System*, 7th ed., ed. Michael Nelson (Washington, D.C.: CQ Press, 2003); and John H. Aldrich, John D. Griffin, and Jill Rickershauser, "The Presidency and the Campaign: Creating Voter Priorities in the 2004 Election," in *The Presidency and the Political System*, 8th ed., ed. Michael Nelson (Washington, D.C.: CQ Press, 2006), 219–234.

13. In previous presidential year surveys respondents between 1972 and 2000 were asked, "What do you think are the most important problems facing the country?" or a very similar version of this question. If they named more than one problem, they were asked which problem was the most important. In 2004, however, they were asked a different question, "What do you think has been the most important issue facing the United States over the last four years?"

14. Of course, 2000 was right at the end of the boom years for economic growth (and the end of the "high-tech stock bubble"). We cannot tell from these data, but it seems reasonable to imagine that this "low" a level of concern about the economy was due to the collective perception that the economy was improving (with Democrats and Republicans differing over the magnitude and distribution of the improvement) and to the fact that in 2004 there were an unusually large number of problems that could reasonably be imagined as candidates for the most important problem facing the country.

15. The 2004 Edison Media Research/Mitofsky International (EMR/MI) exit poll, in which actual voters are interviewed as they leave their polling places, yielded what many saw as one of the great surprises of the campaign—that

"moral values" were the most important problem, a finding that was fodder for a great deal of media speculation shortly after the campaign. While a number of specific problems that voters might have had in mind when they indicated that moral values were their primary concern are undoubtedly included under the social issues category in Table 6-1, we cannot make any direct comparison between "moral values" and these data. In part the reason is that the voter was handed a fixed list of concerns from which to choose, and in part it is that we have no idea what the voters actually had in mind when they selected that response. We will, however, address some aspects of this comparison later in this chapter.

16. These measures were first used in the NES survey of the 1968 election. They were used extensively in presidential election surveys beginning in 1972. The issue measures used in chapter 7 were also used extensively beginning in the 1970s. For that reason, in this and the following two chapters we restrict our attention to the past nine elections.

17. The median is based on the assumption that respondents can be ranked from "most conservative" to "most liberal." The number of respondents who are more liberal than the median (or who see a candidate as more liberal than the median) is equal to the number who are more conservative (or see the candidate as more conservative) than the median. Because there are only seven points on these scales, and because many respondents will choose any given point, the median is computed using a procedure that derives a median for grouped data.

18. Five of the first six scales were used only in the preelection interview. The "government services/spending" scale was used in both the pre- and postelection surveys, but the questions used to place Bush and Kerry were only asked before the election. We therefore used the preelection responses to this scale. The "diplomacy/military force" scale was also used in both the pre- and postelection surveys, but the questions asking respondents to place Bush and Kerry were used only in the postelection survey. We therefore used the postelection responses to this scale. We used the postelection weight when constructing our "balance of issues" measure.

19. In both 2000 and 2004 the median value for the electorate was less than 1, even though 1 was the most egalitarian value respondents could choose. This is not a mistake but results from the way that median values for grouped data are calculated.

20. Morris P. Fiorina, with Samuel J. Abrams and Jeremy C. Pope, *Culture War? The Myth of a Polarized Electorate* (New York: Pearson, Longman, 2005).

21. Campbell et al., *American Voter,* 168–187.

22. In most years, including 2004, respondents were encouraged to reveal an absence of an issue position by the addition to the issue scale question of the wording, "or haven't you thought much about it?" This prompt is designed to remove feelings of social pressure to appear well informed, even if the respondent is not, although the data show that it did not generate a great deal of selection of the "no opinion" option.

23. Before 1996, the NES interviewers did not ask those who failed to place themselves on an issue scale where they thought the candidates stood. Since then, they have asked respondents who did not place themselves on an issue where the candidates stood. Therefore, before 1996 those who failed to meet the first criterion were not able to meet any of the remaining ones. Although some people who express no preference on an issue might know the position of one or both candidates, it is difficult to see how they could vote based on those perceptions if they had no opinion of their own.

24. To maintain comparability with previous election surveys, for 1996, 2000, and 2004 we have excluded respondents who did not place themselves on an issue scale from columns II, III, and IV of Table 6-2. As we do not know the preferences of these respondents on the issue, we have no way to measure the way their issue preferences may have affected their vote.

25. For details, see Abramson, Aldrich, and Rohde, *Change and Continuity in the 1980 Elections*, Table 6-3, 130; Abramson, Aldrich, and Rohde, *Change and Continuity in the 1984 Elections*, rev. ed. (Washington, D.C.: CQ Press, 1987), Table 6-2, 174; Abramson, Aldrich, and Rohde, *Change and Continuity in the 1988 Elections*, rev. ed. (Washington, D.C.: CQ Press, 1991), Table 6-2, 165; Abramson, Aldrich, and Rohde, *Change and Continuity in the 1992 Elections*, Table 6-6, 186; Abramson, Aldrich, and Rohde, *Change and Continuity in the 1996 and 1998 Elections*, Table 6-6, 135; and Abramson, Aldrich, and Rohde, *Change and Continuity in the 2000 and 2002 Elections*, Table 6-4, 137.

26. Although this is evidence that most people claim to have issue preferences, it does not demonstrate that they do. For example, evidence indicates that some use the midpoint of the scale (point 4) as a means of answering the question even if they have ill-formed preferences. See John H. Aldrich et al., "The Measurement of Public Opinion about Public Policy: A Report on Some New Issue Question Formats," *American Journal of Political Science* 26 (May 1982): 391–414.

27. Morris P. Fiorina, *Retrospective Voting in American National Elections* (New Haven: Yale University Press, 1981).

28. We use the phrase "apparent issue voting" to emphasize three points: First, voting involves too many factors to infer that closeness to a candidate on any one issue was the cause of the voter's choice. The issue similarity may have been purely coincidental, or it may have been only one of many reasons the voter supported that candidate. Second, we use the median perception of the candidates' positions rather than the voter's own perception. Third, the relationship between issues and the vote may be caused by rationalization. Voters may have decided to support a candidate for other reasons and also may have altered their own issue preferences or misperceived the positions of the candidates to align themselves more closely with the candidate already favored. See Richard A. Brody and Benjamin I. Page, "Comment: The Assessment of Policy Voting," *American Political Science Review* 66 (June 1972): 450–458.

29. Many individuals, of course, placed the candidates at different positions than the public did on average. Using average perceptions, however, reduces the

effect of individuals' rationalizing their perceptions of candidates to be consistent with their own vote, rather than voting for the candidate whose views are actually closer to their own.

30. Since the 4 response on the diplomacy/military intervention scale was equidistant between the electorate's placement of Kerry and the electorate's placement of Bush, we assigned the 228 respondents with a response of 4 a score of zero on our measure.

31. This procedure counts every issue as equal in importance. It also assumes that what matters is that the voter is closer to the candidate on an issue; it does not consider how much closer the voter is to one candidate or the other.

32. Scores of +5, +6, and +7 were called "strongly Republican," while similarly negative scores were called "strongly Democratic." Scores of +3 and +4 were called "moderately Republican"; –3 and –4 were called "moderately Democratic." Scores of +1 and +2 were called "slightly Republican," with –1 and –2 being called "slightly Democratic." A score of zero was called "neutral." Three respondents who did not have an opinion on any of the seven issues were excluded from the analysis.

33. This is an oddity that appears to be due to the fact that our balance of issue measure counts only whether the respondent is closer to a candidate and does not consider by how much.

34. The EMR/MI exit poll also shows a strong relationship between opinions about abortion and the vote. According to our estimate, about 3,800 respondents were asked their opinion about abortion. Twenty-one percent said it should be legal in all cases, 34 percent that it should be legal in most cases, 26 percent that it should be illegal in most cases, and 16 percent that it should be illegal in all cases. Among major-party voters who said it should be legal in all cases, 74 percent voted for Kerry; among those who said it should be legal in most cases, 62 percent did; among those who said it should be illegal in most cases, 26 percent did; and among those who thought abortion should always be illegal only 22 percent voted for Kerry.

35. See Abramson, Aldrich, and Rohde, *Change and Continuity in the 1992 Elections*, 191; and Abramson, Aldrich, and Rohde, *Change and Continuity in the 1996 and 1998 Elections*, 140.

36. We would like to thank them very much for their generosity. These data are reported in Paul R. Abramson, John H. Aldrich, and David W. Rohde, "The 2004 Presidential Election: The Emergence of a Permanent Majority?" *Political Science Quarterly* 120 (Spring 2005): 53–54.

37. Note, however, that there are limits to the amount of projection, given that so many respondents agreed on at least the ordinal location of the two candidates. "Persuasion," locating oneself close to where a favored candidate stands (especially when it is not "genuine" persuasion but simply rationalization of the vote choice), is another source of limits on the extent of prospective voting.

7. PRESIDENTIAL PERFORMANCE AND CANDIDATE CHOICE

1. By "war" we actually mean the wars in Afghanistan and Iraq and the war against terrorism. For an analysis of what candidates discussed in their campaign speeches over the course of the campaign, see chapter 2, Table 2-1. For a more extensive discussion, see John H. Aldrich, John D. Griffin, and Jill Rickershauser, "The Presidency and the Campaign: Campaigns and Voter Priorities in the 2004 Election," in *The Presidency and the Political System*, 8th ed., ed. Michael Nelson (Washington, D.C.: CQ Press, 2005).

2. See Paul R. Abramson, John H. Aldrich, and David W. Rohde, *Change and Continuity in the 2000 and 2002 Elections* (Washington, D.C.: CQ Press, 2003), chap. 7.

3. Bush became the first sitting vice president to be elected president since Martin Van Buren, the Democratic vice president, was elected in 1836. As Nelson W. Polsby and Aaron Wildavsky point out, a sitting vice president may have many of the disadvantages of being an incumbent without the advantage of actually being president. See Wildavsky and Polsby, *Presidential Elections: Strategies and Structures of American Politics*, 11th ed. (Lanham, Md.: Rowman and Littlefield, 2004), 78–85.

4. See Paul R. Abramson, John H. Aldrich, and David W. Rohde, *Change and Continuity in the 1992 Elections*, rev. ed. (Washington, D.C.: CQ Press, 1995), 203–208.

5. V. O. Key Jr., *Politics, Parties, and Pressure Groups*, 5th ed. (New York: Crowell, 1964), 568. Key's theory of retrospective voting is most fully developed in *The Responsible Electorate: Rationality in Presidential Voting, 1936–1960* (Cambridge: Harvard University Press, 1966).

6. Anthony Downs, *An Economic Theory of Democracy* (New York: Harper and Row, 1957).

7. Morris P. Fiorina, *Retrospective Voting in American National Elections* (New Haven: Yale University Press, 1981), 83. Two recent papers by Christopher H. Achen and Larry M. Bartels argue that the U.S. electorate is too ignorant to make informed decisions consistent with the assumptions of retrospective voting theorists. See Achen and Bartels, "Blind Retrospection: Electoral Responses to Drought, Flu, and Shark Attacks" (unpublished manuscript, Princeton University, January 2004); and Achen and Bartels, "Musical Chairs: Pocketbook Voting and the Limits of Democratic Accountability" (paper prepared for the annual meeting of the American Political Science Association, Chicago, September 1–5, 2004).

8. See Benjamin I. Page, *Choices and Echoes in Presidential Elections: Rational Man and Electoral Democracy* (Chicago: University of Chicago Press, 1978). Page argues that "party cleavages" distinguish the party at the candidate and mass levels.

9. Arthur H. Miller and Martin P. Wattenberg, "Throwing the Rascals Out: Policy and Performance Evaluations of Presidential Candidates, 1952–1980," *American Political Science Review* 79 (June 1985): 359–372.

10. As we point out in chapter 6 (note 13) respondents were asked a different question to determine what they thought the most important problem was.

11. Each respondent assesses government performance on the problem he or she considers the most important. In the seven surveys from 1976 to 2000, respondents were asked, "How good a job is the government doing in dealing with this problem—a good job, only fair, or a poor job?" In 1972, respondents were asked a different but related question (see the note to Table 7-1). In 2004, respondents were asked another question (see chapter 6, note 13) and were given four options for assessing the government's performance: "very good job," "good job," "bad job," and "very bad job." In Table 7-1 we compare the "very good" category with the "good job" category in previous years; the "good" category is compared with the "only fair" category; and we combine the "bad" and "very bad" categories and compare them on the same row as the "poor job" category. We present the full distribution of results for 2004 in Table A7-1A in the appendix.

12. Negative evaluations are not surprising. After all, if you thought the government had been doing a good job with a particular problem, then it probably would not be your major concern. This reasoning seems to underlie the very low proportion of respondents in every survey who thought the government was doing a good job with their most important concern. On the other hand, an "issue" may not have the same connotations as a problem.

13. See Gerald H. Kramer, "Short-Term Fluctuations in U.S. Voting Behavior, 1896–1964," *American Political Science Review* 65 (March 1971): 131–143; Fiorina, *Retrospective Voting*; M. Stephen Weatherford, "Economic Conditions and Electoral Outcomes: Class Differences in the Political Response to Recession," *American Journal of Political Science* 22 (November 1978): 917–938; D. Roderick Kiewiet and Douglas Rivers, "A Retrospective on Retrospective Voting," *Political Behavior* 6, no. 4 (1984): 369–393; D. Roderick Kiewiet, *Macroeconomics and Micropolitics: The Electoral Effects of Economic Issues* (Chicago: University of Chicago Press, 1983); Michael S. Lewis-Beck, *Economics and Elections: The Major Western Democracies* (Ann Arbor: University of Michigan Press, 1988); Alberto Alesina, John Londregan, and Howard Rosenthal, *A Model of the Political Economy of the United States* (Cambridge, Mass.: National Bureau of Economic Research, 1991); Michael B. MacKuen, Robert S. Erikson, and James A. Stimson, "Peasants or Bankers? The American Electorate and the U.S. Economy," *American Political Science Review* 86 (September 1992): 597–611; and Robert S. Erikson, Michael B. MacKuen, and James A. Stimson, *The Macro Polity* (Cambridge: Cambridge University Press, 2002).

14. John E. Mueller, *War, Presidents, and Public Opinion* (New York: Wiley, 1973); and Edward R. Tufte, *Political Control of the Economy* (Princeton: Princeton University Press, 1978). For a perceptive critique of the business cycle formulation, see James E. Alt and K. Alec Chrystal, *Political Economics* (Berkeley: University of California Press, 1983).

15. As an on-line survey conducted in September and October 2004 by the Program on International and Policy Attitudes at the University of Maryland

revealed, Bush and Kerry supporters had dramatically different views on the facts about U.S. foreign policy, including strikingly different views about Saddam Hussein's connection to al Qaeda. See Steven Kull, *The Separate Realities of Bush and Kerry Supporters* (Program on International Policy Attitudes, University of Maryland, October 24, 2004).

16. Fiorina, *Retrospective Voting*.

17. In 1984 and 1988, this question was asked in both the preelection and postelection waves of the survey. Since it is attitudes held by the public before the election that count in influencing their choices, we use the first question. In both surveys, approval of Reagan's performance was more positive in the postelection interview: 66 percent approved of his performance in 1984, and 68 percent approved in 1988.

18. A summary measure of retrospective evaluations could not be constructed using the 1972 NES data. For the procedures we used to construct this measure between 1976 and 2000, see Abramson, Aldrich, and Rohde, *Change and Continuity in the 2000 and 2002 Elections*, chap. 7, note 13, 328. To construct this measure for the 2004 survey, we used the following procedures. First, we awarded respondents 6 points if they approved of the president's performance, 3 if they had no opinion, and zero if they disapproved. Second, respondents received 6 points if they thought the government was doing a very good job in handling the most important problem facing the country, 5 if they thought the government was doing a good job, 1 if they thought the government was doing a bad job, and no points if they thought the government was doing a very bad job. Finally, respondents received 2 points if they thought the incumbent president's party would do a better job at handling the economy [the war on terrorism; keeping us out of war], 1 point if they thought there was no difference between the parties, and none if they thought the challenger's party would do a better job. For the first two questions, "don't know" and "not ascertained" responses were scored as 3, and for the last three questions such responses were scored as 1, but respondents with more than one such response were excluded from the analysis because of missing data. Scores on our measure were the sum of the individual values for these five questions, and 47 respondents were excluded from the analysis. Scores thus ranged from a low of zero (very strongly against the incumbent's party) to a high of 18 (very strongly for the incumbent's party). These scores were than regrouped into seven categories: zero and 1 were strongly opposed to the incumbent party; 2, 3, and 4 were moderately opposed; 5, 6, and 7 were slightly opposed; 8, 9, and 10 were classified as neutral; 11, 12, and 13 were slightly supportive of the incumbent party; 14, 15, and 16 were moderately supportive; and 17 and 18 were strongly supportive. See Table 7-9 for the distribution of the electorate into these seven categories.

19. See Paul R. Abramson, John H. Aldrich, and David W. Rohde, *Change and Continuity in the 1996 and 1998 Elections* (Washington, D.C.: CQ Press, 1999), 158–159 for data on our (different) summary measure from 1972 to 1996, and

see Abramson, Aldrich, and Rohde, *Change and Continuity in the 2000 and 2002 Elections*, 164–165 for this measure in the 2000 elections.

20. The characterization of earlier elections is taken from Abramson, Aldrich, and Rohde, *Change and Continuity in the 2000 and 2002 Elections*, 164.

21. This statement is true even if voters were primarily moderate in their views. It is the parties and candidates, in this view, that create polarized choices, not—or at least not necessarily—the opinions of the voters. For data from the 1976 and 1980 elections, see Paul R. Abramson, John H. Aldrich, and David W. Rohde, *Change and Continuity in the 1980 Elections*, rev. ed. (Washington, D.C.: CQ Press, 1983), 155–157, Table 7-8; for data from the 1984 elections, see Paul R. Abramson, John H. Aldrich, and David W. Rohde, *Change and Continuity in the 1984 Elections*, rev. ed. (Washington, D.C.: CQ Press, 1987), 203–204, Table 7-8; for data from the 1988 elections, see Paul R. Abramson, John H. Aldrich, and David W. Rohde, *Change and Continuity in the 1988 Elections*, rev. ed. (Washington, D.C.: CQ Press, 1991), 195–198, Table 7-7; for data for the 1996 elections, see Abramson, Aldrich, and Rohde, *Change and Continuity in the 1996 and 1998 Elections*, 159–161; and for data on the 2000 elections, see Abramson, Aldrich, and Rohde, *Change and Continuity in the 2000 and 2002 Elections*, 165–166. The small number of seven-point issue scales included in the NES survey precluded performing this analysis with 1992 data.

22. It should be noted that although the electorate's self-placement on the issues was on balance closer to where it placed Kerry than to where it placed Bush, the electorate was closer to the Republicans on the balance of issues measure. This anomaly is discussed in chapter 6, note 33.

8. PARTY LOYALTIES, POLICY PREFERENCES, AND THE VOTE

1. Angus Campbell et al., *The American Voter* (New York: Wiley, 1960). For a recent statement of the "standard" view of party identification, see Warren E. Miller, "Party Identification, Realignment, and Party Voting: Back to the Basics," *American Political Science Review* 85 (June 1991): 557–568; and Warren E. Miller and J. Merrill Shanks, *The New American Voter* (Cambridge: Harvard University Press, 1996), 117–183.

2. Campbell et al., *The American Voter*, 121. See also Morris P. Fiorina, *Retrospective Voting in American National Elections* (New Haven: Yale University Press, 1981), 85–86.

3. For the full wording of the party identification questions, see chapter 4, note 68.

4. Most "apoliticals" in this period were African Americans living in the South. As they were disenfranchised, questions about their party loyalties were essentially meaningless to them. For the most detailed discussion of how the NES creates its summary measure of party identification, see Arthur H. Miller and Martin P. Wattenberg, "Measuring Party Identification: Independent or No Par-

tisan Preference?" *American Journal of Political Science* 27 (February 1983): 106–121.

5. For evidence of the relatively high level of partisan stability among individuals over time, see M. Kent Jennings and Gregory B. Markus, "Partisan Orientations over the Long Haul: Results from the Three-Wave Political Socialization Panel Study," *American Political Science Review* 78 (December 1984): 1000–1018.

6. V. O. Key Jr., *The Responsible Electorate: Rationality in Presidential Voting, 1936–1960* (Cambridge: Harvard University Press, 1966).

7. Morris P. Fiorina, "An Outline for a Model of Party Choice," *American Journal of Political Science* 21 (August 1977): 601–625; Fiorina, *Retrospective Voting*.

8. Benjamin I. Page provides evidence of this. See Page, *Choices and Echoes in Presidential Elections: Rational Man and Electoral Democracy* (Chicago: University of Chicago Press, 1978). Anthony Downs, in *An Economic Theory of Democracy* (New York: Harper and Row, 1957), develops a theoretical logic for such consistency in party stances on issues and ideology over time. For more recent theoretical and empirical development, see John H. Aldrich, *Why Parties? The Origin and Transformation of Political Parties in America* (Chicago: University of Chicago Press, 1995).

9. Robert S. Erikson, Michael B. MacKuen, and James A. Stimson, *The Macro Polity* (Cambridge: Cambridge University Press, 2002).

10. Donald Green, Bradley Palmquist, Eric Schickler, *Partisan Hearts and Minds: Political Parties and the Social Identities of Voters* (New Haven: Yale University Press, 2002).

11. See, for example, Donald Green, Bradley Palmquist, and Eric Schickler, "Macropartisanship: A Replication and Critique," *American Political Science Review* 92, no. 4 (December 1998): 883–899; and Robert S. Erikson, Michael B. MacKuen, and James A. Stimson, "What Moves Macropartisanship: A Reply to Green, Palmquist, and Schickler," *American Political Science Review* 92, no. 4 (December 1998): 901–912.

12. There is some controversy over how to classify these independent leaners. Some argue that they are mainly "hidden" partisans, who should be considered identifiers. For the strongest statement of this position, see Bruce E. Keith et al., *The Myth of the Independent Voter* (Berkeley: University of California Press, 1992). In our view, however, the evidence on the proper classification of independent leaners is mixed. On balance, the evidence suggests that they are more partisan than independents with no partisan leanings, but less partisan than weak partisans. See Paul R. Abramson, *Political Attitudes in America: Formation and Change* (San Francisco: W. H. Freeman, 1983), 80–81, 95–96. For an excellent discussion of this question, see Herbert B. Asher, "Voting Behavior Research in the 1980s: An Examination of Some Old and New Problem Areas," in *Political Science: The State of the Discipline*, ed. Ada W. Finifter (Washington, D.C.: American Political Science Association, 1983), 357–360.

13. See, for example, Martin P. Wattenberg, *The Decline of American Political Parties, 1952–1996* (Cambridge: Harvard University Press, 1998).

14. These surveys were conducted annually between 1972 and 1978; conducted in 1980; conducted annually between 1982 and 1991; and conducted in 1993, 1994, 1996, 1998, 2000, 2002, and 2004. These surveys were conducted in February, March, and April, except for 2004 when they were conducted from September through December. We are grateful to Tom Smith of the National Opinion Research Center for sending us the 2004 results.

15. For evidence on the decline of Republican Party loyalties among older blacks between 1962 and 1964, see Paul R. Abramson, *Generational Change in American Politics* (Lexington, Mass.: D. C. Heath, 1975), 65–69.

16. For the results of the white vote by party identification for the three leading candidates in 1968, 1980, 1992, and 1996, see Paul R. Abramson, John H. Aldrich, and David W. Rohde, *Change and Continuity in the 1996 and 1998 Elections* (Washington, D.C.: CQ Press, 1999), 186–187.

17. See also Larry M. Bartels, "Partisanship and Voting Behavior, 1952–1996," *American Journal of Political Science* 44 (January, 2000): 35–50.

18. Bernard R. Berelson, Paul F. Lazarsfeld, and William N. McPhee, *Voting: A Study of Opinion Formation in a Presidential Campaign* (Chicago: University of Chicago Press, 1954).

19. See Richard A. Brody and Benjamin I. Page, "Comment: The Assessment of Policy Voting," *American Political Science Review* 66 (June 1972): 450–458; Benjamin I. Page and Richard A. Brody, "Policy Voting and the Electoral Process: The Vietnam War Issue," *American Political Science Review* 66 (September 1972): 979–995; and Fiorina, "Outline for a Model of Party Choice."

20. The question measuring approval of the president's handling of economic policy was not asked in NES surveys before 1984. In our study of these earlier elections, an alternative measure of economic retrospective evaluations was created and shown to be nearly as strongly related to party identification. See Paul R. Abramson, John H. Aldrich, and David W. Rohde, *Change and Continuity in the 1984 Elections,* rev. ed. (Washington, D.C.: CQ Press, 1987), Table 8-6, 221. We also found nearly as strong a relationship between partisanship and perceptions of which party would better handle the economy in the data from 1972, 1976, and 1980 as in the later surveys reported here. See Paul R. Abramson, John H. Aldrich, and David W. Rohde, *Change and Continuity in the 1980 Elections,* rev. ed. (Washington, D.C.: CQ Press, 1983), 170, Table 8-6, 173.

21. For a description of this measure, see chapter 6. Since this measure uses the median placement of the candidates on the issue scales in the full sample, much of the projection effect is eliminated. For the relationship between party identification and the balance of issues measure in 1972, see Abramson, Aldrich, and Rohde, *Change and Continuity in the 1980 Elections,* Table 8-5, 171.

22. This earlier measure and its relationship with partisan identification are reported in Paul R. Abramson, John H. Aldrich, and David W. Rohde, *Change*

and Continuity in the 2000 and 2002 Elections (Washington, D.C.: CQ Press, 2003), Table 8-7, 185–186, discussed on 184–189.

23. As we saw in chapter 7, that conclusion is true for those individual components of the measure that are the same as in prior surveys.

24. As in chapter 7, we cannot directly compare the results for 2004 to earlier elections, except in very general terms. For an interpretation and the data over the last seven elections, see Abramson, Aldrich, and Rohde, *Change and Continuity in the 2000 and 2002 Elections*, Table 8-8, 187–188, discussed on 189.

25. See, for example, Aldrich, *Why Parties?* 163–183.

26. Two important articles assess some of these relationships: Gregory B. Markus and Philip E. Converse, "A Dynamic Simultaneous Equation Model of Electoral Choice," *American Political Science Review* 73 (December 1979): 1055–1070; and Benjamin I. Page and Calvin C. Jones, "Reciprocal Effects of Policy Preferences, Party Loyalties and the Vote," *American Political Science Review* 73 (December 1979): 1071–1089. For a brief discussion of these articles, see Richard G. Niemi and Herbert F. Weisberg, *Controversies in Voting Behavior*, 2nd ed. (Washington, D.C.: CQ Press, 1984), 89–95. For an excellent discussion of complex models of voting behavior and the role of party identification in these models, see Asher, "Voting Behavior Research in the 1980s," 341–354. For another excellent introduction to some of these issues, see Richard G. Niemi and Herbert F. Weisberg, "Is Party Identification Stable?" in *Controversies in Voting Behavior*, 3rd ed., ed. Richard G. Niemi and Herbert F. Weisberg (Washington, D.C.: CQ Press, 1993), 268–283.

INTRODUCTION TO PART 3

1. Between 1952 and 1988 seventeen states switched their gubernatorial elections from presidential election years to nonpresidential years. Steven J. Rosenstone and John Mark Hansen estimate that in 1952 nearly half of the electorate lived in states in which there was a competitive gubernatorial election. In the 1988 election, according to their estimates, only 12 percent lived in states with a competitive gubernatorial election. See Rosenstone and Hansen, *Mobilization, Participation, and Democracy in America* (New York: Macmillan 1993), 183. In all eleven gubernatorial elections in 2004, both major parties ran candidates. According to our estimates, 12 percent of the voting-age population lived in these states. Rosenstone and Hansen argue that this change in the scheduling of elections is a major factor contributing to the decline of electoral participation.

2. For a discussion of state-level elections, see James W. Ceaser and Andrew E. Busch, *Red over Blue: The 2004 Elections and American Politics* (Lanham, Md.: Rowman and Littlefield, 2005), 143–168.

3. The Republicans won control of the House in eight consecutive elections from 1894 through 1908, far short of the Democratic winning streak.

4. The Republicans won a majority over the Democrats after the United States, under Democrat Woodrow Wilson, entered World War I, in April 1917. They lost control in 1930, after the 1929 Wall Street crash, which occurred under Republican Herbert C. Hoover.

9. CANDIDATES AND OUTCOMES IN 2004

1. The independent was Bernard Sanders of Vermont, who was first elected to the House in 1990. Sanders had previously been elected mayor of Burlington, Vermont, running as a socialist. For convenience in presenting results, we will treat him as a Democrat throughout this chapter. This seems reasonable because he has received his committee assignments from the Democratic Party, and the Democrats have not fielded a serious candidate against him in recent elections. In 2004, a maverick Democrat ran without party support, receiving only 7 percent of the vote, while Sanders won reelection with 69 percent to 24 percent for his Republican opponent.

2. The independent is James M. Jeffords of Vermont, who votes with the Democrats for organizing the Senate.

3. *Incumbents* here is used only for elected incumbents. This includes all members of the House because the only way to become a representative is by election. In the case of the Senate, however, vacancies may be filled by appointment. We do not count appointed senators as incumbents. In 2004, the only appointed senator who ran for election was Lisa Murkowski of Alaska, who had been appointed in December 2002. We also need to mention Louisiana House races. Louisiana has an unusual, open primary system in which candidates from all parties run against one another in a single primary. If no candidate receives a majority, the top two vote getters, regardless of party, face each other in a runoff in December. In Louisiana contests we count the last round in each district as the controlling race. If that round involved only candidates of a single party, the race is counted as a primary and the winner as unopposed in the general election. If candidates of both parties were involved in the final round, it is treated as a general election.

4. The scandal involved the House bank, in which many members deposited their paychecks. The bank had a policy to honor the checks of members, even if they didn't have sufficient funds in their accounts to cover the checks. During 1991 the public learned about this practice and that there were hundreds of members who had written a total of thousands of these "overdrafts." Many of the members who had written the most overdrafts retired or were defeated in the primary or the general election. For more details see Gary C. Jacobson, *The Politics of Congressional Elections,* 6th ed. (New York: Pearson-Longman, 2004), 172–175.

5. The Republicans had won control of the House in eight consecutive elections from 1894 through 1908, far short of the Democratic series of successes.

6. The regional breakdowns used in this chapter are as follows: East: Connecticut, Delaware, Maine, Massachusetts, New Hampshire, New Jersey, New York, Pennsylvania, Rhode Island, and Vermont; Midwest: Illinois, Indiana, Iowa, Kansas, Michigan, Minnesota, Nebraska, North Dakota, Ohio, South Dakota, and Wisconsin; West: Alaska, Arizona, California, Colorado, Hawaii, Idaho, Montana, Nevada, New Mexico, Oregon, Utah, Washington, and Wyoming; South: Alabama, Arkansas, Florida, Georgia, Louisiana, Mississippi, North Carolina, South Carolina, Tennessee, Texas, and Virginia; Border: Kentucky, Maryland, Missouri, Oklahoma, and West Virginia. This classification differs somewhat from the one used in earlier chapters (and in chapter 10), but it is commonly used for congressional analysis.

7. In 2005 the Senate majority leader is Bill Frist of Tennessee, and in the House the majority leader was, until his at-least-temporary resignation due to an indictment for violating Texas campaign finance laws, Tom DeLay.

8. Over the years changes in the southern electorate have also made southern Democratic constituencies more like northern Democratic constituencies, and less like Republican constituencies North or South. These changes also appear to have enhanced the homogeneity of preferences within the partisan delegations in Congress. See David W. Rohde, "Electoral Forces, Political Agendas, and Partisanship in the House and Senate," in *The Postreform Congress,* ed. Roger H. Davidson (New York: St. Martin's, 1992), 27–47.

9. For a discussion of this poll, see chapter 5, note 3.

10. See Paul R. Abramson, John H. Aldrich, and David W. Rohde, *Change and Continuity in the 1996 and 1998 Elections* (Washington, D.C.: CQ Press, 1999), 207–212.

11. These data were taken from www.pollingreport.com (accessed June 22, 2005).

12. For a discussion of the increased role of national party organizations in congressional elections over the last two decades, see Paul S. Herrnson, *Congressional Elections,* 2nd ed. (Washington, D.C.: CQ Press, 1998), chap. 4.

13. Quoted in Lauren W. Whittington, "No Gold Watches Being Offered," *Roll Call,* January 27, 2003, 24.

14. See Erin P. Billings and Chris Cilliza, "Democrats Lagging in House Recruitment," *Roll Call,* July 10, 2003, 1.

15. *The Hill,* January 22, 2003, 1.

16. *The Hill,* March 11, 2004, 3.

17. *CQ Weekly,* January 10, 2003, 91.

18. *The Hill,* July 22, 2004, 6.

19. *Roll Call,* October 26, 2004, 3.

20. *Roll Call,* September 29, 2004, 22.

21. *Roll Call,* May 5, 2004, 1.

22. For a discussion of the battle over districting following the 2000 Census, see Paul R. Abramson, John H. Aldrich, and David W. Rohde, *Change and Conti-*

nuity in the 2000 and 2002 Elections (Washington D.C.: CQ Press, 2003), 230–233 and 262–264. Also see Sam Hirsch, "The United States of Unrepresentatives: What Went Wrong in the Latest Round of Redistricting," *Election Law Journal* 2 (2003): 179–216

23. For more background on this dispute see ibid., 232–233.

24. *New York Times,* June 27, 2003, A1.

25. See *CQ Weekly,* May 1, 2004, 1019–1020.

26. *Washington Post,* April 20, 2004, A4.

27. *Washington Post,* December 2, 2003, A3.

28. Richard F. Fenno Jr., *Home Style: House Members in Their Districts* (Boston: Little, Brown, 1978). For a discussion of how relationships between representatives and constituents have changed over time, see Fenno, *Congress at the Grassroots* (Chapel Hill: University of North Carolina Press, 2000).

29. For example, analysis of Senate races in 1988 indicated that the political quality of the previous office held and the challenger's political skills had independent effects on the outcome of the race. See Peverill Squire, "Challenger Quality and Voting Behavior in U.S. Senate Elections," *Legislative Studies Quarterly* 17 (May 1992): 247–263. For systematic evidence on the impact of candidate quality in House races, see Gary C. Jacobson, *The Electoral Origins of Divided Government: Competition in U.S. House Elections, 1946–1988* (Boulder: Westview Press, 1990), chap. 4.

30. Data on office backgrounds were taken from various issues of *Congressional Quarterly Weekly Report.*

31. Data on earlier years are taken from our studies of previous national elections.

32. Note that the figures in this paragraph include races in which only one of the parties fielded a candidate, as well as contests in which both did.

33. See Jacobson, *The Electoral Origins of Divided Government;* Jon R. Bond, Cary Covington, and Richard Fleischer, "Explaining Challenger Quality in Congressional Elections," *Journal of Politics* 47 (May 1985): 510–529; and David W. Rohde, "Risk-Bearing and Progressive Ambition: The Case of Members of the U.S. House of Representatives," *American Journal of Political Science* 23 (February 1979): 1–26.

34. L. Sandy Maisel and Walter J. Stone, "Determinants of Candidate Emergence in U.S. House Elections: An Exploratory Study," *Legislative Studies Quarterly* 22 (February 1997): 79–96.

35. See Peverill Squire, "Preemptive Fund-raising and Challenger Profile in Senate Elections," *Journal of Politics* 53 (November 1991): 1150–1164.

36. Jeffrey S. Banks and D. Roderick Kiewiet, "Explaining Patterns of Candidate Competition in Congressional Elections," *American Journal of Political Science* 33 (November 1989): 997–1015.

37. David Canon, *Actors, Athletes, and Astronauts: Political Amateurism in the United States Congress* (Chicago: University of Chicago Press, 1990).

38. See Kenneth J. Cooper, "Riding High Name Recognition to Hill," *Washington Post,* December 24, 1992, A4.

39. See Thomas E. Mann and Raymond E. Wolfinger, "Candidates and Parties in Congressional Elections," *American Political Science Review* 74 (September 1980): 617–632.

40. See David R. Mayhew, "Congressional Elections: The Case of the Vanishing Marginals," *Polity* 6 (Spring 1974): 295–317; Robert S. Erikson, "Malapportionment, Gerrymandering, and Party Fortunes in Congressional Elections," *American Political Science Review* 66 (December 1972): 1234–1245; and Warren Lee Kostroski, "Party and Incumbency in Postwar Senate Elections: Trends, Patterns, and Models," *American Political Science Review* 67 (December 1973): 1213–1234.

41. Edward R. Tufte, "Communication," *American Political Science Review* 68 (March 1974): 211–213. The communication involved a discussion of Tufte's earlier article "The Relationship between Seats and Votes in Two-Party Systems," *American Political Science Review* 67 (June 1973): 540–554.

42. See John A. Ferejohn, "On the Decline of Competition in Congressional Elections," *American Political Science Review* 71 (March 1977): 166–176; Albert D. Cover, "One Good Term Deserves Another: The Advantage of Incumbency in Congressional Elections," *American Journal of Political Science* 21 (August 1977): 523–541; and Albert D. Cover and David R. Mayhew, "Congressional Dynamics and the Decline of Competition in Congressional Elections," in *Congress Reconsidered,* 2nd ed., ed. Lawrence C. Dodd and Bruce I. Oppenheimer (Washington, D.C.: CQ Press, 1981), 62–82.

43. Morris P. Fiorina, *Congress: Keystone of the Washington Establishment,* 2nd ed. (New Haven: Yale University Press, 1989), esp. chaps. 4–6.

44. See several conflicting arguments and conclusions in the following articles published in the *American Journal of Political Science* 25 (August 1981): John R. Johannes and John C. McAdams, "The Congressional Incumbency Effect: Is It Casework, Policy Compatibility, or Something Else? An Examination of the 1978 Election," 512–542; Morris P. Fiorina, "Some Problems in Studying the Effects of Resource Allocation in Congressional Elections," 543–567; Diana Evans Yiannakis, "The Grateful Electorate: Casework and Congressional Elections," 568–580; and McAdams and Johannes, "Does Casework Matter? A Reply to Professor Fiorina," 581–604. See also John R. Johannes, *To Serve the People: Congress and Constituency Service* (Lincoln: University of Nebraska Press, 1984), esp. chap. 8; and Albert D. Cover and Bruce S. Brumberg, "Baby Books and Ballots: The Impact of Congressional Mail on Constituent Opinion," *American Political Science Review* 76 (June 1982): 347–359. The evidence in Cover and Brumberg for a positive electoral effect is quite strong, but the result may be applicable only to limited circumstances.

45. Ferejohn, "On the Decline of Competition," 174.

46. Cover, "One Good Term," 535.

47. More recent research shows that the link between party identification and voting has strengthened again. See Larry M. Bartels, "Partisanship and Voting Behavior, 1952–1996," *American Journal of Political Science* 44 (January 2000): 35–50.

48. The data for 1974–1990 were taken from "House Incumbents' Average Vote Percentage," *Congressional Quarterly Weekly Report,* November 10, 1990, 3800. The 1994 figures are from the *New York Times,* November 10, 1994. The data for 1992 and 1996 are from *USA Today,* November 8, 1996, 4A. The data for 1998–2004 were computed by the authors.

49. For an excellent analysis of the growth of, and reasons for, anti-Congress sentiment, see John R. Hibbing and Elizabeth Theiss-Morse, *Congress as Public Enemy* (New York: Cambridge University Press, 1995).

50. Fenno, *Home Style,* 163–169.

51. However, we note again that these results ignore races that do not have candidates from both major parties. There was a sharp increase in these races in 1998—94, compared with only 17 in 1996 and 52 in 1994. The number was almost as large in 2000—81.

52. The body of literature on this subject has grown quite large. Some salient examples, in addition to those cited later, are Gary C. Jacobson, *Money in Congressional Elections* (New Haven: Yale University Press, 1980); Gary C. Jacobson, "Parties and PACs in Congressional Elections," in *Congress Reconsidered,* 4th ed., ed. Lawrence C. Dodd and Bruce I. Oppenheimer (Washington, D.C.: CQ Press, 1989), 117–152; Gary C. Jacobson and Samuel Kernell, *Strategy and Choice in Congressional Elections,* 2nd ed. (New Haven: Yale University Press, 1983); John A. Ferejohn and Morris P. Fiorina, "Incumbency and Realignment in Congressional Elections," in *The New Direction in American Politics,* ed. John E. Chubb and Paul E. Peterson (Washington, D.C.: Brookings Institution Press, 1985), 91–115.

53. See Jacobson, *The Electoral Origins of Divided Government,* 63–65.

54. The 1990 data were taken from *Politics in America, 1992: The 102nd Congress,* ed. Phil Duncan (Washington, D.C.: CQ Press, 1991); the 1992 data are from the *Washington Post,* May 26, 1993, A17. For both elections the data include all incumbents, not just those who had major-party opposition.

55. See Jacobson and Kernell, *Strategy and Choice in Congressional Elections.*

56. The 2004 spending data were obtained from the Web site of the Federal Election Commission, www.fec.gov.

57. These figures from the Federal Election Commission include a substantial number of races with unavailable spending data for challengers. Thus final data may be somewhat different.

58. Thirteen of the thirty-two targeted representatives (41 percent) lost. *HOTLINE,* November 6, 1997.

59. See Abramson, Aldrich, and Rohde, *Change and Continuity in the 2000 and 2002 Elections,* 215–220, and the earlier work cited there.

60. See Jacobson, *The Electoral Origins of Divided Government,* 54–55; and the works cited in note 52 above.

61. Donald Philip Green and Jonathan S. Krasno, "Salvation for the Spendthrift Incumbent: Reestimating the Effects of Campaign Spending in House Elections," *American Journal of Political Science* 32 (November 1988), 884–907.

62. Gary C. Jacobson, "The Effects of Campaign Spending in House Elections: New Evidence for Old Arguments," *American Journal of Political Science* 34 (May 1990), 334–362. Green and Krasno's response can be found in the same issue on pages 363–372.

63. Alan I. Abramowitz, "Explaining Senate Election Outcomes," *American Political Science Review* 82 (June 1988), 385–403; and Alan Gerber, "Estimating the Effect of Campaign Spending on Senate Election Outcomes Using Instrumental Variables," *American Political Science Review* 92 (June 1998): 401–411.

64. Gary C. Jacobson, "Campaign Spending and Voter Awareness of Congressional Candidates" (paper presented at the annual meeting of the Public Choice Society, New Orleans, May 11–13, 1977), 16.

65. Challengers were categorized as having strong experience if they had been elected U.S. representative, to statewide office, to the state legislature, or to countywide or citywide office (for example, mayor, prosecutor, and so on).

66. Paul R. Abramson, John H. Aldrich, and David W. Rohde, *Change and Continuity in the 1980 Elections,* rev. ed. (Washington, D.C.: CQ Press, 1983), 202–203. See also Paul Gronke, *The Electorate, the Campaign, and the Office: A Unified Approach to Senate and House Elections* (Ann Arbor: University of Michigan Press, 2001).

67. Other Democratic Senate winners in 2000 who spent millions of their own money included Maria Cantwell of Washington and Mark Dayton of Minnesota.

68. Quoted in Angela Herrin, "Big Outside Money Backfired in GOP Loss of Senate to Dems," *Washington Post,* November 6, 1986, A46.

69. See David W. Rohde, *Parties and Leaders in the Postreform House* (Chicago: University of Chicago Press, 1991), especially chap. 3; and Rohde, "Electoral Forces, Political Agendas, and Partisanship in the House and Senate, in *The Postreform Congress,* ed. Rodger H. Davidson (New York: St. Martin's, 1992), 27–47.

70. For discussions of the ideological changes in the House and Senate over the last four decades see John H. Aldrich and David W. Rohde, "The Logic of Conditional Party Government: Revisiting the Electoral Connection," in *Congress Reconsidered,* 7th ed., ed. Lawrence Dodd and Bruce I. Oppenheimer (Washington, D.C.: CQ Press, 2001), 269–292; and Gary C. Jacobson, "The Congress: The Structural Basis of Republican Success," in *The Elections of 2004,* ed. Michael Nelson (Washington, D.C.: CQ Press, 2005), 163–186.

71. See Paul R. Abramson, John H. Aldrich, and David W. Rohde, *Change and Continuity in the 1992 Elections,* rev. ed. (Washington, D.C.: CQ Press, 1995), 339–342; and John H. Aldrich and David W. Rohde, "The Transition to Republican Rule in the House: Implications for Theories of Congressional Politics," *Political Science Quarterly* 112 (Winter 1997–98): 541–567.

72. *Washington Post,* January 4, 2005, A1.

73. *CQ Weekly,* May 2, 2005, 1144.

74. *The Hill,* February 2, 2005, 1.

75. Dan Morgan, "Lewis Gets Appropriations Chair," *Washington Post,* January 6, 2005, A4.

76. Ben Pershing, "Approps Revamp Floated," *Roll Call,* December 12, 2004, 34.

77. *Washington Post,* November 27, 2004, A1.

78. *Washington Post,* March 29, 2005, A4.

79. *CQ Weekly,* April 3, 2004, 790.

80. *Roll Call,* February 14, 2005, 3.

81. *The Hill,* May 10, 2005, 1.

82. *Washington Post,* June 21, 2005, A4.

83. *Washington Post,* January 9, 2005, A4.

84. *Washington Post,* November 4, 2004, A36.

85. *The Hill,* November 18, 2004, 17.

86. *Roll Call,* November 18, 2004, 17.

87. *New York Times,* November 6, 2004, A10.

88. *Washington Post,* November 19, 2004, A6.

89. *The Hill,* January 26, 2005, 1.

90. *The Hill,* March 16, 2005, 6.

91. *CQ Weekly,* May 30, 2005, 1440.

92. Poll data at www.latimes.com (accessed October 25, 2004).

93. *USA Today,* November 23, 2004, 11A

94. Lyn Nofziger, "Bush's Trouble Ahead," *New York Times,* November 7, 2004, WK11.

95. Gary C. Jacobson compiled the data supporting these statements from the first Gallup poll taken after the election of every second-term president from Eisenhower through Bush. See Jacobson, "Polarized Politics and the 2004 Congressional and Presidential Elections," *Political Science Quarterly* 120 (Summer 2005): 215–217.

96. See *CQ Weekly,* June 20, 2005, 1649; and June 27, 2005, 1750.

97. *CQ Weekly,* May 30, 2005, 1444.

98. Earlier research indicated that for these purposes voters may tend to regard a president whose predecessor either died or resigned from office as a continuation of the first president's administration. Therefore, these data are organized by term of administration, rather than term of president. See Abramson, Aldrich, and Rohde, *Change and Continuity in the 1980 Elections,* rev. ed., 252–253.

99. Edward R. Tufte, "Determinants of the Outcomes of Midterm Congressional Elections," *American Political Science Review* 69 (September 1975): 812–826; and Tufte, *Political Control of the Economy* (Princeton: Princeton University Press, 1978); Jacobson and Kernell, *Strategy and Choice in Congressional Elections.*

100. The Jacobson-Kernell hypothesis was challenged by Richard Born in "Strategic Politicians and Unresponsive Voters," *American Political Science Review* 80 (June 1986): 599–612. Born argued that economic and approval data at the time of the election were more closely related to outcomes than were parallel data from earlier in the year. Jacobson, however, offered renewed support for the hypothesis in an analysis of both district-level and aggregate data. See Gary C. Jacobson, "Strategic Politicians and the Dynamics of House Elections, 1946–86," *American Political Science Review* 83 (September 1989): 773–793.

101. Alan I. Abramowitz, Albert D. Cover, and Helmut Norpoth, "The President's Party in Midterm Elections: Going from Bad to Worse," *American Journal of Political Science* 30 (August 1986): 562–576.

102. Bruce I. Oppenheimer, James A. Stimson, and Richard W. Waterman, "Interpreting U.S. Congressional Elections: The Exposure Thesis," *Legislative Studies Quarterly* 11 (May 1986): 228.

103. Robin F. Marra and Charles W. Ostrom Jr., "Explaining Seat Change in the U.S. House of Representatives 1950–86," *American Journal of Political Science* 33 (August 1989): 541–569.

104. In addition, evidence indicates that divided government may also reduce the vulnerability of the president's party in midterms. See Stephen P. Nicholson and Gary M. Segura, "Midterm Elections and Divided Government: An Information-Driven Theory of Electoral Volatility," *Political Research Quarterly* 52 (September 1999): 609–629.

105. *USA Today*, May 24, 2005, 8A.

106. *Roll Call*, May 4, 2005, 11.

107. *Roll Call*, March 10, 2005, 14.

108. *New York Times*, January 16, 2005, A16.

109. *Roll Call*, February 15, 2005, 1.

110. *USA Today*, July 22, 2005, 3A.

111. *New York Times*, October 19, 2004, A13.

112. *National Journal*, February 5, 2005, 384

113. *Roll Call*, June 30, 2005, 13.

114. *Roll Call*, May 24, 2005, 10.

115. *Roll Call*, February 16, 2005, 1.

116. *Roll Call*, April 21, 2005, 14.

117. *The Hill*, March 3, 2005, 1.

118. *USA Today*, December 22, 2004, 3A.

119. *National Journal*, June 25, 2005, 2074-75.

120. *Roll Call*, March 1, 2005, 1.

121. *Washington Post*, July 8, 2001, A5.

122. Ibid.

123. *The Hill*, June 14, 2005, 1.

124. *CQ Weekly*, June 13, 2005, 1590.

125. *Roll Call*, May 15, 2005, 1.

10. THE CONGRESSIONAL ELECTORATE IN 2004

1. As we saw in chapter 5, the 2000 NES survey results slightly overreported the Democratic share of the presidential vote. There is also small pro-Democratic bias in the House vote. According to the 2004 NES survey, the Democrats received 53.0 percent of the major-party vote; official results show that the Democrats received only 48.6 percent of the actual national vote. To simplify the presentation

of the data, we have eliminated from consideration votes for minor-party candidates in all the tables in this chapter. Furthermore, to ensure that our study of choice is meaningful, in all tables except Tables 10-1 and 10-2 we include only voters who lived in congressional districts in which both major parties ran candidates.

2. We will confine our attention in this section to voting for the House because this group of voters is more directly comparable to the presidential electorate. We here employ the same definitions for social and demographic categories as used in chapters 4 and 5.

3. See Larry M. Bartels, "Partisanship and Voting Behavior, 1952–1996," *American Journal of Political Science* 44 (January 2000): 35–50.

4. Paul R. Abramson, John H. Aldrich, and David W. Rohde, *Change and Continuity in the 1980 Elections,* rev. ed. (Washington, D.C.: CQ Press, 1983), 213–216.

5. Among liberal voters who did not see the Democratic House candidate as more liberal than the Republican candidate ($N = 120$), 77 percent voted Democratic; among conservative voters who did not see the Republican candidate as more conservative than the Democratic candidate ($N = 226$), 61 percent voted Republican.

6. Alan I. Abramowitz, "Choices and Echoes in the 1978 U.S. Senate Elections: A Research Note," *American Journal of Political Science* 25 (February 1981): 112–118; and Abramowitz, "National Issues, Strategic Politicians, and Voting Behavior in the 1980 and 1982 Congressional Elections," *American Journal of Political Science* 28 (November 1984): 710–721.

7. Robert S. Erikson and Gerald C. Wright, "Voters, Candidates, and Issues in Congressional Elections," in *Congress Reconsidered,* 3rd ed., ed. Lawrence C. Dodd and Bruce I. Oppenheimer (Washington, D.C.: CQ Press, 1985), 91–116.

8. Robert S. Erikson and Gerald C. Wright, "Voters, Candidates and Issues in Congressional Elections," in *Congress Reconsidered,* 6th ed., ed. Lawrence C. Dodd and Bruce I. Oppenheimer (Washington, D.C.: CQ Press, 1993), 148–150.

9. Robert S. Erikson and Gerald C. Wright, "Voters, Candidates and Issues in Congressional Elections," in *Congress Reconsidered,* 8th ed., ed. Lawrence C. Dodd and Bruce I. Oppenheimer (Washington, D.C.: CQ Press, 2005), 93–95. See also Stephen Ansolabehere, James M. Snyder, Jr., and Charles Stewart III, "Candidate Positioning in U.S. House Elections," *American Journal of Political Science* 45 (January, 2001): 136–159.

10. For the wording of the NES party identification questions, see chapter 4, note 68.

11. Albert D. Cover, "One Good Term Deserves Another: The Advantage of Incumbency in Congressional Elections," *American Journal of Political Science* 21 (August 1977): 523–541. Cover includes in his analysis not only strong and weak partisans but also independents with partisan leanings.

12. It should be noted that the 2004 NES survey may contain biases that inflate the percentage who report voting for House incumbents. For a discussion

of this problem in earlier years, see Robert B. Eubank and David John Gow, "The Pro-Incumbent Bias in the 1978 and 1980 Election Studies," *American Journal of Political Science* 27 (February 1983): 122–139; and David John Gow and Robert B. Eubank, "The Pro-Incumbent Bias in the 1982 Election Study," *American Journal of Political Science* 28 (February 1984): 224–230.

13. Richard F. Fenno Jr., "If, as Ralph Nader Says, Congress Is 'the Broken Branch,' How Come We Love Our Congressmen So Much?" in *Congress in Change: Evolution and Reform,* ed. Norman J. Ornstein (New York: Praeger, 1975), 277–287. This theme is expanded and analyzed in Richard F. Fenno Jr., *Home Style: House Members in Their Districts* (Boston: Little, Brown, 1978).

14. Abramson, Aldrich, and Rohde, *Change and Continuity in the 1980 Elections,* 220–221.

15. Opinion on this last point is not unanimous, however. See Richard Born, "Reassessing the Decline of Presidential Coattails: U.S. House Elections from 1952–80," *Journal of Politics* 46 (February 1984): 60–79.

16. John A. Ferejohn and Randall L. Calvert, "Presidential Coattails in Historical Perspective," *American Journal of Political Science* 28 (February 1984): 127–146.

17. Randall L. Calvert and John A. Ferejohn, "Coattail Voting in Recent Presidential Elections," *American Political Science Review* 77 (June 1983): 407–419.

18. James E. Campbell and Joe A. Sumners, "Presidential Coattails in Senate Elections," *American Political Science Review* 84 (June 1990): 513–524.

INTRODUCTION TO PART 4

1. Some argue that the oracle did not have prophetic powers of her own but that she did have the ability to pass on messages from Apollo. Christians suppressed the worship of pagan deities, and there is no longer an oracle to pass on messages.

2. Nicolò Machiavelli, *The Prince,* trans. Harvey Mansfield Jr., 2nd ed. (Chicago: University of Chicago Press, 1998), 98.

3. The 9/11 Commission, *The 9/11 Commission Report: Final Report of the National Commission on Terrorist Attacks Upon the United States,* authorized edition (New York: Norton, 2004). Note that each of these flights was scheduled for a coast-to-coast flight and thus carried a large amount of jet fuel.

4. In the Japanese attack on Pearl Harbor on December 7, 1941, 2,403 U.S. servicemen were killed, as well as 68 civilians. Of course, the total population of the United States in 1941 was only about 133 million, whereas in 2001 it was about 284 million.

5. Arend Lijphart, *Democracies: Patterns of Majoritarian and Consensus Government in Twenty-one Countries* (New Haven: Yale University Press, 1984). Finland and France could also be considered to have presidential systems, but in Finland the president and prime minister have roughly equal powers. Since

Lijphart's book was written, experience has shown that France is not as much of a presidential system as Lijphart thought. He wrote, "The French president . . . is not only the head of state but also the real head of government; the prime minister is merely the president's principal adviser and assistant." (73). This appeared to be true in 1984, but after the 1996 legislative elections it became clear that the power of the French president is diminished substantially if the president does not have support in the National Assembly.

6. In France a new election is held to select a new president for a full presidential term. This has happened twice—in 1969, when Charles de Gaulle resigned, and in 1974, when Georges Pompidou died in office.

7. Abraham Lincoln never considered postponing the 1864 elections. As he explained, even if there were a constitutional way to cancel or postpone them, "We can not have free government without elections. . . . [I]f the rebellion could force us to forego, or to postpone a national election, it might fairly claim to have already conquered and ruined us." Quoted in David Herbert McDonald, *Lincoln* (New York: Simon and Schuster, 1995), 539.

8. In contrast, in the United Kingdom, the Parliament elected in 1935 had been due to expire in November 1940. But Britain had entered the war in September 1939, and Parliament continued to extend its own life on a year-to-year basis. After Germany was defeated, Winston S. Churchill, the prime minister and Conservative wartime coalition leader, wanted to postpone elections until Japan was defeated. Clement R. Attlee, a leader in the wartime coalition and the leader of the Labour Party, refused. The election was held throughout most of the U.K. on July 5, 1945, six weeks before Japan surrendered. See R. B. McCallum and Alison Readman, *The British General Election of 1945* (Oxford: Oxford University Press, 1947). Despite Churchill's popularity, Labour won a landslide victory.

9. The size of the House is fixed by legislation. According to Article 1, Section 2 of the Constitution, "The number of Representatives shall not exceed one for every thirty Thousand, but each State shall have at Least one Representative." In principle, the House could have as few as fifty members and could have over 9,000. In 1910, Congress passed a self-denying ordinance that limited the House to 435 members. See David Butler and Bruce Cain, *Congressional Redistricting: Comparative and Theoretical Perspectives* (New York: Macmillan, 1992), 18.

11. THE 2004 ELECTIONS AND THE FUTURE OF AMERICAN POLITICS

1. Maurice Duverger, *Political Parties: Their Organization and Activity in the Modern State*, trans. Barbara North and Robert North (New York: Wiley, 1963), 308–309. Throughout this book, we use the term *majority* to mean one more than half the vote. It is clear that Duverger used the term *majorité* to mean what we would call a plurality—that is, more votes than any other party received.

2. *Mapai* is the Hebrew acronym for the Israel Workers' Party. In 1968 Mapai merged with two smaller parties and formed the Alignment. That coalition fell apart. In 2003, Labor ran in coalition with a small centrist party called Meimad.

3. These four countries are examined extensively in a book edited by T. J. Pempel, *Uncommon Democracies: The One-Party Dominant Regimes* (Ithaca, N.Y.: Cornell University Press, 1990). Other democracies that might be classified as having, or as having had, a dominant party include Chile, Columbia, Denmark, Iceland, India, Norway, and Venezuela. See also, Alan Arian and Samuel H. Barnes, "The Dominant Party System: A Neglected Model of Democratic Stability," *Journal of Politics* 36 (August 1974): 592–614.

4. Duverger, *Political Parties*, 312.

5. Duverger was vague about the reasons why dominant parties tend to fall. He suggests that they become too bureaucratized to govern effectively. Although dominant parties clearly fell from power in Israel and Italy, and lost much of their dominance in Sweden and Japan, a variety of factors led to their decline.

6. Asher Arian, *Politics in Israel: The Second Republic*, 2nd ed. (Washington, D.C.: CQ Press, 2005), 124.

7. There was no Knesset election in 2001. The Knesset abandoned the direct election of the prime minister in 2001.

8. For an analysis of the gradual decline of the DC, see Sidney Tarrow, "Maintaining Hegemony in Italy: 'The Softer They Rise, the Slower They Fall!' " in *Uncommon Democracies*, ed. Pempel, 306–332.

9. Maurice Duverger, *Les Partis Politiques*, 3rd ed. (Paris: Armand Colin, 1958), 342. The English-language translation we use appeared in 1963 (see note 1).

10. See, for example, Michael Nelson, "Constitutional Aspects of the Elections," in *The Elections of 1988*, ed. Michael Nelson (Washington, D.C.: CQ Press, 1989), 161–209. See also Byron E. Shafer, "The Election of 1988 and the Structure of American Politics: Notes on Explaining a New Political Order," *Electoral Studies* 8 (April 1989): 5–21.

11. By 1828 every state except Maryland and South Carolina chose its electors by popular vote. The first incumbent to be reelected after that was Andrew Jackson in 1832.

12. The only closer margin was in 1916, when Woodrow Wilson defeated Charles Evans Hughes by a twenty-three-vote margin.

13. Gary C. Jacobson, "The Congress: The Structural Basis of Republican Success," in *The Elections of 2004*, ed. Michael Nelson (Washington, D.C.: CQ Press, 2005), 166.

14. James W. Ceaser and Andrew E. Busch, *The Perfect Tie: The True Story of the 2000 Presidential Election* (Lanham, Md.: Rowman and Littlefield, 2001), 17–47.

15. The Edison Media Research/Mitofsky International (EMR/MI) exit poll found that 37 percent of voters were Democrats, 37 percent were Republicans, and 26 percent were independents. See Paul R. Abramson, John H. Aldrich, and David W. Rohde, "The 2004 Presidential Election: The Emergence of a Permanent Majority?" *Political Science Quarterly* 120 (Spring 2005): 49. If, as surveys show, the Democrats have a lead in the party loyalties of the electorate, these data suggest that the Republicans had higher turnout.

16. John B. Judis and Ruy Teixeira, *The Emerging Democratic Majority* (New York: Scribner's, 2002).

17. Ibid., 116.

18. See introduction to part 1, note 40.

19. See Raymond Hernandez and Patrick D. Healy, "From Seeking Big Change to Taking Smaller Steps: Hillary Clinton's Evolution," *New York Times*, July 13, 2005, A21.

20. Note that the voting-age population had increased from 174 million in 1984, to 221 million in 2004.

21. Quoted in Adam Nagourney, "Putting It Back Together Again," *New York Times*, October 30, 1995, WK, 2.

22. Arend Lijphart, *Electoral Systems and Party Systems: A Study of Twenty-seven Democracies, 1945–1990* (New York: Oxford University Press, 1994), 160–162.

23. "The Mouse that Roared," *The Economist*, September 30, 1995, 32.

24. See *Political Money Line*, www.fecinfo.com/ (accessed July 10, 2005).

25. Under proportional representation, an environmentalist party may be successful with a relatively small share of the vote. For example, in the 1988 German Bundestag election, the Green Party won only 6.7 percent of the votes, but it won 7 percent of the seats and became part of the governing coalition. In the 2002 election the Greens won 8.6 percent of the votes and captured 9 percent of the seats, again becoming part of the governing coalition. In the 2005 election, the Greens won 8.1 percent of the votes and won 8 percent of the seats. As of this writing, it seems unlikely that the party will be part of the next coalition.

26. Joseph A. Schlesinger, *Political Parties and the Winning of Office* (Ann Arbor: University of Michigan Press, 1991).

27. For a discussion of the distinction between selective and collective goods, see Mancur Olson Jr., *The Logic of Collective Action: Public Goods and the Theory of Groups* (Cambridge: Harvard University Press, 1965). For an application of this difference to the study of political parties, see John H. Aldrich, *Why Parties? The Origin and Transformation of Political Parties in America* (Chicago: University of Chicago Press, 1995).

28. We are grateful to Joseph A. Schlesinger of Michigan State University for reminding us of this point.

29. Philip E. Converse, *The Dynamics of Party Support: Cohort-Analyzing Party Identification* (Beverly Hills, Calif.: Sage, 1976).

30. William Crotty, ed., *A Defining Moment: The Presidential Election of 2004* (Armonk, N.Y.: M. E. Sharpe, 2005).

Suggested Readings

(Readings preceded by an asterisk include materials on the 2004 elections.)

Chapter 1: The Nomination Struggle

Abramson, Paul R., John H. Aldrich, and David W. Rohde. "Progressive Ambition among United States Senators: 1972–1988." *Journal of Politics* 49 (February 1987): 3–35.

Abramson, Paul R., John H. Aldrich, Phil Paolino, and David W. Rohde. " 'Sophisticated' Voting in the 1988 Presidential Primaries." *American Political Science Review* 86 (March 1992): 55–69.

Aldrich, John H. *Before the Convention: Strategies and Choices in Presidential Nomination Campaigns.* Chicago: University of Chicago Press, 1980.

Bartels, Larry M. *Presidential Primaries and the Dynamics of Public Choice.* Princeton: Princeton University Press, 1988.

Brams, Steven J. *The Presidential Election Game.* New Haven: Yale University Press, 1978, 1–79.

*Burden, Barry C. "The Nominations: Technology, Money, and Transferable Momentum." In *The Elections of 2004,* edited by Michael Nelson. Washington, D.C.: CQ Press, 2005, 18–41.

*Ceaser, James W., and Andrew E. Busch. *Red Over Blue: The 2004 Elections and American Politics.* Lanham, Md.: Rowman and Littlefield, 2005, 69–105.

Cook, Rhodes. *The Presidential Nominating Process: A Place For Us?* Lanham, Md.: Rowman and Littlefield, 2004.

*Day, Christine L., Charles D. Hadley, and Harold W. Stanley. "The Inevitable Unanticipated Consequences of Political Reform: The 2004 Presidential Nomination Process." In *A Defining Moment: The Presidential Election of 2004,* edited by William Crotty. Armonk, N.Y.: M. E. Sharpe, 2005, 74–86.

Polsby, Nelson W., and Aaron Wildavsky. *Presidential Elections: Strategies and Structures of American Politics,* 11th ed. Lanham, Md.: Rowman and Littlefield, 2004, 89–136.

*Thomas, Evan, and the staff of *Newsweek. Election 2004. How Bush Won and What You Can Expect in the Future.* New York: Public Affairs, 2004, 1–112.

Chapter 2: The General Election Campaign

Brams, Steven J. *The Presidential Election Game.* New Haven: Yale University Press, 1978, 80–133.

*Ceaser, James W., and Andrew E. Busch. *Red Over Blue: The 2004 Elections and American Politics.* Lanham, Md: Rowman and Littlefield, 2005, 107–142.

*Crotty, William. "Financing the 2004 Presidential Election." In *A Defining Moment: The Presidential Election of 2004,* edited by William Crotty. Armonk, N.Y.: M. E. Sharpe, 2005, 87–107.

Hershey, Marjorie Randon. "The Constructed Explanation: Interpreting Election Results in the 1984 Presidential Race." *Journal of Politics* 54 (November 1992): 943–976.

Hillygus, D. Sunshine, and Simon Jackman. "Voter Decision Making in 2000: Campaign Effects, Partisan Activation, and the Clinton Legacy." *American Journal of Political Science* 47 (October 2003): 583–596.

Iyengar, Shanto, and Donald R. Kinder. *News That Matters: Television and American Opinion.* Chicago: University of Chicago Press, 1987.

Johnston, Richard, Michael G. Hagen, and Kathleen Hall Jamieson. *The 2000 Presidential Election and the Foundations of Party Politics.* Cambridge: Cambridge University Press, 2004.

*MacManus, Susan A. "Kerry in the Red States: Fighting an Uphill Battle from the Start." In *Divided States of America: The Slash and Burn Politics of the*

2004 Presidential Election, edited by Larry J. Sabato. New York: Pearson Longman, 2006, 131–164.

Petrocik, John R., William L. Benoit, and Glenn J. Hansen. "Issue Ownership and Presidential Campaigning, 1952–2000." *Political Science Quarterly* 118 (winter 2003–2004): 599–626.

Polsby, Nelson W., and Aaron Wildavsky. *Presidential Elections: Strategies and Structures in American Politics,* 11th ed. Lanham, Md.: Rowman and Littlefield, 2004, 7–86; 137–257.

Thomas, Dan B., and Larry R. Bass. "The Postelection Campaign: Competing Constructions of the Clinton Victory in 1992." *Journal of Politics* 58 (May 1996): 309–331.

Thomas, Evan, and the staff of *Newsweek. Election 2004: How Bush Won and What You Can Expect in the Future.* New York: Public Affairs, 2004, 113–184.

Wlezien, Christopher, and Robert S. Erikson. "The Timeline of Presidential Election Campaigns." *Journal of Politics* 64 (November 2002): 969–993.

Chapter 3: The Election Results

Abramson, Paul R., John H. Aldrich, Phil Paolino, and David W. Rohde. "Third-Party and Independent Candidates in American Politics: Wallace, Anderson, and Perot." *Political Science Quarterly* 110 (fall 1995): 349–367.

Black, Earl, and Merle Black. *The Vital South: How Presidents Are Elected.* Cambridge: Harvard University Press, 1992.

———. *The Rise of Southern Republicans.* Cambridge: Harvard University Press, 2002.

Burnham, Walter Dean. *Critical Elections and the Mainsprings of American Politics.* New York: Norton, 1970.

Kelley, Stanley, Jr. *Interpreting Elections.* Princeton: Princeton University Press, 1983.

Lamis, Alexander P. *The Two-Party South,* 2nd exp. ed. New York: Oxford University Press, 1990.

Mayhew, David R. *Electoral Realignments: A Critique of an American Genre.* New Haven: Yale University Press, 2002.

Miller, Gary, and Norman Schofield. "Activists and Partisan Realignment in the United States." *American Political Science Review* 97 (May 2003): 245–260.

Nardullli, Peter F. *Popular Efficacy in the Democratic Era: A Reexamination of Electoral Accountability in the United States, 1928–2000.* Princeton: Princeton University Press, 2005.

*Sabato, Larry J. "The Election That Broke the Rules." In *Divided States of America: The Slash and Burn Politics of the 2004 Presidential Election,* edited by Larry J. Sabato. New York: Pearson Longman, 2006, 51–120.

Schlesinger, Joseph A. *Political Parties and the Winning of Office.* Ann Arbor: University of Michigan Press, 1991.

Sundquist, James L. *Dynamics of the Party System: Alignment and Realignment of Political Parties in the United States,* rev. ed. Washington, D.C.: Brookings Institution, 1983.

Chapter 4: Who Voted?

Aldrich, John H. "Rational Choice and Turnout." *American Journal of Political Science* 37 (February 1993): 246–278.

Ansolabehere, Stephen, and Shanto Iyengar. *Going Negative: How Attack Ads Shrink and Polarize the Electorate.* New York: Free Press, 1996.

Burnham, Walter Dean. "The Turnout Problem." In *Elections American Style,* edited by A. James Reichley. Washington, D.C.: Brookings Institution, 1987, 97–133.

*Conway, M. Margaret. "Political Participation in the 2004 Presidential Election: Turnout and Policy Consequences." In *A Defining Moment: The Presidential Election of 2004,* edited by William Crotty. Armonk, N.Y.: M. E. Sharpe, 2005, 49–73.

Crenson, Matthew A., and Benjamin Ginsberg. *Downsizing Democracy: How America Sidelined Its Citizens and Privatized Its Public.* Baltimore: Johns Hopkins University Press, 2002.

Highton, Benjamin. "Voter Registration and Turnout in the United States." *Perspectives on Politics* 2 (September 2004): 507–515.

Manza, Jeff, and Christopher Uggen. "Punishment and Democracy: Disenfranchisement of Nonincarcerated Felons in the United States." *Perspectives on Politics* 2 (September 2004): 491–505.

McDonald, Michael P., and Samuel L. Popkin. "The Myth of the Vanishing Voter." *American Political Science Review* 95 (December 2001): 963–974.

Miller, Warren E., and J. Merrill Shanks. *The New American Voter.* Cambridge: Harvard University Press, 1996, 95–114.

Patterson, Thomas E. *The Vanishing Voter: Public Involvement in an Age of Uncertainty.* New York: Knopf, 2002.

Piven, Frances Fox, and Richard A. Cloward. *Why Americans Still Don't Vote: And Why Politicians Want It That Way.* Boston: Beacon Press, 2000.

Putnam, Robert D. *Bowling Alone: The Collapse and Revival of American Community.* New York: Simon and Schuster, 2000.

Rosenstone, Steven J., and John Mark Hansen. *Mobilization, Participation, and Democracy in America.* New York: Macmillan, 1993.

Teixeira, Ruy A. *The Disappearing American Voter.* Washington, D.C.: The Brookings Institution, 1992.

Uggen, Christopher, and Jeff Manza. "Democratic Contraction? Political Consequences of Felon Disfranchisement in the United States." *American Sociological Review* 67 (December 2002): 777–803.

Wolfinger, Raymond E., and Steven J. Rosenstone. *Who Votes?* New Haven: Yale University Press, 1980.

Chapter 5: Social Forces and the Vote

Alford, Robert R. *Party and Society: The Anglo-American Democracies.* Chicago: Rand McNally, 1963.

Alvarez, R. Michael, and Lisa García Bedolla. "The Foundations of Latino Voter Partisanship: Evidence from the 2000 Election." *Journal of Politics* 65 (February 2003): 31–49.

Axelrod, Robert. "Where the Votes Come From: An Analysis of Electoral Coalitions, 1952–1968." *American Political Science Review* 66 (March 1972): 11–20.

Beck, Paul Allen, Russell J. Dalton, Steven Greene, and Robert Huckfeldt. "The Social Calculus of Voting: Interpersonal, Media, and Organizational Influences on Presidential Choices." *American Political Science Review* 96 (March 2002): 57–73.

Burns, Nancy. "Gender: Public Opinion and Political Action." In *Political Science: The State of the Discipline,* edited by Ira Katznelson and Helen V. Milner. New York: Norton, 2002, 462–487.

Campbell, David E. "The Young and the Realigning: A Test of the Socialization Theory of Realignment." *Public Opinion Quarterly* 66 (summer 2002): 209–234.

Dawson, Michael C., and Cathy Cohen. "Problems in the Study of the Politics of Race." In *Political Science: The State of the Discipline,* edited by Ira Katznelson and Helen V. Milner. New York: Norton, 2002, 488–510.

Hamilton, Richard F. *Class and Politics in the United States.* New York: Wiley, 1972.

Huckfeldt, Robert, and Carol Weitzel Kohfeld. *Race and the Decline of Class in American Politics.* Urbana: University of Illinois Press, 1989.

*Leal, David L., Matt A. Barreto, Jongho Lee, and Rodolfo O. de la Garza. "The Latino Vote in the 2004 Election." *PS: Political Science and Politics* (January 2005): 41–49.

Lipset, Seymour Martin. *Political Man: The Social Bases of Politics,* exp. ed. Baltimore: Johns Hopkins University Press, 1981.

Manza, Jeff, and Clem Brooks. *Social Cleavages and Political Change: Voter Alignments and U.S. Party Coalitions.* Oxford: Oxford University Press, 1999.

Miller, Warren E., and J. Merrill Shanks. *The New American Voter.* Cambridge: Harvard University Press, 1996, 212–282.

*Mellow, Nicole. "Voting Behavior: The 2004 Election and the Roots of Republican Success." In *The Elections of 2004,* edited by Michael Nelson. Washington, D.C.: CQ Press, 2005, 69–87.

*Muirhead, Russell, Nancy L. Rosenblum, Daniel Schlozman, and Francis X Shen. "Religion in the 2004 Election." In *Divided States of America: The Slash and Burn Politics of the 2004 Presidential Election,* edited by Larry J. Sabato. New York: Pearson Longman, 2006, 221–242.

*Powell, Richard J., and Mark D. Brewer. "Constituencies and the Consequences of the Presidential Vote." In *A Defining Moment: The Presidential Election of 2004,* edited by William Crotty. Armonk, N.Y.: M. E. Sharpe, 2005, 20–40.

Stanley, Harold W., and Richard G. Niemi. "Partisanship, Party Coalitions, and Group Support, 1952–2000." In *Models of Voting in Presidential Elections: The 2000 U.S. Elections,* edited by Herbert F. Weisberg and Clyde Wilcox. Stanford: Stanford University Press, 2004, 123–140.

Tate, Katherine. *From Protest to Politics: The New Black Voters in American Elections,* enl. ed. Cambridge: Harvard University Press, 1994.

Chapter 6: Candidates, Issues, and Voters

Campbell, Angus, Philip E. Converse, Warren E. Miller, and Donald E. Stokes. *The American Voter.* New York: Wiley, 1960, 168–265.

Carmines, Edward G., and James A. Stimson. *Issue Evolution: Race and the Transformation of American Politics.* Princeton: Princeton University Press, 1989.

Erikson, Robert S., Michael B. MacKuen, and James A. Stimson. *The Macro Polity.* Cambridge: Cambridge University Press, 2002.

Fiorina, Morris P., with Samuel J. Abrams and Jeremy C. Pope. *Culture War? The Myth of a Polarized America.* New York: Pearson Longman, 2005.

Gerber, Elisabeth R., and John E. Jackson. "Endogenous Preferences and the Study of Institutions." *American Political Science Review* 87 (September 1993): 639–656.

*Pomper, Gerald M. "The Presidential Election: The Ills of American Politics After 9/11." In *The Elections of 2004,* edited by Michael Nelson. Washington, D.C.: CQ Press, 2005, 42–68.

Popkin, Samuel L. *The Reasoning Voter: Communication and Persuasion in Presidential Campaigns.* Chicago: University of Chicago Press, 1991.

Shafter, Byron, and William J. M. Claggett. *The Two Majorities: The Issue Context of Modern American Politics.* Baltimore: Johns Hopkins University Press, 1995.

Chapter 7: Presidential Performance and Candidate Choice

*Campbell, James E. "Why Bush Won the Presidential Election of 2004: Incumbency, Ideology, Terrorism, and Turnout." *Political Science Quarterly* 120 (summer 2005): 219–241.

*Conley, Patricia. "The Presidential Race of 2004: Strategy, Outcome, and Mandate." In *A Defining Moment: The Presidential Election of 2004.* Armonk, N.Y.: M. E. Sharpe, 2005, 108–135.

Dalton, Russell J. *Democratic Challenges, Democratic Choices: The Erosion of Political Support in Advanced Industrial Democracies.* Oxford: Oxford University Press, 2004.

Downs, Anthony. *An Economic Theory of Democracy*. New York: Harper and Row, 1957.

Fiorina, Morris P. *Retrospective Voting in American National Elections*. New Haven: Yale University Press, 1981.

Key, V. O., Jr. *The Responsible Electorate: Rationality in Presidential Voting, 1936–1960*. Cambridge: Harvard University Press, 1966.

Kiewiet, D. Roderick. *Macroeconomics and Micropolitics: The Electoral Effects of Economic Issues*. Chicago: University of Chicago Press, 1983.

Lewis-Beck, Michael. S. *Economics and Elections: The Major Western Democracies*. Ann Arbor: University of Michigan Press, 1988.

*Quirk, Paul J., and Sean C. Matheson. "The Presidency: The 2004 Elections and the Prospects for Leadership." In *The Elections of 2004,* edited by Michael Nelson. Washington, D.C.: CQ Press, 2005, 133–162.

Riker, William H. *Liberalism Against Populism: A Confrontation Between the Theory of Democracy and the Theory of Social Choice*. San Francisco: W. H. Freeman, 1982.

Tufte, Edward R. *Political Control of the Economy*. Princeton: Princeton University Press, 1978.

Chapter 8: Party Loyalties, Policy Preferences, and the Vote

Abramson, Paul R. *Political Attitudes in America: Formation and Change*. San Francisco: W. H. Freeman, 1983.

Aldrich, John H. *Why Parties? The Origin and Transformation of Political Parties in America*. Chicago: University of Chicago Press, 1995.

Bartels, Larry M. "Partisanship and Voting Behavior, 1952–1996." *American Journal of Political Science* 44 (January 2000): 35–50.

Campbell, Angus, Philip E. Converse, Warren E. Miller, and Donald E. Stokes. *The American Voter*. New York: Wiley, 1960, 120–167.

Fiorina, Morris P. "Parties, Participation, and Representation in America: Old Theories Face New Realities." In *Political Science: The State of the Discipline,* edited by Ira Katznelson and Helen V. Milner. New York: Norton, 2002, 511–541.

Green, Donald, Bradley Palmquist, and Eric Schickler. *Partisan Hearts and Minds: Political Parties and the Social Identities of Voters.* New Haven: Yale University Press, 2002.

Keith, Bruce E., David B. Magleby, Candice J. Nelson, Elizabeth Orr, Mark C. Westlye, and Raymond E. Wolfinger. *The Myth of the Independent Voter.* Berkeley: University of California Press, 1992.

Miller, Warren E., and J. Merrill Shanks. *The New American Voter.* Cambridge: Harvard University Press, 1996, 117–185.

Wattenberg, Martin P. *The Decline of American Political Parties, 1952–1996.* Cambridge: Harvard University Press, 1998.

Chapter 9: Candidates and Outcomes in 2004

Brunell, Thomas L., and Bernard Grofman. "Explaining Divided U.S. Senate Delegations, 1788–1996: A Realignment Approach." *American Political Science Review* 92 (June 1998): 391–399.

*Ceaser, James W., and Andrew E. Busch. *Red Over Blue: The 2004 Elections and American Politics.* Lanham, Md.: Rowman and Littlefield, 2005, 143–168.

Fenno, Richard F., Jr. *Home Style: House Members in Their Districts.* Boston: Little, Brown, 1978.

Jacobson, Gary C. *The Politics of Congressional Elections,* 6th ed. New York: Pearson Longman, 2004, 1–112; 151–258.

*———. "The Congress: The Structural Basis of Republican Success." In *The Elections of 2004,* edited by Michael Nelson. Washington, D.C.: CQ Press, 2005, 163–186.

*———. "Polarized Politics and the 2004 Congressional and Presidential Election." *Political Science Quarterly* 120 (summer 2005): 199–218.

*Jackson, John S., III. "The 2004 Congressional Races." In *A Defining Moment: The Presidential Election of 2004,* edited by William Crotty. Armonk, N.Y.: M. E. Sharpe, 2005, 161–183.

*Larson, Bruce A. "The 2004 Congressional Election." In *Divided States of America: The Slash and Burn Politics of the 2004 Presidential Election,* edited by Larry J. Sabato. New York: Pearson Longman, 2006, 243–267.

Lau, Richard R., and Gerald M. Pomper. "Effectiveness of Negative Campaigning in U.S. Senate Elections." *American Journal of Political Science* 46 (January 2002): 47–66.

Rohde, David W. *Parties and Leaders in the Postreform House.* Chicago: University of Chicago Press, 1991.

Schlesinger, Joseph A. *Ambition and Politics: Political Careers in the United States.* Chicago: Rand McNally, 1966.

Stone, Walter J., and L. Sandy Maisel. "The Not-So-Simple Calculus of Winning: Potential U.S. House Candidates' Nomination and General Election Prospects." *Journal of Politics* 65 (November 2003): 951–977.

Chapter 10: The Congressional Electorate in 2004

Abramowitz, Alan I., and Jeffrey A. Segal. *Senate Elections.* Ann Arbor: University of Michigan Press, 1992.

Beck, Paul Allen, Lawrence Baum, Aage R. Clausen, and Charles E. Smith Jr. "Patterns and Sources of Ticket Splitting in Subpresidential Voting." *American Political Science Review* 86 (December 1992): 916–928.

Burden, Barry C., and David C. Kimball. *Why Americans Split Their Tickets: Campaigns, Competition, and Divided Government.* Ann Arbor: University of Michigan, 2002.

Dalager, Jon K. "Voters, Issues, and Elections: Are the Candidates' Messages Getting Through?" *Journal of Politics* 58 (May 1996): 486–515.

Fenno, Richard F., Jr. "If, as Ralph Nader Says, Congress Is 'The Broken Branch,' Why Do We Love Our Congressmen So Much?" In *Congress in Change: Elections and Reform,* edited by Norman J. Ornstein. New York: Praeger, 1975, 277–287.

Jacobson, Gary C. *The Electoral Origins of Divided Government: Competition in U.S. House Elections, 1946–1988.* Boulder, Colo.: Westview, 1990.

———. *The Politics of Congressional Elections,* 6th ed. New York: Pearson Longman, 2004, 113–150.

Sigelman, Lee, Paul J. Wahlbeck, and Emmett H. Buell Jr. "Vote Choice and the Preference for Divided Government: Lessons of 1992." *American Journal of Political Science* 41 (July 1997): 879–894.

Chapter 11: The 2004 Elections and the Future of American Politics

*Abramson, Paul R., John H. Aldrich, and David W. Rohde. "The 2004 Presidential Election: The Emergence of a Permanent Majority?" *Political Science Quarterly* 120 (spring 2005): 33–57.

*Ceaser, James W., and Andrew E. Busch. *Red Over Blue: The 2004 Elections and American Politics.* Lanham, Md.: Rowman and Littlefield, 2005, 169–189.

*Cook, Charles E. "Conclusion." In *Divided States of America: The Slash and Burn Politics of the 2004 Presidential Election,* edited by Larry J. Sabato. New York: Pearson Longman, 2006, 279–299.

*Crotty, William. "Armageddon, Just Another Campaign, or Something In-Between? The Meaning and Consequences of the 2004 Election." In *A Defining Moment: The Presidential Election of 2004,* edited by William Crotty. Armonk, N.Y.: M. E. Sharpe, 2005, 236–260.

*McWilliams, Wilson Carey. "The Meaning of the Election: Ownership and Citizenship in American Life." In *The Election of 2004,* edited by Michael Nelson. Washington, D.C.: CQ Press, 2005, 187–213.

*Mileur, Jerome M. "Incumbency, Politics, and Policy: Detour or New Direction?" In *A Defining Moment: The Presidential Election of 2004,* edited by William Crotty. Armonk, N.Y.: M. E. Sharpe, 2005, 136–160.

*Nelson, Michael. "The Setting: George W. Bush, Majority President." In *The Elections of 2004,* edited by Michael Nelson. Washington, D.C.: CQ Press, 2005, 1–17.

*Saletan, William. "Conclusion." In *Divided States of America: The Slash and Burn Politics of the 2004 Presidential Election,* edited by Larry J. Sabato. New York: Pearson Longman, 2006, 269–278.

Index